Ethnic
Economies

Ethnic

Economies

Ivan Light

Department of Sociology
University of California, Los Angeles
Los Angeles, California

Steven J. Gold

Department of Sociology
Michigan State University
East Lansing, Michigan

ACADEMIC PRESS

A Harcourt Science and Technology Company

San Diego   San Francisco   New York   Boston   London   Sydney   Tokyo

This book is printed on acid-free paper. ∞

Copyright © 2000 by ACADEMIC PRESS

All Rights Reserved.
No part of this publication may be reproduced or transmitted in any form or by any
means, electronic or mechanical, including photocopy, recording, or any information
storage and retrieval system, without permission in writing from the publisher.

Requests for permission to make copies of any part of the work should be mailed to:
Permissions Department, Harcourt Inc., 6277 Sea Harbor Drive,
Orlando, Florida, 32887-6777

Academic Press
A Harcourt Science and Technology Company
525 B Street, Suite 1900, San Diego, California 92101-4495, U.S.A.
http://www.apnet.com

Academic Press
24-28 Oval Road, London NW1 7DX, UK
http://www.hbuk.co.uk/ap/

Library of Congress Catalog Card Number: 99-63217

International Standard Book Number: 0-12-287155-3

PRINTED IN THE UNITED STATES OF AMERICA
99 00 01 02 03 04 BB 9 8 7 6 5 4 3 2 1

Contents

Preface

As a new century begins, socialism and inclusive nationalisms have lost much of their ability to unify large and diverse groups into collective projects. Partially filling the void, ethnicity has become a more prominent and acceptable base of personal identity and collective action. Consequently, social cooperation and conflict are more often expressed in ethnic terms than was true a generation ago. Ethnics are now more aware of their own position, economically and otherwise, relative to the positions of others, and they pursue economic or political advantage or redress in the company of their coethnics. Ethnic economies have become an even more conscious vehicle for these goals. Seeking to shape their own fate and to escape discrimination, economically disadvantaged groups, including women, some ethnic minorities, and many immigrant nationalities, start businesses at rates that outstrip those of native-born white males.[1]

When coethnics join together in the pursuit of economic gain, competition among ethnic groups usually increases. First, ethnic employment niches balkanize labor markets, conferring advantage upon insiders while excluding outsiders. Sec-

---

[1] Between 1987 and 1996, women-owned businesses grew by 78%, while all businesses grew at 47%. Between 1987 and 1992, the growth rate for all businesses was 26%; during the same period, the growth rate for black-owned businesses was 46%, the growth rate for Hispanic businesses was 83%, and for American Indian, Alaskan Native, Asian and Pacific Islander owned businesses, the growth rate was 61%. According to the 1990 census, the self-employment rate for the United States was 69.74 per thousand persons age 16 and over, barely exceeding the rate among the foreign-born: 68.29 per thousand. However, many groups, including Koreans, Greeks, Iranians, Canadians, Italians, and Russians, had rates of self-employment close to or in excess of 100 per thousand. Associated Press, "Women own one-third of U.S. Businesses" http://sddt.com/~columbus/Files2/9603278.html (March 27, 1996); MBDA, ND MBDA Business Communities http://www.mbda.gov.stats.html; Paula Mergenhagen, "Black-Owned Businesses," American Demographics June 1996, http://www.demographics.com/Publications/AD/96_AD/9606_AD/9606AF01.htm; A. Portes and R. G. Rumbaut (1996). "Immigrant America: A Portrait" (2nd edition). Berkeley, University of California Press, pp. 72–73.

ond, ethnic business firms are often perceived as colonizing and exploiting social underdogs. Finally, competing ethnic economies seek state-provided advantages or seek to avoid governmental sanctions. The resulting furor animates most political debates of the day, including those surrounding welfare reform, affirmative action, immigration restrictions, charter schools, multiculturalism, and bilingual education. All too often, contention spills out of the political arena or marketplace and into the streets. Real or perceived ethnic economic competition underlies noteworthy instances of civil unrest, violence, and ethnic cleansing at home and abroad.

But the picture is not altogether grim. Granted, the most dramatic evidence of ethnic economies' power can be found in discord, riots, and arson in cities. Nonetheless, ethnic economies also contribute to the general welfare. Ethnic firms provide coethnics and others with improved access to jobs, goods, services, income, and wealth. Ethnic economies also help to maintain neighborhoods, support communal institutions, assist the indigent, train recent arrivals, educate and protect children, build political power, and maintain cultural integrity.

Ethnic economies have drawn the attention of many scholars who, since about 1970, have produced a significant body of research. Indeed, this scholarship has yielded so much useful information that the topic needs consolidation. This book reviews and critically interprets what is known about ethnic economies in the United States while also introducing some new data and new concepts. Our goal is to contribute to the general understanding of ethnic economies and their con-

At left, Ivan Light; at right, Steven Gold.

sequences, *both* positive and negative. We devote more attention to the agency of ethnic actors themselves than to the contexts in which they are embedded, but we address both. Further, while ethnic economies exist in virtually every nation state, we focus upon the United States and Canada because issues of institutional comparability would otherwise make the book unreasonably large and complicated.

Although this book is a collaborative effort, like all real collaborations, it reflects a division of labor. Ivan Light took primary responsibility for Chapters 1–4, 8, and 9, while Steven Gold wrote Chapters 5–7.

The theoretical portion of Chapter 8 is based upon Ivan Light and Carolyn Rosenstein, *Race, Ethnicity, and Entrepreneurship in Urban America* (New York: Aldine de Gruyter, 1995), pp. 149–160. However, Ivan Light added new evidence and interpretation to this version. Chapter 9 derives from Ivan Light and Michelle Pham, "Beyond Creditworthy: Microcredit and Informal Credit in the United States," *Journal of Developmental Entrepreneurship* 3 (1998), pp. 35–52. However, this version is rewritten and reorganized in places and references have been updated.

Acknowledgments

We thank Louise Jezierski, Jan Bokemeier, Maxine Baca Zinn, Marilyn Aronoff, Roger Waldinger, Harry Holzer, Silvia Pedraza, John Bukowczyk, Rubén G. Rumbaut, Mehdi Bozorgmehr, Arlie Hochschild, June Thomas, Bruce Phillips, Cindy Struthers, Philip Kasinitz, Jeff Reitz, Jennifer Lee, Frank Fratto, Brian Fry, and the Social Capital Interest Group at Michigan State for providing materials, suggestions, and critical thinking. Rebecca Kim and Egal Shabaz contributed research assistance.

The Michigan State University Nonprofit Research Initiative and McNair/SROP program funded parts of the research.

Romona Erikson assisted with preparation of the manuscript. Tammy Dennany, Marvey Olson, Rachael Ginsburg, and Sandy Cummings did photocopying and Vivek Joshi solved computer problems.

Our editor, Scott Bentley, provided direction and encouragement.

Ivan Light thanks his wife, Leah, for keeping her cool in the face of multiple errors of commission and omission, some a product of this book.

Steven Gold thanks William and Betty Gold for their warmth. Thanks also to Lisa Gold, who helped sort out many issues and offered consistent encouragement.

Far East National Bank Float, Chinese New Year Parade, Monterey Park, California, 1992. Ethnic banks combine the class resources of capital and financial management skills with the ethnic resources of language competence and coethnic trust. They are well positioned to handle transactions with coethnics beyond the U.S. In this way, ethnic banks rely on the patronage of coethnic customers, who in turn benefit from their services. As a part of the bargain, the coethnic community is a recipient of their philanthropic donations.

Asian Garden Mall, Little Saigon, Westminster, California. Financed by overseas capital and managed by a Chinese-Vietnamese run real estate firm, this enterprise is vital to the social and economic life of the largest Vietnamese settlement outside of Southeast Asia.

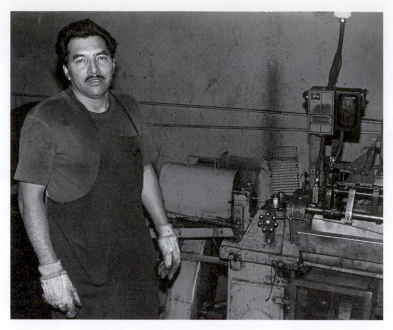

This Mexican-born man working in a wire factory found his job through coethnic referrals. With the exception of the factory's manager and secretary, all of its employees are Mexican immigrants, hired through ethnic networks.

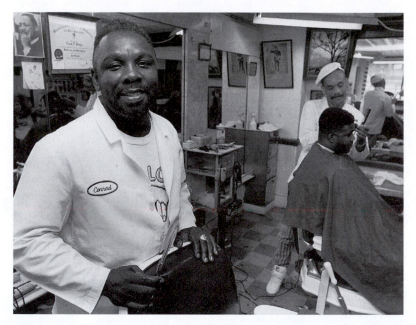

Trinidadian barber, Boston. Historically, discrimination has limited African-American entrepreneurs' access to loans and business locations. However, segregation also provided access to a captive coethnic market for the provision of personal services. Accordingly, barbers, doctors, teachers, ministers, and undertakers have been prominent occupations among the African-American middle class. Barber shops are important community centers in many ethnic communities.

CHAPTER 1

The Ethnic Economy
since Weber

African American entrepreneurs had been unusually successful in Tulsa, Oklahoma, converting the city's black community, Greenwood, into a showplace of enterprise and pride.[1] When a black man was accused of raping a white woman, whites formed a lynch mob outside the jail on May 30, 1921. After exchanging shots with defenders, the white mob invaded Greenwood, burning and looting black-owned homes and businesses. By the time the National Guard broke up the riot, 18,000 homes and businesses had burned, and 304 people were dead. Newspapers blamed the African Americans for the riot.

During the night of November 9, 1938, Adolf Hitler's followers smashed Jewish storefronts in cities all over Germany. The Nazis also looted the stores, torched many, and shot and beat the hapless proprietors and their families. According to Hitler's propaganda minister, Josef Goebbels, "ordinary German citizens" had spontaneously arisen to punish the Jews for economic crimes. The police did not interfere.[2]

The black–Korean conflict in Los Angeles came to the world's attention on April 29, 1992, when rioting and looting broke out in South Central Los Angeles, the heart of the city's black community. In 3 nights of rioting, the worst in American history since 1863, mobs damaged 2073 stores, nearly two-thirds of which were Korean-owned.[3] Of looted stores, 38% were also deliberately burned. Police protection was ineffectual.

When in the spring of 1998 banks closed and the national currency collapsed on foreign markets, irate Indonesians turned against Chinese storekeepers, whom they blamed for the currency's devaluation. Rioters "searching for scapegoats" attacked the Chinese minority.[4] During 3 weeks of rioting, mobs looted Chinese-owned stores and murdered Chinese store owners. Police watched, and some participated in the looting.[5]

In all these cases, angry mobs targeted ethnic businesses. Scholarly interest in the ethnic economy owes much to these horrifying incidents and to others, too numerous to enumerate, that are very similar. On the other hand, the ethnic economy also draws scholarly interest, especially in the United States, from the Horatio Alger tradition. Whatever Alger may really have meant, in American culture the "Horatio Alger tradition" stands for self-help that eventuates in rags-to-riches life stories.[6] When despised and disadvantaged minorities start their own businesses, they progress from employee to business owner, a progression that Abraham Lincoln admiringly called "the true condition of the laborer."

Moreover, when ethnic and racial minorities open business firms, they create new jobs for themselves and others rather than taking jobs from the general labor market. These new ethnic enterprises expand the job supply of the host society, benefiting the ethnoracial majority as well as the minority. One might suppose that, even if prompted by self-interest, others would encourage and support ethnic business. Why should anyone hate those who increase the job supply? However, the historical record indicates that hatred and violence are frequent responses. Ethnic economies have been and still remain controversial. Three generations of social science inquiry have helped to clarify the reasons.

WHAT IS AN ETHNIC ECONOMY?

An *ethnic economy* consists of coethnic self-employed and employers and their coethnic employees. Whatever is not part of the ethnic economy belongs to the general labor market. Simple to define, and useful in studies of immigrant and ethnic minorities, the concept of ethnic economy derives from three feeder traditions. The first originates with the European founders of historical sociology; the second with the literature of middleman minorities that descended from the first; and the third autonomously from African American economic thinkers, notably Booker T. Washington. Although classical economists had no interest in ethnicity, classical sociologists did. Marx, Weber, and Sombart all thought that modern capitalism emerged from and superseded a primitive, ethnic predecessor. Therefore, all three distinguished traditional capitalism and modern capitalism. Sombart declared that a modern capitalist enterprise operates impersonally. That is, decision makers place profit considerations ahead of all purely personal relationships, including relationships of coethnicity. In contrast, "fraternal and communal sentiments" decisively shaped the decision making of traditional firms.[7] The symptoms were favoritism, nepotism, communalism, and exceptionalism in every phase of the traditional firm's operations.

Weber, too, maintained that everywhere in the world precapitalist firms operated a dual-price ethic that reflected underlying loyalties to ethnoreligious groups rather than a determination to maximize profit whatever the social consequences. Weber thought that profit maximization at the expense of all purely social ties was a feature of modern capitalism. Indeed, Weber[8] exculpated the Jews from the charge of inventing capitalism, raised against them by romantic nationalists such as Richard Wagner, the composer, on the grounds that Jews were too traditional in their business outlook to have accomplished the task.[9] Therefore, late-medieval Jews still permitted ethnoreligious relationships to color their business practice. For instance, during the transition from feudalism to capitalism, Jews would still charge a coethnic less than a non-Jew or do business favors for a Jew that they would not do for a non-Jew. Citing these backward practices, Weber pleaded the Jews guilty to minor ethnochauvinism while exonerating them of the disgrace of having invented capitalism.[10] Here Weber's widely shared view converged with the Marxist tradition that distinguished precapitalist business enterprise from capitalist business, reserving to the latter a dynamic role in social change.[11]

Modern capitalism required a decisive break with traditionalism, said Weber, and the Jews could not break out. Weber claimed instead that Protestant sectarians, especially those influenced by Puritanism, had first stripped business enterprise of the fraternal and communal sentiments that had everywhere else in the world prevented the emergence of rational bourgeois capitalism from its ethnic predecessor. Weber believed that its universalism rendered rational bourgeois capitalism superior to traditional capitalism. First, universalism permitted legal regulation of contracts and relationships instead of reliance upon social trust and shared cultural understandings. Second, universalism permitted bureaucracy, itself a key technical innovation. Bureaucracy permitted unlimited expansion of organization size with access to economies of scale, meritocratic appointment to office, official careers, rational cost accounting, and continuous technical innovation. Both Weber and Marx relegated ethnic capitalism to a back burner of sociological interest where, until quite recently, it stayed. After all, ethnic capitalism could not reach vast size, employ bureaucratic methods of organization, appoint workers on the basis of technical qualifications, replace strikers with noncoethnic strikebreakers, accept the judgments of a balance sheet, or promote research and development. Modern capitalism could accomplish all these feats. Because of these advantages, modern capitalism drove out and replaced traditional capitalism. Although traditional capitalism remained significant in underdeveloped countries, even there its days were numbered and its influence continually diminished. Following Weber, mainstream social science endorsed all these conclusions, promoting them virtually to canonical status.

MIDDLEMAN MINORITIES

The literature of middleman minorities developed in this intellectual climate.[12] Oddly, Weber's[13] own concept of "pariah capitalism" had called attention to ethnic minorities that specialized in market trading in precapitalist societies. Unlike proletarian minorities, whom Blauner[14] theorized in terms of internal colonialism and Bonacich[15] in terms of split labor markets, middleman minorities were marginal trading peoples, residing in diasporas, who continued this commercial livelihood into the modern age despite the presumably adverse competitive climate created by modern capitalism.[16] True, Jews were the star illustration of a middleman minority, a centrality that linked middlemen with Weber's concept of pariah capitalism.[17] However, following Howard Paul Becker,[18] who first defined this concept, middleman minority theorists expanded the repertoire to include trading peoples all over the world.[19] Armenians, overseas Chinese, Gypsies, Sikhs of East Africa, the Parsees and Marwaris of India, Ismaili Muslims, the Hausa of Nigeria, and others also represented trading nations that sojourned abroad, performing mercantile roles in a context of old-fashioned ethnic capitalism.[20]

Although old-fashioned ethnic capitalism still worked in backward, Third World regions, survival on the margin did not challenge the mainstream's confidence in the ultimate superiority of modern capitalism. After all, so it was argued, middleman minorities inhabited backward regions still unpenetrated by modern capitalism. As capitalism expanded, big, rationally organized corporations would displace small and medium businesses that operated with traditional rules. Some of these were ethnic businesses; others belonged to the petit bourgeoisie.[21] Both were doomed. A fine example of the mainstream's eschatology is Clifford Geertz's[22] depiction of rotating credit associations as "a middle-rung in development." As Third World countries developed and modernized, Geertz claimed, they would replace the old-fashioned money pools with banks and insurance companies, the progressive financial institutions of modern capitalism. Decades later, rotating credit associations are more powerful and extensive than ever in many parts of the Third World, so the claim that modernization dooms them to oblivion is unpersuasive now.[23]

Actually, a generation ago, when Clifford Geertz was still preaching the conventional view, research had already challenged the supposition that traditional ethnic business conferred only liabilities and no advantages.[24] On the contrary, middleman minorities had developed particularistic resources that supported and enhanced their business success. These resources included entrepreneurial values, beliefs, institutions, and social networks through which the children of middleman merchants easily moved into mercantile roles, continuing the tradition of their family and people. Moreover, as Bonacich[25] argued, the uneasy practice of sojourning abroad inclined middleman traders to intensify their social solidarity, and social solidarity encouraged their business enterprises.

Nonetheless, instructive as it remains, the sociology of middleman minorities perpetuated certain conceptual blind spots.[26] First, middleman theory stressed Third World contexts, implying that advanced market societies no longer had traditional capitalism. This implication mirrored the intellectual context in the shadow of which the theory of middleman minorities had initially developed. That context fashioned a sharp distinction between traditional and modern capitalism, relegating ethnic capitalism to the doomed periphery of the world economy. Representing the cutting edge of capitalist development, the core could then be treated as free of the residues of traditional capitalism.[27] Even if this judgment was in a broad sense correct, it was certainly oversimplified. In actuality, pluralistic societies of North America always contained marginal sectors within which ethnic capitalism continued to flourish, often more luxuriantly than the modern alternative.[28] A simple core–periphery contrast overlooked these ethnic sectors, terribly important though they were to the communities involved.

Second, middleman minority theory could treat only trading peoples with a history of traditional capitalism. Groups such as the Chinese, Jews, India's Marwaris, and Armenians met this qualification. But middleman minority theory could not address the situation of wage-earner groups among whom private business was a peripheral pursuit or who had only recently turned to entrepreneurship.[29] This limitation rendered middleman theory of limited use in the analysis of the economic integration and social mobility of ethnic minorities and immigrants generally.[30] If one wished to discuss the business enterprise of Cubans in Puerto Rico[31] or of Koreans in California,[32] the middleman minority concept was unsuitable because neither of these immigrant nationalities were historic trading peoples. The need to discuss these precise cases and others like them emerged empirically in the developed societies when many immigrant minorities turned impressively to business without a convincing middleman history and tradition. Business-oriented they certainly were, but they had not previously been historic middleman minorities.

Finally, middleman theory had lived comfortably with its own marginality. Middleman theory could explain old-fashioned ethnic capitalism in a Third World still unpenetrated by modern capitalism. However, when entrepreneurial minorities turned up in advanced industrial societies, not just in the periphery, they challenged the accommodation that middleman theorists had worked out within mainstream social theory. After all, the prosperity of middleman minorities in advanced countries implied that the ethnic business formula still worked even in the heartland of progressive capitalism. If so, the vaunted advantages of Fordist capitalism might not be so overwhelming as previously imagined. At a minimum, old-fashioned ethnic business had demonstrated more endurance than an earlier generation of theorists had imagined possible. At a maximum, old-fashioned ethnic business worked better than Fordist capitalism in selected contexts, and could even remedy economic problems (such as disintegrating central cities) that modern capitalism could not. No one suggested then, as they do now,[33] that ethnic capitalism could sometimes outperform multinational corporations in many contexts.[34]

BOOKER T. WASHINGTON

Booker T. Washington[35] was the leading spokesman of black America in the last decade of the 19th century. Unlike his arch-rival for African American leadership, William E. B. DuBois,[36] who stressed political action and education, Washington stressed business ownership and home ownership as strategies for black advance-ment.[37] To this end, he founded the National Negro Business league in 1900. Conceiving of the league as a federation of local black chambers of commerce, Washington hoped the business leagues would improve the economic condition of black America, substituting home ownership for tenancy and business owner-ship for unemployment. Washington's book *The Negro in Business* laid out his economic program, but it also described in empirical detail the advantages of networking in business, a wisdom that American business schools did not receive for another eight decades.

Within the African American community, Washington's political opponents criticized his willingness to compromise with racial segregation. It is true that Washington recommended toleration of legal racial segregation in the South, where most blacks then lived. In actuality, however, Washington did not accept the South's racial status quo as his opponents simplistically alleged. He only believed that the development of black economic power should have priority over black political power and black higher education. A dollar, he once remarked, was worth more to blacks at that moment than was the franchise. Given economic power, he thought, black people would have much less trouble claiming social and political equality than they would without it. Therefore, forced to select a priority, he stressed getting money over getting the vote. This judgment was not complete madness. Reviewing the historical record, Robert Weems now declares that the ideas of Washington "merit serious reconsideration."[38]

Washington's supporters lost a decisive political battle to DuBois, his oppo-nent, at the Niagara Conference of 1905.[39] After this defeat, Washington never recovered his leadership, which was assumed by DuBois's organization, the National Association for the Advancement of Colored People. This organization's programmatic focus was on ballot access and education, not entrepreneurship. Although banished from the leadership of the African American movement, Washington's economic philosophy remained influential among many black intel-lectuals, including Malcolm X, and among African American business faculty, who kept alive and improved his ideas in a series of research monographs.[40] During the 1940s, African American intellectuals were maintaining the only active debate about and research into minority entrepreneurship in the academy.[41] When, years later, interest in ethnic economies reemerged in North America, their writings and those of Booker T. Washington informed and animated the scholarly literature on the topic then available.[42] Still later, as academic interest in immigrant and ethnic minority business spread to Europe, Australia, and Asia from the United States, Washington's legacy became global.

THE ETHNIC ECONOMY

Contemporary ethnic economy literature derives from all these feeder traditions, but owes most to the theory of middleman minorities. Without denying the achievements of middleman theory, which remains a valid case, ethnic economy theory is more general. Every middleman minority has an ethnic economy, but every ethnic economy does not betoken a middleman minority. An *ethnic economy* or, as we shall later call it, an *ethnic ownership economy* exists whenever *any* immigrant or ethnic group maintains a private economic sector in which it has a controlling ownership stake. The size of the ethnic economy affects its significance. A big ethnic economy is of more consequence than a small one. However, size is not a defining feature of an ethnic economy. A small ethnic economy is still an ethnic economy, and every ethnic group has an ethnic economy, including white ethnic groups.[43]

Social science interest in ethnic economies began in 1972 with the publication of *Ethnic Enterprise in America* by Ivan Light.[44] This book compared Chinese, Japanese, and African American self-employment between 1880 and 1940, concluding that social trust supported entrepreneurship. *Ethnic Enterprise in America* anticipated the major theoretical ideas that came later, including social and cultural capital. Additionally it stressed the contributions of rotating credit associations to minority commerce. Rotating credit associations, discussed in chapter 4, still provide the strongest evidence of social capital effects on business.[45] However, *Ethnic Enterprise in America* did not introduce the concept of ethnic economy. Edna Bonacich and John Modell were the first operationally to define ethnic economy.[46] By *ethnic economy,* Bonacich and Modell meant any ethnic or immigrant group's self-employed, its employers, their coethnic employees, and their unpaid family workers. Thus defined, an ethnic economy demarcated the employment immigrant and ethnic minorities had created on their own account from jobs provided them by the general labor market. Thanks to the hard-edge definition, one could measure the size of any ethnic economy in a single percentage. If 16% of all workers (including self-employed and employers) work in an ethnic economy, then 84% of the group works in the general labor market. In this sense, the Cuban ethnic economy of Miami comprises self-employed Cubans, Cuban employers, and their Cuban employees in Miami. The Cuban ethnic economy does not include Cubans who work for wages in the general economy. For example, the Cuban ethnic economy does not include Cubans who work for agencies of government, for multinational corporations, or for private businesses owned by non-Cubans. All of those Cuban employees work in the general labor market.

A puzzling issue is how to define an ethnic group. In principle, everyone is ethnic, including assimilated whites, and Collins[47] rightly complains that the ethnic business literature includes too few whites. As matters stand, whites are the least understood ethnic entrepreneurs. However, as a matter of practice, which is no guide to desirability, ethnic economy researchers have routinely defined ethnic groups in terms of their foreign national origins. Thus defined, the Irish originated in Ireland, a nation; and the Chinese originated in China, another nation. However, ethnic groups need not be defined by national origin. The Irish can be Protestant or Catholic, and each subset further differentiates into county affiliations that have ethnic quality within Ireland. Similarly, the Chinese can be from the mainland, from Taiwan, from Singapore, or from Hong Kong; they can speak various dialects; and they can come from one or another region, all of which have internal ethnic characteristics. Nationality is not a perfect indicator of ethnicity.

Like other indicators of national origin, the terms *Irish, Mexican, Chinese,* and so forth are approximations to real ethnic identities. Ethnic economies depend upon ethnicity not national origins for their boundaries, and national origin is just a convenient indicator of ethnicity, not the real thing. For example, although Chinese-speaking, Shanghainese entrepreneurs played the role of ethnic minority in Hong Kong, a Cantonese city,[48] where their firms composed a Shanghainese ethnic economy. Similarly, Iranians of four different ethnoreligious backgrounds cooperated mainly with coreligionists in Los Angeles, a circumstance that created four thinly linked Iranian ethnic economies, not just a unitary Iranian ethnic economy.[49] Similarly, Guarnizo[50] observes that 70% of Mexican American entrepreneurs in Los Angeles actually hailed from only four districts in Mexico, a provenance that is lost unless we examine internal ethnicity among Mexicans.

An ethnic economy is ethnic because the personnel are coethnics. Intended only to distinguish the internal or external auspices of work creation, the concept of ethnic economy makes no claims about the locational clustering or density of firms, which might, indeed, be evenly distributed among neighborhoods and industries.[51] The concept of ethnic economy is agnostic about clustering. As a matter of definition, the concept also makes no claims about the level or quality of ethnicity within the ethnic economy or between buyers and sellers. Buyers and sellers need not be coethnic in the ethnic economy, nor need they conduct their business in a foreign language. This definition does not focus attention upon trade conducted by owners for the benefit of coethnic buyers, whether at the retail or the wholesale level. Owners are in their own group's ethnic economy regardless of whether their customers are or are not coethnics. The concept of ethnic economy neither requires nor assumes an ethnic cultural ambience within the firm or among sellers and buyers. Bonacich and Modell's[52] research found that those in the Japanese American ethnic economy were more ethnically Japanese than Japanese Americans of the same generation who worked in the general labor market, a finding that O'Brien and Fugita[53] have confirmed. This empirical result was not a matter of definition. The Japanese American ethnic economy would have remained an ethnic economy even had the workers in this economy retained no higher Japanese ethnicity than Japanese Americans in the general labor market.

In the pluralistic societies of North America, immigrant and ethnic minorities have always competed for income, mobility, political power, and prestige. Assimilation theory always assumed that insertion as wage earners into the economic mainstream improved immigrants' earnings chances, and that insertion required and accelerated acculturation.[54] In this view,[55] still the dominant one, ethnic entrepreneurship would not enhance ethnic economic welfare so much as would economic incorporation into the wage-earning mainstream.[56] Wage jobs in the mainstream are deemed likely to pay more than the ownership of small businesses, and jobs outside the ethnic community are deemed better than jobs within it.[57] Reitz and Sklar's comprehensive survey[58] found that the assimilation model's economic assumptions did fit the economic experience of European ethnic and immigrant groups in Canada. Men of European origin paid a penalty of about 10% if they retained ethnic language use, a sign of nonacculturation. However, the assimilation model did not fit the economic experience of nonwhites in Canada, who paid no financial penalty at all when they continued to speak foreign languages in Canada.[59] Acculturated or not, nonwhites experienced economic disadvantage.

Turning to the ethnic economy, we find that some ethnoracial groups have turned heavily to entrepreneurship, others have made average use of it, and still others have made below-average use.[60] In the United States, high-entrepreneurship groups include Arabs, Armenians, Chinese, Gypsies, Greeks, Italians, Japanese, Jews, Indians and Pakistanis, Lebanese, Koreans, and Persians.[61] Immigrants of western and central European provenance have generally displayed only average entrepreneurship in North America, as have Cubans and Latin Americans. Blacks, Mexicans, Vietnamese, and Puerto Ricans have had below-average rates of entrepreneurship in North American towns and cities.[62]

THE ETHNIC ENCLAVE ECONOMY

The concept of an *ethnic enclave economy* resembles the concept of ethnic economy and was often identified with it in the 1980s.[63] However, these are different concepts with different intellectual lineages. Unlike the concept of ethnic economy, which derived from the earlier literature of middleman minorities, the concept of ethnic enclave economy derived from dual labor market theory, itself a product of institutional economics.[64] Dual labor market theory developed in the late 1960s as an effort to explain persistent inequality in employment. Seeking to explain the reduced income and status attainment of women and minorities, dual labor market theory claimed that disadvantaged groups were locked into an inferior, secondary labor market that did not offer egress into more desirable jobs in the primary sector of the labor market.[65] "Labor market segmentation" meant the long-term coexistence of noncommunicating labor markets in which vastly different standards of remuneration and work satisfaction prevailed. Since neoclassical economics declared such a situation impossible, labor segmentation theorists had to concentrate on proof, not theory.[66] Valid as far as it went, dual labor market theory took wage labor as its reality, entirely overlooking self-employment on the grounds, then widely shared, that self-employment was a dwindling phenomenon of negligible importance. In practice, this simplification led to a world view in which self-employment vanished from the consciousness of social scientists.[67]

Sullivan[68] was the first to note that labor market studies could no longer treat self-employment as an anomaly that could be ignored. Somewhat later, Portes and Manning[69] made the case more forcefully, and their view has subsequently prevailed. Although some segmentation theorists still ignore self-employment,[70] informed opinion no longer mistakes such treatment for a comprehensive analysis. First, self-employment is no longer declining in North America, Australia or in western Europe. Second, its prevalence was long underestimated in official documents, a practice that, it is now realized, unwisely encouraged social scientists to ignore the phenomenon.[71] Finally, the effects of self-employment are usually stronger in immigrant and ethnic minority communities than they are in the general economy.[72] Therefore, if self-employment is ignored, no treatment of employment can be comprehensive.

This influence of dual labor market theory is clear in the work of Wilson and Portes,[73] the earliest formulation of the ethnic enclave economy. After a review of the dual labor markets literature, to which they believed themselves contributors, Wilson and Portes[74] introduced the concept of "immigrant enclave," a conceptual ancestor of the ethnic enclave economy. By immigrant enclave, however, Wilson and Portes still meant only the employment of immigrant workers in "the enclave labor market." Workers were in the enclave labor market if their employers were coethnics.[75] Wilson and Portes did not include the self-employed in their study because only employees were of interest to students of labor market segmentation — and the self-employed were not employees.

Wilson and Portes's concept of ethnic enclave economy built upon dual labor market theory's distinction between the competitive and monopoly sectors.[76] Wilson and Portes and his associates argued that ethnic enclave economies obtained some of the economic advantages of the monopoly sector even though, strictly speaking, they belonged in the competitive sector. Ethnic enclave economies obtained these advantages thanks to superior recapture of coethnic spending. This recapture was caused ultimately by vertical and horizontal integration along ethnic lines such that coethnic firms could suck value out of each stage of a product's movement toward the market, losing little or no value to noncoethnic firms. Using the Cubans of Miami as their example, Wilson and Portes showed that Cuban firms bought from and sold to one another to an extent far beyond chance levels. Along *Calle Ocho,* the Cuban economy's main street, Cuban-owned firms bought the semifinished products of other Cuban firms, worked on the products themselves, and then passed the improved products on to other Cuban firms, which finally sold it at retail. These ethnic linkages permitted Cuban firms to extract maximum value from every dollar of final product ultimately sold to non-Cubans. As befits an important idea, analogous enclave situations are easily spotted once someone points out the basics. Tourists can see an analogous process operating on San Francisco's Fisherman's Wharf, where Italian fishermen sell their catch to Italian restaurants that sell seafood meals to visitors. In this manner, San Francisco's Italian ethnic economy monopolizes the whole value of the restaurant business even though the tourist industry has a competitive, small business structure.

The vertical and horizontal linkages that gave the enclave economy its quasi-monopolistic advantage derived ultimately from what social scientists now call *social capital,* a concept we define and use in chapters 4 and 5. Although Wilson and Portes did not utilize that terminology, which had not yet been invented, they did report that Cuban merchants built upon ethnic networks, ethnic trust, and common language for reasons of expediency. That is, Cuban business owners dealt with other Cuban business owners because they already knew and trusted them and could speak to them in their native language. These straightforward and practical business advantages were easy to understand without requiring observers to postulate a Cuban economic conspiracy to bilk or defraud consumers. At this point, Wilson and Portes intersected with the core argument of the ethnic economy according to which ethnic economies evolve naturally because of their operating advantages. True, Wilson and Portes's arguments about the quasi-monopolistic advantages of ethnic economies would have been familiar to African Americans, whose popular economic thought had long stressed like arguments, but their income recapture arguments had never before been empirically traced in formal input−output analysis as Wilson and Portes did.[77]

Portes[78] later expanded the enclave labor market to include the self-employed, the first time dual labor market theorists had done so. According to Portes, immigrant enclaves had two characteristics: spatial clustering, and numerous immigrant-owned business firms that employed many coethnic workers.[79] Even though his new conceptualization included the self-employed, then a conceptual innovation, Portes's emphasis was still upon the numerous workers they employed, not upon the self-employed themselves.[80] This emphasis upon numerous workers was a product of the labor market segmentation tradition. It ignored the question of what was to be done with the self-employed who employed no workers.

Portes and Bach[81] returned to Portes's[82] earlier definition of an enclave economy. However, they[83] operationalized the Cuban enclave economy as "all men indicating employment in firms owned by Cubans," a definition that excluded the self-employed. Later, aggregating self-employed and their coethnic employees, who were not further distinguished, their final operationalization actually followed Bonacich and Modell's earlier definition of the ethnic economy even though it contradicted the definition of enclave economy they offered. In this book, the ethnic enclave economy empirically consisted of the self-employed plus their coethnic employees in Miami. They compared Cubans in the enclave economy with Cubans in the primary and secondary sectors of the labor market in respect to money returns on human capital. They found that after 6 years of residence in the United States, the Cuban immigrants' money returns on occupational prestige and knowledge of English were more favorable in the enclave than in the primary labor market.

Turning to Mexican immigrant men, whom they also followed longitudinally from their arrival, Portes and Bach[84] found no enclave economy at all, a telling result. Cubans had an ethnic enclave economy, and Mexicans did not. Of course, Portes and Bach found self-employment among Mexican immigrants in their sample. In 1979, 5.5 percent of Mexican immigrant men in their sample were self-employed compared with 21.2 percent of Cuban men. However, Mexican self-employment did not create a small immigrant enclave economy to contrast with the Cubans' big one. Such a position would have coincided with the treatment one would have expected from the perspective of Bonacich and Modell's concept of ethnic economy.[85] Instead, they declared that Cubans had an enclave economy and Mexicans did not. As a result, Mexican immigrants had to take their chances as "low wage labor in the open economy," whereas Cubans operated in a "setting dominated by immigrant business networks."[86] The non-existence of a Mexican enclave economy is clear evidence that Portes and Bach's concepts were not the same as those introduced earlier by Bonacich and Modell.

Although Portes and Bach[87] cited Bonacich and Modell, thus indicating familiarity with this earlier work, their treatment of Mexicans diverged from the concept of ethnic economy because they wanted to propose something different. As Portes and Bach conceived it, the ethnic enclave economy was not just the co-ethnic self-employed and their coethnic employees. It also consisted of a *locational cluster* of business firms whose owners and employees were coethnics and whose firms employed a "significant number" of coethnic workers. From this definition, three corollaries followed that excluded the Mexicans from an ethnic enclave economy even though Mexicans clearly had an ethnic economy. First, unlike Cubans in their sample, 90 percent of whom resided in Miami, Mexicans in their sample were more evenly dispersed across the Southwest. Therefore, their ethnic economies were small in scale and could not derive the same benefits from locational aggregation. Second, the scattered Mexican ethnic economies lacked a huge locational cluster like Miami's Little Havana. Third, the Mexican self-employed did not employ a significant number of coethnics in their firms, most of which had no employees at all. For these reasons, Mexicans had an ethnic economy as Bonacich and Modell had defined it, but they did not have an ethnic enclave economy as Portes and Bach defined it.[88]

When attempting to define the ethnic enclave economy, Portes and Bach had in mind the Cuban economy of Miami. One-half the population of Miami is of Cuban origin. Miami's Little Havana contained (still contains) a conspicuous concentration of Cuban-owned firms in which many Cuban employees work. The concentration of the firms in a Cuban business district was conceptually important because of the threshold benefits supposedly derived therefrom. That is, Wilson and Portes[89] and Wilson and Martin[90] had argued that the Cuban ethnic enclave economy was hyperefficient because of vertical and horizontal integration, ethnically sympathetic suppliers and consumers, pooled savings, and rigged markets. Not sharing in this agglomeration benefit, Cuban-owned firms outside the Cuban enclave presumably did not derive any spin-off benefit from their location, so the enclave concept appropriately excluded such firms and their Cuban employees. Indeed, the alleged agglomeration effects of the Cuban ethnic enclave in Miami explained why neither Miami's blacks nor immigrant Mexicans could obtain equivalently high rates of self-employment as did immigrant Cubans.[91]

After much initial confusion during which the concepts were wrongly equated, the literature now distinguishes an ethnic economy from an ethnic enclave economy.[92] These are different concepts. As the concept of ethnic enclave economy matured, the term came to stand for the economic advantages of locational clustering. Economic advantage means the ability of the enclave economy to generate more money for participants than the participants would have been able to obtain without that enclave structure to support them. At this point, the ethnic enclave economy turned into a special case of the ethnic economy, the current view. It is a special case because every immigrant group or ethnic minority has an ethnic economy, but only some ethnic economies are territorially clustered and confer quasi-monopolistic economic advantage.[93] In other words, an ethnic enclave economy requires locational clustering of firms, economic interdependency, and employees, whereas an ethnic economy requires none of these. As a result, researchers conclude that ethnic enclave economies are fewer than ethnic economies.[94]

When ethnic firms are not clustered conspicuously in a neighborhood like Miami's Little Havana, or when firm owners have no employees, or when vertical and horizontal integration do not obtain, then an ethnic economy exists that does not fit the concept of an ethnic enclave economy. Since all three conditions are rarely obtained, the concept of ethnic enclave economy fits far fewer cases than does the concept of ethnic economy. The case of Iranians in Los Angeles illustrates the distinction. The Iranians' ethnic economy is very large. It occupies 61.3 percent of Iranian heads of households in the labor force. However, the Iranian ethnic economy is not an ethnic enclave economy for two principal reasons. First, the Iranian firms are virtually unclustered in space just as Iranian residences are unclustered. The Iranian ethnic economy lacks a business core analogous to Chinatown or Little Havana.[95] Second, the Iranian firms are heavy on owners, but light on coethnic employees. Therefore, the ethnic enclave economy's emphasis upon relative wages misses the main economic effect of the ethnic economy.

INTERACTIONISM

The textbook explanation of entrepreneurship has long maintained that entrepreneurship has a demand side as well as a supply side.[96] That is, the number of entrepreneurs anywhere and their characteristics depend simultaneously upon what customers want and what provider groups will supply. Here what the customers want to buy stands for the demand side of the explanation, and what the provider groups offer stands for the supply side.[97] Both sides belong to a full explanation. However, as the ethnic economy literature developed, emphasis had fallen heavily upon the supply side to the neglect of the demand side. This emphasis made sense in terms of the new subject's need to prove the existence of intergroup variation on the supply side in order to legitimate the whole discussion. Additionally, the practice of holding some factors constant in order to ascertain the effects of others is both essential and legitimate in social science. Nonetheless, some researchers complained that the ethnic economy literature neglected the demand side. They asked for balanced explanations that included both the demand side and the supply side.

In a pioneering statement of this complaint, Waldinger, Ward, and Aldrich[98] observed that a "common objection to cultural analysis" was its lack of attention to "the economic environment in which immigrant entrepreneurs function." They recommended "an interactive approach" that examined the "congruence between the demands of the economic environment and the informal resources of the ethnic population." Since the time they wrote this, that reaction has achieved the strength of a movement of thought in the ethnic economy literature, within which it is now axiomatic that ethnic entrepreneurs emerge from the interaction of supply and demand. At first, this conclusion sounds like the prewar textbook orthodoxy rewarmed. However, the interaction approach does not represent a return to the older textbook generalization that supply and demand coproduce entrepreneurs. That older view makes no reference to the articulation of supply and demand, only insisting that both participate in a complete explanation. In contrast the interaction hypothesis specifies how supply and demand codetermine entrepreneurship—not just that they do so. Specifically, interactionism claims that the entrepreneurial performance of groups depends upon the fit between what they have to offer and what a market requires.[99] The better the fit, the more entrepreneurs; and the same group can experience a good fit in some places and a poor fit in others. Thus, the Chinese operate proportionally more restaurants in New York City where numerous Jews like Chinese food than they do in cities whose predominantly non-Jewish consumers do not share the enthusiasm.[100] This example suggests that the number of Chinese restaurants in any place is a joint product of the number of Chinese in the place and the local public's appetite for Chinese food. In fact, interactionism maintains that every group's entrepreneurship depends upon the fit between what it can do and what the local market demands.

Interactionism imposed a new and stringent methodological constraint upon ethnic economy research. In order to expose supply and demand factors, interactionist research designs must permit simultaneous variation in supplier groups and in demand environments. Some preinteractionist research met this design requirement; most did not.[101] For example, in their research on Asian entrepreneurs in three British cities, Aldrich, Jones, and McEvoy[102] compared the Asians with a sample of white entrepreneurs in respect to directly measured practices thought to reflect ethnic business style. They found few differences between Asians and whites in respect to resource endowment but important differences in business environment among the three cities, with all groups demonstrating higher rates in some than in others. Reviewing the evidence, they concluded that "immigrant business activity" was more shaped by internal than by external forces. "The opportunity structure of the receiving society outweighs any cultural predisposition towards entrepreneurship."[103] Absent simultaneous variation in both supply and demand conditions, this judgment would not have been permissible.[104]

However, most early, interaction-seeking research stumbled over this methodological requirement. For example, in his study of New York City's garment industry, Waldinger stressed the advantages of a balanced treatment that acknowledges "opportunity structures" as well as cultural influences. In this regard, Waldinger[105] mentioned the economic advantages that lured immigrant Dominican and Chinese entrepreneurs into this industry. These economic advantages included low returns on economies of scale, instability and uncertainty of product demand, small and differentiated product markets, agglomeration advantages, access to cheap labor, and vacant niches caused by exodus of ethnic white predecessors. These demand-side attractions did not negate what Waldinger called the "predispositions toward entrepreneurship" of the immigrants, and Waldinger acknowledged the predispositions as well as the economic incentives. Waldinger regarded this conclusion as a balanced one that did justice to supply as well as demand influences.

However, Waldinger's research varied only groups. It did not simultaneously vary demand environments.[106] His multiple groups—one industry design only permitted inductive generalizations about the influence of supply-side resources upon entrepreneurship. It did not permit generalizations about the influence of demand environment, a constant. From a formal point of view, therefore, Waldinger's balanced conclusions were of unequal value. On the one hand, the comparison of Chinese and Dominicans permitted conclusions about the influence of different supply profiles on the groups' entrepreneurship. On the other hand, Waldinger's design did not authorize his conclusions about demand.[107]

To solve the methodological problem, balance-seeking research turned to multigroup, multilocality research designs. In these designs, a plurality of ethnoracial groups represented the supply side, and a plurality of localities the demand side. In the first of these interactionist designs, Light and Rosenstein[108] examined the self-employment rates of five ethnoracial categories in 226 metropolitan regions of the United States. The categories were native white, foreign-born white, Asian, black, and Hispanic. This research did turn up some interactionist results. Metropolitan areas showed considerable variation in respect to the rank order of ethnoracial categories within them. For example, Chico, California, ranked 1st in self-employment rate for Asians and native whites, 3rd for Hispanics, but only 13th for blacks and 35th for foreign-born whites. If local demand just determined entrepreneurship, one would have expected all ethnoracial categories to respond identically to Chico. But, taking interactionism into account, one expects metropolitan areas to produce unequal rates of self-employment among resident ethnoracial categories.[109]

Light and Rosenstein were able to examine the main effects of demand and supply variables net of the supply–demand interaction required by interactionist theory. If interactions were the only influences upon the self-employment of ethnoracial groups, then neither supply variables nor demand variables should exert any direct and unmediated main effects. The results were only partially confirmatory of interactionism. Although interaction strengthened the explanatory power of demand-side variables, when supply variables were omitted, supply–demand interactions only slightly reduced the main effect of supply-side variables such as age, gender, human capital, and ethnoracial category. This result is compatible with the presumption that capacities leap across occupational and industrial boundaries.

Razin and Light[110] compared the self-employment rates of 77 national origin groups in 16 metropolitan regions. This study used national origin groups as the supply-side unit, not ethnoracial categories. Greeks and Koreans were the most consistently entrepreneurial groups in the 17 metropolitan areas. Razin and Light found that mainstream groups' self-employment rates varied closely with the overall self-employment rate of the metropolitan areas, rising where that overall rate was strong and falling where it was weak. But nonmainstream groups had a different pattern. By nonmainstream groups, they meant national origin groups that are not predominantly white, or not predominantly Christian, or not from Europe, or all of these. Nonmainstream immigrants had a much greater propensity to form strong niches in a few low-income retail or service specialties. Razin and Light called these "entrepreneurial niches." The existence of these entrepreneurial niches shows that immigrants of the same nationality were clustering in the same occupations and industries rather than fanning out individually in search of the best opportunities.

THE ETHNIC-CONTROLLED ECONOMY

Bonacich and Modell's concept of ethnic economy frustrates those who wish to build ethnicity or niches into their analytical tools. Therefore, some researchers have redefined the term ethnic economy to suit broader needs, even at the risk of producing terminological confusion. The first was probably Reitz[111] who defined the ethnic economy as any work context in which coethnics utilized a foreign language. Others have wanted to equate the ethnic economy to business firms in which buyers and sellers are coethnics.[112] When ethnics sell to or buy from noncoethnics, the transaction takes place outside the ethnic economy. The ethnic economy would then exist only when ethnics buy from and sell to coethnics.

Jiobu[113] defined "ethnic hegemonization" as a combination of industrial clustering and industrial power. He illustrated his conception by reference to Japanese Americans in California agriculture. Because they were not only numerous in this industry, but heavily clustered within it, especially in strawberries, the Japanese Americans could raise the price of their farm commodities by withholding crops from the market. Therefore, Japanese farmers exercised economic power, and were not just the price takers of economic theory. Successful minorities, Jiobu generalized, "have to hegemonize an entire economic area, both horizontally and vertically." What is noteworthy is that Jiobu referred to an industrial context in which Japanese Americans had ownership authority, but his concept of hegemonization stressed their power, based on their numbers and clustering, not their ownership authority.

About the same time, Light and Bonacich[114] found that Koreans in Los Angeles were heavily clustered both as employees and as self-employed. The heaviest cluster was in soft drinks, in which Korean owners represented more than one-third of all dealers even though Koreans were only 5 percent of all business owners in Los Angeles County. More generally, the clustering of Koreans in self-employment was greater than the clustering of Koreans in wage employment (Table 1.1). Korean employees worked in just 64.7 percent of industries because 35.3 percent of industries had no Korean employees at all. On the other hand, 100 percent of self-employed Koreans worked in just 28.5 percent of industries. A full 71.5 percent of Los Angeles industries contained no self-employed Koreans at all! To equalize the distribution of Koreans among Los Angeles industries,

TABLE 1.1   Korean Representation in Employment and Self-Employment, 232 Industries of Los Angeles County, 1980 (in Percentages)

	Employees	Self-employed
No Koreans in industry	35.3	71.6
Up to 1% Korean	1.3	7.8
More than 1% Korean	63.4	20.7
Total	100	100
N	(232)	(232)

Source: Ivan Light and Edna Bonacich, *Immigrant Entrepreneurs* (Berkeley and Los Angeles: University of California Press, 1988), p. 182. Reproduced by permission.

35.3 percent of Korean employees would have had to move into industries in which no Koreans were actually employed. Conversely, to equalize the distribution of Koreans among the self-employed, 71.5 percent would have had to move into industries that actually contained no Korean firms. The industrial clustering of Koreans, the authors noted, "conferred a potential for moderating competition, exchanging information, and mutual aid."

Zhou and Logan[115] approached the ethnic economy of the Chinese through census data. They first identified industries in which Chinese were overrepresented, and defined the ethnic enclave economy as the sum of these industries. Model[116] used a similar approach to compare Chinese and Cuban ethnic economies. Somewhat later, Logan, Alba, and McNulty[117] redefined an ethnic economy as "any situation where common ethnicity provides an economic advantage."[118] Possible situations included relations among coethnic owners, relations between owners and coethnic employees, and relations among coethnic employees in the mainstream economy. Since this definition of ethnic economy included wage earners in the mainstream, it was broader than what Bonacich and Modell had proposed. In practice, however, Logan, Alba, and McNulty crafted census-based measurements that mimicked the Bonacich and Modell concept of ethnic economy. Studying 10 ethnic groups in 17 metropolitan areas of the United States, they declared that joint overrepresentation of coethnic workers and coethnic employers in any industry would be interpreted as an ethnic-controlled industry, and the sum of the ethnic-controlled industries would represent the ethnic economy. Since the U.S. Census does not provide data on the ethnicity of business owners and of their employees, the authors had to examine clustering rather than ownership. Thus, finding Chinese heavily overrepresented as restaurant owners and restaurant employees, Logan, Alba, and McNulty concluded that the restaurant industry fell within the Chinese ethnic economy. Theirs is a legitimate innovation because issues of data availability and quality impinge very strongly on all social science debates. Their compromise made it possible to count the number of ethnic economies in major cities from existing census data.

To redefine the ethnic economy as ethnic economic advantage invites dialogue with anyone who asserts that ethnicity never confers economic advantage. Timothy Bates[119] makes this claim, alleging that ethnicity is economically neutral, never advantageous. Other economists now dispute this view.[120] However, on Bates's ultraconservative view, the "bedrock" economic resources are only wealth and human capital.[121] People who enjoy wealth, education, and occupational skills prosper thanks to these resources alone. Ethnicity never contributes anything additional. From our perspective, this view is wrong, and rejecting it is a major purpose of this entire book. Just for starters, ethnic entrepreneurs usually cluster in the same occupations and industries.[122] Clustering confers market power above and beyond individual wealth and human capital. For example, Korean business owners monopolized the wig business before federal prosecutors brought suit under the Sherman Anti-Trust Act. While they enjoyed their monopoly, Korean business owners excluded non-Koreans from the wig industry, and raised prices of wigs to consumers.[123] Again, Japanese farmers were able to raise prices for strawberries thanks to their clustering.[124] Cases like these are very common, and all illustrate an ethnic economic resource, market power, that does not depend upon the business owners' human capital or wealth.

Secondly, the redefined concept of ethnic economy (as ethnic advantage) opens discussion of how ethnic employees most advantageously operate outside the ethnic economy, an issue that Bonacich and Modell's concept cannot raise, much less address. For example, what if government employees control hiring for government jobs, but hire only their friends and relatives? These cases have happened with considerable regularity in American history.[125] In a pluralistic society such as the United States, ordinary nepotism produces ethnoracial clustering. When, thanks to nepotism, coethnics get the jobs, noncoethnics are excluded. True, the intent is to advantage friends, relatives, and coethnics rather than maliciously to injure outsiders—even if the effect is the same.[126] In such a case, too, contrary to Bates, workers obtain economic benefit from their ethnicity above and beyond whatever their individual wealth and human capital confer. Following Kessner and Modell,[127] who reached similar conclusions, Waldinger[128] reminds us that exactly this arrangement has long prevailed in the municipal government of New York City.[129] Waldinger studied the history of municipal employment in New York City in the twentieth century. He found that Italian, Irish, and Jewish immigrants obtained municipal employment through coethnic hiring networks. First, the immigrants established ethnic niches within government workplaces, occupations, and industries. For example, construction became an Irish niche, sanitation an Italian niche, and school teaching a Jewish niche. Ethnic niches are just ethnic concentrations at high density.[130] The economic success of white immigrants and their native-born descendants involved "finding a good niche and dominating it."[131] To dominate a niche meant to assure coethnic applicants of preferred access to jobs.

Very informal methods can obtain this end. An Irish contractor in Boston explained[132] his hiring procedure in this manner: "A good number of building contractors drinks in the pub, and the lads comes in and they gives them work." Since the Irish contractors drink in Irish-owned pubs, the lads are reliably Irish. Research recurrently reports that informal social contacts are the most frequent way in which people of all ethnoracial backgrounds find work.[133] Social networks also produce the best jobs. Moreover, once established in this way, ethnic niches are persistent.[134] Lieberson and Waters[135] found that white ethnics' occupational clusters had persisted for 80 years and were still going strong. White ethnics did not own the municipal government of New York City, which employed them, but they managed to control employment in it.

After 1970, African Americans began to enter employment niches that upwardly mobile whites had exited, and they also began to compete with whites for access to government jobs that had once been the exclusive preserve of the whites, and to develop niches of their own.[136] Indeed, Boyd[137] proposes that opportunities for blacks in the public sector siphoned away entrepreneurially endowed workers who would otherwise have started businesses. Although this claim has not been proven beyond the shadow of a doubt, the preponderance of government employment among African Americans is sufficiently strong to create at least a suspicion. Table 1.2 compares the sectoral employment (private, government, self-employment) of African Americans, non Hispanic whites, and selected others in Los Angeles. Heavily immigrant, noncitizens, and lacking political influence, the Asian and Hispanic groups have a much smaller share of government employment than do non–Hispanic whites, who, in turn, obtain only half as much government employment as do blacks.

When coethnic workers control hiring, pay, and working conditions on the job, whether through numbers, trade unions, social networks, legal priorities, or any other advantage, they usurp the legal owners' titular authority to control those decisions. The employees thus obtain de facto control of someone else's property.[138] It does not matter whether the usurpation affects a private corporation, such as the Bank of America, or a government agency, such as the city of New York. Wherever they arise, ethnic niches confer some rights of ownership, but they do not require coethnics to own the premises, industries, or occupations whose hiring, wages, and working conditions they control. Lewin-Epstein and Semyonov[139] even raise the possibility of an ethnic community "gaining hegemony" over portions of the public sector. At this point, business ownership and job control *become equivalent* in respect to the hiring advantage they convey. An

TABLE 1.2   Sectoral Distribution of Ethnoracial Groups in Los Angeles, 1990 (in Percentages)

Groups	Private	Government	Self-employment	Total
Non–Hispanic white	71.7	12.2	16.2	100
Black	69.2	23.7	7.1	100
Chinese	73.0	9.8	17.2	100
Korean	60.1	4.6	35.3	100
Mexican	86.3	7.2	6.5	100
Salvadoran	90.9	3.0	6.1	100

Source: James P. Allen and Eugene Turner, *The Ethnic Quilt: Population Diversity in Southern California* (Los Angeles: Center for Geographical Studies of California State University, 1997), p. 208.

ethnic-owned firm that employs 99 coethnics provides the same employment to coethnics as a state agency that employs 100 coethnics even though the employees do not own the state agency. Small and medium businesses are rarely unionized and they overwhelmingly hire coethnics through word of mouth recruitment. Worker control is uncommon in the ethnic-owned economy.[140] Giant corporations and public bureaucracies are the principal sites in which coethnics usurp de facto hiring authority from owners or managers who are not coethnic.

It is important to note that not all ethnic niches yield an ethnic-controlled economy. If coethnics cluster in a firm or government agency but do not, as ethnics, influence wages, hiring, working conditions, and the like, then an ethnic niche exists, but membership yields no control.

As we wish to address the broader advantages of ethnicity in the economy in this book, not just the advantages of ethnic ownership, important as those are, we require the conceptual means to do it. The Bonacich–Modell concept of the ethnic economy does not provide sufficient means. Therefore, we propose to rename what Jiobu called "ethnic hegemonization," what Logan, Alba, and McNulty called the ethnic economy, *and* what Waldinger[141] and others have called ethnic niches. Instead, we propose the term *ethnic-controlled economy* to encompass all these concepts, and, indeed, all situations and sectors in which coethnic employees (not owners) exert significant and enduring market power in the general economy, usually because of numbers, clustering, and organization, but also, when applicable, because of external political or economic power. In contrast to the ethnic-controlled economy, defined previously, we wish now to rechristen what Bonacich and Modell called the ethnic economy as the *ethnic ownership economy*. These terminological redefinitions permit us to contrast an ethnic economy with its basis in property right, the ethnic ownership economy, with an ethnic economy whose basis is de facto control based on numbers, clustering, and organization, the ethnic-controlled economy (Table 1.3).[142]

TABLE 1.3   Ethnic Economies

Concept	Definition
Ethnic economy	Self-employed, employers, unpaid family workers, and coethnic employees
Ethnic enclave economy	An ethnic economy that is clustered around a territorial core
Ethnic ownership economy	An ethnic economy
Ethnic-controlled economy	Significant and persistent economic power exercised by coethnic employees in the mainstream economy

Our reasons for renaming are several. First, our terminology reduces intellectual clutter without losing content. The ethnic-controlled economy includes all manifestation of economic power based on number, organization, and clustering regardless of exactly what control employees exert. For example, employees may control hiring, wages, working conditions, training, or all of these. Second, different concepts should have different names; otherwise, one sows confusion.[143] Third, Bonacich and Modell's definition of ethnic economy has a valid and legitimate purchase that we retain. Although we change the concept's name to ethnic ownership economy, we leave the content unchanged. Fourth, new terminologies clarify and highlight the latent distinction between ownership and control that has thus far eluded precise identification in the ethnic economy literature. Finally, we believe that the new terminologies invite and open up research questions that will profitably occupy research for some time.

SUMMARY AND CONCLUSION

We have identified three related concepts that derive from the core literature, but that reflect different aspects of the ethnic economy. Of these, the oldest is what we have rechristened the ethnic ownership economy. The ethnic ownership economy consists of business owners and their coethnic helpers and workers. The businesses owned are small and medium in size. This concept permits comparison of the economic integration of ethnic groups now and in the past, in the United States and abroad. The ethnic ownership economy's boundaries distinguish where and how much a group has penetrated a host economy, taking the jobs it made available, and where, how, and how much each group has grafted new firms and jobs onto a host economy. A key feature of any group's economic strategy, this balance between self-employment and wage employment affects the ability of groups to accelerate economic mobility or to evade unemployment. Here the process of ethnic succession in the general labor market creates a baseline of economic mobility against which it is possible to explain why some groups have gone up faster than expected and others slower.[144]

The second concept is the ethnic enclave economy. An ethnic enclave economy is an ethnic ownership economy that is clustered around a territorial core. This concept invites inquiries about the consequences of territorial clustering. Existing literature proposes that territorial clustering permits ethnic communities to capture a higher proportion of sales than would be possible from unclustered firms. In effect, the ethnic enclave economy obtains economic strength that small business firms normally lack, but that monopolies enjoy. The added economic strength accrues to the advantage of the ethnic community, whose workers obtain extra jobs and profit as a consequence. This bonus accelerates their economic mobility above and beyond what unclustered ethnic economies provide.

Finally, we have identified a third sector, the ethnic-controlled economy. The ethnic-controlled economy refers to industries, occupations, and organizations of the general labor market in which coethnic *employees* exert appreciable and persistent economic power. This power usually results from their numerical clustering, their numerical preponderance, their organization, government mandates, or all four. The ethnic-controlled economy is completely independent of the ethnic ownership economy, and its participants exert de facto control, not ownership authority. Control permits coethnics to secure more and better jobs in the mainstream than they otherwise would, to reduce unemployment, and to improve working conditions.[145] In this way, the ethnic-controlled economy accelerates the economic mobility of participants as well as the ethnic group to which they belong.

If we call these three together the ethnic economies, to emphasize their relatedness, their contrast is with the mainstream labor market in which isolated ethnic employees have jobs outside ethnic economies. In these mainstream jobs, coethnics are unclustered, and they exercise no influence as coethnics. Mainstream employment results when immigrants and ethnics fan out in pursuit of individual economic opportunity. Fanning out is exactly what assimilation theorists expected.[146] In the mainstream labor market, immigrants and ethnics get the deal American society offers individuals, and this deal may include discrimination from *other people's* ethnic-controlled economies. For this reason, the general labor market is a more treacherous environment than its enthusiasts acknowledge. Mainstream employment is obviously very important in fact as well as in theory, and we do not ignore it. However, the mainstream labor market has for too long been interpreted as the only way in which ethnics and immigrants can obtain income.

Peter Li[147] asks whether self-employment offers better earning opportunities than wage work, and concludes that it depends on what type of self-employment one specifies. True enough, but the answer also depends, we suggest, on whether employees are in an ethnic-controlled economy or in the general labor market. To assume, as have assimilation theorists, that everyone works in the general labor market is to oversimplify. The prevailing simplification ignores all three ethnic economies in the interest of a homogeneous econospace within which uniform assimilation occurs at a constant speed, a Fordist image that has outlived its usefulness. No wonder that assimilation theory cannot explain why some ethnic and immigrant groups make faster economic progress than others, and why, very generally, intergroup economic outcomes are as divergent as they are.[148] On the whole, sociology's pedestrian answer has been intergroup inequalities of human capital, no doubt a meritocratic aspect of the problem. Still, it is clear that the three ethnic economies powerfully affect economic attainment *net* of individual wealth and human capital endowments. Progress in understanding unequal economic outcomes requires acknowledgment of the diversity in economic situs that actually exists.

CHAPTER 2

The Size of Ethnic Economies

One measure of the size of ethnic economies is how many people work in them. The population of an ethnic ownership economy consists of self-employed, employers, employees of coethnic employers, and unpaid family workers. An ethnic- controlled economy consists of coethnic employees outside the ethnic ownership economy who, thanks to their clustering, numbers, organization, political influence, or all four, exercise significant and enduring market power in workplace, occupation, or industry. Ethnic-controlled economies considerably expand the population of ethnic economies beyond what ethnic ownership economies alone would create. The sum of any group's ethnic ownership economy *plus* its ethnic-controlled economy gives the proportion of coethnic workers whose employment is outside the general labor market. The sum of all the ethnic groups' ethnic ownership economies and ethnic-controlled economies gives the share of the total labor force that works outside the general labor force.

These magnitudes are not easy to estimate. In particular, measuring ethnic-controlled economies encounters the difficulty of evaluating real market power from external indicators such as ethnic clustering. Although occupational and in-dustrial clustering create a basis for market power, neither guarantees it. Nonetheless, the wisdom of investigating them any further depends upon the probable size of ethnic economies. If ethnic economies contain hardly any workers, then increased efforts to improve their measurement might not be cost-effective. On the other hand, if ethnic economies are probably large, possibly even larger than the general labor market, then the case for improving their measurement is compelling. In this chapter, using available materials, we estimate the size of aggregate and group-specific ethnic economies and indicate their probable importance.

ETHNIC OWNERSHIP ECONOMIES

The higher the share of an ethnic ownership economy in any group's total labor force, the more employment that ethnic ownership economy provides coethnics and the less the general labor market provides. In an extreme case, when an ethnic group is an outcast or pariah, its ethnic ownership economy might provide 100% of all the employment that coethnics obtain. In such a case, however wretched their livelihoods, the coethnics would owe all employment entirely to their own ethnic ownership economy. At the opposite extreme, an ethnic economy might employ no coethnics. In such a case, an ethnic ownership economy contributes nothing to the employment of coethnics, whose entire support would depend upon the jobs they find in the general labor market or upon the ethnic-controlled economy. Indeed, in such a case an ethnic ownership economy would not exist at all.

In the American context, ethnic ownership economies only reach either limit, 100% or zero, when ethnic groups are quite small.[1] Otherwise, every ethnoracial group has an ethnic ownership economy. No uncertainty attends this issue, but uncertainty does attend estimates of the actual population of various groups' ethnic ownership economies, and these uncertainties affect their presumptive importance. After all, if ethnic ownership economies are tiny, why study them. The task is to identify which and how many groups actually have significant ethnic ownership economies, where significant means too large to ignore. In turn, too large to ignore means that, when people ignore ethnic economies, they seriously distort reality. If ignoring them does not seriously distort reality, then we may wish to ignore them out of convenience.

The hazards of ignoring ethnic ownership economies are easy to illustrate. Suppose 50% of some ethnoracial or immigrant group work in the ethnic ownership economy, but analysts ignore the topic, concentrating exclusively on coethnic employees in the general labor market. In that case, analysts would wrongly impute to the whole group the earnings modality that actually characterized only half the group. We would really have no proper idea of how this group earns its living, a basic fact about any group, but, worse, we would have accepted misinformation as correct. This case is not speculative. In 1941, when war clouds were gathering, 56.2% of Japanese American men and 44.4% of Japanese American women worked in the ethnic economy.[2] Actually, those estimates are low because some unknown share of persons listed as "wage and salary workers" also had Japanese American employers and so qualified as ethnic economy workers.[3] In view of the large population of the Japanese American ethnic economy in 1941, no one could ignore the ethnic economy without seriously distorting how Japanese Americans were earning their bread.

Admittedly, the Japanese American ethnic economy was unusually large in 1940 relative to many other ethnic economies then and now. Moreover, in view of the decline in self-employment between 1940 and 1974, one might suppose that comparably large ethnic economies no longer exist. Indeed, we thought so ourselves at one time. A complete answer calls for data that systematically compare multiple ethnic economies now and then. Unfortunately, such systematic data are not available, partially because of the unexamined but prevailing assumption that ethnic ownership economies are small and insignificant. However, many contemporary ethnic groups do match and some even exceed the share of the labor force that the Japanese American economy enjoyed in 1940. Among Israelis in Los Angeles, Gold found a self-employment rate of 80%, a proportion far higher than the Japanese Americans had attained in 1940.[4] Min[5] found that 47.5% of Koreans in Los Angeles were self-employed and another 27.6% were their employees in 1989. Portes, Clark, and Lopez[6] estimated that 20% of Cubans in Miami were self-employed, and another 30% worked in Cuban-owned businesses. Table 2.1 shows the population of the ethnic economies that existed among Iranians in Los Angeles in 1988. Overall, 56.7% of Iranians were self-employed, and another 4.6%

TABLE 2.1   Number of Owners and Employees within the Ethnic Economy, Number of Employed in the General Labor Market, and Unemployed: Iranians in Los Angeles, 1987–1988 (in Percentages)

	Iranians	Armenians	Bahais	Jews	Muslims
Ethnic economy					
Owners	56.7	44.5	51.5	81.9	46.1
Employees	4.6	9.5	0.0	3.9	3.3
Subtotal (*n*)	(330)	(74)	(34)	(133)	(89)
General labor market					
Employed	36.8	43.8	45.5	12.2	49.4
Unemployed	1.9	2.2	3.0	1.9	1.1
Subtotal (*n*)	(208)	(63)	(32)	(22)	(91)
Total (*N*)	538	137	66	155	18
Total (%)	100.0	100.0	100.0	100.0	100.0

Source: Ivan Light, Georges Sabagh, Mehdi Bozorgmehr, and Claudia Der-Martirosian, "Beyond the Ethnic Enclave Economy," *Social Problems* 41 (1994), pp. 65–80.

of Iranians worked for them. These two groups created an ethnic economy that encompassed 61.3% of Iranians in Los Angeles.

However, when we disaggregate Iranians into four subethnic groups, we observe even higher self-employment rates. At the top, 81.9% of Jews from Iran were self-employed; another 3.9% of Jews from Iran worked for them. In all, nearly 86% of Iranian Jews worked in the ethnic economy. At the other extreme, 46.1% of Muslims from Iran were self-employed, and these Muslims employed another 3.3% of Iranian coreligionists, bringing the Iranian Muslim economy to 49.4% of their labor force. Clearly, in the cases of the Iranians, Koreans, and Israelis, some contemporary ethnic groups have built ethnic economies as large as the one the Japanese Americans operated in 1940. These cases prove that at least some contemporary ethnic economies are neither obsolete nor insignificantly small when compared with earlier ones.

Ethnic Ownership Economy of Individual Groups

For broad significance, the very best case would exist if all ethnic economies, even the smallest, were sufficiently large to require attention. In that case, ethnic economies would require consistent coverage. Such is the claim we make in this chapter. However, even if some or a few individual ethnic economies were too small to matter, the aggregate ethnic economies of all the ethnoracial and immigrant groups might nonetheless be significant. In that case, we should not ignore ethnic ownership economies in general just because the ethnic economy of some individual groups is insignificant. Finally, in the worst case, even if ethnic economies are generally insignificant and only a few groups had big ones, they could still be influential to at least these groups. In such a case, ethnic economies would be of limited and specific relevance but not of general relevance to the economy. This is probably the prevailing view in social science today, so, if we are right, ethnic economies are of more general importance than is currently recognized.

Getting away from the star cases, such as the Israelis, Iranians, and Koreans,[7] we wish now to assess the broader significance of ethnic ownership economies of American ethnic groups. Star cases do not speak to the general importance of ethnic economies. The literature's protracted emphasis upon the entrepreneurship stars in contrast with nonstars,[8] a legitimate concern, caused some observers wrongly to conclude that the case for ethnic economies rests only upon the stars.[9]

To evaluate the general importance of ethnic economies, we must first define a threshold of substantive significance at or above which ethnic economies are too big to ignore in the interest of convenience. Extrapolating a famous convention, we declare that threshold significance is reached when an ethnic ownership economy occupies 5% or more of any group's civilian labor force. High significance is 10 to 19% of a group's labor force, and extreme significance is 20% or more. Our task in this section is to evaluate how many American ethnic groups' ethnic ownership economies actually reach any level of significance and which and how many do not. The box score thus obtained will help to measure the importance of the ethnic ownership economies in terms of their population.

Easy in principle, this task is difficult in practice because evidence is fragmentary. Fratoe and Meeks[10] compiled a registry of self-employment rates of 50 American "ancestry groups" in 1980. Ancestry groups consisted of the foreign-born persons by birthplace plus native-born persons who claimed a single national origin in the same birthplace. Although they produced the most comprehensive list theretofore assembled, Fratoe and Meeks did not include African Americans, a major omission. Also, since Fratoe and Meeks's registry excludes unpaid family workers and coethnic employees, both participants in an ethnic economy, their list understates the ethnic economy's population by about one-third. On the other hand, because it includes rural and farm residents, it enhances the ethnic economies of farming groups, such as Scandinavians. This expansion occurs because agriculture has much higher self-employment rates than do urban occupations. Therefore, ancestry groups that cluster in agriculture will naturally display larger ethnic economies than urban groups.

Even so, Fratoe and Meeks's list, when properly adjusted, permits a rough estimate of the individual ethnic economies that existed in 1980. To adjust their list, we estimate the ethnic economy's coethnic employees at one-half the self-employed. For example, if the self-employed were 12%, we estimate that these self-employed persons employed another 6% of coethnics. We derive this rule of thumb from Table 2.2. This table shows the number of employers and employees in the three largest ethnoracial categories (Asian, Hispanic, black). On the aggregate, each ethnic minority owner employed about one employee, so if we assume that half the employees were coethnics, then the ethnic ownership economy would encompass the owners plus 50% of their employees. Our method estimates the percentage of each group's labor force that worked in the ethnic economy in 1980. In turn, that estimate suggests among which and what percentage of ethnic groups surveyed the population of the group's ethnic economy was below significance, significant, or highly significant.

Results are easy to summarize. For all 50 groups, the mean self-employment rate was 5.3%, just at the lower limit of significance. Of the 50 ethnic groups that Fratoe and Meeks identified, 26% had self-employment rates below 5%, our threshold of significance. Three-quarters of all ethnic economies identified in Fratoe and Meeks's survey reached or surpassed our threshold. However, when we adjust for coethnic employees, adding one-half of the self-employment rate, only 16% still fell below significance. For all the groups aggregated individually without weighting them according to their actual size, the self-employment rate

TABLE 2.2   Ethnic Economies of Ethnoracial Categories, 1992

	Black	Asian and other[a]	Hispanic	All persons[b]
Ethnic economies				
Owners	620,912	606,426	771,708	17,253,143
Employees	345,193	860,408	691,056	27,403,974
Total	966,105	1,466,834	1,462,764	44,657,117
Civilian labor force, 1992 (thousands)	14,162	5,404	11,338	128,105
Ethnic economy as percentage of civilian labor force	5.6	19.2	9.9	24.1

[a] Asians, Pacific Islanders, American Indians, and Alaska Natives.
[b] Includes nonminorities.

Source: U.S. Bureau of the Census, 1992 Economic Census, Survey of Minority-Owned Business Enterprises, Summary MB92-4 (Washington, D.C.: GPO, 1996), Tables 1 and 12; U.S. Department of Commerce, Statistical Abstract of the United States, 1996 (Washington, D.C.: GPO, 1996), Table 616; U.S. Bureau of the Census, 1990 Census of Population, Asians and Pacific Islanders in the United States CP-3-5 (Washington, D.C.: GPO, 1993), Table 4.

was above 5% and, with the adjustment of estimated ethnic employees, the average estimated ethnic ownership economy was 8.1% in 1980. At the top, 58% of groups had ethnic economies that included 10% or more of the group's entire labor force. In sum, ethnic ownership economies were in the aggregate too big to ignore in 1980; they were also too big to ignore in three-quarters of the individual cases.

Another source of census evidence, more recent than that of Fratoe and Meeks's survey, continues their tabulation of native and foreign persons combined. Table 2.3 assembles the self-employment rates of 12 ethnoracial groups, both native born and foreign born, for which the U.S. Census published data. However, this time the list includes African Americans, whom Fratoe and Meeks did not include. Again we estimate ethnic economies from the self-employment rates given. Of the 12 ethnoracial groups compared in this table, 7 met or exceeded the threshold of significance strictly on the basis of self-employment and without taking into consideration the additional people who also worked in the ethnic ownership economy as employees or unpaid family laborers. Koreans displayed the highest self-employment rate in 1987.[11] When we add estimated employment in the ethnic economy, 75% of groups reach or exceed the 5% threshold. Puerto Ricans, African Americans, and Hawaiians have estimated ethnic economies that remain below significance.

Yoon[12] compiled a list of 99 ancestry groups from the U.S. Census of 1990. Yoon's list included foreign-born and native-born persons. On Yoon's list the mean self-employment rate was 10.2%, and the mean estimated ethnic economy

TABLE 2.3   Business Ownership of Selected Ethnoracial Minorities in the
United States, 1987

	Percentage owners	Estimated employees	Ethnic economy
Korean	19.0	9.5	28.5
Asian Indians	12.6	6.3	18.9
Japanese	11.5	5.8	17.3
Cuban	10.8	5.4	16.2
Chinese	10.4	5.2	15.6
Vietnamese	9.5	4.8	14.3
European Spanish	9.2	4.6	13.8
Filipino	5.1	2.5	7.6
Mexican	3.9	2.0	5.9
Puerto Rican	2.6	1.3	3.9
African American	2.2	1.1	3.3
Hawaiian	1.6	0.8	2.4

Source: U.S. Small Business Administration, Office of Advocacy, *Handbook of Small Business Data, 1994 Edition* (Washington, D.C.: GPO, 1994), Tables 6.7, 6.8, 6.11, 6.12, 6.14, and 6.15; *Statistical Abstract of the United States 1996* (Washington, D.C.: GPO, 1996), Table 616; *1990 Census of Population. Asian and Pacific Islanders* CP-3-5 (Washington, D.C.: GPO, 1993); *1990 Census of Population. Persons of Hispanic Origin in the United States.* CP-3-3 (Washington, D.C.: GPO, 1993).

was 15%. Of the 99 ancestry groups, only 4 ethnic ownership economies failed to reach 5%, our minimum threshold. At the other extreme, 56 ancestry groups had estimated ethnic economies that exceeded 15% of the labor force. Three of Yoon's ancestry groups (Koreans, Israelis, and Palestinians) had ethnic ownership economies that exceeded 30% of their total labor force. Yoon's results suggest that ethnic economies were generally larger than the ones Fratoe and Meeks had measured in 1980, a decade earlier. We believe that, just as these data suggest, ethnic economies did increase in the United States between 1980 and 1990, just as they did in Australia and Europe.[13]

Using published data, we assembled a list of 37 foreign-born groups from the 1990 U.S. Census. The list shows the male, female, and total self-employed and unpaid family workers of each national origin group as a percentage of that group's labor force in 1990. To obtain comparability with our analysis of Fratoe and Meeks's 1980 evidence, we added the same estimate for the coethnic employees that we had added to Fratoe and Meeks's earlier data. When combined with the total self-employed and unpaid family workers, this estimate yields an estimated percentage of each group's labor force that worked in the ethnic economy in 1990. Table 2.4 shows the results.

TABLE 2.4   Ethnic Economies as a Percentage of All Workers for 37 Foreign-Born Groups by National Origin, 1990

Birthplace	Self-employed and unpaid family workers			Estimated employees	Ethnic economy
	Men	Women	Total		
Extreme significance					
Korea	23.5	18.3	20.9	10.5	31.4
Greece	17.9	11.1	15.7	7.8	23.5
High significance					
Iran	14.1	9.8	12.8	6.4	19.2
France	11.9	9.8	10.8	5.4	16.2
Italy	13.1	6.8	10.8	5.4	16.2
Soviet Union	13.1	7.4	10.7	5.4	16.1
Canada	12.2	8.2	10.2	5.1	15.3
Germany	11.3	8.5	9.7	4.8	14.6
Yugoslavia	11.2	6.6	9.5	4.7	14.2
United Kingdom	9.5	7.8	8.7	4.4	13.1
China	9.5	7.4	8.6	4.3	12.9
Taiwan	8.7	8.3	8.5	4.3	12.8
Japan	8.3	8.6	8.5	4.3	12.8
Poland	9.4	6.7	8.3	4.2	12.5
Thailand	9.8	6.9	8.1	4.1	12.2
Cuba	10.1	4.5	7.7	3.9	11.6
Ireland	9.2	6.0	7.7	3.9	11.6
Peru	7.2	6.5	6.9	3.5	10.4
India	7.2	6.2	6.9	3.5	10.4
Significant					
Vietnam	6.1	7.1	6.5	3.3	9.9
Hong Kong	6.8	5.8	6.3	3.2	9.5
Cambodia	6.1	6.0	6.1	3.1	9.2
Honduras	5.5	6.4	5.9	3.0	8.9
Dominican Republic	7.1	3.7	5.6	2.8	8.5
Guatemala	4.5	7.3	5.6	2.8	8.5
Portugal	6.5	3.9	5.4	2.7	8.1
Nicaragua	4.9	5.2	5.1	2.6	7.7
Mexico	5.0	4.9	4.9	2.5	7.4
El Salvador	4.1	6.2	4.9	2.5	7.4
Ecuador	5.6	3.6	4.7	2.4	7.1
Trinidad/Tobago	5.4	3.4	4.3	2.2	6.5
Jamaica	5.3	3.3	4.2	2.1	6.3
Haiti	4.9	2.2	3.7	1.9	5.6
Philippines	4.0	3.1	3.5	1.8	5.3
Panama	4.4	2.7	3.5	1.8	5.3
Below significance					
Guyana	3.4	2.6	3.0	1.5	4.5
Laos	2.6	2.5	2.5	1.3	3.8
All foreign born	8.0	6.5	7.4	3.7	11.1

Source: U.S. Bureau of the Census, *1990 Census of Population, The Foreign-Born Population in the United States* (Washington D.C.: GPO, 1993), Table 4.

Of the 37 national origin groups in the table, 27% had total self-employment rates below 5%. When we add an estimate of coethnic employees to the self-employed, only 5.4% (2 groups) of the 37 groups still had ethnic economies below 5%, our threshold of significance. About 95% of foreign nationalities had ethnic economies that included at least 5% of their total labor force. Of the 37 foreign-born groups, 43% showed ethnic economies between 5 and 10% of their labor forces, 46% showed ethnic economies between 10 and 20% of their total labor force, and 5% had ethnic economies that exceeded 20% of their total labor force. The mean ethnic economy of all the foreign born was 11.1% of the total labor force, and the median was 10.4%.

Table 2.4 also compares the self-employment rates of immigrant women and men. The men's self-employment rate usually exceeded the women's. However, women's self-employment was not inconsequential. In 8 of the 37 immigrant groups, the women's self-employment rate equaled or exceeded the men's. Additionally, if less than that of the men in their own group, the self-employment rate of many women was higher than that of noncoethnic men. For instance, the self-employment rate of Korean women exceeded the self-employment rate of all but the Korean men. Similarly, the self-employment rate of Iranian and French women exceeded the self-employment rate of all but the Italian, Soviet, German, Yugoslav, and Canadian men. One should also read the total self-employment rate as a product, in part, of the sex ratio of the group. That is, female-preponderant groups would normally have slightly lower self-employment rates than male-preponderant groups.[14]

Aggregated Ethnic Economies

Although this evidence shows that the ethnic economies of about three-quarters of all ethnic groups enlist a significant share of the group's labor force, the ethnic economies of two very big groups did not always reach significance. The two groups were Mexicans and blacks.[15] Yoon's[16] estimates of both groups' ethnic ownership economy exceeded ours. Yoon found a Mexican ancestry ethnic economy of 8.4% compared with our estimate of 5.9%. Yoon also estimated the African American ancestry ethnic ownership economy at 5.6%, compared with our estimate of 3.3%. Our estimates put the African American and Mexican ethnic ownership economies below the threshold of significance, whereas Yoon's shows them above the threshold but still small. Without quibbling about the difference, one wonders whether, if all the minority ethnic groups were aggregated, the small ethnic ownership economies of Hispanics and blacks, the two biggest categories, would not reduce the aggregate ethnic ownership economy of all minority groups. If so, a basis would exist for ignoring ethnic economies, at least in studies that involve generalizations about aggregated minority groups.

Fortunately, official statistics of unusual quality are available to assess this issue. Table 2.5 shows the number of firms and the number of employees for black,

TABLE 2.5   Minority-Owned Firms in the United States, 1987

		Firms with employees		
	Number of firms	Number	Percentage of all firms	Number of employees
Blacks	424,165	70,815	16.7	220,464
Hispanics	422,373	89,908	21.3	264,846
Asians and Pacific Islanders	355,331	92,718	26.1	351,345
All minorities[a]	1,213,750	248,149	20.4	836,483

[a]Includes groups not shown separately.

Source: U.S. Bureau of the Census, *1987 Economic Censuses,* MB87-4. *Survey of Minority-Owned Business Enterprise, Summary* (Washington, D.C.: GPO, 1991), Table 1, p. 9.

Asian, and Hispanic groups. We treat firms as equivalent to owners. This treatment understates the true number of owners because each firm is counted only once, whereas in reality some firms have multiple owners. Similarly, we estimate that half the employees of each firm were coethnics. Waldinger[17] declares that ethnic employers prefer coethnic employees for unsentimental reasons, not just group chauvinism. A 50% estimate of coethnics among employees is realistic and even conservative in light of the literature.[18]

Table 2.2 shows much variation among the ethnoracial categories in respect to the share of their total labor force that was in their ethnic ownership economy. In the Asian category, which encompasses Pacific Islanders and indigenous peoples, the ethnic economy included 19.2% of the labor force. Among Hispanics, a hodge-podge of Spanish-speaking groups, the ethnic economy included 9.9% of the labor force. Among African Americans, 5.6% worked in the ethnic economy. When the three minority categories are aggregated, their average ethnic economy includes 9.5% of the aggregated population. That is, 9.5% of Asians, blacks, and Hispanics in the entire labor force worked in an ethnic economy as an owner or coethnic employee. By the standard we adopted earlier, the independent ethnic economy of the blacks, although the smallest of the three categories, is nonetheless significant. The ethnic economy of the Hispanics is highly significant, and that of the Asians is extremely significant. For the aggregate of the groups, the ethnic economy approaches high significance.

On the other hand, when the same method is applied to all persons, including nonminorities (Table 2.2), we find that 24.1% of the entire labor force probably worked in ethnic economies. This estimate indicates that the whites had a 2.5 times higher proportion of their labor force in ethnic economies than did nonwhites in 1992. The direction of this result is compatible with the finding of Logan, Alba, and McNulty,[19] who, using a different technique, concluded that the ethnic ownership economies of non–Hispanic whites included many more industries in 17 metropolitan areas than did those of any other group. Since their industries were more numerous, one presumes that the ethnic economies of the whites also included a higher share of the white labor force than did the ethnic economies of the nonwhites. The use of nonwhite data to illustrate the size of ethnic economies actually understates their true size.

Who Works in Ethnic Ownership Economies?

In all ethnic ownership economies, the self-employed outnumber their employees. The extent of that disparity varies from group to group, but it is usually substantial. Among Iranians the self-employed were 10-fold more numerous than their employees; among Asians, the self-employed were only 1.3 times more numerous. Other groups fell between these extremes. Nonetheless, the invariant surplus of self-employed among these ethnoracial minorities does contrast with the general labor market economy, in which we find 158 employees for every 100 self-employed (Table 2.2). The discrepancy reminds us that the firms of ethnoracial minorities are generally smaller than those of non-minority owners. As one result, they employ many fewer workers.

This point is important for two reasons. First, although the ethnic economy's contribution to income, wealth, and employment is the subject of the next chapter, studies of the economic welfare usually examine the relative wages of employees in the ethnic economy and in the general labor market, ignoring the income of self-employed coethnics. This approach would yield a truer estimate of the economic contribution of ethnic economies if the employees in ethnic economies greatly exceeded the self-employed in number, as they actually do in the general labor market. However, in the economies of ethnoracial minorities that situation occurs infrequently. The self-employed are more numerous than their employees, so estimates of the ethnic economy's economic benefit must include the self-employed to avoid distorting the economic conclusion.

Second, from the point of view of class stratification, it matters whether an ethnic ownership economy of 100 persons consists of 99 self-employed persons and 1 employee or 99 employees and 1 employer. In the first case we confront a small business economy in which all the owners work for themselves, mostly in shirt sleeves, and they direct no hired labor. In the second, a silk-hatted owner supervises 99 employees. Both of these ethnic economies have a population of 100, but the two are qualitatively quite different in many important ways. Since, as the data show, most ethnic economies are strong on owners and weak on employees, contemporary ethnic ownership economies tend to be egalitarian enclaves of the petit bourgeoisie, but the inegalitarian pattern is a developmental possibility. That is, if 98 of the ethnic economy's self-employed become employees of the 1 survivor, we would then have an ethnic economy of 1 employer and 99 workers that used to be an ethnic economy of 1 employee and 99 self-employed. This change would render ethnic ownership economies more inegalitarian.

It would be convenient indeed if ethnic ownership economies consisted entirely of ethnically homogeneous firms. However, ethnic firms need not be ethnically homogeneous and often are not. Rather, ethnic firms are homogeneous at the core, and, as they expand in size, they become less homogeneous.[20] The workers closest to the owner are members of his or her own family. Unpaid family workers are coethnic because they belong to the owner's family and share that family's cultural heritage. Beyond that inner circle, ethnic firms often employ workers related to the owner by blood or marriage. Usually, these employees share the ethnic identity of the owner since they owe their employment to a family relationship. These are also family workers even though they obtain a wage. The next circle consists of coethnics who are not related to the owner by blood or marriage. Such workers share an ethnic affiliation with the owner but they are not also part of that owner's extended family. Finally, ethnic firms hire noncoethnic workers as the need arises, usually when they cannot find enough coethnics.

Table 2.6 shows the proportions of each category that worked in Iranian-owned firms in Los Angeles. Among all Iranian firms, 2.7% of paid employees were actually related by blood or marriage to the owners. Another 35.7% were fellow Iranians who were also coreligionists. That is, the Iranian employee shared the religion of the owner as well as the Persian language skill. Another 19.5% of employees were Persian-speaking Iranians who did not share the religion of the owner. Finally, 42.1% of the employees of Iranian businesses were not Iranians at all. The unequal hiring chances of the categories are clear in these data. Relatives of the owner represented less than 0.0001% of the labor force, so they were

TABLE 2.6   Ethnicity of Self-Employed Iranians' Paid Employees (in Percentages)

Ethnicity of paid employees	Iranian subgroups				All Iranians
	Armenians	Bahais	Jews	Muslims	
Relatives	5.0	0	3.2	1.7	2.7
Iranian coreligionists	65.0	14.3	22.1	48.3	35.7
Other Iranians	5.0	50.0	21.0	12.1	19.5
Non-Iranians	25.0	35.7	53.7	37.9	42.1
Total (%)	100.0	100.0	100.0	100.0	100.0
Total (N)	(40)	(28)	(95)	(58)	(221)

Source: Ivan Light, Georges Sabagh, Mehdi Bozorgmehr, and Claudia Der-Martirosian, "Beyond the Ethnic Enclave Economy," *Social Problems* 41 (1994), pp. 65–80.

represented 21,000 times greater than chance among the paid employees. At the opposite extreme, non-Iranians, who represented 99% of the labor force of Los Angeles, had only 42% of the jobs in Iranian-owned firms. In between, Iranian coreligionists were less numerous than Iranian noncoreligionists, but the coreligionists obtained a larger share of the jobs than did the noncoreligionist Iranians. Clearly the owners gave preference to workers who shared social identities with them.

Most Iranian firms in Los Angeles were less than 10 years old when the data in Table 2.6 were collected. They hired little labor, but what they did hire came principally from their own internal ethnic community. However, as firms and communities mature, they often experience labor shortages that compel changes in hiring policy. First, as more coethnics become owners, fewer are left behind as workers so the coethnic labor pool shrinks. This scenario affected Israeli entrepreneurs in Los Angeles. When 85% of the Israelis had become entrepreneurs, only 15% were left behind as workers. For this reason, as Gold[21] points out, the Israeli entrepreneurs were compelled to hire more and more Mexican workers. A related situation occurred in the London garment industry. In this industry, according to Panayiotopoulos,[22] Greek Cypriot firms had to hire ever more Asian and Afro-Caribbean workers because their expanded firms could no longer be fully supplied with workers by the Cypriot community. The Greek Cypriots had all become business owners, and too few were left behind as workers. As the proportion of noncoethnic employees increased, the proportion of Greek Cypriot and of family workers declined.

The ethnic composition of an ethnic economy's labor force is a significant issue. It would be possible for an ethnic economy to consist exclusively of five major employers, none of whom hired any coethnic labor.[23] As matters stand now, ethnic economies mainly hire coethnics. However, this state of affairs is obviously related to the preponderance of self-employed over employees. Where this preponderance exists, coethnic communities are able to supply all the labor that the ethnic economy needs. For example, Bonacich and Modell[24] found that "sixty percent of the male Nisei in the mid-1960s were employees. Of these 10% were working in firms that they identified as Japanese American." Obviously, there was room for the Japanese American firms to expand without running out of Japanese Americans to hire. However, when ethnic communities run out of workers, who have repatriated or found better jobs, then the heterogeneity of ethnic economies also increases, with potentially dramatic effects upon labor relations in the firms.

The Informal Sector

When we have counted all the owners, unpaid family workers, and employees whom the census enumerates, and estimated those not counted separately, we still have not counted all the workers in ethnic ownership economies of the

United States. This undercount arises because the U.S. Census does not enumerate the informal sector at all, and most of the informal sector belongs also to the ethnic ownership economy. The *informal sector* consists of unregulated and unrecorded economic activity that occurs off the books and on whose proceeds no taxes are paid. An ethnic economy is not an informal sector, although it often overlaps it. An informal sector consists of marginal and distressed workers and petty merchants.[25] Informal businesses typically lack employees, a permanent mailing address, a telephone, regular business hours, tax identities, and inventory. An informal sector is an unmonitored economic sector that coexists with a monitored, official economy in which superior wages and working conditions prevail. Sassen[26] defines the informal sector as "income-generating activities that take place outside the framework of public regulation, where similar activities are regulated." Examples include people who sell at retail in swap meets and on street corners, women who operate unlicensed child care facilities in their homes, vendors of home-brewed liquor, and moonlighting plumbers paid in cash.[27]

Most workers in the informal sector are self-employed. A woman who operates an unlicensed child care facility owns a nursery school. A woman who takes boarders into her house owns a hotel. A man who sells home-brewed beer to his workmates owns a beer distributorship. Since these informal sector workers are self-employed, they participate in the ethnic ownership economy's informal sector. Admittedly, some informal sector workers are employees.[28] In garment and electronic manufacturing, employers sometimes retain many employees off the books. That is, they pay these employees more than they declare to tax authorities or even declare none of what they pay. Since no taxes are deducted from their wages, these employees work in the informal sector. If their employer is a coethnic, these employees work in the ethnic ownership economy's informal sector. If their employer is not a coethnic, but the employees are heavily coethnic, then we are dealing with the *ethnic-controlled* economy's informal sector. The garment industry of the United States is importantly an ethnic-controlled informal sector because employers are disproportionately Asian and employees disproportionately Hispanic.[29]

Portes and Stepick[30] developed multiple ways to measure participation in the informal sector. They identified respondent participation in the informal sector by payment in cash for labor services, or payment without tax deductions, or domestic service employment, or itinerant self-employment, or hourly wages below 80% of the legal minimum. Portes and Stepick's battery operationalized the prevailing treatment of the informal sector as a fully monetarized sector whose transactions are unrecorded in public statistics.

Portes[31] has also reviewed three indirect methods that have been used to estimate the population of the informal sector in the United States. One method uses official statistics to enumerate the employment base of "very small enterprises" that employ fewer than 10 workers. In 1989, 15% of all employees worked in firms this small, but 75% of firms were in this class. If we assume that even one-half the firm owners and one-half of their employees worked part-time in the informal sector on at least one occasion in 1989, we arrive at an estimate of 12% participation. This percentage is the share of the labor force that worked *part-time* in the informal sector and does not include full-time workers, whose numbers, Portes[32] points out, cannot be estimated from an official source.

Another indirect method estimates the size of the informal sector from surveys of consumer purchasing. By ascertaining how and where a sample of consumers spent their income, James Smith and his associates concluded that 83% of all households participated in the informal sector and that these households expended 15% of their disposable income in the informal sector.[33] If we assume that 15% of all expenditures purchased 15% of all labor, then we conclude that the informal sector accounted for 12% of the total work hours of American workers in 1985, the target year.[34] However, because informal sector workers earn less than the average, this method probably underestimates the actual size of the informal sector.

A third, indirect method estimates the size of the underground economy by subtracting from actual spending the currency in circulation required by the formal sector. The difference is the share of the informal sector in total spending. Using this approach, Feige[35] estimated that 18% of adjusted gross income was spent in the informal sector in 1986.[36] If again we assume that 18% of spending bought 18% of labor, a conservative basis, we conclude that 18% of American labor was sold in the informal sector in 1986. This estimate does not mean that 18% of Americans worked full-time in the informal sector. The method cannot reach that conclusion, but it can illuminate what share of their total hours of paid labor Americans worked in the informal sector.

The best estimates of the informal sector derive from labor force surveys that ask respondents to account for their work hours in a target week. Third World countries have made extensive use of labor force surveys to derive estimates of informal sector participation in their country. Estimates range from 20 to 60%.[37] However, direct labor force estimates are not available in the United States, possibly because of the prevailing assumption that the United States cannot have an informal sector. For this reason, ethnographic studies conducted by social scientists contain the documentation on the size of the informal sector in the United States. Ethnographic studies invariably report high levels of informal sector participation in poor neighborhoods, but they rarely provide quantitative estimates.[38]

However, Tienda and Raijman[39] developed quantitative estimates from their survey study of 450 households in an immigrant neighborhood of Chicago. Over three-quarters of neighborhood residents were born in Mexico; the others were mainly Arabs and Koreans. First, Tienda and Raijman enumerated the sampled households' principal economic activities, which are normally reported to census takers and tax collectors. Then Tienda and Raijman distinguished two categories of informal self-employment: general self-employment labor and rental property management. They found that 14% of all households were involved in general self-employment labor, and another 24% in rental property management. In all, 38% of households were involved in the informal sector. Rental property management meant renting furnished rooms in one's home to outsiders, normally coethnics, sometimes with board added. Room and board rentals are a classic source of extra income for immigrant families, and the practice is carefully documented in nineteenth-century descriptions of "the lodger evil."[40] Because the income from renting those rooms escapes taxation and is not reported, this economic activity belongs to the informal sector.

Unemployment and underemployment are more common among visible ethnic minorities and immigrants than is full employment. Most people are underemployed or unemployed. Among immigrants 25–64 years of age in the United States, Zhou[41] finds access to the labor market is easy and labor force participation is high. However, Zhou reports, half the men "of any immigrant group" and "70% of working women are underemployed." Here underemployment means part-time work where full-time work is desired or work below the level for which one's education has prepared one. Under either circumstance, many people seek part-time self-employment in the informal sector. Largely as a result, low-income people have very high rates of informal self-employment. In his study of 1.5 million people in five Midwestern states, Bauman[42] found that "the self-employment rate of persons in poverty who worked full time year round is twice as high as the overall self-employment rate of the full time working population." Tienda and Raijman[43] report comparable results from their study of Mexicans in Chicago. "Whereas 10% of working-age adults are self-employed based on their main economic activity, almost 20% report some form of [part-time] self-employment."

All this part-time self-employment in the informal sector belongs to the ethnic economy. However, census takers have no record of secondary self-employment, contenting themselves with a respondent's main or principal occupation. As a result, official statistics understate the self-employment rates of the poor, of the unemployed, of visible minorities, and of immigrants because these groups' self-employment falls disproportionately in the informal sector. A person who works part-time in the general labor market and part-time as a self-employed mechanic has one foot in the general labor market and another in the ethnic economy's informal sector.[44] We might say that he or she works half-time in one and half-time in the other. Although the classification is simple, the actual numbers of such people are impossible to obtain from existing sources, and we must content ourselves with the knowledge that official self-employment rates, including those cited earlier, considerably understate true self-employment in groups that participate heavily in the informal sector. Since we are attempting in this chapter to measure, however roughly, the extent of actual participation in the ethnic economy, this knowledge is the objective.

Official statistics do show how many business owners worked very short hours and earned very little money. Business owners in this category are likely participants in the informal sector. Among blacks and Hispanics, more than a third of business owners who earned less than $5000 per year also worked very short hours.[45] These owners represented about 12% of all business owners. Women business owners were about as likely as black and Hispanic owners to work few hours for low wages, but the women business owners had the highest percentage of all owners (15%) in this marginal category. White men were at the opposite extreme. Only 5.3% of them worked short hours and earned low incomes. Asians were between white men on the one side and blacks and Hispanics on the other. About 10% earned low incomes and worked short hours. Since this category, short hours and low wages, comes as close to the informal sector as one can get with official statistics, the participation rates in it probably can stand for minimal estimates of the participation of the ethnoracial and gender categories in the real informal sector.

To illustrate the danger of ignoring the informal sector and relying upon official statistics alone, Table 2.7 shows the sectoral representation in 1980 of Cuban Mariel refugees and Haitian refugees in Miami. Derived from the work of Alex Stepick, this table is based ultimately upon official statistics that ignore the informal sector. The three sectors are unemployment, the immigrant economy, and the general labor market of Miami. Cuban Mariel refugees are working-class Cubans, expelled from their homeland, who arrived in a massive exodus in 1979. A significant proportion of these Cuban refugees were black. Haitians are impoverished blacks who claimed political refugee status in the United States but whom the U.S. government defined as economic refugees.

The sectoral representation of Haitians and Cubans was drastically different in 1980 (Table 2.7). Haitian refugees had 0.7% working in the ethnic economy, 58.5% unemployed, and 40.8% employed for wages or salaries in the general economy. In contrast, Cuban Mariel refugees had 46.1% employed in the ethnic economy, 26.8% unemployed, and 27.1% employed for wages in the general economy. In effect, the Haitian population apparently lacked an ethnic economy and so approximated the one-sector economy that we have earlier declared impossible in a group of this size. However, as Stepick[46] shows, the impression is misleading because Haitians in Miami operated a very extensive informal sector that official statistics just ignored. Therefore, no trace of the Haitians' informal sector appears in Table 2.7, giving the erroneous impression that Cubans had an ethnic economy but Haitians did not. Although operated for cash only and without the knowledge of tax collectors,[47] Stepick writes, the Haitians' informal sector amounted to "informal self-employment."[48] Haitian entrepreneurs created jobs for themselves and for other Haitians. Their informal firms were chiefly in

TABLE 2.7   Cuban and Haitian Refugee Employment in Miami, 1980 (in Percentages)

	Cuban Mariel refugees	Haitian refugees
Immigrant economy		
Self-employed	15.2	0.5
Working in coethnic firms	30.9	0.2
General labor market		
Unemployed	26.8	58.5
Employees	27.1	40.8
Total	100.0	100.0

Source: Alex Stepick, "Miami's Two Informal Sectors," in *The Informal Economy,* Alejandro Portes, Manuel Castells, and Lauren A. Benton, eds. (Baltimore: Johns Hopkins University, 1989), Chap. 6. Reprinted by permission.

dressmaking, tailoring, food preparation, child care, transportation, construction, automobile repair, and electronic repair.[49] In point of fact, then, a significant ethnic economy existed among the Miami Haitians as well as among the Cubans, but census takers ignored this Haitian economy whose existence would have gone unobserved except for social science research. Hard to measure does not mean nonexistent.

With these cases in mind, we can return to all the groups with low self-employment rates that our own tables, derived from census data, show as below or close to the 5% significance threshold. Census data show Haitians just above the threshold of significance, with an ethnic ownership economy of 5.6% (Table 2.4). Yet Stepick's ethnography proved Haitians operated a large informal sector, and the same is presumably true of people from Panama, Guyana, and Laos, all of whom the census shows as operating insignificant ethnic ownership economies. In the case of African Americans, who consistently rank low in ethnic ownership, large informal sectors are known to exist.[50] Were these informal sectors to be included in the tables that show self-employment rates, African Americans, Haitians, and the others would rank far higher than they do in the official tables and much above the minimal significance threshold.

The Illegal Enterprise Sector

In addition to the formal sector and the informal sector, the ethnic ownership economy has a third sector, the illegal enterprise sector. The illegal enterprise sector consists of firms that sell proscribed commodities to willing buyers. Examples of proscribed commodities include recreational drugs, pornography, prostitution, gambling, and usurious loans. Providing these proscribed commodities is the core activity of what used to be called organized crime but that analysts now call illegal enterprise in recognition of its affinity with legal business as well as its decentralization. Because it involves the production and sale of commodities to willing buyers, illegal enterprise is a business as well as a crime. Unlike predatory crimes, such as robbery, which require victims, illegal enterprise produces no victims to serve as complainants in a court of law. Therefore, illegal enterprise is a form of victimless crime that is illegal as a matter of social policy.[51]

Illegal enterprise does not occupy the everyday attention of law enforcement personnel. In 1994, arrests for prostitution, drug abuse violations, and gambling combined were only 10% of all arrests.[52] The actual percentage of criminals involved in these activities is probably greater than 10% of the population of professional criminals, but even if it was only 10% the number of people involved would be large. After all, in 1992, 2% of the adult male labor force of the United States was incarcerated, and among blacks the percentage incarcerated was 9% of the labor force.[53] If we look only at young men, among whom crime rates are highest, we find that "37% as many black men aged 18−34" were under the "supervision of the criminal justice system as in the labor force."[54] The number of offenders is sufficiently high that even 10% involvement in the illegal sector would represent 3% of the age cohort. All these workers should be added to the ethnic economy of their group.

Like participation in the informal sector, participation in illegal enterprise is easy to combine with holding a job in the formal sector. George holds a full-time regular job, but he sells recreational drugs on weekends. This pattern is quite common. Ethnographic research shows that legal and illegal work routinely coexist among young men who sell drugs.[55] When George sells drugs on weekends, he operates a retail pharmacy part-time. Therefore, George is a business owner whose part-time enterprise belongs to the ethnic economy of his group. When we seek to identify how many people work in ethnic economies, we must include those who work full- and part-time in illegal enterprises. This issue is quite different from the problem of how many people commit predatory crimes because predatory criminals are not in business. Only the sector of illegal enterprise belongs to the ethnic economy, and this sector occupies only a fraction of the criminal population.

The Italian word *mafia* now refers to any and all ethnically homogeneous syndicates that bring together business owners who manufacture and sell proscribed commodities. Thus, the Italian mafia consists of Italians in illegal enterprise, the Mexican mafia consists of Mexicans in illegal enterprise, and the Russian mafia consists of Russians in illegal enterprise.[56] Mafias are not, as was once supposed, monolithic crime bureaucracies like SMERSH, the archenemy of James Bond. Rather, mafias are chambers of commerce in which various and multiple ethnic crime families assemble to regulate and oversee the trade. Each crime family

consists of fraternal but partially or wholly independent firms that produce or distribute proscribed commodities behind a protective umbrella of corruption and
violence. More even than legal firms in the formal sector, which have access to
courts and police to adjudicate commercial disputes, illegal enterprises require the
enforceable trust that shared ethnicity conveys. Because and to the extent that
mafia firms consist heavily of self-employed workers and their employed coethnics, mafia firms belong to the ownership economy of the owners' ethnoracial
group.

ETHNIC-CONTROLLED ECONOMIES

It remains now to estimate the population of ethnic-controlled economies. An
ethnic-controlled economy consists of coethnic employees in the general labor
market who exert or enjoy significant and sustained market power thanks to
their common ethnic background. Market power enables the coethnic workers
to influence hiring, wages, and job conditions to their own advantage. Influence
on hiring means that workers can reserve jobs for coethnics, reducing the unemployment rate of their group. Influence on wages means that workers can
push wages higher than they otherwise would be, raising the mean income of
their ethnoracial group. Influence on working conditions means that workers
can improve the quality of their work life, reducing or eliminating abusive and
unsafe working conditions, thereby rendering their occupations or workplaces
more attractive.

   Ethnic industrial and occupational niches are the simplest and most common
cause of ethnic-controlled economies.[57] Although the literature on ethnic niches
is venerable as well as international,[58] the idea of actually estimating the population of all the niches is new, and results thus far are crudely approximate at best.
Logan, Alba, and McNulty[59] examined the industrial clustering of 10 ethnoracial
groups and categories in 17 metropolitan areas of the United States in 1980. They
defined ethnic niches as representation at more than 150% of the expected number in an industry.[60] Of the 1360 industries they examined in the 17 metropolitan
areas, Logan, Alba, and McNulty found white niches in one-third. If we assume
that the 451 industries in which whites were overrepresented had 43% of all the
white employees, an algebraic extrapolation, then within the private sector, 43%
of whites worked in industrial niches.[61] The other 57% of whites worked in industries in which whites were not overrepresented. True, some of these white
niches fell within white ethnic ownership economies, so the external white
niches that correspond to what we have called the ethnic-controlled economy included somewhat less than the full 43%.[62]

   Outstanding evidence on contemporary niche formation comes from the research of Jeffrey Reitz[63] in Toronto. Using evidence from the 1971 Canadian census, Reitz examined the concentration of seven ethnic minorities in labor mar-

kets. The groups were Germans, Ukrainians, Italians, Jews, Portuguese, Chinese, and West Indians. Aggregating the seven ethnoracial groups, Reitz distinguished the self-employed, employees of minority business, and mainstream employees. Of the employees of minority business, 70.2% of all men and 68.0% of all women worked for coethnic employers. Of employees in the mainstream, whose employers were not coethnics, 23.3% of men and 23.1% of women reported that at least a quarter of their coworkers were also coethnics. Concentration of coethnic coworkers approximates our definition of an ethnic-controlled economy and can be accepted as an estimate of its size.

Table 2.8 shows the results for the seven aggregated groups. Among men, the combined ethnic ownership economy and ethnic-controlled economy amounted to 52.1% of all workers. Employees of the mainstream were 47.9% of all male workers in the seven groups. Among women, results were comparable; 41% of women worked in the combined ethnic ownership economy and ethnic-controlled economy. Almost 59% of women worked as employees in the mainstream. The difference between the men and women mostly resulted from the women's lower rate of self-employment. Men and women had comparable representation as employees of minority enterprise and as employees in ethnic-controlled occupations of the mainstream.

Reitz's data also bear upon the ethnic economies of four ancestry groups in three generations (Table 2.9). Reitz distinguished owners and employees of minority businesses. These two categories represent the ethnic ownership economy of the four ancestry groups. Additionally, Reitz indicated the percentage who worked in occupations of which at least one-quarter of all workers were coethnics and one-quarter of whose workmates or more were also coethnics. These

TABLE 2.8   Aggregated Ethnic Economies of Toronto, 1971 (in Percentages)

	Male	Female
Ethnic ownership economy		
Self-employed	18.2	7.1
Coethnic employee	10.6	11.1
Ethnic-controlled economy coethnic workmates[a]	23.3	23.1
General labor market mainstream employee	47.9	58.7
Total	100.0	100.0

[a]Employed outside ethnic economy in the general labor market and at least one-fourth of coworkers are coethnics.

Source: Jeffrey G. Reitz, "Ethnic Concentrations in Labor Markets and Their Implications for Ethnic Inequality," in *Ethnic Identity and Equality,* Raymond Breyton, Wsevolod W. Isajiw, Warren E. Kalbach, and Jeffrey G. Reitz, eds. (Toronto: University of Toronto, 1990), Tables 4.10 and 4.12.

TABLE 2.9   Estimated Ethnic Economies of Toronto by Gender and Generation for Four Ancestry Groups, 1971 (in Percentages)

| | Men | | Women | |
| | Ethnic economies | | Ethnic economies | |
	Ownership[a]	Control[b]	Ownership[a]	Control[b]
German				
Immigrant	23.4	5.0	19.8	5.2
Second	16.4	5.1	0.6	0.6
Third	15.5	11.1	0.0	3.4
Ukrainian				
Immigrant	8.7	20.2	2.6	20.9
Second	23.8	16.1	6.7	9.9
Third	15.5	11.3	10.3	16.5
Italian				
Immigrant	44.3	90.6	17.4	89.7
Second	39.6	42.6	18.3	55.0
Third	32.2	39.8	17.6	9.9
Jewish				
Immigrant	61.4	55.7	54.1	52.1
Second	56.0	51.7	40.6	42.9
Third	68.4	54.9	63.1	67.3

[a]Combines self-employed and employees of minority-owned business of whom 70% are coethnics. These categories are mutually exclusive, but both categories can also be counted in ethnic occupations and ethnic workmates.

[b]Combines working in a 25% or more coethnic occupation and having coworkers on the job 25% of whom or more were also coethnics. These two categories are not mutually exclusive.

Source: Jeffrey G. Reitz, "Ethnic Concentrations in Labor Markets and Their Implications for Ethnic Inequality," in *Ethnic Identity and Equality,* Raymond Breyton, Wsevolod W. Isajiw, Warren E. Kalbach, and Jeffrey G. Reitz, eds. (Toronto: University of Toronto, 1990), Table 4.16, p. 186. Reproduced by permission.

two indicators can stand for the ethnic-controlled economy of the mainstream. The trouble is, in Reitz's data these categories are not mutually exclusive. About 42% of the self-employed worked in heavily ethnic occupations, and another 36% of employees of minority businesses had coethnic workmates. Therefore, the ethnic-controlled category of Table 2.9 includes people from the ethnic ownership economy, exaggerating the size of what we have called the ethnic-controlled economy.

Nonetheless, we reproduce Reitz's data because of the unparalleled insight they offer into generational changes in ethnic economies and the opportunity to examine specific intergroup differences (Table 2.9). According to assimilation theorists, ethnic economies disappear with successive generations as the children and grandchildren of immigrants join the melting pot. Indeed, Nee, Sanders, and Sernau[64] have provided cross-sectional evidence that immigrant Asians in San Francisco were gradually transferring from the ethnic ownership economy to employment in the mainstream during their *own* lifetimes. Furthermore, the Toronto data offer partial support to assimilation theory's prediction. Among the German men and women and the Italian men, the proportion in ethnic ownership economies declined monotonically with successive generations after immigration, just as assimilation theory predicts. However, among the Ukrainian men and women, the Italian women, and the Jewish men and women, the ethnic ownership economy either increased or remained stable after the immigrant generation. This result is not what assimilation theory predicts.

Turning similarly to the issue of coethnicity in occupations and workplaces, called the ethnic-controlled economy, we find declines among German women, Ukrainian men and women, and Italian men and women. This result is compatible with the possibility that, as they assimilated and acculturated, the children and grandchildren of immigrants moved into mainstream occupations in which their chances depended less upon ancestry and more upon their wealth and human capital. However, German men and Jewish men and women did not experience reduced workmate or occupational coethnicity in successive generations after immigration. This result is not compatible with assimilation theory.

Apart from complete intergenerational assimilation or, strictly speaking, the lack of it, another issue is the size of ethnic economies. Of immigrant groups in North America, Germans have been among the most assimilated.[65] This was partially a result of cultural compatibility, but the historical record shows that World War I and World War II drastically undermined what had been strong and durable ethnic communities among Germans. During the two world wars, German ethnic associations and newspapers were shut down. Indeed, just speaking German in public was regarded as subversive.[66] Whatever the causes, compared with the other immigrant nationalities, the Germans had rather small ethnic economies in Toronto, and these tended to decline with successive generations, suggesting an ethnic group that moved into total assimilation. By contrast, Italians started with huge ethnic economies that declined with assimilation but remained big into the third generation.[67] Finally, the only middleman minority of these four groups, the Jews started in Toronto with large ethnic economies that they maintained despite acculturation to Canadian society. Among the Ukrainians, ethnic-controlled work sites and occupations declined with assimilation, but ethnic ownership economies increased, possibly because of upward mobility among what had been a working-class immigrant group. The quite different trajectories of these four Canadian ethnic groups show how cautiously one must specify with historical detail the blanket predictions of assimilation theory.

Ethnic niches are not a recent development. Lieberson[68] analyzed the ethnic composition of occupations in 66 nonsouthern cities in 1900. After standardizing group size to eliminate compositional effects, Lieberson presented data that confirmed many occupational stereotypes. Blacks constituted 74% of all domestic servants in the 66 cities, Germans constituted 72% of brewers, and Irish constituted 26% of policemen. In the same manner, 82% of Boston's laborers and 74% of its domestic servants were Irish in 1850.[69] Historian Oscar Handlin[70] provided data on ethnic occupational clustering among 43,567 Boston workers in 1850. If we define ethnic niches as an *average* representation of workers in occupations that exceeded 10 times chance, a stiff standard, then 100% of blacks worked in niches in 1850, as did 100% of Latin Americans, 100% of Poles and Russians, 100% of Scandinavians, and 100% of Italians.

DISCUSSION

Ethnic economies have only two sectors: ownership and control. The ownership sector comprises the self-employed, owners, and their coethnic employees. The control sector consists of employees outside the ownership sector who work in occupations, industries, or workplaces in which coethnics enjoy market power thanks to their numbers, their organization, their political power, or all three.[71] However, both the ownership and the control sectors have three subsectors. These are the formal, the informal, and the illegal. The formal subsector consists of firms that pay taxes and have official recognition. The informal subsector contains firms that, producing legal commodities, produce them illegally because they evade taxation and the labor code. The illegal subsector consists of firms that manufac-

TABLE 2.10   Ethnic Economies and Sectors

Ethnic ownership economy			Ethnic-controlled economy		
Formal sector	Informal sector	Illegal sector	Formal sector	Informal sector	Illegal sector
1	2	3	4	5	6

Examples

1   Owners of dry-cleaning retail store and their coethnic employees

2   Owner-operators of 'off-the-books' garment factory and their coethnic employees

3   Owner-operators of illegal betting parlor and their coethnic employees

4   Coethnic employees of a giant corporation who enjoy market power thanks to their coethnicity

5   Coethnic employees of 'off-the-books' garment manufactory owned by a noncoethnic

6   Coethnic employees of illegal betting parlor whose owners are noncoethnics

ture or distribute proscribed commodities. Table 2.10 illustrates this typology with examples.

Official statistics give some access to the formal sector since they permit us to ascertain the formal sector's self-employment rate, the unpaid family workers who work in the formal sector, and, in some cases, the number of employees of ethnic firms in the formal sector. Official statistics are of no use in estimating the population of the ethnic economy's informal sector, but social science research makes possible rough estimates of participation. For obvious reasons, the illegal sector's population is even harder to illuminate than is the informal sector's. But the roughest calculations suggest that, although the smallest of the three sectors of the ethnic economy in terms of population, even the illegal enterprise sector cannot be ignored.

Although all ethnoracial groups have ethnic ownership economies, and the formal sectors are clearly quite different in size, we cannot be sure which groups' ethnic ownership economies are largest in population. It is plausible to suppose that the participation of ethnoracial groups in the informal and illegal sectors varies inversely with their entrepreneurial resources. By entrepreneurial resources we mean those resources of skill, money, acumen, and network that permit groups to own and operate legitimate enterprises in the formal sector. Just from the evidence we have reviewed, one can see that low-ranking ethnoracial groups with the lowest participation in the formal sector have higher participation in the ethnic economy's informal sector and probably have higher participation in the ethnic economy's illegal sector as well. This possibility harmonizes with the classic view that as ethnic racketeers acquire resources of money and education, they transfer their assets from the illegal to the legal sector, thus leaving behind a vacancy in illegal enterprise for lower-ranking ethnic minorities to occupy.[72]

However, our purpose in this chapter has not been to investigate how ethnic economies work, but only to estimate how many people work in them. The null hypothesis is the claim that so few people work in ethnic economies that social science can legitimately ignore the whole subject. This null hypothesis is, in fact, the old-fashioned view that informed social research in the previous generation and that continues, to some extent, even today. Rejecting this claim, we have shown that, even when we restrict our attention to the formal sector, three-quarters of ethnic groups have self-employment rates in excess of 5%. When account is taken of employment in the ethnic economy's formal sector, virtually all ethnic groups have ethnic economies that reach a 5% threshold. For the average ethnic group in our review, about 11% of the whole group's labor force works in the ethnic ownership economy.

The formal sector does not exhaust our case. Beyond the formal sector, we have shown that ethnic economies also exist in the informal sector and in the illegal sector. Although participation rates in the informal sector are impossible to quantify with confidence, available evidence suggests that rates of informal sector participation reach or exceed 10% for an average ethnic group. In this case, participation in the ethnic economy's formal sector plus participation in the informal sector would come to 20% for the average ethnic group. When we consider that an additional percentage must be added to the ethnic economy because of its illegal enterprise sector, our concluding estimate for the average ethnoracial group's ownership economy reaches 21% of the labor force. As we shall see in the next chapter, these estimates of labor force share are compatible with estimates of gross domestic product share that others have reached.

Even the ethnic ownership economy does not exhaust our case. Beyond ethnic ownership economies, there exist ethnic-controlled economies. In ethnic-controlled economies, coethnic employees influence hiring, wages, and working conditions in the mainstream thanks precisely to their coethnicity. The concept of ethnic-controlled economy is harder to measure than is the concept of ethnic ownership economy, which has a firm definition in law. Moreover, available evidence is even more fragmentary and harder to mobilize. Nonetheless, the literature of social science permits no escape from the conclusion that big ethnic-controlled economies exist now and have existed in the past. Reviewing the available evidence, we conclude that about a fifth of the average ethnoracial group now works in ethnic-controlled economies. This proportion is higher for some than for others, and assimilation reduces it, but a fifth represents a conservative estimate.

When we add the ethnic ownership economy and the ethnic-controlled economy, we obtain an estimated participation rate of 41% outside the employment mainstream. This estimate applies to the average ethnic group and is higher or lower for individual cases. Additionally, as we have suggested, ethnoracial groups have unequal participation in the formal, informal, and illegal subsectors of the two ethnic economies. Nonetheless, our overall estimate suggests a phenomenon that is too large to ignore, and that, fervently to echo Fawcett and Gardner,[73] should "receive more serious attention" from the research community in the future than it has in the past.[74] The question is not whether our rough-hewn methods are conclusive, but only whether they make a case for more adequate coverage of this phenomenon.

Ethnic economies exist because of the scarcity of jobs. Ethnic economic behavior is a rational response to job scarcity. The general labor market does not offer now, and never has offered in the past, enough jobs to employ everyone to his or her full satisfaction. In all probability, the general labor market will *never* provide enough good jobs for all in the future either. Although the inadequacy affects everyone to some extent, even the native-born white majority, the burden of scarcity falls most heavily upon the less assimilated or acceptable white groups, visible minorities, non-Christians, refugees, and immigrants.[75] For affected individuals, who are numerous, the inadequacy of the general labor market leaves scant alternative to utilizing their own resources to improve their economic chances. Evans[76] concludes that ethnic ownership economies "buffer the most disadvantaged" from the "limited opportunities they would confront on the open labor market." We agree, but note that, in expanding opportunities to coethnics, ethnic-controlled economies diminish the opportunities available to noncoethnics whereas ethnic ownership economies do not.[77] Arguably people should not create ethnic-controlled economies, which balkanize labor markets, but they rationally do.[78]

Wealth, Income, Employment

Ethnic economies have three ways of rewarding participants. These ways are job creation, job capture, and accelerated mobility. Ethnic-controlled economies capture jobs that noncoethnics would otherwise obtain. Ethnic ownership economies create altogether new jobs. Sometimes created or captured jobs are exceptionally lucrative, but even when they are not, they are extra jobs. Whether created or captured, extra jobs expand the job supply available to coethnics.[1] After all, coethnics get all jobs that the ethnic-controlled economy captures and most jobs that ethnic ownership economies create, but they only get *some* of the jobs in the general labor market.[2] Insofar as ethnic economies recruit the unemployed or the nonemployed, such as former housewives, they draw into paying jobs people who would otherwise have earned no income. The upshot is an ethnic community in which a higher proportion of the adult population enjoy paying jobs than would have been possible without any ethnic ownership economy or ethnic-controlled economy. This community will have more earners and fewer nonearners thanks to job creation and job capture.

The third way in which ethnic economies reward participants is to accelerate economic mobility beyond what the general labor market would have provided. The components of economic welfare are wealth, income, and working conditions, including security of employment. If ethnic economy participants earn more of all rewards (income, wealth, working conditions) or, conversely, earn less, then our judgment is simple. In the first case, the ethnic economy accelerates their economic mobility; in the second case, it retards it. But what if ethnic economies only improve one of the three superior rewards, or they improve two, but the third reward is better outside? In that realistic case, we would confront trade-offs in which ethnic economy participants get more of one value than they would have in the general labor market, but they would get less of another.

To complicate the judgment still more, we may have to weigh the advantages of job capture and extra jobs against those of income, wealth, and working conditions. In the best case, of course, ethnic economies capture jobs that are also superior to what participants could have obtained in the general labor market. Imagine how advantageous it would be for any ethnoracial group, say Puerto Ricans in New York City, to capture an additional 100,000 jobs, each of which is paid twice what its incumbent would otherwise earn in the general labor market. In the worst case, ethnic economy jobs relegate participants to inferior jobs on which the general labor market could improve if only the unfortunate coethnics, languishing in their ghetto, would apply for them. This is not the worst imaginable case, but it is the worst case for ethnic economies.[3] However, cases need not be so extreme and usually are not. Ethnic economies can deliver job capture and job creation even while they fail to accelerate mobility, or vice versa. In any mixed case, we again confront trade-offs in which some benefit is matched by some disadvantage. Additionally, group A may obtain one set of benefits from their ethnic economies while group B obtains another and group C still another. Facing all these realistic complexities, one sees that reaching a blanket conclusion about ethnic economies is challenging.

For this reason, the ethnic economy has generated a lengthy and often polemical literature bearing upon its economic desirability. Ignoring the heat that this literature has generated,[4] we focus on the light, attempting only to present the most faithful account of what the evidence actually conveys about economic mobility, wealth creation, income attainment, and employment in ethnic economies and outside them. This is the course of social realism that, as Alan Wolfe puts it, just seeks to understand the world "no matter how distasteful, politically objectionable, or immoral that world may be."[5]

ETHNIC OWNERSHIP ECONOMIES

Economic Mobility and Wealth

Portes and Zhou[6] define assimilation as a "mechanism for socializing culturally diverse groups into common normative expectations so that they can join the mainstream." Assimilation theory originated as interpretation of the cultural and social change through which European immigrants had passed in the first half of the twentieth century.[7] Although assimilation theory continues to develop, it still proclaims that economic self-interest prompts immigrants to acculturate and then to assimilate.[8] That is, in order to obtain well-paid jobs in the general labor market, adults forsake their childhood ethnic attachments, including their old neighborhood and native language. As one immigrant put it, "You wanna da mon, you gotta speaka da ing." Assimilation theory enthusiastically agrees.[9] Someday this immigrant's grandson will have a good job and perfect command of English. In order to obtain these, he will, so argues assimilation theory, have abandoned his grandparents' cultural heritage and married a noncoethnic wife who has abandoned her grandparents' cultural heritage too. Over a sequence of generations, so the theory continues, everyone will have individually forsaken her or his ethnic attachments out of materialist motives. The ethnic groups whence they emerged will disappear into the melting pot.

Unsentimental though it is, assimilation theory is still the mainstream view. It is also importantly true, and our own review concurs with much of what assimilation theory proclaims. Nonetheless, classic assimilationist generalization now seems overstrong, so we propose modification. In at least some cases, we now realize, ethnic ownership economies render slow assimilation more lucrative than fast, and nonassimilation more lucrative than assimilation.[10] In such cases, the motive of economic self-interest does not promote acculturation as assimilation theory expects. On the contrary, it promotes retaining the ethnic cultural heritage and staying out of the economic mainstream. An important complication derives from the economic advantages that self-employment confers. Ethnic economies make ethnicity lucrative for at least some of the people all of the time.

Conventional wisdom proclaims that self-employment accelerates economic mobility and wealth creation. This conventional wisdom actually enjoys some scientific support.[11] One reason is the importance of self-employment in wealth generation. The self-employed amass and own more wealth than do wage and salary earners. Here we distinguish wealth and income.[12] In contrast to income, which is a regular infusion of money or goods, wealth is a household's store of valuable assets.[13] These stored assets are either fully monetarized, as are bank accounts, or are convertible to money, as are houses, jewelry, and vehicles.[14] Although high incomes make wealth creation easier, and the two often go together, wealth and high income are not identical in that a person or household can have one without the other.[15]

Table 3.1 compares the nonfinancial assets of American families in 1992. Approximately 91% of families had nonfinancial assets; the most common form was motor vehicles, owned by 86.4% of families. The largest single source of wealth for American families was their owner-occupied residence, whose median value was $81,800. Only 20% of families owned investment real estate, and only 14.9% owned a business. The average value of businesses these families owned was 21% of the average of all nonfinancial assets Americans owned. The average value of investment real estate was 72% of the average value of all nonfinancial assets. Since the ownership of a business and the ownership of investment real estate are both products of self-employment, these statistics show that the self-employed had unique access to distinctive forms of wealth.

TABLE 3.1   Nonfinancial Assets Held by Families by Asset Type, 1992

Value of assets	Median dollar value	Percentage who own asset
Any nonfinancial assets	69,500	91.3
Vehicles	6,900	86.4
Primary residence	81,800	63.8
Investment real estate	50,000	20.0
Business	14,900	14.9
Other	8,500	8.5

Source: Statistical Abstract of the United States, U.S. Bureau of the Census, Washington, D.C.: Government Printing Office, 1996: Table 741.

Oliver and Shapiro[16] found that the self-employed own "from two to 14 times as much net worth as their salaried counterparts." The advantage of the self-employed in wealth greatly exceeds their advantage in income. Self-employed whites earned 73% of what upper-white-collar whites earned, but the self-employed whites had nearly three times more net financial assets than did the upper-white-collar whites.[17] The reasons for this disparity are simple. The self-employed own businesses; their business represents personal and household wealth to its owners. Indeed, the income of the self-employed is obtained from the proceeds of their business *after* the cost of servicing their loans and their return on equity investment has already been deducted. Therefore, as the self-employed pay off any loans, their equity share in their own business grows, and as it grows, their wealth increases. Every pay period, the self-employed receive income *plus* any growth of their equity share, whereas employees receive only their paycheck.[18] Additionally, as Blau and Graham point out, the self-employed are also more likely than wage earners to have inherited business property from self-employed parents.[19] Here are two reasons why the self-employed own so much more wealth than do employees. Even if the after-tax incomes of the self-employed were identical to those of employees, the self-employed would hold and amass more wealth than employees for these two reasons.

Business Owners' Incomes

To estimate whether ethnic business owners earn more in business than they would have in wage employment, one could simply ask them. They should know. However, that ingenious question has only been posed in Australia, where two-thirds of immigrant entrepreneurs, male and female, said they were "better off in terms of money" as a result of operating a small business than they would have been had they worked for wages. By contrast, only one-third of native-born Australian entrepreneurs said they were financially better off as owners than they would have been as employees.[20] Collins concludes that business ownership was more advantageous to entrepreneurs of non–English-speaking background than to those already fluent in English, a result that should generalize to North America.

However, North American researchers have gone to census data rather than to business owners for the answer to this question. Early research simply assumed that self-employment fetched higher incomes than did wage employment. Only in the 1980s did this assumption undergo scrutiny. Early evidence tended to show, as expected, that the self-employed earned higher incomes than coethnic wage earners. The key contribution was that of Portes and Bach.[21] In a statistical comparison of working-class men of Cuban and Mexican origins, Portes and Bach found that the Cuban men experienced much more rapid economic advancement because an ethnic enclave economy in Miami encouraged their entrepreneurship. Net of human capital, the Cubans in the ethnic enclave economy earned more than Cubans employed in the general labor market. Additionally, Wilson and Portes[22] and Portes and Bach[23] found that participants in the ethnic enclave actually earned higher education–adjusted wages than did their coethnic counterparts in the general economy. This finding challenged the accepted wisdom, and made the ethnic enclave economy seem even more advantageous since employees as well as employers earned high money returns in it.

Sanders and Nee[24] opened a useful debate on this subject. Although they wrongly conceded that entrepreneurs earned higher human capital adjusted earnings than wage workers, Nee and Sanders[25] disputed Wilson and Portes's claim of positive returns on human capital for immigrant workers in the ethnic enclave economy. Instead, they reported that an ethnic enclave economy financially benefited a group's employers but harmed its workers. In partial rebuttal, Zhou[26] pointed out that workers often accept low-wage employment in ethnic economies in preference to the general labor market because of the symbolic reassurance it offers, the advantage of being able to work longer hours and to evade taxes, as well as the possibilities they perceive for training in hard-to-acquire entrepreneurial skills. Ethnic economies are the West Point of future ethnic entrepreneurs.[27] Nonetheless, in narrowly economic terms, Sanders and Nee first showed that the effect of an ethnic enclave economy might be mixed or even negative rather than wholly beneficial.

A lengthy debate ensued. Although empirical tests of relative wages have sometimes failed to substantiate Portes's enclave economy findings, the debate about employee earnings was slightly misspecified because most participants in ethnic economies are self-employed or employers, not employees. The nonemployer self-employed are the largest class, and the debate over employees' wages had simply overlooked the self-employed themselves. Coethnic employees are less numerous than the self-employed. Therefore, as discussed in the preceding chapter, the economic welfare of the ethnic economy's employees is less significant than the welfare of its self-employed and employers. An ethnic economy increases the wealth of the ethnic community so long as the self-employed are more numerous than employees. Among all minority-owned firms, only 20.4% had any employees in 1987. Furthermore, the relative earnings of coethnic employees depend upon industry, gender, locality, the ratio of self-employed and employees, and so forth. For example, women employees may earn relatively more than men, San Francisco's Chinatown may pay more than New York's, Mexicans have more employees than do blacks in San Jose, and the Asian ethnic economy generates more income than does the black ethnic economy.[28]

In addition, Sanders and Nee stipulated that ethnic entrepreneurs in the enclave earned more than their counterparts in the general labor market. Their's was then the common view. Actually, to estimate the earnings of the self-employed is a bigger problem than they or others realized because raw census data are unreliable. As Reitz[29] points out, census income data on self-employment are not fully comparable with those on employed persons.[30] First, the income of the self-employed requires a year-end accounting because one must subtract costs from receipts. The self-employed may not even know what their current income actually is. Additionally, one must decompose the income of the self-employed into a component derived from their work and a component derived from their equity investment. For example, if a business owner had invested $100,000 in her business, and later has earned $40,000 after she has paid all her costs, we cannot declare the whole $40,000 proprietor's income. After all, her $100,000 equity investment would have yielded $8000 if invested in government bonds. Therefore, an accountant would declare $8000 of her $40,000 income a return on capital, leaving only $32,000 as proprietor's income.[31] Census data ignore this issue.

These considerations suggest that census income data overstate the incomes of the self-employed. Moreover, even census data show that the self-employed earn less than wage and salary workers in the majority of cases.[32] True, evaluating specific cases, Portes and Zhou[33] showed that Cuban, Chinese, Japanese, and Korean self-employed earned more than comparably productive coethnics in the general labor market. Light and Roach[34] obtained the same results in Los Angeles. These results demonstrate that entrepreneurship has enabled many American ethnic groups to increase their mean income above what wage and salary employment in the general labor market would have provided. This was an important lesson. Yet those cases are exceptional because, on average, the self-employed earn slightly lower money returns than equally productive wage and salary workers.

Maxim's[35] statistics demolished the assumption that self-employment was always superior to wage employment in respect to income. The finding certainly weakened the claim that ethnic ownership economies always accelerated the income growth of business owners above and beyond what the mainstream labor market would have provided. Low proprietor incomes made the ethnic economy resemble what Wiley[36] called a "mobility trap." A mobility trap looks inviting, but those who enter later find their career prospects worse inside it than they would have been outside. This issue has produced a flood of empirical studies intended to show just how much the self-employed and their coethnic employees earn relative to coethnic employees in the general labor market.[37] On the side of the ethnic economy are amassing wealth and the prospect of future entrepreneurship for trainees; on the side of the general labor market are high wages. The ethnic ownership economy trades off benefits and costs.

The plausibility of the negative conclusion has declined in response to arguments that take unemployment into account. After all, even low wages and long hours in the ethnic economy are superior to unemployment in the general labor market. When ethnic ownership economies pay owners and employees little, the participants have usually been recruited from workers with diminished or negligible employment chances in the general labor market. If either employers or employees earn *less* in the ethnic ownership economy than in the general labor market, then new entrepreneurs and new employees can only be recruited from the unemployed, the underemployed, or those previously not in the labor force.[38] In either case, an ethnic economy raises the earnings of the formerly unemployed or nonworkers above zero. Conversely, if the self-employed or employed earned *more* in the ethnic economy than in the general labor market, as they often do, then the more who moved into the ethnic economy, the richer the group would become. Therefore, whether earnings in the ethnic economy are more or less than those in the general labor market, an ethnic economy confers benefit. The benefit is great when entrepreneurs and/or their coethnic employees earn more than do counterparts employed in the general economy. It is small when entrepreneurs and their coethnic employees earn less.

Table 3.2 illustrates four earnings scenarios that compare the relative earnings of self-employed and coethnic employees in the ethnic ownership economy with counterparts in the general labor market. When the workers earn more in the ethnic economy than in the general labor market, Table 3.2 shows a plus sign; when the workers earn less in the ethnic economy, Table 3.2 shows a minus sign.

TABLE 3.2   Relative Earnings Scenarios in the Ethnic Ownership Economy

	Scenario	Self-employed	Employers	Employees
1	Best case	+	+	+
2	Next best case	+	+	−
3	Next best case	−	−	+
4	Worst case	−	−	−

+ Earn more
− Earn less
Source: Ivan Light and Stavros Karageorgis, "The Ethnic Economy, in *Handbook of Economic Sociology,* Neil Smelser and Richard Swedberg, eds. (Princeton: Princeton University Press, 1994), p. 654.

There are four main scenarios. In scenario 1, the most favorable, self-employed, employers, and coethnic employees all earn more than equally productive coethnics in the general labor market. When this situation obtains, the more workers who switch from the general labor market into the ethnic economy, the higher the average income of their group. This ethnic economy increases the economic mobility of the group above what full general labor market employment would offer. Scenario 1 is what Portes and Bach[39] reported in their study of the Cuban ethnic economy in Miami.

Scenario 4 illustrates the worst case. Employees, employers, and the self-employed *all* earn less than equally productive counterparts in the general labor market. In this worst case, the more of the group's workers who can obtain entry into the general labor market, the higher will be the mean income of the whole group. However, even *this* ethnic economy raises group incomes so long as participants would otherwise have been underemployed, unemployed, or nonworkers. In such a case, an ethnic economy does not accelerate income growth above what full employment would provide, if full employment could be attained, but it does increase mean group income in the face of unemployment and underemployment. Even a poorly remunerated ethnic economy shields resource-poor and disadvantaged groups from unemployment.

Scenarios 3 and 2 are mixed. In scenario 2, employers and the self-employed experience income increase, but their coethnic employees only obtain relief from unemployment. Scenario 2 is what Sanders and Nee[40] found in their study of American Chinatowns. Since the self-employed and employers are more numerous than the employees, scenario 2 accelerates the income growth of the group albeit less than scenario 1. In scenario 3, employers and the self-employed just obtain relief from unemployment while their coethnic employees, few in number, actually earn more than counterparts in the general labor market. Scenario 3 is not just fanciful. When ethnic economies are heavily informal, and employer firms few, as among the Haitians in Miami, coethnic employees in the ethnic economy may earn higher productivity-adjusted money returns than do the self-employed.

Successful self-employment depends upon entrepreneurial capacity.[41] Entrepreneurial capacity requires resources.[42] But self-employment *sometimes* increases income all by itself. Portes and Zhou compared the incomes of employees in the general labor market and self-employed Cubans, Chinese, Japanese, and Koreans in 1979.[43] They found that self-employment significantly increased incomes in each group net of age, sex, human capital, hours of labor, length of residence in the United States, and marital status. That is, when all of these variables were controlled, Portes and Zhou found that the self-employed of these groups *still* earned more than equally productive coethnics who were employees.[44] For these groups, and others like them, self-employment, and thus participation in the ethnic economy, increased income and wealth, just as the folklore of capitalism proclaims. However, in other cases (e.g., those of blacks and Puerto Ricans, among whom income scenario 4 has long obtained), self-employment only helped the under- and unemployed to reduce their poverty, an economic service, but not one that increased income generation or wealth above what full employment would have provided.

Guarnizo usefully distinguished three sectors of the ethnic ownership econ- omy and measured their size. The sectors are subsistence, growth, and transition. Businesses in the subsistence sector provide a sparse living for the owner, but they do not provide a means of upward mobility. Subsistence firms were 43% of the Mexican-owned businesses in Guarnizo's sample. "In spite of their scanty economic returns and possibilities, entrepreneurs at this level remain in business either because their only alternative is unemployment, or because of an ideologi- cal conviction that if they persevere, they will eventually make it."[45] At the oppo- site pole, growth firms were vehicles for the upward mobility of their owners. About 21% of Mexican firms were growth firms whose owners enjoyed income mobility. Transition firms were those in the middle, wavering between growth and subsistence. These were 36% of all firms in Guarnizo's sample. These results display the continuum along which ethnic-owned firms array, reminding us that ethnic ownership economies confer a wide range of benefits.[46]

Employment Creation

An ethnic economy's contribution to employment creation depends upon how successfully it meets three challenges. The first challenge is to generate busi- ness firms whose owners have a reliable job in the firm they own. The higher the rate of self-employment, the more jobs an ethnic economy offers as a business owner. Thus, Cubans had 154.1 business owners for every 1000 workers in 1992. Conversely, in the same year, Puerto Ricans had 44 business owners for every 1000 workers. The Puerto Rican rate was only 28% of the Cuban rate. Overlooking for the moment the issue of what might have caused this inter- group difference of rates, a subject we approach in Chapters 4 and 5, one con- cludes that Cubans were creating jobs for business owners at a more rapid rate than were Puerto Ricans. If Cubans and Puerto Ricans had the same employ- ment chances in the general labor market, Cubans had more employment chances overall than did Puerto Ricans just because their ethnic ownership economy was bigger.

A second challenge involves maximizing the number of employer firms. Unless employer firms have been created, an ethnic economy consists exclusively of nonemployer self-employed. Ethnic economies can expand coethnic employment by adding jobs to firms, not just by self-employed. Generally speaking, the higher the share of employer firms in an ethnic ownership economy, the more employ- ment that economy offers. Employer firms offer the potential for drastically increasing the employment of ethnic economies. Among all American self-employed persons in 1992, 181 employer firms existed for every 1000 firms. Therefore, operating at the same rate, if an ethnic economy contained 1000 firms, it would contain 181 employing firms and 819 nonemployer firms.[47] However, ethnocultural or ethnoracial groups do not convert firms into employer firms at the same rate much less at the average rate. Comparing groups, we find that their ethnic economies contain quite different proportions of employing firms.

For instance, Cubans had 192 employer firms per 1000 firms in 1992, whereas Puerto Ricans had only 130 employer firms per 1000 firms in that year (Table 3.3).[48] However, to explain why Cubans had relatively more employer firms than Puerto Ricans, we must mention two prior challenges, not one. The first challenge involved the Cubans' prior ability to convert civilian labor force into firms that give employment to their owners; the second involves the Cubans' secondary ability to generate employer firms.[49] Because the Cubans could make firms more easily than Puerto Ricans, their ethnic economy offered self-employment to more coethnics. Because the Cubans could also generate a higher proportion of employer firms than could Puerto Ricans, Cubans had a second advantage in employment creation, wage jobs. However, Cubans would have had more employer firms than Puerto Ricans even if they did not have a superior ability to convert firms in general to employer firms. That is, if Cubans had 200 firms and Puerto Ricans only 100, then even if Cubans and Puerto Ricans had the same proportion of employer firms, the Cubans would still have twice as many employer firms as would Puerto Ricans. However, if Cubans also convert firms into employer firms at a rate higher than Puerto Ricans, then Cubans would have *more than twice* as many employer firms as would Puerto Ricans even though Cubans had only twice as many firms in general. In fact, as Table 3.3 shows, Cubans generated employer firms more abundantly than did the American economy as a whole so that their observed share of employer firms exceeded their share of all firms.

The third challenge of employment creation requires job creation. Success here depends upon *how many employees* the average employing firm hires. The more employees the average employing firm hires, the more employment that ethnic economy offers. After all, even if employer firms are numerous, they will not create much wage employment if the average employer firm hires only one worker. In fact, a small base of employer firms could create more total employment than a big base provided the firms in the small base economy hire more workers on average than do firms in the big base economy. In the U.S. economy, all employer firms averaged 8.74 employees per firm in 1992. Ethnic economies that surpass this standard converted employer firms to workers at a more rapid rate than did employer firms in general. To establish an ethnic economy's success in this conversion, we need only multiply its employer firms by 8.74 and compare the hypothetical result with the actual number of employees that the ethnic employer firms reported.

Successive Challenges

Table 3.3 accomplishes this exercise. It compares the ethnic economies of two ethnoracial categories (Asians and Pacific Islanders, Hispanics) and four ethnic groups (Blacks, Mexicans, Puerto Ricans, Cubans) in 1992. Using published data, Table 3.3 displays each group's actual business parameters in the observed column. Next to that, in the expected column, Table 3.3 displays the number that, given its civilian labor force, each group would have created had it generated this resource at the average rate of the whole American economy. For example, blacks had 620,912 firms in 1992, but they would have had 1,907,621 if blacks had generated firms from their civilian labor force at the same rate as did the entire American economy. Similarly, blacks had 64,478 employer firms in 1992, but they would have had 346,615 employer firms if they had reached the expected number of firms in 1992 and had generated employer firms from that number at the same rate as did the entire American economy. The last column of Table 3.3 shows the observed number as a percentage of the expected. For example, the actual number of black-owned firms was only 32.5% of the number that would have been expected had blacks generated firms at the same rate as did the entire U.S. economy. Similarly, the number of black-owned employer firms was only 18.6% of what it would have been had blacks generated employer firms from all firms at the same rate as did the entire U.S. economy. These employer firms hired only 11.4% as many employees as would have been expected had black-owned employer firms been as numerous as expected *and* had they hired workers at the same rate as did all employer firms, two prior challenges.

Since Table 3.3 piles up contingencies, ethnic firms that fall short of the first fall farther behind in the second, and failing the second, fall farther behind in the third. Reading down the third column, one notes successive shortfalls in a declining percentage. That is, where a percentage is lower than was the percentage directly above it, the ethnic or racial group or category fell farther behind at this point. Thus, we read that black-owned firms were 32.5% of expected, but black-owned employer firms were only 18.6% of the expected number. Had blacks constructed employer firms at the same rate as the American economy, then black-owned employer firms would have been 32.5% of the expected too. Because blacks constructed fewer employer firms than the economy's average and *also* created firms at a lower rate than the economy's average, their observed employer firms' share of the expected number was even lower than the share of their observed firms to the expected number of all firms. Similarly, had black-owned employer firms hired employees at the same rate (8.74 employees per firm) as all employer firms, then the employees of black-owned firms would have been 18.6% of the expected number rather than 11.4%. That black firms' employees were an even lower share of the expected number than were the black-owned employer firms indicates that black-owned employer firms, few in number, were

TABLE 3.3   Observed and Expected Ethnic Economy Statistics by Ethnicity for the United States, 1992

	Observed	Expected[a]	Observed as percentage of expected
Blacks			
All firms	620,912	1,907,621	32.5
Employer firms	64,478	346,615	18.6
Employees	345,193	3,029,415	11.4
Payroll ($000)	4,807,000	57,880,002	8.3
Hispanics			
All firms	771,708	1,527,228	50.5
Employer firms	115,364	277,497	41.6
Employees	691,056	2,425,328	28.5
Payroll ($000)	10,768,000	46,345,015	23.2
Mexicans			
All firms	378,614	980,751	38.6
Employer firms	56,277	178,202	31.4
Employees	323,883	1,557,489	20.2
Payroll ($000)	4,533,844	29,761,694	15.2
Puerto Ricans			
All firms	47,401	144,533	32.8
Employer firms	6,162	26,262	23.5
Employees	33,797	229,527	14.7
Payroll ($000)	621,742	4,386,041	14.2
Cubans			
All firms	93,096	81,359	114.4
Employer firms	17,839	14,783	120.7
Employees	120,477	129,203	93.0
Payroll ($000)	2,105,136	2,468,553	85.3
Asians and Pacific Islanders			
All firms	606,426	727,867	83.3
Employer firms	136,351	132,253	103.1
Employees	860,408	1,155,891	74.4
Payroll ($000)	13,327,883	22,084,453	60.3

[a]Expected statistics are generated by multiplication of base numbers derived from the "all persons" statistics. Civilian labor force of each ethnoracial group in 1992, expressed in thousands, is multiplied by 134.7 to obtain the expected number of all firms. The mean number of firms per 1000 persons in the civilian labor force is 134.7. The expected number of all firms is multiplied by 0.1817 to obtain the expected number of employer firms from the expected number of all firms. Among all persons, employer firms are 0.1817 as numerous as all firms. The expected number of employer firms is multiplied by 8.74 to obtain the expected number of employees. Among all persons, there were an average of 8.74 employees per employer firm. The expected number of employees is multiplied by $19,106 to obtain the expected payroll. Among all employer firms, the average payout per employee was $19,106.

Source: U.S. Bureau of the Census, *1992 Economic Census, Survey of Minority-Owned Business Enterprises, Hispanic* MB92-2 (Washington, D.C.: GPO, 1996), Table 2; *1992 Economic Census, Survey of Minority-Owned Business Enterprises, Black* MB92-1 (Washington, D.C.: GPO, 1996), Table 1; *Statistical Abstract of the United States 1996* (Washington, D.C.: GPO, 1996), Table 616; *1992 Economic Census, Survey of Minority-Owned Business Enterprises, Asians and Pacific Islanders, American Indians and Alaska Natives* MB92-3RV (Washington, D.C.: GPO, 1996), Table 1.

also hiring fewer employees per firm than did all employer firms in the American economy.

For the most part, Table 3.3 displays ethnic economies that perform below national norms. Five of six ethnic economies recorded fewer firms than expected; four of six recorded fewer employer firms than expected. All six ethnic economies recorded fewer employees and smaller gross payrolls than expected. Even Cubans, who had *more* than the expected number of firms and even of employer firms, just as Portes and his coworkers have reported, had fewer employees than expected from national norms and smaller gross payrolls than expected. Since Table 3.3 includes some very large and important groups, its dismal message is of substantive importance: some of the largest ethnoracial minorities have small ethnic economies. This is a critical fact. However, one cannot generalize from the results of Table 3.3 to ethnic groups that are not included because the U.S. Bureau of the Census published no economic data about them. It is likely that Koreans, Greeks, Iranians, and Chinese had larger ethnic economies than the ones recorded in Table 3.3, but no published data prove it.

At the same time, Table 3.3 shows considerable range in the employment generation of the ethnic economies it compares. At the top end, the Cubans had more employers and self-employed than expected and 93% of the employees expected. Adding the self-employed, the employers, and the employees, the Cubans had generated employment in their ethnic economy above the national rate. Where they expected an ethnic ownership economy of 210,562, the Cubans actually had an ethnic ownership economy of 213,573. At the bottom end, African Americans had fewer firms, fewer employers, and fewer employees than would have been expected from national norms. Expecting an ethnic economy of 4,937,036, the African Americans actually had an ethnic economy of only 966,105. The other categories and groups fell between the Cubans and the blacks.

Expanded Ethnic Economies

One way to assess the importance of the ethnic economies' employment contribution is to ask how large that *expected* ethnic economy's employment was relative to each category's and group's *real* unemployment problem in 1992. This exercise shows whether the expansion of a group's or category's ethnic economy to the national average might have reduced that group's or category's unemployment. Accordingly, we compare the expected employment that each group would have generated had it reached national norms with its actual unemployment problem, ascertaining how much of that unemployment an expanded ethnic economy could potentially have absorbed. An *expanded ethnic economy* is the expected ethnic economy minus the observed. This quantity indicates by how much a group's employment would have expanded over the observed if that ethnic economy had met national averages. If the expanded ethnic economy surpasses a category's total unemployment, we can conclude that expansion of the ethnic economy to the national average, were that possible, might reduce unemployment among coethnics.

Table 3.4 compares the observed and expanded ethnic economy with total unemployment and the unemployment rate for the five ethnoracial groups for whom the U.S. Bureau of the Census published economic data. Among blacks, Hispanics, Mexicans, and Puerto Ricans, the expanded ethnic economy greatly exceeded total unemployment of coethnics in 1992, indicating that expanding the ethnic economy of these groups and categories had some potential for reducing group unemployment.[50] In fact, expansion of the African American ethnic economy beyond its actual size to *half* the expected size would have created 2,011,000 new jobs and businesses in 1992, enough potentially to employ the entire population of unemployed blacks in that year. A comparable expansion of the Hispanic ethnic economy to 50% of the economy's average would also have created enough new jobs and businesses to employ all the unemployed Hispanics.

However, although expansion of an ethnic economy has the potential to reduce a group's unemployment, the case of the Cubans suggests that even strong expansion of an ethnic economy need not *eliminate* unemployment. That is, the Cuban ethnic economy had exceeded national norms in 1992, but 7.8% of Cubans still remained unemployed in that year. We do not know how much or even whether drastic expansion of the Cuban ethnic economy beyond this level would ultimately have eliminated unemployment among Cubans. But it is clear that merely exceeding national norms did not achieve this goal in 1992. This result should not surprise us. After all, the well-developed ethnic economies of the

TABLE 3.4   Unemployed and Ethnic Economy Employment, 1992

	Unemployment		Ethnic economy	
	Number	Rate	Observed	Expanded[a]
Blacks	2,011,000	14.2	966,105	3,970,931
Hispanics	1,311,000	7.7	1,462,764	2,489,792
Mexicans	782,000	10.7	702,497	1,835,743
Puerto Ricans	141,000	13.1	81,198	374,060
Cubans	47,000	7.8	213,573	− 3,011

[a]The expanded ethnic economy = (ES + EW) − (OS + OW), where ES is a group's expected total self-employment, EW is a group's expected wage employment, OS is a group's observed self-employment, and OW is a group's observed wage employment.

Source: U.S. Bureau of the Census, *1992 Economic Census, Survey of Minority-Owned Business Enterprises, Hispanic* MB92-2 (Washington, D.C.: GPO, 1996), Table 2; *1992 Economic Census, Survey of Minority-Owned Business Enterprises, Black* MB92-1 (Washington, D.C.: GPO, 1996), Table 1; *Statistical Abstract of the United States 1996* (Washington, D.C.: GPO, 1996), Table 616; *1992 Economic Census, Survey of Minority-Owned Business Enterprises, Asians and Pacific Islanders, American Indians and Alaska Natives* MB92-3RV (Washington, D.C.: GPO, 1996), Table 1.

non–Hispanic whites had not eliminated unemployment among whites in 1992 either. One obvious reason is the ethnic pluralism of the actual employment base, a reality that census data do not expose. Although ethnoracial particularism is a strong factor in small firms' hiring, even ethnic firms hire noncoethnics; Cubans hire some non–Cubans, African Americans hire some nonblacks, Koreans hire some non–Koreans, and so forth. In the preceding chapter, we estimated that 50% of the employees of ethnic firms were coethnics, and the other 50% were not. Therefore, expansion of an ethnic economy's wage sector need not reduce unemployment among coethnics beyond any actual preference or advantage that the coethnics receive in hiring. In an extreme case, actually documented in the literature,[51] where ethnic entrepreneurs *prefer* noncoethnic employees, even drastic expansion of the ethnic employers' employment base will not reduce coethnic unemployment at all.

Nonetheless, within this limitation, expansion of ethnic ownership economies reduces coethnics' unemployment rate and increases their labor force participation. Indeed, the existence of ethnic economies shows that some of this reduction has already occurred. In the case of African Americans, whose ethnic economy is small, Table 3.4 shows that nearly a million workers owed their employment to it in 1992. A thought experiment makes the point. If this African American ethnic economy had disintegrated all at once on January 1, 1993, would all of those 966,105 workers have found jobs in the general labor market on January 2, or would some of them have become unemployed? If even half of them would have become unemployed, then the African American economy in 1992 had already reduced African American unemployment by nearly 15% below what it otherwise would have been. If all of them would have become unemployed on January 2, then the African American ethnic economy had already reduced unemployment among coethnics by about 30%. Thus, even in this relatively small one, the ethnic ownership economy's contribution to coethnic employment was appreciable and should be considered an economic contribution in conjunction with its contribution to wealth, income, and wages.

Wages in the Ethnic Economy

Returning now to wages in the ethnic economy, discussed previously, we find useful evidence in Table 3.3. This table shows that for all six of the ethnoracial groups and categories, payroll was the weakest performer among all ethnic economies. Compared with the ethnic economies' production of employer firms and of employees, which was generally weak, the ownership economies' production of payroll was even weaker. For example, in the case of African Americans, their ethnic economy generated only 11.4% as many employees as it would have had the African American ethnic economy generated employees at the same rate as the general economy. However, the African American ethnic economy generated only 8.3% of the expected payroll. This amounts to 27% less payroll than employees.[52] These are low-paying jobs. Even Cubans, whose employer firms and employees exceeded national norms in number, produced only 85% of the expected payroll. The Cubans' payroll was 8% below their employment.

The implication is straightforward: ethnic economies pay lower wages than the general labor market. However, although all ethnic economies pay badly, some pay worse than others. The Puerto Rican ethnic economy, small in size, paid the highest wages, reaching 96.5% of the expected level. At the opposite extreme, the African American ethnic economy's payroll was only 72.8% of what it would have been had the African American ethnic economy paid wages at the average level of the general labor market. Other groups fell between Puerto Ricans at the top and African Americans at the bottom. Although the data in Table 3.3 are not comprehensive, and the possibility exists that some ethnic economies for whom the U.S. Bureau of the Census did not report economic data actually meet or exceed national payroll levels, the results in Table 3.3. warrant the conclusion that payroll is the weakest performance dimension of ethnic economies and that major ethnic economies pay wages that are below the average level in the general labor market.

From these conclusions one might infer, as Sanders and Nee[53] did, that employers are the only economic beneficiaries of ethnic economies and that employers in ethnic economies exploit their coethnic workers by paying them very low wages. This conclusion fits some individual ethnic economies in some localities, but it would be premature to embrace the generalization. First, the real issue is not whether ethnic economies generate payroll at the same rate as does the general labor market but whether ethnic economies reward employee productivity as generously as do American firms in general. If employees in ethnic economies are the least productive, least skilled, and least educated of coethnics, then it would be no wonder if they were paid less on average than more qualified coethnics employed in the general labor market. Exactly this situation prevails in the ethnic economy's informal sector, whose workers are, on average, less educated than those in the formal sector.[54] Moreover, the evidence on productivity-adjusted wages is equivocal. Some researchers report that ethnic economies pay productivity-adjusted wages that match those in the general economy to all their employees; others report that male employees in ethnic economies receive productivity-adjusted wages that are as high as those in the general labor market, but female employees do not; still others report that no employees obtain productivity-adjusted wages that equal those paid in the general labor market.[55] Conclusive evidence is not yet available.

Additionally, even when ethnic economies pay productivity-adjusted wages appreciably lower than those in the general labor market, the possibility exists that the low wages are a condition of the job's existence. In that case, the low wages and the job itself represent contributions of the ethnic economy to employment of coethnics, and the low wage exceeds the general labor market's counteroffer,

zero. Consider a situation in which 500 Chinese waiters in Los Angeles's Chinatown average only $6/hour whereas 5 Chinese waiters outside of Chinatown av-
erage $20/hour.[56] This situation is unfair, and it suggests that Chinese restaurant
owners are exploiting their coethnic waiters by paying them less than what they
would obtain outside Chinatown.[57] Unfortunately, it may turn out that there are
no more waiters' jobs outside Chinatown, and, worse, the Chinatown restaurants
obtain business by price competition with restaurants outside Chinatown. The
low prices bring customers into Chinatown restaurants and are a condition of
existence for the Chinatown restaurants. In this case, a realistic one, the highly
unequal productivity-adjusted wages inside and outside Chinatown do not *prove*
that Chinese restaurant owners exploit Chinese waiters.[58] Possibly the inexpensive
Chinese restaurants they created had created 500 low-wage jobs for waiters,
taking 500 people off the unemployment rolls to fill them. Karl Marx would
agree that unless we know the owners' profit, we cannot infer exploitation from
low wages alone.[59]

Finally, more than half of the participants in most ethnic economies nonemploying self-employed. In the African American ethnic economy, for example, we
find 556,434 nonemployer self-employed, 64,478 employers, and 345,193 employees (Table 3.3). Even if all the employers exploit all their workers, only 42%
of those in the African American ethnic economy would be exploited or ex-
ploiters. Approximately 58% of the workers in the African American ethnic economy are nonemployer self-employed who, employing no workers, cannot exploit
any workers. To the extent that these nonemploying self-employed obtain wealth
and income that facilitate their economic mobility, the African American ethnic
economy enhances the economic welfare of most of its participants even if, for
the sake of argument, we stipulate that all the ethnic economy's coethnic employees are exploited. Under the circumstances, evidence that ethnic economy wages
are low cannot support the inference that bosses exploit workers or that ethnic
economies benefit only employers.

These conclusions are only strengthened when we include the ethnic economy's informal economy sector in our assessment of the overall economic advantageousness of ethnic ownership economies. The economic information reported
by the U.S. Bureau of the Census (Table 3.3) completely excludes the informal
economy, and this exclusion most understates the ethnic economies of poorer and
less resource-endowed groups such as Mexicans and African Americans. Self-
employed workers in the informal sector are prevailingly those who have less skill
and productivity in the first place, and, to that extent, the low money returns of
the informal economy are comparable to what they might earn in the general labor market. Additionally, people in the informal economy are mostly underemployed or unemployed. They are people to whom the general labor market offers
either no income or not enough. Many are desperate. Therefore, they undertake
self-employment to obtain some money where otherwise they would have none.
Under the circumstances, the ethnic economy's informal sector just adds

employment to the ethnic group and reduces real unemployment and underemployment. Finally, most people in the informal sector are self-employed, not employees. The garment manufacturing industry is the major exception. Therefore, most informal economy workers cannot be exploited by bosses. If the ethnic economy's informal sector just disappeared tomorrow, then the economic welfare of the participants, who are usually recruited from the poorest ethnoracial minorities, would immediately decline. It makes no sense to reject the economic contribution of the ethnic economy's formal sector, declaring it exploitative, without rejecting that of the ethnic economy's informal sector too. We regret that market capitalism does not now and rarely has in the past provided full employment. However, ethnic economies relieve this situation.

Illegal Enterprise

Illegal enterprise is the ethnic economy's third sector, and we are bound to ask, following the logic of this inquiry, whether racketeers would not prosper better if they had wage jobs in the general labor market. On its face, this question is preposterous. The Godfather does not want a loading job in a warehouse! However, when they have matured out of youthful recklessness, many successful racketeers prefer legitimate business to illegal business. Indeed, for those most successful in organized crime, the usual way out of the rackets is not through police suppression, the legend of Elliott Ness notwithstanding, but rather through the slow intergenerational transfer of assets from illegal business to legal business.[60] Once reinvested in Nevada real estate or casinos, dollars that originated in illegal drug deals create a legal business whose owners are entrepreneurs, not racketeers. Thanks to the fluidity of American society, even one generation away from crime, the children of successful racketeers can move into elite status. The archetype is President John F. Kennedy, whose father made the family fortune by bootlegging liquor during the Prohibition era, 1919–1933.[61] What Daniel Bell once called a "queer ladder of mobility" has permitted many illegal entrepreneurs, their children, and grandchildren to break into respectability.[62]

Of course, everyone in the illegal economy is not the Godfather; whether employed or self-employed, most organized criminals earn modest incomes in crime careers that are interrupted by imprisonment and shortened by violent death. Gang members expect to die young. From a narrow economic standpoint, a warehouseman's job would usually be more lucrative than a gangster's if only because a warehouseman can anticipate more earning years thanks to his longer life span. In illegal enterprise as in crime generally,[63] the excitement and the enjoyment of power, not just the money, are major attractions that bring people to the life. However, for most youthful offenders who survive the adolescent years, when heart means everything, maturation breeds reflection upon the incarceration and brutal death that await them. At this point, the decision to remain in illegal enterprise does compete with economic alternatives available in the general labor market as well as with legal sectors of the ethnic economy.[64] By age 28, 85% of ex-delinquents have exited crime forever.[65] Were more legitimate options available to mature criminals, possibly more would retire from illegal enterprise than actually do so. To that extent at least, the employment creation capability of the illegal sector locks some participants into lifelong careers in illegal enterprise. Realistically speaking, the ethnic economy's legal sector is the most likely employer for such disillusioned gangsters, whose educational attainment is weak. Since their educational credentials are weak, the ex-racketeers cannot get jobs in the general labor market. The attraction of former racketeers into legitimate business is an unrecognized contribution of ethnic economies to social order.

THE ETHNIC-CONTROLLED ECONOMY

Job Capture

Turning now to ethnic-controlled economies, we first address job capture. *Job capture* means mainstream jobs that are reserved to coethnics. Job capture mainly occurs when coethnic employees in the general labor market obtain the ability to control hiring. Craft unions capture jobs in this way. However, job capture also occurs when persons outside the workplace mobilize political or economic power to reserve hiring for certain mainstream jobs to members of designated ethnoracial groups or categories. Affirmative action policies capture jobs in this way.[66] Of course, even without job capture, coethnics have a legal right to compete for jobs, but in a fair competition only as many coethnics succeed as win the competition. Job capture reserves hiring for coethnics, releasing them from competition with noncoethnics and tilting the odds in their favor. The advantages of job capture accrue as much to the whole ethnic group as to the successful job candidates.

Here is how job capture tilts the odds of employment. Suppose that A and B are ethnic groups, each of which is sending 50 workers to compete for jobs in an industry that offers only 50 jobs. That means 100 workers are competing for 50 jobs. On their merits, group A members will get 25 jobs, group B members the other 25, and both groups will have 25 unemployed. However, if group A creates an ethnic-controlled economy that reserves 10 of the 50 jobs to group A members, excluding group B members, then group A will get 30 jobs (10 + 40/2) and group B will get 20 jobs. As a result, the unemployment rate of group A will decrease, and that of group B will increase. The average income of group A will also increase. As a result of the job capture, 5 more group A members will have employment than would otherwise have had it.

If group B obtains the same hiring advantage in another equivalent-sized industry, then the balance of welfare will not have changed. Group A's captures counterbalance group B's. Each group has exactly as many jobs as they would have had under a regime of equal employment opportunity. However, even when this equality of job captures reigns, members of both group A and group B would now experience discriminatory treatment when they attempt to get jobs in the other's ethnic-controlled economy. In an extreme case, where a whole economy was divided into A jobs and B jobs, anyone who ventured outside his or her group's sector would encounter discriminatory exclusion. Discrimination would increase rejectees' consciousness of ethnic group membership as well as their dislike of the other ethnic group. Worse, neither group A nor group B could unilaterally dismantle its own ethnic-controlled economy without economic disadvantage. On the other hand, the prospect of creating more ethnic-controlled economies in new industries would offer possible advantages for both groups, thus encouraging their efforts to extend existing ethnic-controlled economies and to create new ones. In this Hobbesian economic world, permanent disadvantage of group B would arise when group A had established many more ethnic-controlled economies than had group B. As a result, group A would successfully exclude members of group B from more jobs than group B would exclude group A members from.

We distinguish full and partial job capture. *Full job capture* arises when all the jobs in some occupation, industry, or workplace are reserved for coethnics. Full job capture is unusual except in legally segregated societies such as the Union of South Africa once was. *Partial job capture* occurs when only some jobs are thus reserved, and others are available to any applicants, regardless of ethnic origin, on the basis of merit. Thus, if coethnics have captured 1/10 of the jobs, they have *not* captured 90% of the jobs, which are open to all. However, where they would otherwise routinely expect to get only 1/20, capture of 1/10 of the jobs doubles their share. Partial job captures obviously expand group welfare less than full captures, but partial captures can be increased over time, and, from the point of view of the capturers, partial job capture is superior to equal hiring opportunity.

Job capture has a long history.[67] The most egregious contemporary cases come from the construction industry, where craft unionism still prevails. Craft unions require employers to hire only union members, and they exclude from union membership applicants who are not related by blood or marriage to current or past union members.[68] These work rules indirectly link ethnic origins to union membership since only those who intermarry acquire the qualification to join the union.[69] In the nineteenth century all unions were craft unions. This situation no longer exists, and most unions are not craft unions anymore. However, in the building trades, most unions still are craft unions. The work rules of the building trades craft unions *capture* jobs for coethnics. This outcome is not fortuitous. Ethnic consciousness is close to the surface in the building industry's craft unions. As a result of government efforts to open opportunities for black construction workers, building trades unions have engaged in 30 years of defensive litigation, and governments, writes Waldinger, have failed to change hiring very much.[70]

Fire departments tend also toward nepotistic qualification that perpetuates ethnic job capture. Waldinger[71] writes that "Firefighting enjoys a well-deserved reputation for intergenerational succession." Although governments have attempted to open fire departments to blacks (as well as to women), their success has not been great. New York City's fire department was 93% white in 1990, down from 96% white 30 years earlier. Admittedly, fire departments are public sector occupations, recruitment to which requires applicants to pass competitive examinations. Few blacks and few women apply to take fire department examinations, and even fewer pass the examinations. Therefore, the process of intergenerational transmission of this occupation does not depend, as it does in the building trades, upon nepotistic work rules. Rather, existing fire department personnel virtually monopolize the skills and motivation to do this job, and they are very well organized to insert their kin into the hiring process. These are cultural resources. The example makes the point that job capture is not necessarily against the public interest since the most qualified applicants are apparently getting the jobs thanks to an occupational culture that reproduces competence in the younger generation.

Occupational and industrial clustering commonly bespeak job capture. In an effort to ascertain how advantageous had been occupational clustering, Suzanne Model[72] and John Logan[73] independently reviewed the occupational and industrial history of New York City's ethnic minorities and white immigrants between 1910 and 1960. Model proposed that occupational and industrial clusters were either neutral or positive in their long-term economic effect on men, never negative. She advanced two grounds for expecting positive long-term economic effects of clustering among male employees in the mainstream.[74] First, coethnic clusters facilitate coethnic job searches. Second, coethnic clusters facilitate unionization, which improves wages and working conditions. We accept Model's points, but wish to slightly clarify their import. Facilitating job searches leads to job capture. Job capture is, we submit, the real advantage to which the facilitation of coethnic job searches really leads. Beyond job capture, the advantages of coethnic clustering among employees also leads, we agree, straight to unionization, and, short of caste formation, coethnic craft unions are the farthest terminus of this progression. However, even work settings in which coethnic clusters do not create coethnic unions, employers know that the clusters can confer market power upon nonunionized employees. Market power enhances the ability of even nonunionized workers to raise wages and improve working conditions.

Model's evidence confirmed the contribution of ethnic-controlled economies to group welfare. "At one or another point in time, each group studied here profited from one or more niches."[75] However, blacks and Puerto Ricans did not form so many niches as had earlier white immigrants and so did not equivalently profit from them. In fact, Model understands affirmative action policies, which began in the 1970s and built African American clusters in the public sector, as attempts to redress the lack of ethnic-controlled economies ("niches") among blacks.[76] An interesting exception is the Brotherhood of Sleeping Car Porters, which was a black-controlled railroad union in the days of Pullman sleeping cars. Only blacks worked in this occupation; all joined the union. Union members earned wages 20% higher than those externally prevailing among southern blacks.[77] Malcolm X was once a member of this union, and one supposes that, if African Americans had enjoyed 20 more such unions, their economic welfare would have been higher than it actually was.

Assessing the contribution of clusters to the economic welfare of white immigrants and their descendants in roughly the same period earlier studied by Suzanne Model, John Logan[78] found that native whites enjoyed more niches than immigrant whites in 1920.[79] Later the immigrants caught up, and native-white niches declined in number. Like Model, Logan interpreted a shortfall of clustering as indicative of economic disadvantage, but, in this case, the immigrant whites were disadvantaged vis-á-vis the nonimmigrant whites. The clusters of the white immigrants persisted over three generations, affecting the life chances of their grandchildren. The surprising persistence resulted, Logan[80] supposed, because "group members consciously build upon ethnic social networks to find jobs, to attempt to control access to those jobs . . . and to do all the other things that affect success or failure in the economy." The protracted survival of these ethnic-controlled economies suggests that they enhanced income because city people do not stay in underpaid industries or occupations over three generations.

If ethnic-controlled economies conferred only benefits, and no disadvantages, assimilation theory would simply collapse. Assimilation theory predicts that ethnic-controlled economies should not survive the immigrant generation. After that, the descendants of immigrants will find their economic interest best served if they move into the general labor market. As Reitz[81] put it, "Mobility to high-status occupations usually means mobility out of ethnic specializations." Obviously, the results of Logan and of Model do not confirm assimilation theory, but other research has been kinder. In his study of seven immigrant groups in Toronto, Reitz isolated what amount to ethnic-controlled economies although he did not use that terminology. His is the only research that has used this approach. For male employees, the correlation between working in ethnic-controlled economies and income was .086 and for female employees, −.26. For men, the correlation between having many coethnic workers and income was −.10 and for women, −.152. These results range between mixed for men to strongly negative for women. However, when Reitz turned to regression, a stricter technique, he found that ethnic-controlled economies slightly increased the earnings of male employees but had no effect upon the earnings of women.

SUMMARY AND CONCLUSION

The research debate has focused heavily on the issue of how economically advantageous ethnic economies are to participants. An important position maintains that ethnic ownership economies benefit employers but reduce the economic welfare of their employees. Reviewing the topics of wealth generation, proprietor's income, employment creation, and wages, we have revisited this debate, adding some new census-derived evidence. The issue of wealth creation has not received so much attention in the research literature as it deserves. Available evidence shows that the self-employed have 10 to 14 times the wealth of employees. This situation colors our interpretation of the equivocal research results about the relative money incomes of self-employed and equally productive employees. Although outcomes vary among localities, research literature generally shows that the self-employed fall slightly behind equally productive employees in income. Nonetheless, the self-employed's compensation of 10 to 14 times the employees' wealth is quite generous. Many self-employed persons have higher incomes as well as higher wealth; others have only higher wealth. On balance, then, the joint income and wealth situation of the self-employed considerably surpasses the situation of employees. As a result, except during depressions, increases in the proportion of self-employed within ethnoracial minorities transfer workers from less to more rewarded occupations, accelerate the long-term generation of wealth that will be intergenerationally transmissible, and increase the economic welfare of the group.

The extent of worker exploitation in ethnic economies has attracted much debate. Our census-derived evidence shows that ethnic economies pay lower wages than does the general labor market, apparently confirming superexploitation within ethnic economies. However, the real issue is productivity-adjusted wages, not just relative wages. Research studies show that productivity-adjusted wages in ethnic economies sometimes exceed, sometimes match, and sometimes fall behind wages in the general labor market. Because research results are mixed, one cannot reach a final judgment about the productivity-adjusted wages within ethnic economies. Moreover, to the extent that ethnic economies create jobs for the unemployed and underemployed, ethnic economies put money in the hands of people who would otherwise have none. Even when the wages paid them fall below those of equally productive coethnics in the general labor market, ethnic economy employees know and often state that their rotten job stands between them and destitution. Additionally, most of the workers in ethnic economies are non-employer self-employed who cannot exploit any employees. The debate about worker exploitation just does not engage this modal group. Finally, ethnic economy firms are not very profitable, and there can be no exploitation without profits.

Unlike the formal sector, in which this issue is uncertain, the ethnic economy's informal sector definitely pays workers and self-employed less than they would earn in the general labor market. However, in this sector, more than in the formal sector, the ethnic economy's workers are aware that their informal sector work is their only realistic alternative to underemployment and unemployment. Within the ethnic economy's illegal sector, successful racketeers earn high incomes while the rank and file just get by, contenting themselves with the nonfinancial rewards of their jobs. However, for successful entrepreneurs of illegal business and their descendants, the main exit from illegal enterprise is into the ethnic economy's formal sector, which alone offers realistic alternatives to their illegal occupations.[82] Laundered money, contributed by racketeers, is an influential source of capital in the formal sector of ethnic ownership economies.[83]

Ethnic-controlled economies are occupational and industrial clusters of employees in the mainstream. Whereas assimilation theory predicts that such clusters should disintegrate over generations, as their former participants scatter into the mainstream, the research of Waldinger, Model, and Logan all found long-term persistence in New York City. Historical persistence implies a continuing contribution to the welfare of participants over three generations. Of course, one cannot build an entirely convincing case around one city, even if it is New York. Unfortunately, only Reitz's study of Toronto takes us outside the Big Apple. Using a cross-sectional, nonhistorical design, Reitz found weak support for the income advantages of ethnic-controlled economies among men and none among women. Possibly women derive no advantage from ethnic-controlled economies because women are harder to unionize than men. At any event, Reitz's results do show some modest advantages of ethnic-controlled economies among men. Among women, Reitz found no advantage to either working in the mainstream or working in clusters, a neutral result.

In a world of full employment and nondiscrimination, ethnic ownership economies and ethnic-controlled economies would be unnecessary because everyone would obtain a suitable job in the general labor market. However, market capitalism has never offered such a world in the past and probably will not do so in the future. Given unemployment and discrimination, ugly realities of the work world, successful ethnic ownership economies accelerate wealth creation, income generation, and employment options for coethnics. Even unsuccessful ethnic economies, small and concentrated in the informal sector, move participants from starvation to survival, a kind of economic mobility. The formal sector of ethnic economies is the only real economic competitor to illegal enterprise and probably sucks more gangsters from racketeering crime than do the police, courts, and prisons. Big and successful ethnic economies produce more wealth and income than small and struggling ones, but even small and struggling ethnic economies confer significant economic benefit upon the ethnoracial communities to which they are adjunct.

Ethnic-controlled economies capture jobs; they do not create them as do ethnic ownership economies. Job capture tends to balkanize labor markets and to aggravate intergroup relations. These consequences are undesirable from the point of view of social policy. However, if we ask whether ethnic-controlled economies produce income advantages for participants, available evidence suggests that the answer must be yes. First, they give jobs to those who otherwise would lack them. Second, at least for men, ethnic-controlled economies increase incomes over what equally productive coethnics obtain in the general labor market. That is why they persist over generations. If so, employees are defending and promoting their economic self-interest when they build and defend ethnic-controlled economies.

Family business. This Chinese-Vietnamese family owns an herb and tea shop in Southern California. Family members pooled their money and labor to purchase this business and a home, and to pay for their children's college tuition. Ties to relatives and coethnics overseas facilitate their importation of perishable goods for sale.

The number of women entrepreneurs, such as this Vietnamese food distributor and this Soviet Jewish cardiologist, has been growing at a rapid rate since the late 1980s. Through self-employment, some women can escape from the limited range of social and economic options available in the larger society.

Ethnic media. A billboard advertising a "salsa rock" radio program on Sixth Street between downtown Los Angeles and Boyle Heights, a Chicano enclave. A profit-making enterprise, ethnic media do much to provide ethnic communities with entertainment, guidance, and information unavailable elsewhere in the host society. In recent years, Latino ownership of AM radio stations has increased.

Women fundraisers at a Jewish community festival, Detroit suburbs, 1996. In recent years, women have been of increasing importance in philanthropic activities, contributing both funds and volunteer efforts in growing amounts.

Class Resources

The previous chapter defined *entrepreneurial capacity* as the ability to open and operate numerous, large, and lucrative business firms.[1] Entrepreneurial capacity means having whatever it takes to succeed in business, but what exactly does it take? In addition to being in the right place at the right time, partially a matter of luck, it takes resources. Entrepreneurs need resources. Useful as far as it goes, the concept of entrepreneurial capacity is just a cipher for the resources that create it, and the real task of explaining ethnic ownership economies requires one to identify and classify the needed resources. Here the key distinction is between class resources and *ethnic resources*.[2] This distinction does not imply mutual exclusivity such that some entrepreneurs use ethnic and others use class resources. Rather, when they build ethnic ownership economies, ethnoracial groups and ethnic entrepreneurs have and utilize both class and ethnic resources albeit in differing proportions. Although real ethnic economies blend class and ethnic resources, this chapter addresses class resources, leaving ethnic resources to the next chapter.

In classical Marxism, a bourgeoisie owns the means of production and distribution within market economies.[3] Narrowly defined, a bourgeoisie consists of all the employers in an economy's formal sector. Marxists also distinguish a large and small bourgeoisie, depending upon the size of their firm; Marxists include nonemployer self-employed among the small bourgeoisie.[4] Marxists do not include in the bourgeoisie any employers or self-employed in the illegal sector nor any business owners in the informal sector. Since we wish to include all business owners, a Marxist bourgeoisie is too narrow. Therefore, we broaden the Marxist bourgeoisie to include business owners in each of the three sectors, formal, informal, and illegal. This concept we call *the class of business owners* to distinguish it from the Marxist concept of bourgeoisie. The class of business owners consists of all business owners in any sector: formal, informal, or illegal. A bourgeoisie consists only of employers in the formal sector. A bourgeoisie is the elite of the business class.

Class resources are the vocationally relevant cultural and material endowment of bourgeoisies.[5] Business owners possess class resources, too, but in lesser amounts. Class resources enable entrepreneurs to initiate and to run business firms in the formal sector. A defining feature of class resources is universality. Class resources lack distinctive ethnic or cultural character. The bourgeoisie of Finland possesses them just as does the bourgeoisie of Taiwan. Every bourgeoisie possesses the same class resources but not necessarily the same resources in the same quantities. Class resources are material or cultural. On the material side, class resources include private property and wealth. In the Marxist lexicon, the bourgeoisie's property was its only resource.[6] Neoclassical economists now add human capital to this list of material resources because human capital requires a prior financial investment.[7] For that reason, an individual's ownership of human capital imposes a money cost.

On the cultural side, class resources include occupationally relevant and supportive values, attitudes, knowledge, and skills transmitted in the course of socialization from one generation to another. Since the occupation of bourgeoisies is to initiate, own, and operate business firms, their occupational culture contains all the skills they need to practice their occupation.[8] Bourgeois occupational culture means cultural endowment (values, skills, attitudes, knowledge) characteristic of bourgeoisies around the world, and which, furthermore, distinguishes bourgeoisies from nonbourgeois coethnics while linking the bourgeoisie to noncoethnic bourgeoisies elsewhere.[9] The ability to communicate in English is a good example. In non–English-speaking countries, bourgeoisies learn English because English is now the lingua franca of international business. Whether in Taiwan or Finland, bourgeoisies learn English, and their knowledge of it represents a class resource precisely because and insofar as all business owners share this knowledge.[10] However, when they speak Finnish or Chinese to coethnic employees, Finnish or Chinese business owners avail themselves of linguistic knowledge that is ethnocultural in origin. Bourgeoisies are ethnic, and they have ethnic resources, but their ethnicity does not define their class status.

FORMS OF CAPITAL

All class resources are forms of capital.[11] Capital is any store of value that assists production and productivity. The classic form of capital is financial capital. Money

and wealth are the two main forms of financial capital. Ethnoracial and ethnoreligious groups possess unequal financial capital; some are wealthy, others poor, and
still others middling. It is not newsworthy to observe that wealthy groups respond
more successfully to opportunities for formal sector entrepreneurship than do
poor groups. They build larger and more successful ethnic ownership economies
in consequence. Clearly, the unequal financial capital access of ethnoracial groups
and categories importantly explains the very intergroup and interlocal variations
in ethnic entrepreneurship we documented in Chapters 2 and 3. We acknowledge
the big role that financial capital plays in building ethnic economies. For example,
whites own and operate more and bigger businesses than blacks. The superior
financial resources of the whites importantly explain why their ethnic ownership
economies are bigger. Because whites are wealthier than blacks, whites can inject
more equity capital, and they can borrow more debt capital. The key question,
however, is whether financial assets, a class resource, provide a complete explanation for black–white differences and, indeed, for all intergroup differences in
ethnic ownership economies. If so, we would have a class only explanation that
depended exclusively upon intergroup differences in wealth, a class resource, to
explain why one group's ethnic economy surpassed another's.

   A financial explanation of black–white differences in self-employment is more
than 125 years old, and this explanation still recurs in casual treatments of this
important topic.[12] This argument explains black–white differences in ethnic
ownership economy on the basis of the blacks' low incomes, their societal victim-
ization, and the racial discrimination of white bankers.[13] That is, blacks lack the
capital to start up their own businesses, and they cannot borrow it either. Persua-
sive as far as it goes, and, as we show in Chapter 9, importantly true, this argument
falls short of completeness. First, other immigrant and ethnic minority groups are
or have been poor and subject to discrimination by bankers and employers, yet
some poor groups have built bigger ethnic ownership economies than others.[14]
Oftentimes groups subjected to equal discrimination are unequally successful in
entrepreneurship. Indeed, some ethnoracial minorities outperform the entrepreneurship of the white majority.[15] Similarly, if wealth or access to debt capital simply explained entrepreneurship, then the native born ought to evidence higher
entrepreneurship than the foreign born, but we observe the opposite. The foreign
born are more frequently self-employed than the native born among every ethnoracial group and category.[16]

   Finally, scholars have known for half a century that small business start-ups
depend upon the owner's savings rather than upon bank loans.[17] Blacks also have
started businesses from personal savings rather than from loans.[18] Table 4.1 shows
that 70% of business owners of all ethnoracial groups did not borrow money in
order to start their own businesses.[19] Of those who did borrow, as many borrowed
from family, friends, and kin as borrowed from banks. Bank loans influence the
start-up of big and medium business; they do not influence small business.
Therefore, however reprehensible, banker discrimination cannot explain much
intergroup difference in ethnic small business because bankers' role in small

TABLE 4.1   Sources of Borrowed Capital for Business Firms, 1987

	Spouse, family, and friends	Bank loan	Government	Did not borrow[a]
Hispanic	10.5	8.7	0.4	70.3
Black	6.8	9.5	0.9	69.6
Asian[b]	22.8	12.2	0.5	58.6
Women	7.4	10.5	0.3	73.7
White men	9.8	16.0	0.5	66.8

[a]Owners who did not require capital to start their businesses or who did not borrow the required capital.

[b]Includes Pacific Islanders and American Indians.

Source: U.S. Bureau of the Census, *1987 Economic Censuses: Characteristics of Business Owners* CBO87-1 (Washington, D.C.: GPO, 1991), Table 17C.

business funding has long been minimal. As we document more completely in Chapter 9, bankers have historically ignored the capital needs of small business owners of every ethnoracial background. Therefore, small business start-ups have always depended most upon the savings of owners and secondarily upon loans from kin and friends.[20] Bank loans have always been less important than the other two in funding small business start-ups. Savings depend upon the savings rate within one's group. Thrifty communities generate more financial capital than others. Of course, economic conditions, interest rates, and income level also affect the savings rate of every ethnoracial group. However, net of economic conditions and income level, some groups save more and lend more than others. The causes of intergroup disparity in savings rate include values and attitudes that bear upon saving and lending, the size and integrity of the group's kinship system, and the availability of rotating credit associations.[21] These are not class resources.

Likewise, the ability of small entrepreneurs to borrow depends upon their integration into cultures whose norms endorse philanthropic lending within families. Some cultures encourage lending to family members; others do not. According to Yen-Fen Tseng, "the Chinese are more likely to finance their businesses with capital borrowing from parents and relatives than the general [American] population."[22] Similarly, the remarkable entrepreneurship of the Pennsylvania Amish relies squarely on normatively prescribed lending.[23] American culture does not meet the Chinese or the Amish standard for lending or saving.[24] Family size matters too. The larger these family units, the larger the pool of people from whom small entrepreneurs might borrow.[25] Pennsylvania Amish couples average 10 children per couple, and each child has 75 first cousins, each of whom is available as a potential lender.[26] Since the size of families, their integration in networks, and their borrowing norms are cultural issues, the ability of entrepreneurs to borrow from families depends upon the cultural group to which they belong. Some cultural groups provide entrepreneurs with greater access to family capital than do others. Zimmer and Aldrich reported that Asian shopkeepers in London borrowed money from family and friends to a greater extent than did whites.[27] In Bradford, 49% of Asian owners but only 3% of white owners acknowledged the use of money borrowed from friends. Zimmer and Aldrich conclude that "Asians and whites differ significantly in how they mobilized capital."[28] Even Bates concedes that Asians borrowed from kin and friends three times more frequently than white Americans.[29] Young and Sontz similarly found that only 24% of Hispanic grocers received help from friends or family when starting up, but 57% of Korean grocers had received that help.[30]

Beyond the family and extended family stand formal and informal ethnic group institutions of savings and credit. Tenenbaum has shown how much the prewar entrepreneurship of Jews benefited from the Hebrew Free Loan Associations, a unique philanthropic institution of the Jewish communities.[31] Similarly, rotating credit associations have supported the entrepreneurship of Asians and West Indians in North America.[32] Since poor whites and blacks lacked either cultural tradition, Jews and Asians had the advantage of unique business-supporting financial institutions.[33] When ethnic institutions of saving or credit affect the creation of ethnic economies, we cannot explain why one group's ethnic ownership economy surpasses another's just on the strength of prior differences in financial wealth.

HUMAN CAPITAL

Like the classical economists, his contemporaries, Karl Marx considered money, commodities, and physical capital the only forms of capital.[34] Contemporary social science has rejected this nineteenth-century view. Social scientists now recognize three additional forms of capital of which human capital is the elder brother. Recognizing this priority, Balkin declares that human capital gives "the basic conceptual framework" to studies of entrepreneurship.[35] *Human capital* means an individual's investment in personal productivity. Productivity is a person's ability to add value by doing work. Education and work experience are the basic forms of human capital.[36] For example, to become a computer programmer, one needs first to learn programming. The human capital of the computer programmer consists of programming knowledge, and this knowledge renders that person productive on the job. Insofar as formal education really increases personal productivity, an unproven but plausible assumption, then those who have human capital make more effective entrepreneurs than those who lack it.[37] Human capital improves the productivity of entrepreneurs as well as of their employees. Much evidence shows that among all ethnoracial groups and categories, human capital increases rates of entrepreneurship.[38]

The impact is easy to illustrate. The average level of education among American business owners is higher than the average level of the feeder population for all ethnoracial and gender categories except Asian high school graduates (Table 4.2). This result indicates that higher educational attainments increase the individual's likelihood of business ownership. Categories with higher educational levels have higher self-employment rates than categories with lower average educational levels. Moreover, within the population of business owners, employers have slightly higher educational levels than do nonemployers in all categories except black high school graduates (Table 4.2). The difference is about 10% on average. Even among business owners, additional human capital increases the likelihood of owning a bigger business.

The advantages of education are easiest to illustrate for Hispanics, the ethnoracial category with the lowest average educational level. Table 4.2 shows that Hispanic business owners had higher educational attainment than did Hispanics in general. Nearly 30% of Hispanic employers were college graduates compared with only 8.8% of the Hispanic adult population. This was the biggest gap of any ethnoracial category. This educational advantage of the business owners held true for both employers and nonemployers, but the gap was bigger for employers. Nonetheless, despite the big educational gap between Hispanics and Hispanic business owners, the Hispanic business owners had only about three-quarters the educational level of the other four ethnoracial categories. Clearly, this low educational level of the Hispanics helps to explain why Hispanic self-employment rates were low as well as why Hispanics had fewer employer firms than others: Hispanic self-employment rates were reduced by the low educational levels of the Hispanic population. We arrive at a thought experiment. If the Hispanics had had twice as high a proportion of college graduates as they actually did, would Hispanics have generated more entrepreneurs and employer firms? If yes, we must acknowledge that financial capital is not the only class resource of entrepreneurship.

Now, comparing the entrepreneurship of blacks and whites, the locus classicus of this debate, we recognize that, in addition to their advantage in financial capital, the whites had more human capital than the blacks. That is, the average years of education of whites were still somewhat greater than the average among blacks even though blacks were closing this gap.[39] Did this human capital advantage give the whites an additional advantage in entrepreneurship above and beyond the advantages conferred by their superior financial capital? The answer is most likely yes. Like the financial capital advantage of the whites, the human capital advantage of the whites is a class resource that translates into higher rates of entrepreneurship. In fact, when human capital endowments are statistically controlled, the huge differences in self-employment rates that divide whites and blacks are actually reduced by 30%.[40] That is, if blacks had the same average human capital endowments as do whites, the difference between black self-employment rates and white self-employment rates would be only two-thirds as large as it actually is. When combined with the effects of unequal financial capital, the effects of unequal human capital evidently accentuate black–white differences in entrepreneurship.

Although the impact of human capital upon entrepreneurship is unambiguous, the meaning of this relationship requires clarification.[41] Collins complains that economists' use of human capital "does not capture either the economic advantages, or disadvantages of cultural knowledge and cultural practice in the economy."[42] The objection has merit because economists treat human capital as though it were just a financial investment.[43] Their justification is straightforward. At least in market economies, human capital costs money.[44] Investment in human capital takes two forms. One is direct costs of instruction, lodging and meals away from home, transportation to classrooms, and so forth. The second is the opportunity cost of being a student. The opportunity cost of being a student means the money a student could have earned had that student held a job instead.[45] Even students who pay no tuition, learning at home from unemployable parents, must pay an opportunity cost for being students, so, in that sense, their education imposes money costs too.

Agreeing that human capital is importantly a class resource, like financial capital, we cannot call it a *financial* resource. Human capital is importantly

TABLE 4.2   Educational Attainment of Owners and All Persons by Race and Ethnoracial Category, 1987 (in Percentages)

	Hispanic		Black		Asian[a]	
	HS+[b]	College+[c]	HS+[b]	College+[c]	HS+[b]	College+[c]
Business owners						
No employees	61.5	20.2	70.8	25.7	80.5	47.2
With employees	64.5	22.9	69.3	28.6	82.2	51.4
All persons	49.1	8.8	62.4	11.2	80.4	39.9

	Women		Nonminority men	
	HS+[b]	College+[c]	HS+[b]	College+[c]
Business owners				
No employees	84.5	34.2	80.8	33.3
With employees	86.0	33.0	82.8	38.6
All persons	75.1	17.0	77.2	24.5

[a]Includes Pacific Islanders and American Indians.
[b]HS+, completed 4 years of high school or more.
[c]College+, completed 4 years of college or more.
Source: U.S. Bureau of the Census, *Statistical Abstract of the United States: 1996* (Washington, D.C.: GPO, 1996), Tables 241 and 242; *1987 Economic Censuses: Characteristics of Business Owners* CBO87-1 (Washington, D.C.: GPO, 1991), Table 6C.

nonfinancial in origin. People's decision to purchase human capital and their learning capacity if they do purchase it both depend upon class culture much more than upon income.[46] Income has a modest effect upon educational attainment. Comparing educational attainment across income groups, Susan Mayer concludes that "doubling parental income" would raise a poor child's "eventual years of education by about a fifth of a point."[47] Indeed, Mayer shows that, if we could raise the children of the lowest income quintile into the second lowest income quintile, we would raise their years of education at age 24 by only 2%. If we moved the poorest children into the highest income quintile, we would raise their expected years of education at age 24 by only 10%.[48]

Additional evidence derives from research on educational attainment. This research has increasingly contrasted economic and noneconomic explanations, concluding that income does not explain educational attainment. In his study of elementary school children, George Farkas found the white children learned and achieved more in school than did the black children, the usual research result. However, when Farkas statistically controlled for the cognitive level of the children's parents, the learning differences between white and black children vanished.[49] Black children learned as well as white children if their parents had equivalent cognitive skills. Farkas concluded that the children whose parents demonstrated strong cognitive skills benefited from an informal curriculum at home that paralleled and reinforced the curriculum at school. However, the whites had more such children in these curricula than did the blacks. As a result, the cultural environment of the white homes supported and encouraged classroom attainment more than did the culture of the black homes.

In addition to money, which confers the ability to buy human capital, affluent people possess a class culture that encourages them to want human capital. This class culture furnishes an outlook that broadly supports educational attainment. Pierre Bourdieu calls this outlook a habitus. By habitus, Bourdieu means mental structures "through which we apprehend the world."[50] In reality, a class culture's encouragement of education extends to the habitus it provides as well as to financial means. Take Josephine Smith, who recently completed an MBA at Yale. True, Smith paid for her education. In that sense, her degree embodies human capital that Smith purchased. Nonetheless, her prior knowledge of that degree's economic value in the marketplace, the academic motivation that produced her high grade point averages, her materialistic outlook on life, and her knowledge of and comfort with business careers and ambience are all features of class culture that prepared and conditioned Smith's enthusiastic investment in human capital. Following Pierre Bourdieu, we call the educational sequence that eventuated in Smith's business degree a class "strategy."[51] Except for this strategy, known to and practiced by people of her class, Smith might have done something else with her money. Possibly, she would have donated her money to the needy; alternatively, she might have squandered it on drugs, motorcycles, and tattooed boyfriends.

Smith's money did not invest itself in human capital; Smith made the choice. To that extent, human capital investments reduce to prior class cultures, which must be invoked to explain the investment decision.

CULTURAL CAPITAL

This observation requires the identification of a third form of capital, cultural capital. Like human capital and financial capital, cultural capital is a class resource in that those of higher class status normally possess it. However, although a class resource, cultural capital is not a material resource and one can have cultural capital without financial capital, or vice versa. The developer of the concept of cultural capital, Pierre Bourdieu, defines it "as competence in a society's high-status culture."[52] High-status culture emphasizes art, music, dance, and literature, but it also includes furniture, architecture, cuisine, and fashion. Knowledge of these arts represents capital, Bourdieu maintains, and not just snobbish affectation, because—and to the extent that—this knowledge can be turned to the owner's financial advantage at multiple points in the owner's life span.[53] For example, when Josephine Smith wears the right suit, handbag, and shoes to a job interview on Wall Street, she makes a favorable impression and lands the job.[54] Josephine's mother and peers taught her how to dress, a culturally monitored skill that paid off when she landed a lucrative job.[55]

In Bourdieu's formulation, people acquire cultural capital in the family *and* in formal schooling. The home curriculum and the school curriculum partially co-incide, but they importantly diverge. The parallel curriculum of the home teaches class knowledge that the school ignores. The parallel curriculum gives children of the affluent a superior endowment in cultural capital. However acquired, at home or in school, cultural capital is converted to income in several ways, of which the principal means is educational certification.[56] Although formal education culminates in diplomas, degrees, and certificates, cultural capital is quite different from human capital, which also emerges from formal education. The difference between human capital and cultural capital resides in how the capital benefits its owner. Human capital increases its owner's productivity, a competence employers reward with wages. In contrast, cultural capital conveys prestige recognition on the strength of which people get desirable jobs, marriages, and business contacts. Therefore, the same diploma has value as human capital and as cultural capital; the difference depends upon whether we emphasize the real vocational competencies that a diploma represents or the prestige recognition it commands for its owner. Every diploma has both. When a person's education has bestowed both enhanced productivity and prestige recognition, that person has two forms of capital (human and cultural), both of which can be converted into money. If an education has bestowed only snob value or only enhanced productivity, the graduate has only one form of capital, not two. Obviously it is better to have both cultural capital and human capital than to have only one or the other, but it is better to have one or the other than neither.

Although Bourdieu analyzed the high culture of the bourgeoisie, calling this cultural capital, he neglected the occupational culture of the bourgeoisie.[57] This disjuncture led George Farkas to complain that the sociologists' cultural capital was an empty "shell game" that ignored competence.[58] Culture is a tool kit, complains Farkas, who looks for its provision of "real skills for real production."[59] We agree that cultural tools confer competencies. Bourdieu's narrow concept of cultural capital stresses aesthetic judgment as if entrepreneurs had only to attend art openings and poetry readings.[60] This view requires amendment.[61] Business owners run the market economy, and to discharge this real responsibility requires real competence. Granted, some well-connected people obtain lucrative jobs on snob appeal alone, but an economy cannot run on snob appeal. It requires real skills for real production. What Brigitte Berger has called "the culture of entrepreneurship" is an occupational culture, not an aesthetic standard.[62] The occupational culture of the bourgeoisie is the skills, knowledge, attitudes, and values that bourgeoisies need to run the market economy. Their occupational culture transmits and maintains the practical knowledge of how to start and to run business firms.[63] This occupational culture includes relevant and supportive values, attitudes, knowledge, and skills transmitted in the course of socialization at home as well as in school. Bourgeois occupational culture means cultural traits (values, skills, attitudes, knowledge) characteristic of bourgeoisies around the world, and that, furthermore, distinguish bourgeois from nonbourgeois coethnics while linking bourgeois coethnics to bourgeois noncoethnics elsewhere. An established bourgeoisie equips its youth with appropriate class resources.[64] Having them, the youth prosper in and reproduce a market economy. Entrepreneurship is the occupational culture of bourgeoisies.

Evidence for this conclusion appears in Table 4.3. Derived from the 1987 census of business owners, this table shows the percentage of current business owners whose "close relative" owns or had owned a business.[65] Of those whose close relative owned a business, the table also shows the percentage who had themselves earlier worked in that close relative's business.[66] When a close relative owns a business, a young person may acquire an informal education in entrepreneurship without actually working in the business.[67] This informal education includes skills and knowledge as well as attitudes and values. For example, a child might acquire from an entrepreneur aunt or uncle the value of vocational independence. Additionally, a child might acquire from an entrepreneur relative a role model. In this manner, just having entrepreneur kinfolk conveys occupationally relevant cultural capital.

When, additionally, a young person works in a relative's business, the young person acquires exposure to the occupational culture of entrepreneurship. Of course, any young person working in this business would obtain some human

TABLE 4.3   Cultural Capital of Business Owners by Race and Gender for the United States, 1987 (in Percentages)

	Owner's close relative owned a business	Owner worked for self-employed relative
Hispanic	30.7	40.6
Black	27.8	37.6
Asians[a]	35.3	38.8
Women-Owned	47.0	37.3
Nonminority male	48.0	50.7

[a]Includes Pacific Islanders and American Indians.

Source: U.S. Bureau of the Census, *1987 Economic Censuses, Characteristics of Business Owners* CBO87-1 (Washington, D.C.: GPO, 1991), Table 10A.

capital from the work experience. Nonetheless, when working in a relative's business, a young person acquires cultural capital as well as human capital. First, getting the job is much easier when one is a close relative of the owner, so the vocational education is much more available to kin than to nonkin. Second, a child identifies more with a relative entrepreneur than with a nonrelative entrepreneur. A relative entrepreneur is "Uncle Harry." A nonrelative entrepreneur is "the boss." Finally, entrepreneurs identify with kinfolk too, and offer them access to business skills, techniques, and outlook above and beyond the narrow requirements of their job.

For these reasons, having a close relative who owned a business and having worked in that relative's business are two indicators of childhood access to the culture of entrepreneurship. Table 4.2 shows that of black and Hispanic business owners, about 30% had had close relatives who were also business owners. Since the self-employment rate among blacks and Hispanics was between 3 and 6% a generation earlier, the table shows that current black or Hispanic business owners were 10 times more likely to have had a close relative who was a business owner than were blacks and Hispanics in general. A comparable inference can be drawn about Asians except that, among Asians, the previous generation's self-employment rate was higher. Among women and white men, the percentage of business owners who reported a self-employed relative is appreciably higher than among ethnoracial minorities. This elevation is unsurprising because the actual rate of self-employment among women and whites was about 8%, more than twice as high as the self-employment rate among the ethnoracial minorities. Therefore, women and white men actually had a higher probability of having a self-employed relative than did blacks and Hispanics.

Women business owners and white male business owners were about six times more likely to have had a close relative who was self-employed than were women in general or white men in general. This disproportion indicates the impetus toward self-employment that the vocational culture of entrepreneurship conveyed to them. That is, if a woman or a white man had close relatives who were business owners, that woman or white man had a six times better chance of becoming self-employed than did women or white men in general. By implication, if blacks and Hispanics had had the same self-employment rates in 1947 as did white men and all women, these two minorities would have enjoyed higher self-employment rates in 1987 than they actually exhibited. One reason the self-employment rates of the contemporary minorities fell below those of whites was apparently the minorities' prior lack of access to an equivalently large pool of self-employed relatives from whom they could informally acquire the occupational culture of business owners.[68] If these conclusions are justified, then even human capital and financial capital do not exhaust the class-derived advantages in entrepreneurship that whites had over minorities.

Results are very similar when we turn to the issue of what proportion of owners had actually worked for their own self-employed close relatives. Such work conveyed additional business education. Of the minority and women business owners who had reported self-employed close relatives, about 39% had actually worked for those relatives. Among nonminority male owners, who had the highest self-employment rate, about 51% had worked for their self-employed relatives. Clearly the opportunity to work for a relative depends in part on the size of that relative's business. The more employees a close relative has, the more opportunities his or her business affords for employment of kinfolk. Size of business might explain why the white men had a higher employment rate than did the minorities, whose relatives owned smaller firms on average than did the relatives of the white men. A more likely explanation is gender. Women and men did not differ in the percentage who had self-employed relatives, but white men were about one-third more likely than women to have worked for those relatives. Young men were more likely than young women to seek and to obtain informal vocational training in business and thus acquire more fully the occupational culture of their self-employed relatives.

SOCIAL CAPITAL

Social capital is a fourth capital resource.[69] Ostrom defines social capital as "the arrangement of human resources to improve flows of future income."[70] We distinguish class-derived social capital from ethnic-derived social capital. *Class-derived social capital* is ownership of class-derived social relationships that facilitate entrepreneurship.[71] Social capital's simplest form is a social network of strong and weak social ties.[72] The contribution of social networks to entrepreneurship is the most important research discovery in the last generation. Entrepreneurs make extensive and important use of social networks when starting and running a business.[73] Unlike financial capital, which is exhausted by use, social capital increases with use.[74] Unlike cultural capital, which a learner absorbs, social capital remains an external resource. Social capital is inherited or acquired. *Inherited social capital* conveys a class-derived advantage in entrepreneurship when the inheritor matures into advantageous social relationships as a result of the entrepreneur status of parents. Being related to an entrepreneur by blood or marriage most facilitates one's own entrepreneurship when one can take over a parent's business relationships and reputation (Table 4.2). In the case of Sam Walton, founder of Wal-Mart, the youthful entrepreneur borrowed start-up funds from his wife's wealthy father.[75] Everyone does not have a wealthy father-in-law to finance his or her start-up. In the case of Donald Trump, New York real estate mogul, young Trump inherited his father's business connections and established reputation in the construction and real estate industry as well as his father's great wealth.[76] Of business relationships that belonged to Donald Trump's father, some became accessible to young Trump too, and these inherited relationships conferred economic advantage upon the youthful Trump at an early stage of his entrepreneurial career.

Acquired social capital represents a class resource when it reflects the owner's class status rather than the owner's ethnocultural identity.[77] Even those most endowed with inherited social capital acquire their own class-defined social capital as their work career proceeds.[78] As Donald Trump's career unfolded, he utilized social capital that he had acquired in the Wharton School of Finance in addition to social capital that he inherited. Alumni ties are common sources of acquired social capital because they reflect the graduate's class-linked acquired network. Naturally, alumni ties also reflect a graduate's ability to pay for higher education plus her or his cultural capital plus the social capital of parents who may have used influence to arrange a dullard's university admission. In that sense, current alumni connections reduce to the class background of an entrepreneur's parents. However, even entrepreneurs who inherit class resources have to perform work in order to renew social capital resources for their own lifetime use. The work of creating their *acquired* social capital from opportunities to form it and of recreating and renewing their *inherited* social capital is essential because inherited social capital does not last a lifetime without renewal, and acquired social capital requires effort to develop and maintain.[79]

The entrepreneur's social capital resource resembles the Chinese concept of *guanxi*.[80] *Guanxi* means literally a social relationship or social connection.[81] Indeed, this ancient Chinese economic idea, part of the folk culture of China, anticipated social science by a millennium. *Guanxi* is the ability to build useful social relationships, to stockpile these relationships, and then to call upon them for business help.[82] *Guanxi* is by no means limited to entrepreneurs, but it is certainly important in Chinese business. *Guanxi* is not the same as corruption. Corruption occurs when an entrepreneur pays for improper or illegal help. For example, if an entrepreneur bribes an inspector to overlook fire hazards on her premises, she has corrupted the official.[83] The corruption conveys a business advantage because competitors will have to remedy fire hazards, paying whatever it costs and adding the cost to the price of their commodity. This business advantage benefits bribers to the disadvantage of nonbribers. Corruption is a naked quid pro quo.[84]

In contrast, *guanxi* involves prior targeting of potentially useful individuals, who are cultivated in the hope of developing a genuine personal relationship.[85] Naturally, cultivation involves the normal exchange of favors and gifts that accompany real friendships, but this exchange is mutual. For example, if an entrepreneur makes a friend of the fire department's inspector, anticipating that her help may someday be needed, then she has built social capital or *guanxi* with that inspector. Should a fire inspection turn up hazards on the entrepreneur's business premises, her inspector friend will not require a bribe to ignore or minimize them.

The cultural capital of an entrepreneur includes the knowledge of what social capital is, how to obtain it, and how to use it. Every American does not understand social capital equally well. Among those who understand it best, entrepreneurs are overrepresented. This advantage arises from the entrepreneurs' repertoire of class culture. But thanks also to social science's discovery of the advantageousness of networking among entrepreneurs, the simplest utilization of social capital, some business schools now teach networking to entrepreneurship students. In the United States strategic networking is a restricted skill linked to entrepreneurship. In China, by way of contrast, skill in strategic networking is more universal. Therefore, it is an ethnic resource. Chinese entrepreneurs' wide familiarity with *guanxi* certainly reflects Chinese culture, not just class culture, and the Chinese are more knowledgeable than Americans about *guanxi*. To this extent, Chinese entrepreneurs' social capital (real *guanxi*) is a product of Chinese cultural capital (knowledge of how to make *guanxi*). Nonetheless, we distinguish social capital and cultural capital on the ground that knowledge of how to obtain and use a resource and the actual possession of that resource are different matters. One can know how to use an ax to cut wood but have neither wood nor ax. In the same sense, cultural capital provides the entrepreneur with knowledge of *social capital*, but that entrepreneur's actual stock of social capital, and her skillful disposition of it, is a separate resource.

In the same sense, we argue, following James Coleman, that social capital *creates* human capital, which economists treat as a strictly financial resource.[86] Social capital creates human capital by strengthening the ability of parents to monitor and control their children's study habits and friendships.[87] This ability increases children's success in school and increases graduation rates. To the extent that this practice works, we can reduce an entrepreneur's human capital to her or his parents' social capital. That is, parents' social capital becomes children's human capital, which becomes children's self-employment, which becomes children's prosperity. That reduction would eliminate entrepreneur human capital as a separate and distinct class resource, wholly subsuming it under social capital. This view is extreme. Again, we choose to deal with real resources in hand rather than reducing them to their often complex antecedents. However engendered, human capital is a separate resource from social capital, especially if we stress the entrepreneur's armament rather than the armament's manufacture.

DEFECTIVE RESOURCE CLUSTERS

We have identified four class resources that encourage entrepreneurship. All are forms of capital. These are financial capital, cultural capital, human capital, and social capital.[88] A bourgeoisie usually enjoys all four forms simultaneously, but occasional separations occur. When the separations occur, a bourgeoisie does not have all the usual class resources. These *defective resource clusters* illustrate the importance of distinguishing the separate forms of class capital that bourgeoisies usually assemble. For example, Portes reported that the earliest pre–Mariel Cuban refugees in Miami were disproportionately of bourgeois origin.[89] Their parents had been wealthy entrepreneurs and business managers in Cuba, as were they themselves. However, after the Cuban Revolution of 1958, the Cuban refugees arrived penniless in Miami. Communists had seized their property and money. The refugees escaped with their lives. Nonetheless, the impoverished Cuban refugees in Miami reinserted themselves in business. Within a generation, the Cuban refugee bourgeoisie had reconstituted itself as a property-owning class and had rebuilt its wealth.[90]

How was this reconstruction possible? If financial capital were the only resource of entrepreneurship, as nineteenth-century social scientists believed, then the Cubans in Miami created an ethnic economy out of nothing. *Ex nihilo nihil fit.* Only a miracle creates something out of nothing.[91] However, if we recognize that, although stripped of their property and their wealth, the Cuban refugees in Miami retained their social capital, their human capital, and their cultural capital, we can appreciate that the penniless Cuban refugees were not without class resources after all. These class resources permitted them to regain their property and their wealth within a generation, but the achievement, impressive as it was, was no miracle. Rather, the Cubans' achievement illustrates the basic point of this chapter: class resources are productive resources. Human capital, social capital, and cultural capital contribute to entrepreneurship. Inherited wealth is not a sufficient explanation of entrepreneurship.

These considerations also explain why the penniless Haitian refugees in Miami have not been so successful in business as the penniless Cuban refugees in creating a prosperous ethnic enclave economy.[92] True, both Cuban refugees and Haitian refugees were penniless upon arrival, but there the similarity ends. The working-class Haitian refugees did not have the class resources of the Cubans. Specifically, the working-class Haitians lacked the class-derived social capital, cultural capital, and human capital that the Cuban refugees already had when they landed. For this reason, the Haitians were actually poorer than the Cubans even though their level of material deprivation was initially the same. We do not imply that the Haitians cannot build these class resources. In fact, Haitians are doing that. However, building class resources takes time, even generations, and, courageous as they were, the Haitians had to start with the resources they had on hand.

Similarly, if we ask what happened to grand prize lottery winners or retired boxing champions, we usually learn that they squandered their wealth and, within a decade, were back in the working class.[93] Wacquant's hustling informants were very aware of the problem, but they could not explain it. In reality, the explanation is easy. These individuals of working–class origin came into great wealth without also acquiring the knowledge of how to husband it. Benjamin Franklin once wrote that "a fool and his money are soon parted." Franklin's caustic judgment is too harsh because he deprecated as fools those who lack class-derived social capital, cultural capital, and human capital, usually for no fault of their own. Nonetheless, implicit in Franklin's epigram is a valid distinction between having money and knowing how to use money. The former is a material resource; the latter is a culture resource. Those who gain money but do not understand its use lose their money. Boxing champions have this problem.[94] We submit that Franklin's folk wisdom expands into the four class resources, each a form of capital, and that many entrepreneurs acquire these forms of capital through their class connections.

CLASS EXPLANATIONS AND CLASS THEORY

If one attempts to explain ethnic economies strictly on the basis of class status, then one utilizes a *class explanation* since all variables in the explanation are indicators of class status. Neoclassical economists such as Timothy Bates champion a class explanation of ethnic ownership economies.[95] Indeed, in the preceding comparison of Cubans and Haitians, we offered a class explanation of their ethnic economies, alleging that the Cubans built a bigger and more successful ethnic economy because of their superior class resources. Similarly, when explaining how low average education level retards Hispanic business ownership, we explained the Hispanics' small ethnic ownership economy by reference to their low class resources. When, going beyond a *class explanation* of a case, one asserts that class resources are the *only* resources of entrepreneurship, then one has produced a class theory of entrepreneurship. The difference between a class explanation and a class theory is their scope. A class explanation addresses selected cases, explaining them on an ad hoc basis. A class theory frames the entire debate, laying down generalizations that purportedly cover *all the cases*.

A strict class theory claims that interethnic differences in ethnic ownership economies result from unequal access to class resources. Class theory reduces ethnic difference to class difference. Class theory is certainly the old–time religion, and it still has defenders among Marxists and neoclassical economists alike. But how successful is class theory from a scientific point of view? The answer depends, first of all, upon how broadly one throws the class net. Class theory works best when class is broadly defined to include all four class resources. In that case, a class theory utilizes financial capital, cultural capital, social capital, and human capital. All figure in explanations. Class theories that utilize some but not all of these class resources in their explanation will be less successful than those that use all the variables. Karl Marx believed that "circulation of commodities" was the only form of capital, and he meant physical commodities.[96] Entrepreneurs were just the inheritors of money and property, their only economic resources. Marx's was a strict, if limited, class theory of entrepreneurship.

Later theorists expanded class theory to include human capital as well. Foremost is the economist Timothy Bates, who proposes a class theory of ethnic entrepreneurship that includes only financial capital and human capital.[97] That is, Bates claims that human capital and financial capital are the only class resources, and the only ones that ever affect intergroup disparities in size of ethnic ownership economies.[98] This theory encounters predictable problems. One is the ambiguous character of human capital. Like most economists, Bates treats human capital as if it were a producer's commodity purchased in expectation of a future money return. Although human capital costs money, and its purchasers expect a money return, ability to pay does not fully explain anyone's decision to purchase human capital. The other determinants of human capital are cultural capital and social capital, both of which are nonfinancial.[99] Putting it together, bourgeoisies usually have the money, the cultural capital, and the social capital with which to obtain human capital for their youth. Once obtained, this human capital becomes an advantage in entrepreneurship and employment just as Bates suggests, but the source of the human capital is importantly the sociocultural side of class. Therefore, Bates's version of human capital clandestinely imports class culture and class-derived social capital into what purports to be a purely financial explanation.

Returning to Josephine Smith, whose MBA at Yale University we previously celebrated, Table 4.4 shows in abbreviated and schematic terms the genealogy of her human capital. Smith's social capital played a role in that, knowing Yale alumni, Smith acquired an informed and favorable view of Yale. This information caused Smith to apply, an essential step on her road toward graduation. Additionally, Smith's cultural capital contributed to her access to a Yale MBA. Thanks to

TABLE 4.4   Genealogy of Human Capital

Social capital	Knows alumni	Learns about Yale	
Cultural capital	Good student	Admitted to Yale	Obtains human capital
Financial capital	Rich	Pays tuition	

this cultural capital, passed on from her parents, Smith acquired the motivation and skills to succeed in secondary school and in college. But for this academic success, Smith could not have matriculated at Yale's business school. Finally, Smith's family paid for her education. With all the elements in place, financial, cultural, and social, Smith emerged with a degree that stands for *bona fide* business skills but also commands prestige recognition in the marketplace. The money reward that Smith will obtain from her human capital depended as much upon her inherited social and cultural capital as it did upon her inherited money. Were any lacking, Smith would not have obtained the valuable certificate.

Another objection to a limited class theory arises from the attack that Bates and Servon launch against microcredit schemes. Bates and Servon claim that microcredit schemes fail because they lend to poor people who lack the human capital to utilize money.[100] It would be more effective, say Bates and Servon, to lend that same money to middle-class people who may create real firms that will employ the poor.[101] This classically liberal view Panayotopoulos and Gerry call a strategy of "wagering on the strong."[102] We call it trickle-down economics.[103] Of course, we agree that poor people routinely lack the class-derived human capital, social capital, and cultural capital that promote and facilitate entrepreneurship and must, to this extent, rely upon others to employ them.[104] This lack importantly explains why the ethnic ownership economies of predominantly working-class ethnoracial categories and groups are smaller than those of preponderantly middle-class ethnoracial groups. When Green and Pryde bewail the absence of "an entrepreneurial culture" among African Americans, much of their complaint reduces to the shortage of class-derived social capital, cultural capital, and human capital among this predominantly working-class racial minority.[105]

The same reasons importantly explain why the ethnic ownership economy of Cubans in Miami exceeded that of Haitians in Miami. Predominantly upper- and middle-class ethnic groups such as Cubans have and transmit class resources that are much less available among predominantly working-class groups such as Haitians.[106] However, when making this explanation, why stop with human capital as Bates does? Why not also include class-derived social capital and cultural capital? These are components of human capital and also direct and independent influences upon entrepreneurship. Networking and money management belong much more to the class culture of the bourgeoisie than they do to an elementary school curriculum in the ghetto.[107] That is, the parallel but informal curriculum of middle-class culture inculcates and teaches networking and money management more effectively than do public schools in ghettos. Indeed, it is precisely this educational shortfall that impels the Ewing Marion Kauffman Foundation to fund innovative classroom instruction in entrepreneurship in the hope of increasing thereby the self-help capability of downtrodden American minorities.[108] The Kauffman Foundation hopes to strengthen the classroom's impact on entrepreneurship in order to compensate the children of the working class for a class culture that ignores the whole topic.

CRITIQUE OF CLASS THEORY

That class theory is best that includes all class variables, and Bates's version includes financial capital and human capital, but it does not include class-derived cultural capital and class-derived social capital. Recognizing the shortfall, other economists are seeking to expand class explanations by expanding human capital. George Borjas tries to bring ethnic resources within an expanded definition of human capital. Gary Becker tries to bring cultural capital inside human capital.[109] Jumping ship as they have, other economists have left Bates behind, the last exponent of an obsolete theory. In this chapter, we have shown that social capital and cultural capital expand the scope of what class can explain about intergroup differences in entrepreneurship. Moreover, we have shown that human capital, though often treated as a commodity purchase, actually includes indispensable contributions of cultural capital and human capital, a conclusion that even Gary S Becker acknowledges.[110] That is, people enjoy human capital today because they earlier enjoyed social capital and cultural capital. Money alone does not explain human capital acquisition. To that extent, economistic definitions of human capital illegitimately smuggle the effects of social capital and cultural capital into their analysis without crediting the sources. In general, the effects of class on entrepreneurship considerably exceed what wealth alone can explain.

Although we have expanded class theory beyond the conventional boundary, enriching it in the process, even expanded class theory still offers an inadequate theory of entrepreneurship and even, we should add, of income attainment. In fact, human capital only explains about a third of the income gap between men and women and between blacks and whites.[111] When it comes to both entrepreneurship and income attainment, human capital just does not explain everything. Therefore, class theory, even at its best, much less in the anemic Bates version, offers an incomplete explanation of interethnic differences in entrepreneurship. First, class theory implies that ethnic groups and ethnoracial categories must already have class resources before they can build an ownership economy. More accurately, it implies that ethnic groups can build ownership economies only in strict proportion to the class resources they already possess. If it were so, only those could become entrepreneurs who already were middle class. If groups must already have class resources in order to develop ethnic economies, then entrepreneurship is impossible for poor people, a conclusion Timothy Bates enthusiastically endorses.[112] Prepared to acknowledge that economic mobility through entrepreneurship is difficult for poor people, and always has been, we deny that it is *impossible*, especially if they have supportive ethnic resources. Moreover, if we include the illegal sector and the informal sector along with the formal sector, expanding the referent economy, entrepreneurship has been a classic route out of poverty, and it still functions that way.[113] Zelizer points out, for example, that in 1900, New York City's guardians of the poor regarded poor Italian immigrants as "unintelligent" in their use of money.[114] Ten decades later, Italians have moved into middle-class status, importantly on the basis of their entrepreneurship, and Elaine Garzarelli is the country's foremost stock market expert. In exactly this sense, America's historical experience refutes a class-only theory of social mobility through entrepreneurship.

Second, and more basically, class theory ignores ethnic resources, the subject of the next chapter. Ethnic resources importantly contribute to entrepreneurship independent of class. A theory that excludes ethnic resources cannot be complete.[115] *Ethnic resources* are sociocultural and demographic features of the whole group that coethnic entrepreneurs actively utilize in business or from which their business passively benefits.[116] Ethnic resources characterize a whole group, not just its isolated members and not just its bourgeoisie. For example, writing of Jews in western Pennsylvania before World War II, Morawska found that "a desire for self-employment" was virtually universal.[117] In about a third of the cases, this motive characterized families that had been self-employed in Europe. In this third of cases, we could declare the aspiration for entrepreneurship a class resource of the Jewish bourgeoisie. But in two-thirds of cases, the aspiration for self-employment characterized Jews who had *not* been self-employed in Europe and who were not then self-employed. In effect, the whole Jewish community aspired to self-employment, not just the Jewish bourgeoisie. Mavratsas makes the same claim for Greek Americans, alleging that their nearly universal "desire to become self-employed" is "clearly a function of the Greek's traditional value of independence."[118] In both these cases, the aspiration for entrepreneurship was an ethnocultural resource, not just a class resource.[119]

Conversely, if Mr. Kim, a Korean entrepreneur in Los Angeles, enjoys a resource that his working-class coethnics do not, Kim's resource is not ethnic. If Mr. Kim's working-class coethnics work little and save little, but Mr. Kim works and saves much, then one cannot explain Mr. Kim's saving by reference to his ethnocultural resources. After all, Kim's behavior would be unique among coethnics, whereas those who utilize ethnocultural resources are typical of their coethnics in so doing. Typical ethnic resources include kinship and marriage systems, relationships of trust, ethnic-derived social capital, cultural assumptions, religion, native language fluency, a middleman heritage, entrepreneurial values and attitudes, rotating credit associations, relative satisfaction arising from nonacculturation to prevailing labor and living standards, reactive solidarities, multiplex social networks, employer paternalism, an ideology of ethnic solidarity, and a generous pool of underemployed and disadvantaged coethnic workers.[120] If one observes, for example, that Chinese work long hours under unsafe conditions, trust one another more than outsiders, save more than others, express satisfaction with low wages, help one another to acquire business skills and information, follow one another into the same trades, combine easily to restrain trade, utilize rotating credit associations, or deploy multiplex social networks to economic advantage, one is calling attention to the manner in which ethnic resources promote entrepreneurship of all the Chinese, not just the Chinese bourgeoisie.[121] As the constituent resources

are shared, ethnic entrepreneurship acquires a communitarian rather than individ-
ualist character.[122]

Martin Marger proposes that Canadian business immigrants operated strictly on
the basis of their wealth and human capital, ignoring the immigrant communities
to which they titularly belonged.[123] For capital, they went to banks; for labor, they
accessed the general labor market; and for information, they hired experts. Business immigrants applied directly to the Canadian government for priority immigration, to gain which they were required to have abundant money, business
experience, and plans to invest in Canada. Marger proposes that abundant money
and business skills permitted the business migrants to forego reliance on ethnic
social capital. True, Bruederl and Preisendoerfer did not find any substitution of
ethnic for missing class resources, but let us suppose that Marger is right about all
the facts.[124] His theoretical conclusion ignored cultural capital that fed into the
entrepreneurship of these elite immigrants through kinship, a cultural system.[125]
Kinship is cultural. Kinship explains why class resources never affect ethnic
ownership economies without ethnocultural resources also being present.

To ignore ethnic resources, focusing exclusively on class variables, is to take as
one's model of the general what is, at best, an extreme and uncommon situation.
Indeed, no one has ever adduced any ethnic ownership economy that fits a class-
only theory.[126] All the ethnic ownership economies in evidence are mixed cases.
All use class and nonclass resources. Even the contrast of Haitians and Cubans in
Miami, which we couched in class terms for illustration, has distinct ethnic content when one examines the cases more closely.[127] Since no class-only cases are in
evidence despite much searching, we conclude that all ethnic ownership
economies depend upon mixed class and ethnic resources albeit with different
preponderance. Some are class-preponderant; others are ethnic-preponderant.
These mixtures are types 3, 4, and 5 in Table 4.5. These three types are the only
realistic types; types 1 and 5 never occur in real-world ethnic ownership
economies. Ethnic resources always combine with class resources in ethnic
ownership economies.[128] Theoretical explanation must build upon the cases in
evidence, which are types 3, 4, and 5.

Although mixed together within the same group, ethnic and class resources
need not be of equal importance. In some mixed cases, class resources predomi-

TABLE 4.5   Ethnic and Class Resources of Entrepreneurship

	Ethnic	Class
1. Class-only	0	C
2. Ethnic-only	E	0
3. Mixed	E	C
4. Mixed: class predominant	E	C
5. Mixed: ethnic predominant	E	C

nate; in other mixed cases, ethnic resources predominate; in still others, ethnic and class resources are of equal importance. The important debate is no longer whether class and ethnic resources combine, but how they combine and in what proportions. In an important discovery, In-Jin Yoon found that ethnic resources were more important than class resources in the start-up phase of Korean business firms in Chicago.[129] Older Korean firms relied more upon class resources than did younger firms, but the older firms' very survival had created the class resources upon which they later came to rely. The life cycle of the firm determined the relative importance of ethnic and class resources. Similarly, ethnic resources are more important in the entrepreneurship of impoverished groups than in the entrepreneurship of the affluent, and as formerly impoverished groups ascend the social hierarchy, in partial response to the success of their ethnic economy, their entrepreneurship relies more upon class resources.

CHAPTER 5

Ethnic Resources

INTRODUCTION

The last chapter discussed how class provides group members with financial, human, cultural, and social capital that permit them to produce ethnic economies or, in other words, to create small businesses and control job opportunities in existing firms or the public sector. The chapter concluded that all ethnic economies depend upon mixed class and ethnic resources. This chapter examines ethnic resources and their role in shaping ethnic economies. Ethnic resources are features of a group that coethnics utilize in economic life or from which they derive economic benefit. They include identifiable skills, organizational techniques, reactive solidarity, sojourning orientation, and other characteristics based in group tradition and experience. Conceptually, ethnic resources are distinguished from class resources—those cultural and material assets, outlooks, and skills possessed by all persons of a common class position, regardless of their ethnic background.[1]

Neoclassical economists and Marxists tend to downplay ethnic resources, regarding class as the only factor that determines economic relationships. However, this chapter argues that ethnic resources, in conjunction with class resources, contribute financial, human, cultural, and social capital to members of ethnic groups in such a way as to facilitate their building ethnic economies.

The most important feature of ethnic resources is their ability to contribute to economic survival and achievement among groups lacking class-based endowments of skill, education, or capital. This is because ethnic resources are generated as a part of normal group life. In effect, they offer an inexpensive and accessible solution to a costly problem.

Ethnic and Class Resources as Ideal Types

Although the ideal type definition of ethnic resources suggests that these are available to all members of a group, empirical observation indicates that this is often not the case. Every ethnic setting is in some ways unique and as such will develop among its constituents different skills, outlooks, and experiences: New York's Chinatown is in various ways (historically, economically, culturally, linguistically, politically) unlike San Francisco's, Detroit's black community contrasts with that of Atlanta, and so on. Hence, the particular meanings of ethnicity and the kinds and quantity of ethnic resources generated within these environments will vary. Further, ethnic culture is in constant flux. The meanings, skills, cultural forms, tastes, and symbols associated with groups change over time, producing differences in outlook across generations and cohorts. As a case in point, 20% or more of U.S. Latinos, numbering almost 7 million persons, have abandoned Catholicism in favor of evangelical Christianity, generally practiced within co-ethnic congregations.[2] Luis León, who studied one such church consisting of Mexican migrants and Chicanos in East Los Angeles, asserts that these converts are replacing "the collective drama and tragedy of Mexican Catholicism" with "the American Protestant myth of prosperity and success." Through religious conversion, members are equipping themselves with ethnic resources previously unavailable within their group.[3]

Moreover, class and ethnic resources are inextricably intertwined. Development of ethnic resources is often linked to one's class position. On the one hand, learning ethnic culture generally involves money costs associated with education, diet, language skill, travel, and ritual involvement. Consequently, those lacking money will be limited in their ability to fully develop ethnic membership and the ethnic resources with which it is associated. The Jewish community, for example, has long worried about the costs of maintaining a Jewish life, which requires the expense of a religious education for children, synagogue membership, celebration of Jewish holidays, kosher food, not working on the Sabbath, instruction in Hebrew, purchase of ritual articles, charitable contributions, and travel to Israel.[4] On the other hand, many elements of ethnic identification, such as occupational concentration, residential location, and strategies for coping with disadvantage are associated with low income—a lack of class resources. More educated and affluent members who deploy class resources to avoid these experiences and settings may be unversed in important forms of ethnic knowledge and subjectivity.[5]

Finally, many social settings, including some that would appear to be defined strictly by class, bear a significant ethnic stamp. Studies of minority men and of women entering high-status occupational settings have consistently found that competence in the folkways of the male white Protestant upper middle class (patterns of sociability, taste, dress, hobbies, joking behavior) are vital to success, even if such skills are unrelated to actual job performance.[6] The woman, minority group member, or graduate of an urban public university who is unfamiliar with golf, social drinking, or Ivy League attire will have difficulty building the social contacts needed to function effectively.[7] In her classic *Men and Women of the Corporation*, Rosabeth Kanter cites such a case: "In one industrial organization, managers who moved ahead needed to be members of the Masonic Order and the local yacht club, not Roman Catholic; Anglo-Saxon or Germanic in origin and Republican."[8] Hence, jobs in corporate management have been traditionally filled on the basis of religion, national origins, and leisure styles (as well as the possession of educational credentials)—criteria that are linked to both class and ethnicity. While rooted in the upper middle class, elite law firms and corporate management suites are, like garment districts, often marked by ethnic forms of attachment, loyalty, and sociability. Both can be considered ethnic economies.[9]

In sum, the separation of class and ethnic resources, while theoretically instructive, is virtually impossible in the real world, since every social setting is characterized by both class position and ethnic membership.

Tool Kit and Boundary Perspectives

Scholars offer two interpretations of how membership in an ethnic group can yield economic resources. One perspective stresses the unique skills and outlooks shared by members of an ethnic group in their homeland or enclave: the "tool kit" of symbols, stories, rituals, and worldviews that people may use in varying configurations to direct action and solve different kinds of problems.[10] Ivan Light calls this the "orthodox" view of culture.[11]

This conception is valuable for understanding ethnic economic life because group-specific approaches, outlooks, and assumptions often have clear economic implications. For example, members of various ethnic groups, by virtue of their socialization, come to possess specific forms of knowledge and skill: Jamaican immigrants know about Reggae music, Mexican immigrants can cook Mexican food, and Israelis are well prepared to work as Hebrew teachers. In American society, there is a demand for Reggae music, Mexican food, and instruction in Hebrew. Hence, members of these ethnic communities have the ability to market their ethnic skills in order to obtain economic rewards.[12] The tool kit may also include norms that facilitate pooling money, sharing resources, or working together.[13] Finally, ethnic groups maintain unique means of evaluating the costs and rewards of economically relevant activities—which endeavors are desirable or prohibited for which persons.[14] Such techniques, norms, and outlooks may prove valuable when group members engage in entrepreneurial, philanthropic, or community building activities, especially in a context in which those with whom they compete either lack such traditions or are oriented toward other goals.[15]

A second model accounting for the economic value of ethnicity emphasizes the way a group establishes *boundaries*, and hence cooperation and solidarity, among its members.[16] Ethnicity is a powerful determinant of cooperation and solidarity because it is regarded as biological in origin, is reflected in social stratification, shapes numerous elements of social life, is frequently institutionalized (in religious practice, language, nationality, residential location, group myths, and government policy), and often constitutes a basis of personal identity. In contrast to tool kit or orthodox traits, Light and Rosenstein describe this form of ethnicity as *reactive*: arising "in response to alien status in defense of the collective self-esteem of group members . . . ethnicity is itself an ideology of solidarity."[17] In other words, when faced with challenges, group members share resources and create collective and mutually beneficial responses. Reactive theories explain why certain immigrant groups such as Koreans, Soviet Jews, and Greeks who had low rates of pre-migration self-employment become highly entrepreneurial in the United States.[18]

Although some scholars emphasize either the tool kit or the boundary making aspects of group culture as most vital to the maintenance of ethnic solidarity, for the purpose of understanding ethnic resources, we hold them complementary and interconnected.[19] Even if culture functions mostly as a source of solidarity-making social boundaries, there has to be some content—language, appearance, customs, religion, nationality, or heritage—that group members feel they share with each other and do not have in common with outsiders. Similarly, proficiencies highlighted in the tool kit approach must be acquired and exercised in collective settings. Returning to our earlier example, one cannot perform or sell Reggae music, prepare and sell Mexican food, market Hebrew lessons, or raise money in an ethnic rotating credit association unless one has coethnics and coethnic settings in which to learn and practice these skills.[20] These two dimensions of the culture—its role in providing groups with specific skills and orientations as well as its ability to delineate social bonds of mutual obligation, loyalty, and trust—are vital for the analysis of ethnic economies. In many cases, both tool kit and boundary making elements of ethnic solidarity transcend class boundaries, uniting groups marked by different class positions and interests. Ethnic-based cooperation delivers resources to persons without the financial or educational means otherwise required for their acquisition.

HOW DO GROUPS CREATE ETHNIC RESOURCES?

Ethnic resources are created, maintained, and reproduced as part of the collective lives of group members. Specific skills, outlooks, and rules for interaction are taught as part of family and communal life. Maintaining in-group loyalty, coethnics join together in cooperative activities either to make up for their inability to access economic resources used by the mainstream society or simply because they value coethnic interaction. The concept of reactive solidarity suggests that members of minority groups who lack the skills, credentials, language ability, cultural knowledge, legal status, work histories, social ties, or money required to access economic opportunities in the larger society have few social avenues beyond their own numbers to turn, and so develop community-based means of advancement.

Theories of ethnocentrism and privilege maintenance propose that social boundaries are perpetuated because group members feel drawn to one another as a result of shared outlook, interest, and values. A wide array of ethnic groups such as Orthodox Jews, Amish, Mormons, Fundamentalist Protestants, Nation of Islam members, and upper-class WASPs maintain self-segregation through informal interaction patterns and because of religious teachings that stress avoidance of worldliness and disengagement from nonbelievers.[21] As a result, members of many ethnically defined communities prize coethnic connections. Since such units are often small, coethnic interaction becomes intense and deeply involving. Further, among ethnic communities, various spheres of life often overlap. Individuals live near one another, meet in business and leisure pursuits, rely on the same religious and communal institutions, and consume ethnic media.[22] In groups as varied as affluent Jewish adults and working-class Latino teenagers, informal pressure encourages in-group devotion while punishing excessive attachment to the larger society. Because alternative venues for social and economic interaction are either few in number or rejected as inappropriate, there is a high likelihood that group standards will be maintained.

Discrimination underlies many instances of unification, but high-status groups not subject to ill treatment also restrict eligibility for full membership in order to maximize the rewards of group participation.[23] For example, after 1890, the American WASP elite established social boundaries: "Excluding all but WASPs, this national upper class gained a profound self-consciousness through a network of exclusive clubs, boarding schools, resorts, and Ivy League colleges that promulgated a subculture of common values and common norms of behavior."[24] Through such involvements, a strong notion of shared fate and trust develops among members. It is this ethnic-based trust that provides numerous competitive advantages while excluding outsiders from access thereto.

Forms of Capital and Ethnic Resources

In Chapter 4, we discussed how class provides access to resources vital for creating ethnic economies, including financial, human, cultural, and social capital. Ethnic resources acquired through membership in an ethnic group also provide comparable assets.

Ethnic groups regularly provide their members with financial capital through personal loans, rotating savings and credit associations (ROSCAS), loan societies, and other cooperative endeavors, all of which rely on reputation and enduring relationships as collateral.[25] In general, they have extremely low rates of default.[26] Insofar as ethnic groups and families provide their members with useful skills, they deliver human capital. This generally takes place in a rather informal context, such as a parent teaching a child how to run a business, cook traditional foods, or perform a craft. There is, however, a sizable network of religious and ethnic educational institutions, such as Howard, Brandeis, Notre Dame, Loma Linda, and Brigham Young, that provide group members with formally recognized academic credentials in a coethnic context. A law degree from Howard reflects both ethnic and class resources. Moreover, insofar as these ethnic and religiously oriented universities have been established to further the education of the coethnic population, a student's ethnic membership becomes a resource in the acquisition of a degree.

Ethnic groups also provide their members with cultural capital, in both its "high culture" form and what we described as "vocational culture" in Chapter 4. For example, a Japanese American child trained in traditional culture and language by her parents will be knowledgeable about sushi (considered a gourmet food by sophisticated Americans of diverse ethnic origins) while also being linguistically and culturally equipped to market American machine tools to Japanese manufacturing firms. Finally, ethnic groups are capable of providing members with social capital.[27] Denoting the web of connections, loyalties, and mutual obligations (shared fate, solidarity, and communal membership) that develop among people as part of their regular interaction, social capital refers to the sense of commitment that induces people to extend favors, expect preferential treatment, and look out for one another's interests.

Within ethnic settings, actors rely upon social capital created by their common membership to reach economic ends. Groups' collective resources, including trust and cooperation, help them overcome the disadvantages of outsider status and maximize the value of their human and financial capital in order to achieve economic stability or betterment.[28] In many cases, ethnic-based trust offers definite advantages over the impersonal and legalistic forms of cooperation that underlie modern economic exchange. The benefit of ethnic-based trust can be attributed to the flexible human relationships in which this trust is embedded. Further, because the use of social capital tends to reinforce the relationships from which it originates, its consumption may actually increase rather than deplete its availability in a given context. Finally, unlike resources availed through impersonal market transactions, social capital is often delivered within an environment of human caring and concern.[29] At the same time, however, social capital can only be created at a cost, in terms of money, effort, or the exchange of favors. A woman can only expect preferential treatment from her sorority sisters, coworkers, or teammates if she is a member in good standing—a status achieved by attending events, contributing effort, and paying dues. Forms of mutual obligation involved in the maintenance of social capital can diminish the value of resources by limiting individual freedom, requiring assets to be shared, mandating contributions to community welfare, permitting "free riding," and the like.[30]

The ethnic basis of social capital becomes apparent when cooperation and mutual aid develop among group members of disparate class origins, who would be unlikely to cooperate without common ethnicity. For example, employers often provide coethnics with higher wages and better benefits than out-group workers. For their part, workers may treat coethnic employers with exceptional consideration and respect. Wong describes the case of a Chinese garment factory that closed without paying coethnic employees. When a legal case instigated by union activists yielded back pay, "some workers returned their checks to the owners" in a gesture of loyalty and gratitude for good treatment.[31] Similarly, in the following quote, an Israeli building contractor in Los Angeles describes how coethnic loyalty shapes his hiring decisions:

> I'll put it this way. I have a few circles around me. And of course, the Israeli circle is closer to me than the Jewish circle. And the Jewish circle is closer to me than the Gentile circle, okay. And the human race is closer to me than, I don't know, the planet. I would say it comes about in this kind of degree and people from my own Kibbutz are closer to me than people from Israel in general. So I hire them and I am glad to see them doing well.[32]

Census data appear to validate this man's assertion of ethnic resources economically benefiting Israelis in Los Angeles. Although Israeli men have generally lower rates of education and a greater fraction employed in blue-collar occupations[33] than other Middle Eastern groups in Los Angeles (Arabs and Iranians), they nevertheless earn substantially higher incomes.[34] Since it would appear that Arabs and Iranians have greater class resources than Israelis, we may attribute Israelis' greater earnings to their ethnic resources. These ethnic resources include a long tradition of middleman entrepreneurship, being accustomed to minority group status, being socialized in a country that emphasizes ethnic collectivism and cooperation, access to a sizable community of native-born coethnics (American Jews), and familiarity with Western-style social norms, including women working outside of the home.[35] [A group's maintaining Western notions of gender equality, resulting in women's education and labor force involvement, can be considered an ethnic resource (see Chapter 6).]

In contrast, despite their higher levels of education, Arabs and Iranians are characterized by certain ethnic-based economic liabilities. Some Arabs and most Iranians are traumatized exiles, not voluntary immigrants like Israelis. Moreover, they are generally less familiar with Western-style social life. Because of recent conflicts between the United States and their countries of origin, and their generally Islamic faith, Arabs and Iranians are more likely to confront discrimination in the United States. Finally, they have considerably lower rates of female labor force participation than is the case among Israelis.[36] As a consequence of these "negative ethnic resources" Arabs and Iranians earn less than Israelis in Los Angeles despite their superior educational credentials (see Table 5.1).

Ethnic resources may yield benefits to an entire group. However, financial, human, cultural, and social capital are often most extensively amassed and shared among subcollectivities wherein control is greater and malfeasance less likely.[37] Granovetter demonstrates that the value of social capital is often enhanced when it is confined within specific boundaries or, in other words, constrained by both "coupling and decoupling."[38] In order to optimize their economic position, group members benefit not only by cooperating among themselves, but also by minimizing obligations to others, such that gainful action will be unfettered. Limiting their engagement with the consumption patterns, leisure styles, status con-

TABLE 5.1 Israeli Men Have Lower Class Resources but Higher Earnings Than Other Middle Eastern Men in Los Angeles, 1990

Men	Iranians	Arabs	Israelis
4+ years college	64.9%	42.4%	39.5%
Employed	84.0%	81.8%	87.0%
Managers and professionals	51.3%	42.0%	45.1%
Clerical and sales	29.1%	29.8%	23.3%
Blue collar	19.6%	28.2%	31.6%
Self-employed	33.3%	26.8%	35.0%
Earnings			
Median	$27,540	$23,871	$29,484
Mean	$34,107	$30,230	$40,250

Women	Iranians	Arabs	Israelis
4+ years college	33.7%	26.7%	32.3%
Employed	47.6%	45.5%	59.7%
Managers and professionals	41.7%	36.8%	53.3%
Clerical and sales	41.4%	45.7%	31.3%
Blue collar	16.9%	17.5%	15.4%
Self-employed	14.4%	15.1%	14.1%
Earnings			
Median	$13,770	$14,580	$14,580
Mean	$17,441	$17,218	$18,619

Source: 1990 Census, PUMS data for Los Angeles, cited in Mehdi Bozorgmehr, Claudia Der-Martirosian, and Georges Sabagh, "Middle Easterners: A New Kind of Immigrant," in *Ethnic Los Angeles*, Roger Waldinger and Mehdi Bozorgmehr, eds. (New York: Russell Sage Foundation, 1996), p. 356.

cerns, social taboos, reservation wages, and collective obligations of the larger society, group members can seize opportunities that are deemed unacceptable by
the majority. For example, Oxfeld describes Chinese tanners in India who are
unconcerned with the religious taboos that constrain locals from engaging in
the lucrative if stigmatized trade in leather.[39] It is often advantageous for group
members to experience a degree of decoupling from coethnics as well in order to
avoid profit-draining familiarity. In the section that follows, we describe several
economic resources that are a product of ethnic group membership.[40]

SKILLS AND MOTIVATIONAL RESOURCES

By virtue of their life experience and formal and informal socialization, members
of various ethnic groups often possess culinary, linguistic, aesthetic, or handicraft
skills (otherwise described as human and cultural capital) that may be of economic value. This skill base often results in ethnic occupational concentration.
Lieberson's data illustrate the importance of group-specific resources in creating
economic niches:

> [I]t is clear that most racial and ethnic groups tend to develop concentrations in
> certain jobs which either reflect some distinctive cultural characteristics, special skills
> initially held by some members, or the opportunity structure at the time of their
> arrival. In 1950, among foreign-born men of different origins there were many such
> examples: 3.9% of Italians in the civilian labor force were barbers, eight times the level
> for all white men; 2.5% of the Irish were policemen or firemen, three times the rate for
> all white men; more than 2% of Scottish immigrants were accountants, about two and
> one-half times the level for whites; 9.4% of Swedish immigrants were carpenters, nearly
> four times the national level; 14.8 percent of Greek immigrant men ran eating and
> drinking establishments, 29 times the national level; and 3.3% of Russian immigrant
> men were tailors or furriers, 17 times the rate for all white men.[41]

Over time, some economically concentrated groups are able to achieve what
Gans calls "niche upgrading" by taking hold of more prestigious and well-paid
positions within the vocations they initially accepted because of lack of competition.[42] Their original willingness to take tasks other groups found uninviting
ultimately yields access to more desirable positions. For example, Jews who
formerly operated sewing machines in the garment industry are now designers,
manufacturers, and retailers in the same enterprise.[43] Similarly, southern California
Armenians who became involved in the garbage business early this century now
own economically vital landfills and run law and engineering firms that specialize
in environmental concerns. (Recently arrived coethnics continue to hold non-
professional jobs in the waste industry.) Finally, exemplifying the ethnic-controlled
economy, African Americans, who entered government employment at the lowest
rungs during the 1930s, are now heavily employed in government in well-paid
professional positions.[44] For African Americans, coethnic incumbency, affirmative

action hiring, and low rates of suburban dispersion (for city jobs that include residency requirements) all contribute to their high representation in government.

As groups upgrade their occupations, members may lose the motivation to accept low-level jobs and hence abandon realms of previous occupational concentration. In turn, these positions are taken up by less-advantaged groups in a process called ethnic succession. In a historical comparison of several groups, two sociologists found that rates of self-employment decline with each additional generation in the United States, largely because the migrants' American-born offspring find satisfactory positions in the existing economy. Although the rate of self-employment declined among all groups, the ranking remained the same over generations, indicating ethnic economic persistence.[45]

However, economic competition, legal restrictions, or a reduced demand for niche-produced goods and services may forestall niche upgrading for some. William Julius Wilson's work details the difficulties encountered by black Americans who have been concentrated in the declining manufacturing sector.[46]

FINANCIAL CAPITAL

Capital is most commonly discussed as a prerequisite for self-employment. However, funds are also required to acquire work in the existing economy. Obtaining a job hinges on the availability of education, clothes, tools, equipment, an automobile, and sometimes the possession of a license. Applying for a job is in itself often a costly endeavor, demanding access to job listings, travel to job sites or interviews, presentable attire, and the mailing of resumes, transcripts, and the like. Because many members of immigrant groups are noncitizens, their employment often mandates the acquisition of legal status, which involves payment of government fees as well as for the services of an immigration lawyer. Finally, working frequently entails costs of carfare, child care, and lunch money.

The literature is rich with examples of ethnic groups providing their members with the funds needed to obtain employment, whether it be tuition for a training program, capital to expand a factory, travel to a location where workers are needed, or simply the price of a pair of work boots. For example, in his study of Korean businesses in Chicago, Yoon found that entrepreneurs relied on several coethnic capital sources: 35% got loans from kin, 19.8% from friends, 13.7% from Korean American banks, and 27.9% from *kyes* (Korean rotating credit associations).[47] Similarly, Trankem found that 40% of Vietnamese entrepreneurs in Orange County, California, used ethnic sources of investment capital. Demonstrating its vital role for both Korean and Vietnamese entrepreneurs, coethnic funding was the only sizable source of business capital beyond personal savings.[48] As will be discussed in the chapter on gender and families, inheritance patterns can be important resources in ethnic economies. Sociologists, anthropologists, and historians have contributed research that demonstrates how ethnic norms regarding the distribution of land, money, and other family assets have important implications for landholding patterns and the viability of rural communities.[49]

Ethnic Credit

One of the most extensively studied ethnic economic resources is group-specific techniques for the accumulation and distribution of capital. These resources include rotating savings and credit associations (ROSCAs) as well as other ethnic-based institutions for saving and distributing funds. Anthropologists and sociologists have identified rotating credit associations among a broad variety of ethnic populations including those from East Asia, Latin America, the Caribbean, the Near East, and Africa.[50]

A *rotating credit association* is defined as "an association formed upon a core of participants who make regular contributions to a fund which is given in whole or in part to each contributor in turn."[51] This system is described in the following example. A leader organizes among friends, neighbors, relatives, or fellow workers an association in which four other persons agree to contribute a set amount of $10 a week. The order in which resources are distributed is decided by lot or by the sequence in which the members agreed to join. Each person receives $40 once from the ROSCA. Each person will have contributed to the others $40, at the rate of $10 per week. The total life of the ROSCA will be 5 weeks.[52] Relying on confidence and mutual trust, ROSCAs are often embedded in existing social networks, such as alumni associations, neighborhoods, family or hometown associations, or among employees of the same company. Through the use of such associations, group members are able to amass the funding required for personal spending, entrepreneurial investment, or other consumption. ROSCAs also foster forced saving, another economic benefit. Rooted in a trust-based social milieu, such activities provide their participants with many of the services of a bank, but in a more personal environment. They often exist in settings in which consumer-oriented banks are unavailable.

In a detailed study of ROSCAs among Mexicans in both the United States and Mexico, Carlos Vélez-Ibañez found that the *tanda* (Mexican ROSCA) is understood by a broad sector of the population and used toward multiple ends that reflect local needs. For example, Mexican and Chicano garment workers in Texas use rotating credit associations to amass the capital required to open their own sweatshops. When recruiting members, they are more concerned with trustworthiness and ability to pay than ethnic exclusivity and sometimes involve Central Americans, Filipinos, or Anglos. In contrast, urban middle-class Mexican women participate in credit associations for the opportunity to establish a select clique and, as such, maintain strict social criteria for membership. Saving money is not their primary goal, even though funds may be used to purchase expensive birthday gifts for members.[53]

There is some debate regarding the current applicability of ROSCAs to business financing. That they were important in an earlier era is clear. In his historical study of ethnic economies, Light concluded that

> Immigrants to the United States from southern China and Japan employed traditional rotating credit associations as their principal devices for capitalizing small businesses. West Indian blacks brought the West African rotating credit association to the United States; they too used this practice to finance small businesses.[54]

Recent migrants including Chinese, Vietnamese, West Indians, Mexicans, and Koreans continue to be active in ROSCAs. However, their application to small business varies. Some authors contend that these organizations generate too little capital for business start-ups and are often considered risky or illegal. With the increasing availability of other sources of funding—banks, investor networks, personal savings, and the like—the importance of the ROSCA is no longer central as a source of capital.[55] On the contrary, Park as well as Light and Deng found that "*kyes* (Korean ROSCAs) raised substantial sums of money, and that this money often supported the capitalization and expansion of Korean-owned business firms."[56]

The dispute about the current importance of ROSCAs notwithstanding, numerous studies of ethnic entrepreneurship find that coethnic capital sources remain vital to ethnic economies. With growing economic globalization, some ethnic groups make use of overseas capital sources as well as contacts with affluent coethnics and ethnic economic institutions in the United States. Further, because ethnic funding sources tend to have close relationships with loan recipients, they often provide additional resources, including business advice and referrals.[57]

Loan Societies

Various ethnic groups have developed financial practices intended to meet communal needs. Drawing upon biblical injunctions to aid impoverished coreligionists as well as traditions of ethnic self-help brought from eastern Europe, Jewish immigrants created *Hebrew Free Loan associations.* Following religious instructions, these organizations charged no interest. Free loan societies relied on a system of endorsers to achieve exceptionally low default rates—only about 1%. The communal importance of such associations was greatest early this century, when Jews—noted for their high rates of self-employment—had special need for borrowing, yet found commercial credit through banks to be either unavailable, excessively costly, or unpredictable due to frequent bank failures. The latter made these organizations crucial during the lean years of the Great Depression. Often affiliated with synagogues, Jewish communal agencies, or *landsmanshaften* (hometown lodges), Hebrew Free Loan societies provided Jewish women, who had fewer economic resources than men, with a modicum of financial independence.[58]

Hebrew Free Loan societies continue to exist, offering loans to needy coethnics as well as Jewish immigrants and members of other ethnic groups. In suburban Detroit, a program devoted to community stabilization offers loans to Jews willing to purchase homes in transitional communities. Ukrainians, Poles, Slovaks, Serbs, Croats, Slovenes, and African Americans also created fraternal, insurance, and mutual benefit societies.[59]

Borrowing and lending money is an issue capable of provoking awkwardness, embarrassment, and considerable discomfort.[60] Accordingly, involvement in communal arrangements such as a Hebrew Free Loan Society or a Mexican *tanda* provides members with a socially acceptable means of acquiring funds without shaming themselves or incurring awkward obligations to others. In effect, such institutions transform the isolating act of accepting a loan into the socially approved and social capital building endeavor of joining a network marked by trust and shared confidence.

Smaller-Sized Capital Sources

In addition to formalized bases of economic support, such as loan societies and rotating credit associations, ethnic groups also maintain informal networks based upon family relationship, friendship circles, or common occupation that provide funds for investment and consumption. These sources furnish group members with the cash they need to survive day to day. In her study of recently arrived Vietnamese in Philadelphia, Kibria found that "the pooling or sharing of resources, concentrated within the household or co-residential unit, was in fact one of the central economic practices by which Vietnamese Americans worked to survive and realize economic expectations."[61]

Members of ethnic groups often encourage the arrival of relatives or cultivate relationships with acquaintances (in effect, investing in social capital) in order to increase the size of cooperative networks. For example, in the late nineteenth and early twentieth centuries, eastern Europeans and Scandinavians frequently paid for the transport of their countrymen to the United States, while Latino, Asian, and Middle Eastern groups continue to do so.[62] Sometimes, however, this strategy backfires as relatives and friends absorb more resources than they contribute.[63]

Within many ethnic groups, extended families or "pseudo-families" (groups of unrelated persons) share common households, combining their resources to pay for food, utilities, and rent and to care for children, the elderly, or the sick.[64] Carpooling is also a common practice within low-income ethnic groups. Ethnics also raise funds by engaging in informal economy entrepreneurship directed at coethnics. For example, for a fee, they may fix cars, offer job training, do tailoring work, provide child care, sublet residential space, or use their cars as pseudo-taxis.[65] In her study of Puerto Rican and Dominican businesses in

Boston, Levitt found that these entrepreneurs felt their role was to support the community at large:

> Latino business owners . . . are not simply motivated by profit maximization—they also try to achieve approval, status and power within the community. The economic act is not merely an exchange of goods—it is also an exchange of respect and trust. These practices make such businesses work.[66]

LABOR

In addition to furnishing capital, ethnic economies also play important roles in organizing labor. There is a long tradition of union activism among ethnic groups, and coethnics often exert considerable influence over hiring and subcontracting practices in such a way as to direct employment and procurement to their fellows.[67] Many ethnic economies rely on trust and solidarity to manage conflicts among ethnic entrepreneurs and between employers and workers.[68] In communities in which employment of coethnics is common, conflict between owners and workers is regulated through a "deferred compensation" process whereby employees are paid low wages for a period and then remunerated by being helped to start their own, noncompeting business at a later date. This practice, which is based in ethnic trust, ensures the loyalty and low cost of workers, limits the creation of competitors from among the ranks of former employees, and facilitates the sharing of capital, advice, and credit. Working simultaneously, these factors foster the upward mobility of ethnic workers and the expansion of the ethnic economy.

Training Systems and Ethnic Solidarity

Bailey and Waldinger's discussion of *training systems* provides a tool for understanding cooperation between coethnic owners and workers. Training is an investment an employer makes in his or her workforce. An employer needs skilled workers to achieve high productivity. However, hiring employees who already possess needed skills is expensive—if they are available at all. Accordingly, employers often seek to hire unskilled workers and train them. The investment in training pays off over time as the skilled worker performs his or her task for the employer. If the trained worker leaves to take another job, the employer's investment in training the worker is wasted. The proposition for the worker is also risky "since, to the extent that workers pay for their training (through lower than average wages at the early stages of a job), they can only gain a return if they remain employed in the firm or industry for which the training is relevant."[69]

Enter ethnic solidarity. Ethnic coupling engenders mutual obligation between boss and worker. Coethnic employees know that their work is needed, and employers can be confident that trained workers will not leave. The investment in training is thus less risky for both parties. Hence, the institution of training explains an advantage ethnic economies possess over the larger economic system: workers and employers are bound together by trust that yields more stable and less costly relations between paid staff and business owners. Despite the role played by ethnic solidarity, however, there is a long history of conflict among owners and workers marked by the same ethnic membership.[70] Several recent studies have reported that workers and owners of the same ethnic origins make concerted efforts to avoid working together.[71]

Hiring and Referral Networks:
The Ethnic–Controlled Economy

Ethnic communities rely upon networks to locate jobs. Referral by friends removes some of the uncertainty associated with finding a job with unfamiliar employers and reduces chances of being abused or not being paid. Friends provide transportation, show the new worker how to perform the job, and look out for his or her interests. Employers realize that this practice is beneficial for them as well. Little cost or effort need be expended when new workers are located through employees' contacts.

> In the absence of unusual shortages or other strong pressures, managers fill vacan-
> cies in the easiest way . . . overwhelmingly on word of mouth—the natural cheapest
> route to a reliable labor supply. Information passes through informal networks of kin,
> friends and co-workers, which, of course, are based on ethnic, religious and racial
> groups and social strata.[72]

Moreover, such hires are likely to be competent and reliable, since present workers must accept responsibility for them.

A growing body of research reveals that employers make hiring decisions on the basis of racial and ethnic preferences, often preferring foreigners over natives, Latinos and Asians over blacks or whites, and the undocumented over legal migrants or citizens, largely because of the preferred groups' greater compliance and willingness to accept low wages.[73] Since employers seek an ethnically defined workforce, they find coethnic networks to be an efficient means of locating prospective employees. The practice of hiring through workers' contacts has become so widespread that it is no longer strictly the province of small operations. When photojournalist Ed Wheeler obtained a "worm" (assistant) job on a Gulf Coast oil platform in order to make a photo documentary, he confronted the informal constraints of an ethnic labor market. Although the oil rigs are owned by multinational oil companies, hiring networks ensure that nearly all the laborers on the rigs are Cajuns. Ethnic loyalty was so strong that non-Cajun Wheeler found himself subject to the scorn of workers who believed that his very presence was depriving a fellow Cajun of employment.[74] Finally, Waldinger demonstrates how hiring networks among Indian workers have resulted in their rapid entry into technical and professional positions in the New York City government, despite the agency's reputation as a constricted bureaucracy that changes at a snail's pace. During the 1980s, while total employment in the city's Transport Department little more than doubled, the employment of Asians increased by a factor of 4.5, ultimately accounting for a fifth of all workers.[75]

CONSUMER DEMAND AND SOURCES OF GOODS TO MEET IT

Ethnic-specific demand for native language services and traditional products plays a key role in the development of ethnic economies because it shields the newly established proprietor from competition with more experienced and better capitalized majority-owned businesses. "The special demands of ethnic consumers (for example lasagna noodles, kosher pickles, won ton soup) created protected markets for ethnic tradesmen who know about things their countrymen wanted."[76]

The relative importance of ethnic consumers in developing meaningful ethnic economies is subject to some contention. Several authors have argued that ethnic populations are too small in number and too limited in spending power to support major ethnic economies on their own.[77] For example, Bates asserts that black-owned retail and service businesses directed at the coethnic market have little earning potential, whereas African American firms that service the general market, other businesses, and government are highly profitable.[78]

Moreover, since the provision of ethnic-specific goods is often the occupation of choice among fledgling ethnic business owners, cannibalistic competition often develops among them. Conversely, it is asserted that groups that provide goods and services to the larger society have achieved significant rates of self-employment. Such has been the case among Chinese restaurateurs and laundrymen, Japanese truck farmers, Jewish retailers, and, most recently, Korean retailers, Cuban light manufacturers and construction firms, and Amish craftspeople.[79]

Despite the limitations associated with serving ethnic-specific markets, many groups have used these protected niches to establish their businesses. Further, especially since the 1980s, very sizable ethnic populations, numbering in the hundreds of thousands, have entrenched themselves in major cities. For example, when combined, the Mexican- and Asian-origin populations of Los Angeles and Orange County, California, exceed 4 million persons.[80] Totaling the demand for ethnic-specific goods and services, nonethnic goods and services delivered by coethnic entrepreneurs (e.g., Spanish- or Cantonese-speaking purveyors of health care, insurance, real estate, and auto parts), and ethnic products (such as piñatas or Thai food) consumed by noncoethnics, there is clearly a gigantic ethnic consumer demand. Latinos spent $216 billion on consumer goods and services in 1991, an amount that is expected to grow rapidly in the future.[81]

As a case in point, consider the broadcast media industry. Since the mid-1990s, the radio station with the largest audience in the entire United States has been a

Spanish language station in Los Angeles. The first Latino station to hold the number-one spot (KLAX) specialized in "Banda"—Mexican country music. Most recently, another Los Angeles station, KLVE, has occupied first place, playing "family oriented humor and romantic ballads" in Spanish. The 10 Spanish language radio stations in Los Angeles take in about $75 million annually, or 15% of the region's total radio market.[82]

The market potential of serving ethnic consumers is demonstrated by the fact that certain ethnic groups specialize in satisfying the unmet consumer demand of others; the most common example is when ethnic entrepreneurs establish businesses in underserved inner-city locations because corporate businesses are unwilling to locate branches there. Koreans, for example, the ethnic population with the highest rate of self-employment in the United States, established their economic foothold in the States by marketing wigs and other fashion items to urban blacks and Latinos. As is well known, this instance of economic concentration has yielded significant conflict between Korean entrepreneurs and black customers.[83] Sassen asserts that an important role played by ethnic economies involves their provision of goods and services to other low-income populations.[84]

Whether catering to a handful of consumers in a mom-and-pop store or mass marketing goods and services to ethnic consumers with billions to spend, ethnic entrepreneurs use their linguistic and cultural skills and international connections to import consumer items of the type desired by ethnic consumers in the United States. Since labor costs are often much lower in developing nations, imported agricultural and manufactured goods and cultural products are often inexpensive when compared with those made in the United States.

Imported and Wholesale Goods

The connection between U.S.-based businesses and overseas production finds its highest level of development among groups such as Taiwanese, Chinese, and Koreans, who are characterized by both an export-oriented country of origin and an entrepreneurial immigrant community in the United States.[85] In the 1970s, Korea became a major manufacturer of wigs and Korean Americans monopolized their importation and sale.[86] Since that time, Korean entrepreneurs have continued to be involved in the import and sale of Asian-made consumer goods, but no longer limit themselves to wigs or Korean-made merchandise. Min estimated that as of the mid-1990s in New York and Los Angeles, there were approximately 1100 Korean-owned import firms that provided merchandise for some 5700 coethnic retail shops in these two cities.[87]

Similarly, due to the arrival of thousands of highly educated Jews from the former Soviet Union, Israel, as of 1995, had 135 scientists and engineers per 10,000 residents, compared with 85 in the United States and 80 in Japan. U.S. computer companies have wasted little time in using American-based workers with social and linguistic links to Israel to take advantage of this highly skilled and relatively inexpensive labor force. The design specifications for Intels 286, 386, and MMX Pentium were all devised in Israel, home to major plants for IBM, Intel, Microsoft, and DEC.[88]

Because certain food products preferred by ethnic consumers are not generally exported to the West, personal contacts are vital for organizing their acquisition and shipment. Importers claim that organizing international trade in such perishable commodities is extremely risky and would be virtually impossible without their language competence, coethnic connections, and travel. The same is true with trendy cultural products such as popular music, videotapes, and seasonal clothing. Dealers in this merchandise have little competition and thus find the endeavor to be profitable. Consequently, ethnic entrepreneurs and their trading partners are bringing various products and firms into the world economy for the first time.[89]

Ethnic connections are also valuable for obtaining preferable deals on merchandise available within the United States. Immigrant entrepreneurs facilitate success through horizontal and vertical integration. *Horizontal integration* involves ethnic business owners cooperating to choose store location, avoid competitive pricing, pool information, and engage in collective buying. *Vertical integration* occurs when a whole package of business services — ranging from credit, wholesale goods, and maintenance to parking, transportation, real estate, manufacturing, and import − export concessions — are provided by coethnics. Through vertical and horizontal integration, ethnic entrepreneurs can support each other, strengthen coethnic ties, share information, avoid cannibalism, and generally contribute to the interlocking business orientation of the entire immigrant community.[90]

POLITICAL RESOURCES

Ethnic-based notions of trust, cooperation, and shared fate that yield economic resources are also valuable assets for political activity. Since ethnic groups are often involved in conflicts and seek to both obtain state-provided benefits and limit government actions that could reduce their economic viability, ethnic political organization is an important economic resource for ethnic groups.

One of the earliest American examples of the significance of politics in shaping an ethnic economy involved some of the first Jews to set foot in North America. In the 1600s, when Sephardic Jews began to settle in New Amsterdam, Peter Stuyvesant, the governor of the New Netherlands, tried to prohibit their entrance. He petitioned his employer, the Dutch West Indies Company of Amsterdam, to ban their arrival, claiming that they were disloyal and had an "abominable religion." However, the migrants defended themselves before the company (which had several Jewish stockholders) and were permitted to stay.[91] Without this application of influence on the political process, these early arrivals (whose descendants would eventually develop a significant ethnic economy) would not have been able to establish a foothold on the continent.

Throughout U.S. history, various ethnic groups have used political power to access jobs and income. Such was the function of urban political machines early this century. They introduced newcomers to the American political system while relying on both patronage and the civil service to furnish government employment. More recently, the Civil Rights movement increased opportunities for blacks and other groups. Government has now become a dominant employer of American blacks. In 1980, a majority of black college graduates "held jobs tied to federal government spending."[92] "In Los Angeles, as in all cities across America, African Americans have been overrepresented in government employment. About one-fourth of all black men and nearly one-third of all black women in the Los Angeles region worked for the government in 1970, 1980, and 1990." By 1990, these jobs were highly professionalized and well paid, employing a third of college-educated black men and 43% of college-educated black women. Government jobs offered fewer opportunities for less educated blacks, however, because the public sector has little need of workers lacking a high school diploma.[93]

Political connections have also been vital in directing government spending to ethnic economies. Through their involvement in political machines, Irish politicians secured public works contracts for coethnic construction companies. As early as 1870, the Irish constituted a fifth of building contractors in the United States. Irish employers and workers "shared job opportunities only with their sons and compatriots." In this way, ethnic solidarity provided a link between the ethnic-controlled economy in government jobs and the ethnic ownership economy in construction firms.[94]

During the 1980s, 110 years later, major cities throughout the United States had dedicated significant fractions of their purchasing—Richmond, Virginia, allocated 40%—to women- and minority-owned businesses. As a result of minority set-aside programs, in 1992, 5% of American black-owned businesses derived more than one-half of their revenue from state and local government, while 17% derived more than one-half of their revenue from the federal government. Further, once a minority-owned enterprise has secured a contract to provide goods and/or services to a major corporation or the government, it may then become eligible for credit. For example, the Business Consortium Fund of New York City loaned more than $40 million in contract financing to minority-owned businesses and created 3488 full-time jobs between 1989 and 1994.[95] As further evidence to the role of political factors in contributing to the growth of ethnic economies, Bates found that big cities with black mayors have higher rates of black business ownership than cities with mayors of other races.[96]

As noted by Kasinitz and Vickerman in their study of Caribbean immigrants in New York, black migrants can qualify for politically derived affirmative action programs and have used this option for their economic advancement.

> Affirmative action programs at many schools increased educational opportunities. Both public- and private-sector enterprises found themselves under political pressure to hire more blacks after the late 1960s, and West Indians seem frequently to have been the preferred choice. . . . Twenty percent of Jamaican-born people in the city and 28 percent in the regional labor force work in the government and not for profit sectors. . . . The economic importance of public and not for profit sector jobs may also explain the disproportionate amount of political activity on the part of Afro-Caribbean immigrants (particularly Jamaicans) compared to other recent immigrants.[97]

Latinos and Asians, too, have used political mobilization to generate economic resources. Padilla describes how Mexicans and Puerto Ricans in Chicago joined forces to demand affirmative action programs from major employers.[98] Asian American college students and faculty at several universities have fought against discriminatory criteria for admissions and tenure, and a broad coalition of Asian interests worked to resist zoning regulations that would restrict the growth of Asian businesses in southern California.[99] Finally, Native American groups have developed significant ethnic economies through their right to run gambling casinos and ability to harvest otherwise prohibited fish, game, minerals, and other natural resources. "Today, 97 tribes in 22 states are operating more than 200 casinos and bingo parlors, earning an estimated $2.7 billion in annual profits." The Mashantucket Pequots of Connecticut, who number only a few hundred, operate a casino that employs 10,000 people and is exceeded only by the federal government as a contributor to the state's treasury.[100]

Because of the many interethnic conflicts involving Korean American businesses, Koreans have been forced to become active in political life. Business owners' organizations such as New York's Korean Small Business Service Center lobbied on behalf of ethnic entrepreneurs, demanding fair prices from wholesalers and reduced user fees and police protection from government. The need to deal more effectively with the larger society after the Los Angeles riot of 1992 led to a major generational shift in the control of the Korean American community. Prior to the riot, community spokespeople were successful business owners who had been educated in Korea. However, the older generation "had difficulty communicating the position of the Korean community either orally or in writing." Following the uprising, the importance of "maintaining successful public relations with the mainstream media, government agencies and other American organizations" became a top priority, thus propelling a younger cohort of American-educated Koreans to positions of leadership and advocacy.[101]

Although ethnic political activism has yielded benefits for group members, it has also produced conflict with other groups. In many cases, each actor in a contemporary urban political struggle represents a distinct ethnic constituency. Often established groups such as white ethnics and blacks find themselves pitted against recent arrivals as well as one another. Hence, ethnic political movements intended to further economic interests may initiate hostile responses that then require further political action.

Refugees

Refugee status, a political and economic advantage, yields significant resources for those eligible.[102] In the post–World War II era, more than 2 million refugees have entered the United States.[103] This category not only endows recipients with legal status—itself a valuable economic resource—but also provides incumbents with a wide range of economic benefits including cash assistance, health care, housing, training, and job placement. Refugee status is given to specific populations, and denied to others, as the result of political decisions that are influenced by mobilized ethnic groups and their allies.[104]

Government funds pay for resettlement agencies and community-oriented service provider positions (doctors and other health professionals and job training programs) that are frequently staffed by refugees themselves.[105] Medical doctors are especially dependent upon ethnic customers because as foreign medical graduates, they find it difficult to obtain the certification in a medical specialty that is required for employment in most hospitals and health maintenance organizations (HMOs). Private practice, then, becomes the only option for employment. Taking advantage of refugees' eligibility for Medicare, the practices of refugee doctors are frequently directed toward refugee communities.[106]

In addition to supporting themselves, physicians and other professionals sustain other sectors of the ethnic economy, including medical supply companies, commercial real estate, dental labs, pharmacies, and, most notably, ethnic media industries whose newspapers, magazines, cable TV programs, and ethnic "yellow pages" carry their advertisements. For example, a quarter of the more than 900 businesses listed in the *1988 Vietnam Business Directory of Southern California* were medical professionals, including 133 doctors, 66 dentists, and 21 pharmacists. Nearly half (45) of the 115 advertisements in the *1988 Los Angeles Russian Language Telephone Directory* offered various medical services. In turn, ethnic media contribute to community solidarity and economic growth.

Jobs directly or indirectly supported by government benefits are the foundation of refugee communities' middle classes and a key element in their political life. Several groups that entered the United States as refugees, including Iranians, Vietnamese, Soviet Jews, Armenians, and Cubans, are noted for their powerful ethnic economies, which were developed on the basis of legal status and assistance provided to them by the U.S. government.[107]

THE MIXED BLESSINGS OF ETHNIC RESOURCES

Although they confer numerous advantages, patterns of mutual obligation that underlie ethnic economies also incur significant costs that can diminish the value of group resources. In their study of entrepreneurship among Pennsylvania Amish,

Kraybill and Nolt make the distinction between a group's *cultural resources* "that are available to empower the work of prospective entrepreneurs" and *cultural restraints* "that impede entrepreneurial activity." They point out that the benefits of coethnic loyalty and cooperation are not free. Often, they can only be realized by providing coethnics with expensive rewards and by conforming to communal standards that preclude one's cashing in on lucrative opportunities. The Amish, for example, are disallowed "litigation, politics, individualism, commercial insurance and higher education" as well as free interaction with the outside word, the use of many forms of modern technology, and aggressive advertising, resources that most non–Amish business owners find vital in operating their firms.[108]

In addition, although group-specific business skills and techniques can yield valuable dividends in certain circumstances, they may be ill-suited for dealing with challenges posed by doing business in a diverse, rapidly changing, and highly regulated business environment. It is important to point out that most problems encountered in ethnic economies are not specific to the application of ethnic resources alone but are shaped by class resources as well. However, the section that follows is limited to difficulties specifically linked to the use of ethnic resources.

Coethnic sources provide investment capital and business advice. However, because such services are generally delivered within an unregulated and informal context in which trust is assumed, they are subject to malfeasance. Ethnic entrepreneurs report being swindled by coethnics through fraudulent deals, stolen investment funds, and illegal surcharges. Ethnic entrepreneurs are also vulnerable to protection rackets from ethnic gangs. In certain settings, the risk of coethnic exploitation is so great that entrepreneurs disassociate themselves from their fellows to avoid blackmail.[109] As a case in point, Portes and Rumbaut cite the instance of a Vietnamese owner of a large electronics company who, in an effort to escape coethnic extortionists, hires few countrymen and goes by the name of George Best.[110]

Ethnic communities provide their entrepreneurs with loyal consumers. However, businesses embedded in coethnic settings are required to return the favor. Levitt found that Dominican and Puerto Rican shop owners in Boston accept their obligations to coethnics and are compensated for their generosity with status and prestige. In contrast, Geertz, Granovetter, and Lyman describe how ethnic entrepreneurs seek to reduce the costs associated with coethnic involvement: "Chinese American professionals have for the most part chosen to practice their professions outside Chinatown" in order to "escape from having to give special favors and free or cheaper services to kin and friends in the Ghetto."[111]

Ethnic entrepreneurs often complain that communal obligations demand that they hire coethnics rather than workers from the general labor market who possess needed skills and characteristics. For example, coethnics may lack the language, management, legal, or marketing skills and knowledge required for successful and legal business operation. Further, as the experience of many middleman entrepreneurs reveals, business owners who fail to employ workers of their customers' ethnicity are especially likely to encounter resentment and conflict. In either case, reliance on a strictly coethnic labor force can limit businesses success. Finally, employers often assert that coethnic employees hope to open their own business—which will directly compete with that of their former boss. Like the Israeli building contractor quoted in the following, they may avoid coethnic hiring in order to limit training future rivals.

> You see, Israelis, they want to also become self-employed. So there was sometimes friction and also they care too much about the details of how I run my company. If I need to be somewhere else for a while and a potential customer comes to the work site and asks for a contractor and they (my employees) give their card or leave their number—that's cheating. I need to be careful of Israelis, and now I hire Mexican workers more.[112]

The preceeding is illustrative of problems associated with coethnic labor from an employer's point of view. Workers also encounter difficulties in ethnic economies, including low wages, long hours, and poor working conditions. Further, working in the ethnic economy yields few opportunities to learn English, which is normally required to move beyond bottom-rung jobs. Ethnic employment also means that the types of benefits provided by unions or government regulations are usually unavailable. Contradicting Portes and Bach's contention that employment in the ethnic enclave economy is beneficial to coethnic workers, two studies of Vietnamese adaptation determined that employment in the ethnic economy was associated with low wages and lack of promotions.[113] Under these circumstances, ethnic solidarity may actually function as a liability to ethnic economic development, causing ethnic entrepreneurs and workers alike to seek out more favorable relations with employers and labor or consumer markets beyond their own community.

Cannibalistic Competition

Depending on the common tool kit of business skills and techniques, most ethnic entrepreneurs rely on the same markets for supplies, capital, labor, and consumers; sell the same type of goods and services; and use comparable business practices. Accordingly, businesses run by coethnics are similar and, as such, prone to fierce competition. Without the ability to control competition, ethnic businesses can become antagonistic. This lack of variety is noted as a source of business failure among East Indian entrepreneurs.

> East Indian businessmen demonstrate imitative behavior when they follow practices of buying from the same wholesalers, locating in the same locale, catering to the same ethnic market and using the same brands and assortments of merchandise as their competitors. This hardly provides them the opportunity to differentiate their enterprises from others in order to build customer loyalty and patronage.[114]

As the foregoing discussion reveals, the regulation of competition and the development of cooperative relations between workers and employers require extensive communication, viable community ties, trust, and loyalty. Some groups limit conflict among coethnic businesses by coordinating and integrating the types and locations of businesses such that each will not reduce the profitability of the other. Conflict between coethnic owners and workers is minimized by providing workers with financial and in-kind benefits, by offering promises of help in starting their own businesses, or by hiring out-group members to perform unpleasant and poorly paid tasks. However, such extensive cooperation can be considered an ideal type rather than a common practice. Several studies indicate that it is most highly developed among ethnic subgroups already bound by trusting relations and other forms of social capital.[115]

Finally, ethnic resources may be organized and distributed in ways that benefit some members of a group at the expense of others—women may do the lion's share of work while men receive the income, a paternalistic elite may control the labor of a rank and file, and the demand for family labor may hinder children's educational advancement. Hence, some ethnic resources are obtained at the cost of self-exploitation.[116]

CONCLUSIONS

Thanks to both their cultural orientation and their trusting relations with coethnics, members of ethnically defined groups are able to mobilize resources that help them in economic life. Class resources alone cannot explain how undocumented, non-English-speaking Mexican migrants can quickly find jobs in many U.S. locations, why the incomes of Israelis in southern California exceed those of other Middle Eastern groups even though they have fewer years of education, why Chinese–Vietnamese entrepreneurs in the United States can efficiently locate and import large shipments of perishable foodstuffs previously unknown outside of Southeast Asia, how Cuban refugees with meager financial assets could open businesses within a few years of their U.S. arrival, or why African Americans went from being greatly underrepresented in New York City government employment in the 1960s to holding such jobs in excess of their proportion of the city's population by the 1980s, even at professional levels. In each of these cases, ethnic resources allow for the achievement of significant goals.

Ethnic connections reduce the costs of doing business and provide investment capital, advice, raw materials, training, and access to customers. Networks render job referrals and training, and ethnic-based trust reduces conflict between workers and owners. Ethnic-based feelings of shared fate provide a basis for political action that can permit groups to win concessions from government agencies and establish a common standpoint for addressing conflicts with opposing groups and interests. These resources provide group members with financial, human, cultural, and social capital, which yield a path to economic progress that would have been unavailable in their absence. Moreover, to a substantial degree, they are distributed along ethnic lines and cannot be seen simply as the product of class.

Despite these many benefits, ethnic resources may come into being within a context that may limit freedom and impose restrictions that constrain gainful activities. Finally, it is important to remember that ethnic resources do not exist in a vacuum. Their potential benefits and liabilities alike are to a large extent determined by the social, legal, and economic context in which groups exist.

CHAPTER 6

Gender and Families in Ethnic Economies

INTRODUCTION

This book's main assertion is that ethnic-based collectivism makes a difference to the economic status of immigrant and minority groups in the United States. In the last two chapters, we have discussed how groups deploy class and ethnic resources to develop ethnic economies. However, the link between broad and imprecise social categories such as ethnicity and class and the actual situations and behaviors of groups and individuals is abstract. Family plays a vital intermediary role.

This chapter concerns families and gender arrangements in ethnic economies. Like ethnicity, family and gender relations are social forms based upon loyalty, intimacy, shared fate, social prescriptions, and relational ties. In entrepreneurship, farming, formal and informal production, inheritance, remittances, allocation of responsibility and reward, and even organized crime, ethnic families blur the distinction between production and consumption, employer and worker, exploitation and self-interest, and public and private that underlie contemporary models of economic life. Max Weber declared that families practiced "household communism," typified by "solidarity in dealing with the outside and communism of property and consumption of everyday goods within."[1] Individualistic, cost–benefit models of human behavior offer limited insight into the conduct of families, gender groups, and ethnic communities because these units' goals and their means of achieving them frequently elude the logic of selfish preference upon which conventional economic thought is based.

The gender and family characteristics of ethnic groups are fundamental in determining their economic fate. Families are among the basic units of social life, wherein economic plans are developed and carried out, class and ethnic resources are created and distributed, work roles are defined, and consumption takes place. Ethnic families are an important point of intersection among individuals, generations, genders, ethnic communities, and the larger society. And within such families, activities and outlooks oriented toward economic gain, affection, intimacy, preservation of group culture, and striving toward both loyalty and independence are intertwined. Hence, it is within families that structures of economic opportunity most directly encounter personal circumstances.

Precisely because ethnic families reject individualistic and cost–benefit models for determining their behavior, they are often able to endow (and occasionally deprive) their members with class and ethnic resources, including strategies for survival under adverse circumstances. However, ethnic families' unique economic logic is not always celebrated. Social activists and policymakers sometimes criticize their collectivist orientation, arguing that such practices either hinder the progress of the entire ethnic community or privilege certain family members at the expense of others.[2] Just as ethnic solidarity may obscure communal conflicts, so goes the argument, families conceal intergender, intergenerational, and interpersonal strife.[3]

Research demonstrates a link between a group's family and gender composition and its economic status.[4] However, the factors underlying family composition are complex and often the result of available opportunities, historical processes, economic developments, and policy choices, not just of cultural preferences. Moreover, families are not simply cooperative economic units. Rather, they are made up of men and women and generations with different—sometimes opposing—interests, needs, and resources. Consequently, families are locations of conflict and negotiation among members with regard to the allocation of prestige, responsibility, assets, decision making, group identity, and moral credibility. Although ethnic groups maintain very different patterns of communal organization and participation, every group incorporates family arrangements, making such units of special relevance to the comparative understanding of economic outcomes among diverse groups.

When we speak of gender and families[5] in ethnic economic life, we are addressing three sets of interrelated issues: the obligations, rights, and duties specified for men and women; families as units of collective action, socialization, consumption, and production; and the intergenerational dimensions of family (in terms of division of labor and reward, continuity, and the passing on of knowledge and resources). Finally, families are in constant flux, both with regard to their composition at any given moment in time and to historical changes in their meaning, functioning, and context.

Culture, Context, and Process

Ethnic families rely upon culture and traditions to provide their members with economic resources (and sometimes liabilities). However, cultural explanations of group behavior that do not address the importance of context, history, and process are incomplete. Although popular debate emphasizes family values and gender roles as being central to groups' economic fate, relatively little systematic research has been devoted to examining the economic patterns of ethnic families.[6] As a consequence, many assertions regarding the role of gender and families in ethnic life overemphasize the consequences of intractable group culture on economic outcomes while disregarding contextual effects. Further, many scholars wrongly assume that group culture strictly determines human behavior. More often, culture and ethnic traditions are highly malleable, allowing groups to creatively develop the diverse forms they need to cope with diverse circumstances. Consider Korean women's economic behavior. Korean women have an extremely low rate of labor force participation in Korea, but a high one in the United States.[7] Aphorisms about invariant "Korean family values" are thus incapable of accounting for such a dramatic transformation in family arrangements. Instead, the importance of a group's experience and adaptability in the face of contextual challenges must be considered.[8]

A final challenge encountered when trying to generalize about racial and ethnic families is that they reflect myriad social forms and practices in terms of almost every possible measure. As Rumbaut[9] points out, "various immigrant nationalities [and racial–ethnic groups] account for at once the *highest* and *lowest* rates of education, self-employment, home ownership, poverty, welfare dependency, and fertility" (emphasis in original). Moreover, although the families of any two ethnic groups may reveal certain similarities, they may be very different in other dimensions.[10] Given the great diversity that exists among ethnic family and gender patterns and the many circumstances in which they are embedded, it would be impossible to constitute a comprehensive evaluation of their broader functioning. More modestly, the following discussion identifies important features of ethnic families and gender arrangements with regard to ethnic economies. Our goal is to establish that ethnicity, class, gender, and family type do make a difference to the economic fate of ethnic groups in American society. We pose this position as an alternative to the assertion that class is the sole determinant of economic outcomes.

Because gender and families affect ethnic economies in so many realms, the discussion that follows is organized in terms of three levels of analysis: the macro or structural realm of broad sociodemographic conditions, the midrange of group behavior in context (involving family economic strategies), and the micro territory of interaction within families and among individuals. It is important to note that we use these categories for analytic convenience. The social factors and relationships that shape actual ethnic families' economic activities have simultaneous impacts on multiple levels.

MACRO FACTORS

To a considerable extent, the family and demographic makeup of a group determines its resources, needs, and the kinds of jobs for which group members can qualify. In addition, the legal status of foreign-born persons is often related to family relationships. Hence, regardless of a group's culture, educational level, or access to ethnic and class resources, its family characteristics partly determine its economic standing.

Groups Differ in Their Family and Gender Composition

Ethnic economic life is influenced by groups' demographic characteristics. Groups vary in their sex ratios and, as a result, their records of family formation, outmarriage, and economic adaptation.[11] Some groups are youthful, others are older. They also differ in their fertility, household size, and rates of marriage and divorce. In turn, these factors contribute to social patterns. Family and household composition often affect economic outcomes by both defining needs and fixing resources that can be mobilized to achieve goals. Soviet Jewish and Cuban American families often include three generations but have few children. This family composition, which can be traced to residential patterns in their socialist countries of origin and to U.S. refugee policy (which fosters the entrance of intact families), yields a high ratio of adults to children. The presence of grandparents (who are able to assist in child rearing and culturally inclined to do so) allows these refugee families to devote extensive resources to children's care and socialization, a practice conducive to their educational achievement.[12] In contrast, children of families lacking social capital are likely to encounter more educational difficulty.[13]

It is well-documented that age and gender are associated with levels of education and earnings: male and older workers make more than female and younger workers. Hence, insofar as families differ in these dimensions, so too will their economic patterns. However, there are important variations. Among immigrants from Taiwan, the United Kingdom, China, Korea, and India, men are much more likely to be professionally employed than women. Among Greeks and Italians, men and women have roughly similar rates, and among Filipinos, Cubans, Canadians, and Mexicans, women have higher rates of professional employment than men.[14]

Finally, immigrant families maintain social and economic behaviors that are distinct from those of individual migrants. For example, single migrants are more likely to send remittances and less prone to settling than are migrant families.[15] Historically, female migrants have been more likely to settle in urban locations, and not return to the country of origin, whereas migrant men have been more often associated with rural locations and sojourning.[16]

Gender and Involvement in Economic Life

In recent years, women's involvement in paid employment has increased at a rapid rate. In 1900, only 20% of adult women worked for wages. In 1992, the figure was 58%. This augmentation has been especially the case for mothers, who now have a higher labor force participation rate than women in general. Most rapid in growth is the labor force participation of mothers of young children. In 1975, only 31% of married women whose youngest child was under 2 years of age were in the labor force. By 1990, the figure had risen to 54%. A major consequence of women's growing labor force participation has been a decline in married women's dependency on their husbands' income.[17]

These trends are true with regard to women with jobs in existing firms and especially for the self-employed, whose numbers have grown at a very rapid rate. In the 5 years from 1987 to 1992, for example, the number of businesses owned by women in the United States increased by 43%.[18] By 1996, women owned a third of all U.S. businesses, and those businesses provided more jobs than the *Fortune* 500, or 26% of the U.S. labor force.[19] Women-owned businesses are heavily concentrated in labor-intensive sectors; hence, they require less capitalization and create more jobs than capital-intensive operations.

Although women's growing labor force participation is noted among all groups, this trend is especially evident among ethnic women. Because immigrant and ethnic groups are usually disadvantaged in the labor market, the economic contributions of women and other family members are vital for survival.[20] Women also provide considerable unpaid labor that maintains families, cares for children, supports ethnic businesses, and builds communal environments.[21] As Gabaccia[22] notes, married ethnic women earned money at home, often in the informal economy, as they continued traditional forms of subsistence production. "Although they were called housewives, their domestic work little resembled that of middle class American women." For this reason, she identifies them as "bread-givers." And as women's economic contributions have grown, jobs for men with less than a high school education have become increasingly scarce, yielding major consequences for families, especially those of native-born minorities, including blacks and Puerto Ricans.[23] One study attributed about a quarter of the recent reduction in the wage gap between male and female workers to "the decline in the average real earning of male workers, due to the loss of many well-paid male blue-collar jobs."[24] Despite the shrinking number of jobs for low-skilled male workers, a recent study of earnings among undocumented workers found that women who were locked into domestic service (generally in the informal sector) had little chance for mobility. In contrast, men found jobs in food retailing. While initially low-paying, such positions eventually offered more chances for advancement.[25]

Gender, Family, and Employment Patterns

In opposition to neoclassical economic models, which assume that all job seekers compete freely for available work, dual labor market theory argues that "informal social expectations and formal institutional mechanisms" protect native-born, majority and male workers from having to take low-level jobs.[26] While high-status workers avoid low-level positions, at the same time, "market economies create a permanent demand for workers willing to labor under unpleasant conditions, at low wages, with great instability and little chance for advancement." Such jobs are filled by persons defined by ethnic status (immigrants and native minorities) as well as age and family status (women and teenagers, who have few options in the labor market and, consequently, have low expectations). According to Massey *et al.*[27] women and teenagers are willing to accept such jobs because their primary identity is derived from family relationships rather than from job status. Of course, persons characterized by both highly visible ethnicity and family status are especially likely to be steered into such low-level occupations. In sum, the gender, age, and marriage status of a group determines the number of persons available for positions that seek workers defined according to these criteria.

Many economic endeavors within which immigrant and ethnic group members concentrate are organized by gender. In fact, several occupations within both ethnic ownership economies and ethnic-controlled economies are female dominated.[28] With recent economic changes yielding a decline in unionized and well-paid manufacturing jobs, and growth in low-paid service and manufacturing jobs, women—often ethnic and immigrant women—have experienced a growing job demand.[29] For at least a hundred years, immigrant and ethnic women have been concentrated in domestic service and garment industries. For example, between 1950 and 1990, foreign-born women (mostly Latinas and Asians) increased their representation in Los Angeles from 3.2% of all manufacturing jobs to more than 15% of the total. At the same time, as the fraction of women—especially foreign-born women with low levels of education—increases in an occupational sector, wages tend to shrink.[30]

This trend continues. As increasing numbers of women enter the labor force, ethnic women are employed in the informal economy to care for homes, families and children. Immigration policy reflects the demand for female workers by granting special visas to nurses, a heavily female occupation.[31] At the same time, ethnic women are employed in growing numbers in new types of service jobs, such as food service, clerical occupations, and entertainment. Ethnic women also play vital roles in ethnic businesses and are active in home-based entrepreneurship. The networks and businesses that comprise ethnic economies are very often family-based. In many cases they are also oriented around a single gender group and grounded upon sociability, trust, and networks rooted in gender and family relationships.[32]

The family and gender makeup of an ethnic group shapes its economic adaptation. Family labor provides clear economic benefits.[33] Ethnic families with many workers per household tend to have higher incomes and rates of home ownership and lower rates of welfare dependency than those with fewer workers per household.[34] Asian and Latino groups with more married, cohabiting members have higher rates of self-employment than those with fewer married couples. Sanders and Nee[35] examined the relationship between family status and self-employment in New York and Los Angeles among four Asian groups (Chinese, Koreans, Filipinos, and Indians) and three Latino populations (Cubans, Mexicans, and Puerto Ricans). They found that "being married and living with the spouse increases the odds of self-employment for each ethnic group." For both men and women, being married increases one's chances for self-employment by 20%, with an even greater impact among Koreans and Cubans. The number of teenage relatives in the family is also positively associated with self-employment. Further, being married is correlated with receiving on-the-job training, an important prerequisite for both promotion and self-employment.[36] However, for African Americans, being married is not associated with higher rates of entrepreneurship. "Blacks in married couple families are no more likely to be self-employed than are blacks in nonfamily or single-parent households." This finding is attributed to the different patterns of family involvement in business maintained by blacks and by Latino and Asian immigrants, as well as the groups' contrasting sets of job alternatives.[37]

Compared with the native-born, immigrant families are more often headed by married couples, more frequently extended, and more likely to reside in relatively affluent regions of the country (neither rural nor southern). Consequently, they are more likely than natives to escape poverty status through the use of secondary wage earners.[38] However, large families are not always an economic asset. A study examining school attainment among adult men of seven racial and ethnic groups (blacks, Asians, American Indians, Cubans, Mexicans, and Puerto Ricans) that controlled for both parental schooling and father's occupation found that "the number of siblings had a consistently significant negative effect on various measures of educational attainment, except among the Asians."[39] In one Asian group, the Vietnamese, children commonly assist each other with homework, making numerous siblings an asset to achievement.[40]

Families headed by single women—a family form that in 1990 accounted for 43% of blacks, 37% of Puerto Ricans, 12% of whites, 11% of Koreans, 9% of Chinese, and 4.5% of South Asians—are at a significant economic disadvantage "given the persistent gender gap in wages, low child support payments and reduced access to social and cultural capital."[41] Despite these liabilities, immigrant women who head their own households are less likely to receive public assistance and more likely to work for wages than native-born female heads of households.[42]

Several studies have argued that while women's labor makes ethnic families more affluent, the increased affluence and leisure time generated by female labor often accrue to men. Greta Gilbertson[43] epitomizes this position:

> Dominican and Colombian women do not benefit from working in Hispanic-owned firms in New York City. . . . Our results suggest that ethnic ties do not confer advantages to women workers. Thus, some of the success of immigrant small-business owners and workers in the ethnic enclave is due to the marginal position of immigrant women. Stated more plainly, enclave employment is most exploitative of women.

However, this point has been contested.[44] Zhou and Logan,[45] in their study of earnings in New York's Chinese enclave, offer the following argument:

> Viewed from an individualistic perspective, the enclave labor market appears exploitative of women. But we must remember that Chinese culture gives priority not to individual achievement but to the welfare of the family and community. . . . [F]emale labor force participation is part of a family strategy. It is not obvious that the Chinese immigrant community has better options in the face of limited opportunities and discrimination in the mainstream economy.

A similar sentiment is expressed by Elvira Gómez, a Cuban woman who contributes to family coffers through homework in the ethnic garment industry: "It is foolish to give up your place as a mother and wife only to go take orders from men who aren't even part of your family. What's so liberated about that? It is better to see your husband succeed and to know you have supported one another."[46] Suggesting a different trajectory, George[47] notes the experience of Christian Indian nurses, whose occupation provides their families with both immigrant status and most of their income, making them far more powerful than their husbands. The men compensate for their lost status through church involvement.

Accepting that immigrant women did have conflicts with coethnic men, Gabaccia[48] argues that resources were also available to them in the ethnic community. "Immigrant women resembled women of America's racial minorities in viewing family ties as resources supporting female power and ethnic solidarity." Moreover, just because ethnic traditions stress unequal gender arrangements, that does not mean that ethnic families always maintain them. "Kinship also facilitated women's struggles against culturally specific traditions of misogyny."[49]

Family Policy and Economic Outcomes

American social policies generally take for granted the existence of "traditional," nuclear families with a male breadwinner and a female homemaker as the norm.[50] This view assumes that parents will marry and cohabit, that women and children will receive support from a husband–father, and that adolescent mothers and their children will be cared for by their parents and grandparents. However, this family arrangement, which applies to an ever-shrinking portion of the U.S. population, is an especially inaccurate depiction of ethnic families, which often exist within a cultural and economic environment distinct from that associated with the native-born, heterosexual, white middle class. In 1990, less than 20% of all American families conformed to the traditional nuclear family cited earlier.[51] Almost 75% of women with children age 6–17 were in the labor force.[52]

The consequences of these policies are that gender divisions are reinforced and nontraditional family forms are not acknowledged in policymaking, even if such arrangements create special needs or yield practical benefits. Thus, state policies have the effect of rewarding some family arrangements while taxing others.[53] A significant body of literature, for example, discusses the effects of U.S. public assistance policy on family type and its relationship to patterns of cohabitation, age, marriage, female-headed households, fertility, and labor force participation.[54] And although the majority of recipients of public assistance are native-born and white, public debates about "welfare" are generally framed in terms of ethnically defined and—in recent years—immigrant populations.[55]

Legal resident and work status for immigrants is of clear economic importance and is very often allocated in relation to one's family status. Regardless of their parents' nationality, children born in the United States are citizens. Their citizenship confers important benefits on the entire family and may provide a route for the legalization of relatives. Marriage to a citizen also offers a quick and direct path to legalization. In fact, each year, the overwhelming majority of legal immigrants enter the United States through family-based criteria as determined by their relationship to U.S. citizens or permanent residents. In fiscal year 1992, out of a total 810,000 entrants, more than 500,000, or 62%, entered as family immigrants.[56]

Partly because of these policies, in existence since the 1930s, the majority of U.S. immigrants have been women (see Table 6.1). Gabaccia[57] notes that despite eugenic fears that childbearing by foreign women would outpace that of "the Anglo-American race," every U.S. law restricting immigration by race included some provision for family reunification. On the other hand, because Americans worried about "the moral and economic risks" (prostitution and indigence) of independent female migration, women who migrated alone or were not met by their husbands upon arrival in U.S. ports were singled out for harassment.

What is more, U.S. policies intended to restrict or control immigration have also fixed on family status. The Bracero Program, which recruited temporary Mexican workers from 1942 to1964, was oriented toward "physically able adult male" workers but excluded women and children to reduce social costs and make deportation easier.[58] Similarly, in 1994, Californians voted for Proposition 187 in order to deny undocumented immigrants' eligibility for public assistance, education, and health care—services most likely to be consumed by immigrant families (including women, children, and the elderly) rather than single adults.

However, although male immigrants without families are thought to incur few social costs and be more likely to repatriate, they are often associated with

TABLE 6.1   Percentage Female Among Immigrants to the
United States, 1820–1980

	Percentage female	Total immigration
1820–1829	31.0	128,502
1830–1839	37.6	508,381
1840–1849	44.5	1,497,277
1850–1859	41.2	2,670,513
1860–1869	39.8	2,123,219
1870–1879	39.0	2,742,137
1880–1889	38.8	5,248,568
1890–1899	38.4	3,694,294
1900–1909	30.4	8,202,388
1910–1919	34.9	6,347,380
1920–1929	43.8	4,295,510
1930–1939	55.3	699,375
1940–1949	61.2	856,608
1950–1959	53.7	2,499,268
1960–1969	55.6	3,213,749
1970–1979	53.0	4,336,001

Source: Donna Gabaccia, *From the Other Side: Women, Gender, and
Immigrant Life in the U.S., 1820–1990* (Bloomington and Indianapolis:
Indiana University Press, 1994), p. 28.

disruptive behaviors such as gambling, fighting, substance abuse, and frequenting
brothels. Some European nations have attempted to reduce the incidence of
antisocial acts through family unification policies.[59] Most recently, federal welfare
reform legislation has sought to deny benefits to noncitizens. (Eligibility for
public assistance, social security, and other social programs has always been linked
to family and household status for citizen and immigrant alike.) Hence, family
status has been fixed upon by policymakers to determine one's eligibility for legal
residency and public assistance.

THE MIDDLE RANGE

As we have seen, the macrolevel demographics of an ethnic group condition
its economic status. In this section, we consider how groups' economic standing
is also shaped through the interactions between ethnic families and the larger
society and economy through entrepreneurship, job seeking, resource pooling,
inheritance patterns, cultural innovation, and the like.

The New Economics of Migration

Although early work on ethnic economies largely ignored families, recent research has understood that families are vital to economic adaptation. Much of this scholarship seized on the notion of the family not simply as a passive or reactive unit but rather as a rational agent capable of developing various strategies to cope with the contingencies presented by social and economic circumstances. "Families are depicted as developing strategies precisely because there exist constraining economic, institutional and social realities in the larger opportunity structure. . . . [F]amilies remain creative actors on a sometimes barren, sometimes hostile stage."[60] One of the most influential of such models is called "the new economics of migration."

This perspective contends that economic decisions are typically made by "families or households—in which people act collectively not only to maximize expected income, but also to minimize risk and loosen constraints associated with a variety of market failures." Such units "control risks to their well-being by diversifying the allocation of household resources."[61] Consequently, some family members may work in the local economy, while others are sent abroad where they can find income sources and amass savings in an environment largely independent of regional economic fluctuations and levels of inflation.

A major claim of the new economics of migration is that wage levels alone do not shape migration decisions or other economic behaviors. Rather, families and households consider the stability of earnings as well: "The source of the income really matters, and households have significant incentives to invest scarce family resources in activities and projects that provide access to new income sources, even if these activities do not necessarily increase total income."[62]

Consistent with these assertions, one study of the relationship between gender and migration among Mexican families demonstrated that ownership of specific assets exerts differential influence on the propensity of men and women to migrate. Land ownership ties women to their homes, freeing men to travel abroad. Business ownership has the opposite effect, tending to keep men in the country of origin while increasing the likelihood of women's migration.[63]

Family and Gender Behaviors and Strategies

Groups maintain different norms and standards with regard to how members should conduct economic life and allocate specific economic roles and responsibilities. Cultures emphasize economic priorities and define which family members should control economic resources while social networks clarify expectations and strategies. For example, Irish, Scandinavian, east European, Caribbean, Central American, and African American women have worked in domestic employment at higher rates than others.[64] Although domestic work is poorly paid, constraining, and demands separation from one's own family, it also offers a degree of flexibility and an opportunity for immigrants to learn American culture. Terry Golway[65] traces Irish women's entry into the American middle class well before coethnic men to these advantages.

In contrast to the groups listed, Middle Easterners have notably low rates of women working outside of the home, a consequence of both cultural preferences and husbands' relatively high earnings.[66] First-generation Italian women and girls also had low rates of employment outside the home but were extensively involved in home-based production. Whereas young boys worked as bootblacks, sold newspapers, or assisted their fathers with peddling, a 1911 congressional report found that 80% of Italian girls under age 14 worked with their mothers at home, either full-time or after school in garment work, making artificial flowers, shelling peanuts, or other tasks.[67] Settlement house staff often attributed Italian parents' desire to have their daughters at home to their chaste morality. In reality, however, families needed to keep their girls busy at work in order to make ends meet.[68] In another adaptive pattern, ethnic groups including Orthodox Jews, Pennsylvania Amish, and Vietnamese in the United States and Chinese in Britain opt for self-employment at least partially as a means of keeping families together while limiting contact with the larger society.[69]

As Milkman and Townsley[70] note, "Outwork, paid domestic service, and petty trade are also far more prominent female activities in the Third World than elsewhere." Accordingly, country and region of origin and length of time in the United States are relevant in conditioning the economic activities that ethnic women find acceptable because women evaluate their current economic options in view of previous work experience.

Cultural preferences are often malleable. Families develop pragmatic approaches to women's employment such that women will work outside of the home when funds are needed and compensation is adequate, while remaining out of the labor market or working at home when rewards are too low or domestic support is required. For example, while Punjabi farm families in California are party to a strong tradition against women's employment, many Punjabi women work seasonally in the United States in order to increase family income. These women would often prefer to work year-round but find that "seasonal labor has its advantages because it allows these women to work in the summer, when their children are out of school, and to be at home during the school year tending to their families' needs."[71] Similarly, in her research on overseas Chinese entrepreneurs, Oxfeld[72] found that parents disregarded the openly patrilineal (male-oriented) focus of their cultural traditions (wherein daughters are regarded as "a small happiness") and placed high value on daughters because they (and their families) were seen as uniquely able to offer emotional closeness, joyful family gatherings, and extensive social contacts.

Fernández-Kelly and Garcia[73] describe the contrasting strategies adopted by two groups of Latinas (Mexicans and Cubans) who share several "perceptions and expectations about sex roles" and both work in the garment industry, but are characterized by contrasting class, communal, and family contexts. Because of their lack of class resources, Mexican women in southern California seek employment to address "long-term financial needs" associated with the loss of male support and "the proletarian status of the ethnic group to which they belong." While it pays poorly, garment work does provide the option of homework, allowing these women to earn money while caring for their children. In contrast, "Cuban women who arrived in southern Florida as exiles saw garment jobs as a transitory experience aimed at recovering or attaining middle-class standards of living." Their goals included both earning money and sustaining traditional gender arrangements.[75] Relying on their class and ethnic resources of education, entrepreneurial know-how, and intact families, women supported the household while their husbands started businesses. Over time, Cubans created an ethnic enclave economy that ultimately "allowed women a marginal advantage in the labor market."[76] As their families became more economically stable, they left wage work, often at the husband's request.

Fernández-Kelly and Garcia conclude that while the Mexican women were more free from male authority than were Cubans, their lack of class resources, husbands' incomes, and the ethnic enclave's benefits meant that their situation was economically far worse. At least in this case, power came not through autonomy, but rather from cooperation rooted in traditional definitions of manhood and womanhood. "Many Cuban women interpret their subordination at home as part of a viable option ensuring economic and emotional benefits."[77]

Based on opportunities, resources, and needs, groups vary widely in their family and gender involvement in self-employment. Koreans frequently run enterprises that rely upon family labor. In contrast, groups such as like West Indians and Filipinos have very high rates of labor force participation, especially among women, but low rates of self-employment.[78] The explanation? Because Koreans have a hard time speaking English, they experience difficulty in finding well-paid jobs in the United States. Many discover that self-employment is a relatively rewarding alternative. In contrast, West Indians and Filipinos are much more familiar with the English language and are able to find satisfactory employment in service industries.[79] Revealing a third pattern, Israelis, who tend to speak English quite well, exhibit a rate of self-employment almost as high as that of the Koreans. However, they rely less upon family labor. Men run businesses, whereas women most often find jobs as teachers in American Jewish institutions, where their Hebrew proficiency is in demand.[80] Finally, among Vietnamese and Salvadorans, women have higher rates of self-employment than men.[81]

Families and Entrepreneurship

A wide range of literature describes how ethnic families make use of their collective resources and traditions to run small businesses. Among the advantages associated with family firms, Wong[82] notes ease of training family members in business operations, control of information and trade secrets, family members' willingness to put in long hours, access to financing, and kin serving as an important labor pool. In addition, family firms offer the flexibility required for business survival in competitive, seasonal, and changing markets, such as garments and restaurants, in which ethnic groups often concentrate. Reflecting the importance of family in providing business capital is the following quote from a Soviet Jewish entrepreneur in San Francisco: "I have over 30 relatives in San Francisco and they didn't have a choice [about giving money]. They were my relatives, . . . I just said 'I gotta have it.' "[83]

Working in or knowing about a family enterprise—a class resource—is an important source of business skill and contacts that facilitates self-employment (see Chapter 4). To quote from a Small Business Administration (SBA) publication, "Many entrepreneurs have had parents or other relatives who were self-employed as business owners . . . who were viewed as role models upon whom children could pattern their lives. . . . Potential entrepreneurs often receive informal training in a relative's business." [84] Wong[85] elaborates on family firms as sources of business training: "A mistake by a son or daughter is tolerated; he or she will be given another chance and is expected to learn from the mistake." Further, because businesses, unlike wage employment, can be readily passed on to one's offspring, families may provide not only occupationally relevant resources and training but firms themselves.

A 1982 Characteristics of Business Owners (CBO) survey found that for men, nonminorities, followed by Asians, Hispanics, and blacks, were most likely to have close relatives who owned businesses and to have worked for them.[86] Although cultural traditions and family-based business training foster self-employment, groups such as Greeks and Koreans not party to these traditions in the country of origin also adapt their family patterns in the United States to achieve remarkable rates of self-employment.

As noted, Korean immigrants have among the highest rates of self-employment of any American ethnic group. Korean men generally held white-collar positions in the country of origin, but due to language difficulties, lack of American credentials, and discrimination are unable to find professional employment. As an alternative to low-level work, a large fraction have become self-employed in the United States. Although Korean immigrants have little premigration experience with either self-employment or women working outside of the home, in the United States "a typical Korean business is a small family business usually operated by the husband and wife and in some cases with the additional help of children."[87] While women's labor is vital to Korean businesses in the United States it reflects a "radical difference" between Korean and Korean immigrant families. Min cites three factors in accounting for this change in family economic behavior: the necessity of women's work for economic survival, especially among the self-employed; the greater economic rewards of labor in the United States; and being influenced by American sex-role ideologies. "The advantage of dual career families for economic mobility and the importance of Korean women for the Korean immigrant-family economy have led many Korean immigrants to discard the traditional view that the husband should be the only or primary breadwinner."[88]

However, while Korean women have taken on responsibilities for earning income in the United States, surveys suggest that their husbands (like the men of most groups) have not increased their involvement in domestic labor such as cooking, cleaning, or child care.[89] As a result, "double roles give the Korean immigrant working wives role pressure and role conflicts."[90] In fact, such tensions are quite common within ethnic businesses. Family enterprises are often a viable means to achieve economic stability. However, as Zenner points out, strains are pervasive and often limit the longevity of family businesses.

> [U]nder modern corporate capitalism, small businesses of a family-kin type often have short lives. . . . While several studies of Jewish kinship in North America support the tie to independent enterprise, they also demonstrate the tensions which spill over from business to family life when the two are connected.[91]

Despite the importance of children's labor in family businesses, little research has been devoted to this issue. However, Miri Song's[92] study of Chinese children growing up in take-away restaurants in England has shed some much needed light on the topic. She found that their experience is marked by ambivalence — associated with positive feelings of loyalty, autonomy, and ethnic identification, on the one hand, and resentment over work demands, lack of freedom, and being forced to serve hostile, often inebriated customers in a racially tense atmosphere, on the other. Few children received a cash wage, but families did contribute to their educational expenses. Despite children's feelings of constraint and exploitation, there were few limits on the amount of work they were "guilt tripped" into contributing to the enterprise. This pattern of work can be traced to family and ethnic norms, which preclude economic negotiation across generations. In addition, the close quarters of the home–business setting, the necessity for Chinese–English translation, and the need to save on labor costs generally impede employing a nonrelated counter person until the child leaves home. As these cases demonstrate, family-based entrepreneurship is a complex matter. Involving exploitation, financial support, and strong feelings of mutual obligation, it is vital to the functioning of ethnic economies, yet eludes the kind of cost–benefit theorizing associated with impersonal market models.

Women-Owned Businesses: Exploitation or Empowerment?

Ethnic businesses are often assumed to be owned by men or grounded in families. However, there is also a significant number of women-owned enterprises. Like African Americans, who have traditionally specialized in captive markets maintained by racial segregation (barbers, ministers, undertakers, entertainers, and doctors), some of the earliest niches for immigrant women's entrepreneurship were associated with female concerns, including home-based production, midwifery, and prostitution. And just as black entrepreneurship was restricted by Jim Crow laws, home production, midwifery, and sex work were all prohibited by the social reforms of the Progressive Era.[93]

Some scholars contend that ethnic businesses are consistently exploitative of women.[94] They assert that such enterprises rely on women's unpaid labor and use family traditions to prevent women from gaining access to the wealth and power normally associated with income generation. Under such conditions, women remain within the "helper" role, while husbands reserve business assets and decision making for themselves. In the case of the husband's death, divorce, or abandonment, women may find themselves with nothing to show for a life of work.[95] "Mere work in economic activity (or even ownership of economic resources) does not translate into the economic leverage . . . if the person derives no control of economic resources thereby."[96]

Reflecting an opposing trend, recent figures indicate that business ownership by ethnic women (and by women generally) is growing much faster than all businesses. From 1987 to 1996, women-owned business grew at a rate between 150 and 220% faster than all businesses in the 50 largest U.S. cities (see Tables 6.2 and 6.3).[97] From 1987 to 1996 the number of minority-women-owned businesses grew by 153%, their employment increased by 276%, and their revenues expanded by 318%. Currently, they account for 13% of all women-owned businesses in the United States.[98] Women-owned firms comprise 38% of all minority-owned firms in the United States and produce 30% of their employment and 25% of their sales. Since "minority" in this study was defined as Asian, African American, Hispanic, and Native American, this number greatly underestimates the total number of self-employed *ethnic* women because the latter includes ethnic groups such as Jews, Armenians, Iranians, Arabs, southern and eastern Europeans, and the like, who are known to have high rates of self-employment but are defined as white. Given that women own almost 40% of all minority businesses in the United States, we presume that a sizable fraction of women involved in the ethnic economy have avoided exploitative, helper roles and, instead, are able to control assets and make business decisions. This position is reflected in a recent survey of white and minority women business owners. It determined that around half felt that the chief reward of self-employment was "being their own boss."[99] Along with their desire for flexibility and independence, female entrepreneurs of all races left their previous jobs "due to frustrations with the 'glass ceiling,' lack of challenge or being unhappy or uncomfortable."[100]

Census data analyzed by the National Foundation for Women Business Owners revealed that 37% of minority-women-owned businesses are owned by blacks (405,200), 35% are Hispanic-owned (382,400), and 28% are owned by Asians, American Indians, or Alaskan Native heritage women. More than half of these businesses are in the service sector, 19% are in retail trade, and 8% are in finance,

TABLE 6.2   Relative Growth in the Number of Women-Owned and All Firms,
1987–1996

Metropolitan statistical area	Women-owned firms	All firms	Absolute difference	Relative difference
New Orleans, LA	73.4	34.5	38.9	2.2:1
Oklahoma City, OK	55.7	25.3	30.4	2.2:1
Riverside–San Bernardino, CA	121.8	63.1	58.7	1.9:1
Tampa–St. Petersburg–Clearwater, FL	89.0	47.3	41.7	1.9:1
Phoenix–Mesa, AZ	93.9	51.2	42.7	1.8:1
Sacramento, CA	99.3	58.7	40.6	1.7:1
Salt Lake City–Ogden, UT	86.9	50.9	36.0	1.7:1
Los Angeles–Long Beach, CA	77.9	45.4	32.5	1.7:1
Nassau–Suffolk, NY	72.8	42.6	30.2	1.7:1
San Diego, CA	74.2	44.5	29.7	1.7:1
San Antonio, TX	70.3	43.4	26.9	1.7:1
Orlando, FL	131.1	82.0	49.1	1.6:1
Ft. Lauderdale, FL	109.1	69.1	40.0	1.6:1
Nashville, TN	94.0	59.5	34.5	1.6:1
Seattle–Bellevue–Everett, WA	88.3	56.5	31.8	1.6:1
Norfolk–Virginia Beach–Newport News, VA	82.0	52.1	29.9	1.6:1
Cleveland–Lorain-Elyria, OH	82.4	53.0	29.4	1.6:1
Ft. Worth–Arlington, TX	74.6	47.1	27.5	1.6:1
Orange County, CA	69.0	42.8	26.2	1.6:1
Miami, FL	117.3	76.4	40.9	1.5:1
West Palm Beach–Boca Raton, FL	113.6	76.8	36.8	1.5:1
Columbus, OH	100.2	68.0	32.2	1.5:1
Cincinnati, OH–KY–IN	85.2	56.5	28.7	1.5:1
Indianapolis, IN	82.1	53.7	28.4	1.5:1
Chicago, IL	88.0	59.9	28.1	1.5:1
Bergen–Passic, NJ	76.2	52.2	24.0	1.5:1
Philadelphia, PA–NJ	70.2	47.4	22.8	1.5:1
Oakland, CA	63.9	41.6	22.3	1.5:1
San Francisco, CA	61.4	39.7	21.7	1.5:1
Pittsburgh, PA	68.6	39.7	21.7	1.5:1
San Jose, CA	59.2	38.3	20.9	1.5:1
Kansas City, MO–KS	57.1	37.1	19.6	1.5:1
Hartford, CT	56.2	37.7	18.5	1.5:1

(Continues)

TABLE 6.2 (*Continued*)

Metropolitan statistical area	Women-owned firms	All firms	Absolute difference	Relative difference
Denver, CO	56.9	38.6	18.3	1.5:1
Atlanta, GA	112.7	78.1	34.6	1.4:1
Portland–Vancouver, OR–WA	121.2	88.7	32.5	1.4:1
Charlotte–Gastonia–Rock Hill, NC–SC	104.8	73.6	31.2	1.4:1
Greensboro–Winston–Salem–High Point, NC	87.4	61.8	25.6	1.4:1
Houston, TX	81.3	56.8	24.5	1.4:1
Austin–San Marcos, TX	79.2	55.4	23.8	1.4:1
Dallas, TX	74.3	51.3	23.0	1.4:1
Baltimore, MD	82.6	60.8	21.8	1.4:1
Detroit, MI	74.2	53.0	21.2	1.4:1
New York, NY	67.8	47.5	20.3	1.4:1
Milwaukee–Waukesha, WI	67.2	47.1	20.1	1.4:1
Newark, NJ	64.6	45.7	18.9	1.4:1
St. Louis, MO–IL	62.9	44.8	18.1	1.4:1
Washington, DC–MD–VA–WV	87.6	69.6	18.0	1.3:1
Boston, MA–NH	58.5	43.4	15.1	1.3:1
Minneapolis–St. Paul, MN	78.0	62.6	15.4	1.2:1

Source: National Foundation for Women Business Owners, using data published by the U.S. Bureau of the Census, http://www.nfwbo.org/rr012t4.html.

insurance and real estate. Despite the rapid growth of women-owned enterprises, women of all ethnic backgrounds continue to encounter difficulty in the key area of access to credit. While nearly half of both female and male business owners have access to bank credit, men have access to larger amounts. About 43% of female-owned as compared with 37% of male-owned businesses had access to less than $25,000 in credit, and women were less likely to have used credit in the last year than men (27% versus 34%). For women of color, credit circumstances were even worse. Only 50% of women of color had bank credit as compared with 60% of Caucasian women business owners.[101] Perhaps as a result of their limited access to credit and other resources, "Women continue to be leaders in capitalizing on non-traditional ways of doing business" including home-based operations, which account for almost half of all women-owned businesses.[102] In 1982, women founded their businesses with about half the capital used by men ($10,505 versus $20,717).[103] However, men and women were about equal (80%) in the fraction who started their business from scratch as opposed to buying it.[104]

At least among whites, marriage was associated with a woman's greater likelihood of getting a loan from a bank and reduced reliance on family-based loans, even though marriage would seemingly increase the pool of relatives from whom one might borrow money. Hence, along with its other economic benefits, being married is also allied with better access to bank loans for women. In 1982, married nonminority women were much more likely to have received bank loans for business start-up than were never-married women, who tended to rely on family funds.[105] For married women, 63% received bank loans as compared with only 44% of never-married women. In contrast, 42% of never-married women used family loans while only 26% of married women relied on them. Married women tended to be older, while never-married women had higher levels of education.[106] According to a survey of 679 female business owners, 29% of black women, 37% of Asian women, 45% of Native American and Alaskan Native women, 49% of Caucasian women, and 51% of Hispanic women borrowed funds for business start-up.[107]

In sum, the rapid growth in women's business ownership is an encouraging trend, clearly yielding income and creating jobs. However, female entrepreneurs, like those of minority groups in general, continue to face serious obstacles. Their businesses are disproportionately home-based, labor intensive, service oriented, and lacking in capital, especially from banks (see Chapter 9). Accordingly, while many observers contend that increasing numbers of women do find autonomy and economic rewards in self-employment, those skeptical about the potential for self-employment to solve the economic problems of disadvantaged groups insist that the growth of self-employment reflects a desperate, if creative, attempt on the part of women, minorities, and others to earn a living in an economy in which good jobs are increasingly scarce, especially for those lacking degrees in business or engineering.[108] The economist Timothy Bates,[109] for example, argues that ethnic businesses that come into being through communal funding (a pattern common among ethnic women with limited access to capital) are the most likely to fail. Further, he concludes that even if viable, most such operations should not be considered successful, but rather as instances of underemployment.

However, according to the SBA,[110] "top growth industries of women-owned business between 1987 and 1996 were construction, wholesale trade, transportation, communications, agribusiness and manufacturing"—enterprises not associated with the "pink collar ghetto." Accordingly, evidence indicates that although women in general and ethnic women in particular continue to face challenges as entrepreneurs, the growing rate of women-owned businesses provides increasing numbers with opportunities and working conditions that they find desirable.

Families and Transnationalism

In recent years, an approach called *transnationalism* has been advanced by scholars to comprehend contemporary migration and ethnic behavior.[111] Stressing the increasing globalization of political, economic, social, and cultural life, the speed and low cost of modern communications and transportation, and the growing acceptance of expatriates in the polity of many nations, the concept of transnationalism

TABLE 6.3   Percentage Share of Women-Owned Firms by Metropolitan Area, 1996

Metropolitan area	Percentage share of women-owned firms	Overall ranking
Phoenix–Mesa, AZ	40.6	1
Seattle–Bellevue–Everett, WA	40.0	2
Oakland, CA	39.8	3
Denver, CO	39.8	3
Portland–Vancouver, OR–WA	39.8	3
Washington, DC–MD–VA–WV	39.5	6
Tampa–St, Petersburg–Clearwater, FL	39.4	7
Norfolk–Virginia Beach–Newport News, VA	39.1	8
San Francisco, CA	39.0	9
Sacramento, CA	39.0	9
West Palm Beach–Boca Raton, FL	38.6	11
Riverside–San Bernardino, CA	38.5	12
San Diego, CA	38.2	13
Ft. Lauderdale, FL	38.2	13
Orlando, FL	38.0	15
Salt Lake City–Ogden, UT	38.0	15
Baltimore, MD	37.9	17
San Jose, CA	37.7	18
Oklahoma City, OK	37.6	19
Los Angeles–Long Beach, CA	37.3	20
Minneapolis–St. Paul, MN	37.3	20
Indianapolis, IN	37.2	22
New Orleans, LA	37.1	23
Kansas City, MO–KS	37.0	24
New York, NY	36.7	25
Columbus, OH	36.7	25
Atlanta, GA	36.6	27
Orange County, CA	36.6	27
St. Louis, MO–IL	36.6	27
Chicago, IL	36.5	30
Ft. Worth–Arlington, TX	36.2	31
Detroit, MI	36.0	32
Milwaukee–Waukesha, WI	36.0	32
Austin–San Marcos, TX	36.0	32
Dallas, TX	35.7	35

(*Continues*)

TABLE 6.3 (*Continued*)

Metropolitan area	Percentage share of women-owned firms	Overall ranking
Miami, FL	35.7	35
Cincinnati, OH–KY–IN	35.4	37
San Antonia, TX	35.3	38
Houston, TX	35.0	39
Hartford, CT	35.0	39
Boston, MA–NH	34.9	41
Cleveland–Lorain–Elyria, OH	34.9	41
Nashville, TN	34.4	43
Charlotte–Gastonica–Rock Hill, NC–SC	34.2	44
Greenboro–Winston–Salem–High Point, NC	33.9	45
Nassau–Suffolk, NY	33.5	46
Philadelphia, PA–NJ	33.4	47
Newark, NJ	33.0	48
Bergen–Passic, NJ	32.6	49
Pittsburgh, PA	31.7	50

Source: National Foundation for Women Business Owners, using data published by the U.S. Bureau of the Census, http://www.nfwbo/org/rr012t3.html.

emphasizes the various networks and links (demographic, political, economic, cultural, familial) that exist between two or more locations. From this perspective, migration is not a single, discrete event involving movement from one geographically and socially bounded locality to another. Instead, transnational communities embody and exchange concerns, relationships, resources, needs, and often people immersed in multiple settings. "Transmigrants take actions, make decisions and develop subjectivities and identities embedded in networks of relationships that connect them to two or more nation states."[112]

Because migrant families often maintain social ties with relatives in other settings, they are key actors in transnational processes. Such ties play important roles in shaping ethnic economic arrangements. For example, remittances are often sent home, links to family members overseas provide resources for importing or exporting goods and/or capital, and eventual plans to either return or unite in the host society shape economic behavior. Transnational networks bring in workers with needed skills as well as those willing to accept low-level jobs that more seasoned family members reject. Finally, high repute enjoyed during respites in the home country allows migrant workers to tolerate disesteemed jobs and stigmatized status in the country of settlement.

Transnationals can be very innovative, introducing new products and ways of doing business in countries of origin and settlement.[113] For example, rather than accepting minimum wage jobs in the United States or Canada, Dominican, Chinese, or Korean immigrants get together with relatives and compatriots to form businesses that import and market goods supplied by partners overseas.[114] In some cases, these enterprises are created with resources of offshore capital and advice.[115] As migrants and their relatives and associates at home mix formal and informal economic endeavors to produce transnational entrepreneurship, with loans, goods, business techniques, standards of consumption, and workers crossing borders in both directions, they often take advantage of economic, political, and cultural differences between nations. By providing information and lowering the cost of migration, such networks allow their members a means of escaping the constraints generally associated with regional or national economic conditions. As such, transnationalism offers a potential challenge to the economic platitude "capital is mobile and labor is fixed."[116] Nonini and Ong[117] describe this as "guerrilla transnationalism"—a strategy used by families and groups to resist the nation-states and global corporations that would limit their economic options.

The literature generally describes transnationalism as a strategy by which disadvantaged groups "resist incorporation into the bottom of the racial order in the United States" or elude other social obstacles, such as undocumented status.[118] However, the use of transnational family arrangements is not limited to poor migrants. Some legal, prosperous, and high-status groups—including Chinese, Koreans, Israelis, and South Asians—employ them as well.[119] In his book on Chinese entrepreneurs, Bernard Wong[120] asserts "The very rich, out of economic necessity, have globalized their families along with their businesses." Hence, we might conclude that while a group's low rank in the American racial hierarchy can contribute to their preservation of extranational identities and affiliations, the maintenance of transnational ties by relatively comfortable groups shows that other factors are involved as well.

Families from diverse nationalities (Dominicans, Israelis, Trinidadians, Puerto Ricans, Taiwanese, Indians, Haitians) have been noted for their maintenance of international networks used by family members to shuttle between the United States and the country of origin in order to maximize economic opportunities, expose children to multiple cultural environments, attend to economic holdings, and access an optimal mix of educational and health services. In his study of Haitians in the United States, Alex Stepick[121] describes children as "social cement": "Central to all Haitian families and non-family relationships are children. . . . Haitians view children as intrinsically delightful and critical to establishing social ties among adults." Family-based transnationalism is further reflected in the increasingly common practice of "astronaut" parents and "parachute" children who reside on different continents in order to access an ideal combination of economic and educational opportunities and cultural environments, all the while relying on recurrent air travel to maintain family unity.[122] However, although multinational links provide families useful options and resources, it is important to note that they may also yield multiple obligations that are additional sources of strain and conflict.[123]

Generational Effects on Ethnic Economies

Generational relations are another important, family-related element in ethnic economies. Children are a major economic resource and a determinant of consumption in ethnic families. Through forms of sponsorship and inheritance, economic opportunities are passed on or lost. Family members provide their children with economic skills (including class and ethnic resources), introduce them to occupational contacts, and give them businesses, land, and other holdings. For example, many well-paid, unionized occupations—such as auto assembly or dock work—can be acquired only through the referral of an employed relative.

Generational exchange of economically relevant resources links members of ethnic families together. Children comply with parental (and often communal) standards in order to inherit such resources. At the same time, taking an interest in the economic institutions that they have developed, the older generation becomes deeply involved with and committed to their heirs, who are those most capable of preserving the family legacy. And children often provide economic support for elderly relatives.

However, with each additional generation, conflicts within family businesses tend to increase and rates of self-employment decline.[124] For example, a 1994 survey found that issues of contention between generations nearly doubled between the first and third generation.[125] Similarly, children may reject economic activities that parents have selected for them in ethnic ownership or ethnic-controlled economies. However, intergenerational conflict is not always the reason for children abandoning their parents' economic niches. In many cases, parents feel that their career path is an undesirable one. They make conscious efforts to keep offspring away from the family occupation and instead encourage educational achievement as a path to other careers.[126]

In a significant body of work on Illinois farm families, the historian Sonya Salamon found important differences among communities made up of U.S.-born farmers of German and Anglo-Saxon ancestry. The German "yeoman" communities, which were established during the nineteenth century by chain migration from common sources, placed a high value on stability. Through conjoint church membership, strong, often ethnically exclusive communal ties, limited but lifelong commitment to a select few local institutions (church, school, and village), and inheritance patterns that stressed retaining family land ownership, the German families maintained viable communities and held onto their relatively small farms.[127]

In contrast, the Anglo-Saxons' approach to farming was more innovative, individualistic, and profit-oriented. Their settlements, which were established by persons lacking previous ties, reflected less commitment to the community per se. Many Anglo-Saxons developed greater landholdings than did German farmers. Moreover, their involvement in local businesses, schools, and churches was more extensive but sustained only as long as required to achieve specific goals associated with children's education or business growth. As a consequence, their communities were less permanent. Former residents became absentee landlords as farmers retired in the Sun Belt and their children pursued urban careers. Salamon argues that the importance of the yeoman tradition is often overlooked by agricultural economists, who are trained to assume that all farmers operate as profit-maximizing entrepreneurs. She asserts that ethnic preferences "must be taken seriously in explaining the direction family farms and rural communities will take in the future."[128]

Not only are the yeoman farm communities more viable than those of other groups, but according to Salamon's estimates from the 1980 census, the Midwest farm population is over one-half German, and descendants of Germans now account for over one-fourth of all farms in the United States.[129] Hence, this case study reveals an enduring ethnic economy not among foreign-born workers and entrepreneurs in the expanding service economy of a "gateway city" but, rather, in the rural Midwest among the descendants of nineteenth century "old immigrants."

Of course German farmers in Illinois are not the only American ethnic group that effectively allocates resources toward securing its children's futures. The economist Barry Chiswick[130] argues that several U.S.-born groups (including Jews, Chinese, Japanese, and Caribbean blacks) with low fertility rates, urban residence, relatively high education levels, and low labor force participation rates by mothers when children are small have done especially well with regard to "schooling, earnings and rates of return from schooling" as compared with other ethnic groups not following these behaviors. This pattern reflects "parental investments (implicit and explicit) in the home-produced component of child quality" and appears to be an especially successful means of intergenerational transfer of assets.[131]

In his book on Latino gangs in southern California, Vigil demonstrates that family members—often uncles—train their nephews in economically relevant skills of gang life, that gang involvement is often multigenerational, and that gangs offer family-like support for both boys and girls lacking it in their families of origin.[132]

In a study of Jewish philanthropy in metro Detroit, Gold interviewed a leading volunteer who described how his grandmother promised to give each of her grandchildren a sum of money on the condition that the child participate in Jewish education until graduation from high school. Not only did the respondent go on to receive his grandmother's gift, but he continues to dedicate much of his time to Jewish communal service.[133] Jews are noted for their intergenerational economic continuity in both philanthropy and self-employment. This involvement is based in families.[134]

In fact, familial- and gender-based patterns of volunteerism and philanthropy are documented among various ethnic groups. Gender is often vital to the intergenerational exchange of resources because women generally outlive men, and therefore play especially important roles in allocating family assets to both charities and inheritors. Further, many philanthropic organizations are arranged according to participants' gender, age, and marital status. Finally, several studies reveal that women view philanthropy in a manner distinct from men.[135]

Families, Assimilation, and Segmented Assimilation

Ethnic groups vary in the degree to which they both attempt to and succeed at passing economic and cultural skills, identities, and resources on to future generations. Parents may hope that children maintain group-specific cultural outlooks, religious affiliations, linguistic skills, and occupational orientations. However, assimilation is a very powerful force in American society, and children often reject the patterns of their parents in favor of those of the peer group and the larger society.[136] Among many ethnic groups, for example, rates of intermarriage approach 50%, reducing ethnic continuity. And even when the younger generation chooses to retain their ethnic membership, they may express belonging in ways that separate them from the social and economic orientations of their elders.

A significant body of research describes the process of segmented assimilation, wherein racially defined immigrant youth often adopt the oppositional cultural and economic orientation of their native-born, coethnic peers, rather than that of the white majority. In so doing, they may also reject their parents' social and economic strategies.[137] From this perspective, the context of assimilation and the possession of class resources have important effects on economic mobility. When immigrant children assimilate into racialized "underclass" settings where enthusiasm for schoolwork is berated as "selling out" or "acting white," retaining the mobility-oriented outlook and "adherence to traditional family values" of the ethnic group may enhance life chances.[138] "In such a situation, ethnicity itself can be a resource; indeed it may be the only resource available."[139] In contrast, those ethnic youth whose families "have sufficient human capital or financial capital [to move into middle-class suburbs] may find immediate assimilation to the host society advantageous."[140]

MICRO DIMENSIONS

Much of the research summarized earlier views families as aggregates and assumes that they maintain mutually beneficial practices with regard to the sharing of work and assets. While this may be the case for some, a growing body of scholarship suggests that economic arrangements involving families are not always marked by cooperation, egalitarianism, and distributive justice. Rather, work, reward, and decision making are often allotted in very inegalitarian ways within families, making them locations of conflict, negotiation, exploitation, and frequent realignment. In fact, dissatisfaction with or exclusion from family-based economic arrangements is often both a motive for migration itself and the driving force behind the creation of ethnic economic institutions, such as women's rotating credit associations, mutual support networks, gangs, and collectivities among the disaffiliated.[141]

Working within a micro tradition, a number of scholars have critically examined economic relationships within ethnic families and gender groups. They present a detailed picture of compromise, cooperation, and renegotiation that exists within ethnic families, households, and gender groups. Such studies have been critical of the new economics of migration perspective, seeing it as simplistic and offering a unitary depiction of family dynamics and an overly economistic understanding of family behavior.[142]

Central to many such studies is a concern with the complex, gender-based processes of negotiation and realignment—within both families and ethnic communities—that shape patterns of adaptation. For example, Hondagneu-Sotelo criticizes the view that migrant families are harmonious, cooperative units with common orientations and interests, pointing out that because they operate "under the implicit assumption of the household model—that all resources, including social ones are shared equally among household and family members—studies imply that married women automatically benefit from their husbands' social resources and expertise."[143] Another scholar takes an even stronger position, arguing that exploited female labor is the key to flourishing ethnic economies: "Those ethnic groups deemed to be more 'successful' in the business world than others are characterized by social structures which give easier access to female labor subordinated to patriarchal control mechanisms."[144]

In direct contradiction to the preceding assertion, several studies indicate that the more affluent an ethnic group, the *lower* the rate of women's labor force participation. For example, in a regression analysis of 1980 census data on Korean, Filipino, other minority, and native-born and foreign-born white women in Los Angeles, Lee and Karageorgis[145] determined that "the higher a husband's earnings, the lower the likelihood that his wife worked, regardless of ethnicity." Although female labor is central to many ethnic economies, including those of Koreans, Dominicans, and Colombians, it does not appear to be a universal resource.[146] Israeli men, for example, have the second highest rate of self-employment in the United States, and earnings that far exceed the average for all foreign-born men. (Israeli men's earnings surpass even those of native-born whites in Los Angeles, one of their principal points of settlement.) Yet Israeli women have much lower rates of involvement in ethnic businesses than men and rates of labor force participation that are lower in the United States than those maintained in the country of origin.[147] Hence, Israelis' affluence is achieved without heavy dependence on Israeli women's labor.[148] The same pattern exists among other Middle Eastern groups as well, which reveal high rates of self-employment but limited female participation. Among Armenians, Arabs, and Iranians in Los Angeles, female labor force participation rates all fall below 50%.[149]

Detailed observations suggest that women—whether migrating alone or with families—often have very different opportunities, resources, concerns, and reactions to migration than men and, accordingly, follow distinct adaptive strategies.[150] "Men and women in the same family may use different network resources, sometimes at cross purposes. These networks are significant for both migration processes and settlement outcomes."[151] As a result of this body of research, we understand better how family negotiation is vital in shaping ethnic families' economic adaptation.

It is often asserted that men's identity is most strongly associated with work, whereas women have multiple sources of identity, reflecting their concern with income as well as important relationships.[152] A study investigating gender and satisfaction with American society among Vietnamese refugees, for example, found that men's contentment was directly predicted by economic concerns such as employment, financial well-being, availability of health care, and ability to speak English. For women, however, these factors had "the least influence" on their sense of satisfaction with the host society. Instead, they were most concerned with their relationships to significant others.[153] Hence, men and women may evaluate successful adaptation according to distinct criteria, with men focusing on economic issues alone and women considering a broader range of consequences.

There is some debate on how the labor and earnings of men and women are distributed. The new economics of migration view suggests that all members of the family benefit. Another body of findings argues that men often spend savings on leisure, including beer, leaving women to perform domestic labor and purchase necessities.[154] Finally, a third body of work submits that men often provide basic sustenance for the family, while women's earnings and especially their labor—which to a considerable degree are beyond men's control—are devoted to maintaining status, reputation, and cultural production according to standards determined by women themselves.[155] For example, among Pakistani migrants in England, Werbner[156] found that male income was used to fulfill basic needs, whereas women's earnings were used for gifts and savings, and this "extra" consumption was vital for establishing family prestige.

An additional flaw with the new economics position uncovered by in-depth fieldwork is that it overlooks the difficulties and trade-offs families encounter when their members pursue specific economic strategies: Going abroad, working long hours, or otherwise seeking economic stability and advancement entail sacrifice and adjustment. In her study of black immigrants in New York City, Waters determined that family solidarity and children's life chances were sometimes impaired by financially motivated migration and separation:

> Many families are composed of single working mothers and children. These mothers have not been able to supervise their children as much as they would like, and many do not have extended family members or close friends available to help them with discipline and control. . . . The generational conflict which often ensues tends to create greater pressure for students to want to be 'American' [in terms of aspirations, consumption, and work ethic] to differentiate themselves from parents.[157]

Paradoxically, then, the parents' economic plans are rejected by the children who are its intended beneficiaries.

Negotiation within Families

As ethnic families confront new social and economic circumstances, members' access to resources is transformed. In response, families renegotiate gender-based and generational roles and responsibilities, decision-making processes, and the nature of ethnic identity. Fine-grained studies examining this process have found that in most cases, as women's independent income increases, so does their power within the family.[158] Pedraza's review concluded that though paid work, many Latinas and Asian women gain both income and family power even though they frequently lacked a premigration tradition of wage work, were often undocumented, and had to accept low-level jobs in the United States.[159] Such women preferred to stay on in the United States even though male members of their families wanted to return home, where they had more gender-based power and were not subject to racism.[160] Such women often used their newfound resources to support rather than directly challenge their husbands in order preserve family stability and their own reputation.[161] "Although immigrant women created female ethnic organizations, their collective action fostered community solidarity, not female autonomy."[162]

Among impoverished female immigrants, entry into the labor market grants them additional funds and family power. In contrast, more economically advantaged women from Israel and Iran, whose family resources permitted them to remain outside of the labor market, encountered a great deal of difficulty in the United States. Freed from economic responsibilities, these women were charged with the task of creating a congenial environment for their families within American suburbs. However, lacking extensive knowledge of American society or access to familial or coethnic networks, they found this to be a daunting task. As a result, these Middle Eastern exiles develop a variety of coethnic women's activities. Despite the vitality that women-built organizations bring, among Israelis, it is women rather than men who want to return home.[163]

Male immigrants, especially those from relatively prestigious strata in the country of origin, sometimes become heavily involved in compensatory status-building activities in the United States, leaving to women the task of supporting the family. For example, Soviet Jewish, Vietnamese, Korean, and South Asian male immigrants who were professionals prior to migration often suffer status loss in the United States. Their wives support the family while the husbands engage in communal activism, religious ritual, or the acquisition of professional employment to boost their self-image.[164] A recent Canadian study found that immigrant wives have especially high rates of labor force participation upon arrival, suggesting that "wives in immigrant families help finance their husbands' human-capital investments."[165] Some of this division of labor may be externally imposed rather than freely chosen: When ethnic business networks are male-dominated, even if a woman is the owner of an enterprise, access to network-based resources can only be acquired by her husband.[166] On the other hand, women may posses advantages as well. Dallalfar[167] states that within the Iranian community, the potential to run businesses from home is only available to women. Men's economic pursuits must be carried out in a separate location, at additional cost.

Changes in Gender Expectations by Generation

In his pivotal article, James Coleman[168] stresses the importance of social capital in ethnic families' transferring human capital to their children. Among a variety of ethnic groups (as well as native-born whites), patriarchal traditions have favored the provision of sons with more means than daughters. However, scholars observing immigrant families adapt to the American environment frequently record a reformulation of such traditions in only one generation. Parents who were raised in an environment of gender inequality and maintain this pattern among themselves, nevertheless treat their sons and daughters equally with regard to education and devote as many resources to their daughters' development of prestigious credentials and successful careers as to their sons'. Min[169] notes that among foreign-born Koreans, almost twice as many men completed college as women (47 to 26%). However, their U.S.-born children are marked by only a 5% difference in their graduation rates (39% for men versus, 34% for women). This rapid change can be attributed to both a shift in parental attitudes and their realization that women have more career opportunities in the United States than was the case in the country of origin.

Still, a fully egalitarian outlook has yet to develop. Korean American parents continue to enforce different expectations on daughters and sons in terms of housework, with girls facing more extensive demands. In addition, parents maintain gender stereotypes in leisure as well, encouraging boys to become active in sports while favoring music as an appropriate extracurricular activity for girls. Party to a less patriarchal culture than Koreans, Filipino daughters receive even greater familial pressure for achievement than their brothers, which provides them with opportunities as well as a high level of stress.[170] A similar pattern is noted among Vietnamese. Prior to migration, Vietnamese women had less access to education and were far more likely to be illiterate than Vietnamese men. However, in the United States, unmarried Vietnamese women have lower dropout rates and were more likely to be in college than married or unmarried Vietnamese men. Data collected in a New Orleans Vietnamese enclave revealed that girls had much higher grade point averages than their male peers. The study's authors attribute this transformation to a combination of familial and communal support for achievement as well as the presence of educational opportunities unavailable in the country of origin.[171]

Finally, another group with a tradition of gender equality—African Americans—has been able to provide its daughters with a degree of insulation against the commonly reported decline in achievement motivation experienced by white and Hispanic girls around the onset of puberty.[172] This factor may be behind black women's recent record of accomplishment in higher education and earnings as compared with both black men and white women.[173]

Conflict within Gender Groups

Although some studies of ethnic families assume that conflicts will be between genders, this is not always the case. Among many groups, gender-based social roles are enforced by same-sex elders. For Indian and Pakistani immigrants, for example, migration allows younger women to escape the domination of older female relatives who impose inflexible social mores. In Western settings, young women earn their own money, develop personal networks, and protect their daughters from limiting expectations. In two studies, Indian migrant "wives were found to be more satisfied with their marriages than their husbands. This may be due to freedom from the social control and authority of elders in the extended family."[174] For some women, this freedom came as a mixed blessing. "It was true that by migrating to the United States, young women escaped harsh mother-in-laws and felt 'freed from the elders' but also found themselves farther away from the mothers and sisters they loved."[175]

In adjusting to an environment defined by individualism, immigrant sons and daughters from collective cultures battle their parents over ownership of wages. In various groups, sons purchase a measure of freedom by paying their mothers half their wages. As a consequence, "[c]onflict over daughters' wages became the most common source of generational conflict, pitting daughters against mothers as often as against fathers."[176] Another source of generational conflict among women is courtship. Although it varies among nationality groups, ethnic parents generally seek to protect daughters' virginity and sexual innocence, as well as to control their choice of partners. The availability of wages is a central issue, since self-supporting daughters are less subject to familial authority than are those lacking an independent income. "Here too, daughters often wrestled power from their mothers as well as from their fathers; they challenged not patriarchy but traditions of family oligarchy."[177]

Evading the Ethnic Family

As a result of family conflicts, the sons and daughters of ethnic families sometimes limit their connections with the ethnic community, accepting native-born peers as a reference group and associating with them in work, social life, and courtship.

Marriage patterns evidence this larger pattern. By the 1930s and 1940s, about a quarter of all immigrant sons and daughters married outside of their nationality, most often to other second-generation coreligionists: Irish with Polish, Lutheran Germans with Lutheran Finns, German and Polish Jews, and so forth.[178] This propensity has increased in terms of both numbers and social distance between partners. According to the 1990 census, less than 50% of native-born Chinese, Japanese, Korean, or Filipino married women age 25–34 in Los Angeles were married to a man of their own nationality.[179] Similar rates of intermarriage are reported for Latinos and Jews.[180]

While immigrant groups often have lower rates of divorce than the native born, a significant body of research suggests that the stress associated with adaptation to the United States precipitates family conflicts and domestic abuse, leading to divorce.[181] This finding is consistent with the high rates of family dissolution found among native-born minority groups generally attributed to the extensive social and economic stress they confront.[182] As a result of intermarriage and divorce, the nature and meaning of ethic families are transformed economically and otherwise.

CONCLUSIONS

This chapter has shown that family and gender factors are of clear importance to ethnic economic life, determining patterns of economic integration and family adjustment on micro-, midrange, and macro levels. The gender and family characteristics of ethnic groups differ greatly, as do customs, class and ethnic resources, and strategies for coping with economic concerns. Nevertheless, forms of family-based cooperation and strategizing generally offer valuable economic benefits to group members.

Family-based bonds, traditions, and shared goals often provide ethnic groups with a degree of stability otherwise unavailable. While families frequently bear the burden of difficult economic circumstances and are marked by conflict among their members, the links among their members offer a basis of endurance, involvement, and mutual support. Hoping to survive and to increase their income, family workers may accept exploitative conditions that would not be tolerated by unrelated employees. At the same time, family members use their influence to improve their lot or protect the next generation from exploitative conditions while maintaining traditions that they see as important.

The array of ethnic family and gender patterns reveals many approaches to the problems of social and economic adaptation. To earn a living, Koreans, Cubans, and Middle Easterners rely on entrepreneurship, while Filipinos and West Indians sustain high rates of labor force participation, both with a good degree of success. To foster children's educational achievement, Cubans and Soviet Jews maintain close physical proximity among several generations. In contrast,

Caribbeans (Haitians, Trinidadians, Jamaicans, Dominicans) maintain broadly inclusive family networks that involve fictive kin and extended transnational families to care for and educate their descendants. To maintain family solidarity and religious continuity, the Amish prohibit education past the eighth grade. Several populations rely heavily on women's work in family businesses and wage labor, whereas others achieve substantial incomes with lower rates of female labor force participation. Even groups marked by severe disadvantages—including inner-city blacks, Hmong, and undocumented Mexicans and Central Americans—are able to mobilize needed resources through familial- and gender-based ties.

Finally, it is important to note variations in family strategies over time and generation. Groups whose first generation is characterized by high rates of self-employment often reveal a substantial reduction by the second generation; migrant nationalities maintaining significant differences in the education of men and women adopt an egalitarian approach within years of arrival; and the children of immigrants reject the economic strategies of their parents, develop new ways of demonstrating group affiliation, and marry outside of the ethnic populations as often as within. And while pundits praise the mobility-fostering power of certain ethnic family forms, academic research and autobiographical accounts reveal the tension, ambivalence, and discomfort experienced by those growing up within them.[183]

Families are collective agents. Their collectivism is usually beneficial, and the class and ethnic resources that they provide are vital to ethnic economies and to group survival, even if the costs and benefits thereof are distributed in unequal ways. In this light, it may be most productive to understand the family and gender arrangements of ethnic groups as settings wherein group strategies are defined and deployed, not in terms of individual outcomes. Further, we should remember that ethnic family and gender norms are in constant flux. In time, past inequalities may be redressed or resolved. For example, women-owned businesses are growing rapidly, suggesting that women do have the potential to achieve autonomy. Many "problems" associated with ethnic family and gender arrangements may be temporary and the result of the larger society and economy, not the group itself. As a consequence, the ethnic family and community often provides a ready, if imperfect, shelter in an otherwise hostile world.

As the historian Donna Gabaccia notes in her study of women, gender, and immigrant life in the United States, the adaptation of ethnic families involves a process of optimizing social and economic resources presented by both group-specific contexts and those of the larger society. "[T]he main challenge was . . . to claim new forms of power—whether in the form of an individual wage, the choice of a spouse, or leisure time—without losing older . . . modes of influence within community and kinship networks."[184]

Voter registration campaign at the annual Arab-American community festival in Dearborn, Michigan. The event is supported by numerous ethnic businesses and community organizations.

Arab-American produce stall, West Side Market, Cleveland, Ohio. Arabs specialize in food-related businesses in the U.S. In earlier generations, most of these stalls were run by Italians and Eastern Europeans. Arab entry into this niche reveals the process of ethnic succession.

Detroit firemen demonstrate firehouse cooking at the Michigan Folklife Festival, 1998. Irish, African-American, and several other groups have developed ethnic-controlled economies in public employment.

Vermont Avenue, Los Angeles, 1992. During the urban unrest following the acquittal of the police officers who beat Rodney King, thousands of ethnic businesses were looted and burned. Korean-American enterprises, like these in Koreatown, bore the brunt of the violence.

Russian drug store, West Hollywood, California. Soviet Jews, an elderly refugee group with eligibility for government health care subsidies, consume a considerable amount of health care services. Coethnic doctors, pharmacists, and other service providers cater to their needs.

Tzofim (Israeli scouts), Los Angeles, 1992. Rather than merge into the larger American Jewish community, Israeli immigrants in Los Angeles maintain an element of cultural autonomy through activities such as this. Many of these children's parents are self-employed, and their self-employment facilitates ethnic independence.

CHAPTER 7

Ethnic Economies and Ethnic Communities

INTRODUCTION

This chapter addresses the broader relationship between ethnic economies and ethnic communities. Ethnic economies provide coethnic communities with benefits and liabilities beyond the direct assignment of jobs or their creation through self-employment. Such benefits include the allocation of social welfare (health care, burial benefits, loan funds, legal advice, food, social services), education, the building of ethnic institutions, communal leadership and advocacy, cultural innovation and maintenance, and the establishment of neighborhoods.

In return, communities contribute the ethnic context. As discussed in Chapter 5, communities provide ethnic economies with labor, loan funds, and consumers. In addition, they establish and maintain the notions of group culture, trust, and solidarity that allow ethnic economies to exist, fill ethnic neighborhoods and other social spaces, and grant status and legitimacy to major actors in ethnic economies—philanthropists, unionists, party bosses, real estate developers, and the like.[1] Accordingly, the relationship between ethnic economies and ethnic communities is often symbiotic. Expressing this sentiment, a Dominican business owner in Boston told the sociologist Peggy Levitt[2] that "[I]t is the role of the businessperson to give back a little of what they have received from the community."

In many cases, the non-job-related communal impacts of ethnic economies affect far more people than are employed within them. For example, many more Jews in New York or Chinese in San Francisco (as well as members of the larger society) make use of coethnic institutions, agencies, businesses, and neighborhoods than earn their living in these ethnic economies. In fact, some of the primary beneficiaries of ethnic communities, including children, the elderly, the infirmed, recently arrived immigrants, the jobless, and homemakers are not employed at all. However, through their grant of effort, funds, and in-kind donations, nonemployed persons are also major contributors to enriching the quality of ethnic communal life.

Ethnic solidarity provides group members with a common commitment and common purpose. And unlike most bases of collective organization in American society that bring together people already sharing commonalties of class, age, lifestyle, and ideology, ethnic communities often comprise a socially diverse membership. In *Habits of the Heart,* Bellah *et al.*[3] assert that in contrast to the narcissistic "lifestyle enclaves" that dominate American life, ethnic communities maintain support, mutual responsibility, and a genuinely collective outlook. At their best, they constitute "an inclusive whole, celebrating the interdependence of public and private life and the different callings of all." Drawing from his research on Cubans in Miami, Alejandro Portes[4] makes a similar point about ethnic inclusiveness, contending that migrant communities marked by class diversity—those including complementary subgroups such as entrepreneurs and workers, leaders and constituents, the settled and the recently arrived—are well-suited for the creation of extensive ethnic economies.

Several authors have observed that ethnic communal life features a moral element that mandates mutual obligation and prosocial behavior.[5] For example, Light[6] reveals that welfare activities conducted by Chinese and Japanese immigrant regional associations were run on a "moralistic rather than professional" footing. As such, the local community rather than a distant bureaucracy was responsible for service delivery. Potential for abuse is limited, since benefits that kin and associates know are not needed will not be delivered. Ethnic obligations are understood to be mutual rather than based on charity or noblesse oblige. Moreover, ethnic organizations could compel coethnics to care for their own relatives, thus relieving the broader community of this burden. Along the same lines, ethnic fraternal and rotating credit associations also maintain moral authority, because membership within them is based on a good reputation. Those who fail to conform to group standards are denied access.[7] In addition to their maintenance of informal moral obligations, many religious communities require specific contributions to the public good, such as tithing, providing interest-free loans, volunteer effort, ritual giving, and the like.[8] In return, gifts are celebrated within these ethnoreligious contexts.[9]

As expressed by the concept of bounded solidarity, members of ethnic communities realize that regardless of personal standing, their social, economic, and political fate is attached to those with whom they share group membership.[10] Upwardly mobile members understand that their own status is linked to the coethnic rank and file who are their customers, employees, and political constituents. At the same time, those of more humble means know that their contacts with the larger society are likely to be mediated by the coethnic elite—generally the only persons in the larger society with whom they have any influence or contact. Even ethnic gangs maintain strong attachments to the coethnic community.[11]

A review of historical research reveals that entrepreneurs play significant roles in the founding of communal activities.[12] However, there is also a link between ethnic economies and communal development among many populations lacking a substantial self-employment sector. The scholars of ethnic labor and political movements Kornblum,[13] Kantowicz,[14] and Delgado[15] all demonstrate the importance of collective action by workers as providing a vehicle for self-help, political incorporation, and economic mobility.

For example, Gorelick[16] argues that it was immigrant Jews' "socialism and labor militancy" that forced "businessmen, educators and politicians" to open up "ladders of mobility" prior to this group's extensive involvement in self-employment in the United States. Similarly, Karni[17] describes how socialist Finnish miners in the western Great Lakes region assembled a variety of consumer cooperatives, sources of credit, and newspapers in an explicit effort to support strikers and further "the interests of the working class."[18] In 1917, they established the Central Cooperative Exchange, which provided basic necessities, including Scandinavian-style foods, at a low cost. Because the organization was boycotted by capitalist suppliers, it had to create its own line of products. These products bore the image of a red hammer and sickle nestled within a yellow star. By the mid-1920s, Finns had established not only a network of ethnic organizations but also a successful cooperative economy, so extensive that a Finn "did not even have to shop at a non-Finnish store."[19] In each of these cases, ethnic communal organizations were created not by entrepreneurs but by another part of ethnic economy: labor movements. Ethnic concentration in industrial settings provided a context whereby labor activism (based on ethnic solidarity) could shape communal life. Such a context is clearly consistent with what we name the ethnic-controlled economy.

Although ethnicity is defined in terms of ascriptive criteria, such as language, religion, or nationality, that does not mean that all ethnic organizations necessarily promote forms of solidarity and organization that include the total ethnically defined population. Instead, ethnic communities and the organizations they create often reflect numerous class, ideological, regional, religious, gender, generational, and demographic differences included in the population.[20] Several studies suggest that political and economic entrepreneurs often make special efforts to respond to the unique needs and interests of such subgroups.[21]

The symbiotic relationship between ethnic economy and ethnic community becomes especially clear when we consider that ethnic communal ties frequently outlast a group's concentration in specific industries, unionized occupations, economic niches, or other areas of economic congregation. As a case in point, Waldinger[22] describes how Jewish New Yorkers retain patterns of economic concentration despite their abandonment of earlier areas of economic activity for newer realms of specialization. Prior to the 1970s, Jews were centered in garment industries, government employment, and petty entrepreneurship. "By 1990 Jews had entirely transformed their niche, all the while maintaining a distinctive economic role." Education, legal services, publishing, advertising, public relations, and theaters were the new niches. Areas of self-employment in which Jews were overrepresented were now limited to a few high-level professions—doctors, dentists, and engineers. The small business fields they had previously occupied are now the property of more recent immigrants. Suggesting the value of ethnic consolidation, Jews employed in niches earned more than those employed in areas of lesser Jewish density. Hence, for Jews, it appears that the benefits of flexible and enduring ethnic communities have been retained even when areas of earlier economic dominance have been replaced with new, more rewarding areas of concentration. Similarly, an array of migrant groups—including Jews, Cubans, West Indians, Lebanese, Chinese, Iranians, and Mexicans—have used premigration social solidarity to rapidly develop ethnic economies in new regions of settlement.[23]

In fact, the ability of ethnic economies to create social benefits for community members is a major reason that scholars find this topic to be worthy of exploration and analysis.[24] Those who disparage ethnic economies because of their limited ability to create numerous well-paying jobs fail to consider the many benefits ethnic economies provide in addition to employment. For example, in his discussion of social capital and self-employment, Timothy Bates[25] hopes to determine "if self-employment, in the aggregate, has accelerated or held back Asian immigrants' *adaptation* to life in the United States." (emphasis added). He seeks the answer to this question solely in terms of the earnings of the self-employed. This approach ignores the many benefits that ethnic businesses and ethnic communities provide to their members beyond earnings alone, as well as the fact that adaptation includes more than making a living per se.

In sum, the history of immigrant and ethnic groups' adaptation to the United States is to a very large extent the history of ethnic self-help built upon a symbiotic relationship between an ethnic population and its ethnic economy—broadly defined. "The ability of the American industrial economy . . . to nurture and sustain kinship and ethnic ties has been demonstrated to underscore that ethnic and family solidarity certainly has an economic base."[26]

In pointing to the broader benefits produced by ethnic economies, we do not claim that all of the impacts of ethnic economies on coethnic communities are positive, nor that ethnic communities are able to generate all the resources they require to resolve their most serious problems. Ethnic communities can and do limit social, political, and economic options for their members and, in most cases, are unable to provide all of their members with needed resources. Ethnic elites frequently manipulate the broader group for their own selfish benefit. Further, as we have noted elsewhere, demands made by ethnic communities on their economies sometimes impair those enterprises' and networks' ability to function. Finally, ethnic communities vary in both their level of communal strength and the areas in which their activism is focused. Nevertheless, in many cases, ethnic economies do offer valuable resources to their members.

MUTUAL ASSISTANCE ASSOCIATIONS

Every immigrant and ethnic population in the United States has created mutual aid associations, ranging from Japanese *tanomoshi,* to Polish and black churches of the nineteenth century, to today's new immigrant religious congregations.[27] Typically, such organizations began by providing insurance, small loans, or burial benefits and, with time, were able to offer more extensive resources. These fraternal organizations, secret societies, regional lodges, churches, and schools facilitated the development of ethnic communities and allowed members to maintain their language and cultural orientation in such a manner as to ease adjustment to American life.[28] Internal migrants, including blacks moving from the rural South to the urban North, Native Americans from Oklahoma settling in California, Mexicans migrating from Texas to the Midwest, and Jews moving from the Northeast to the Sun Belt also created organizations.[29]

Ethnic self-help reduces dependency on external entities and reduces external control.[30] This self-reliance is an important concern, because out-group help may be unavailable, carry restrictions, or be dispensed with a large measure of paternalism. Further, as the following quote indicates, within many populations the acceptance of aid from the larger society is considered to be a source of shame.

> Every Pole who accepts the help of American institutions is thus considered not only disgraced personally as a pauper, but as disgracing the whole Polish colony. . . . No individual who has preserved some self-respect will accept it [charity] from an American institution unless his traditional conceptions have been obliterated owing to the new conditions and to insufficient contact with the Polish-American group.[31]

Ethnic self-help organizations were normally led or supported by the coethnic elite, which consisted of major players in the nascent ethnic economy—shop owners, doctors, artisans, and the like. "The very earliest leaders and entrepreneurs in immigrant communities frequently achieved recognition in the larger community through their role in the establishment and running of fraternal organizations."[32] Such "fraternal associations preceded even the formation of churches and labor organizations."[33]

This pattern was remarkably consistent over a broad array of ethnic populations and locations. Most Czech and Italian fraternal heads in Chicago, as well as the core of German leaders in nineteenth-century Cincinnati, were artisans, small businessmen, craftsmen, and shopkeepers, while leaders of Bavarian, Slavonian, Polish, and Jewish groups across the United States also revealed the connection between small business ownership and communal guidance.[34] Among Chinese immigrants, "the clan was organized around a leading merchant's store. The merchant usually assumed leadership of his clan, established a hostelry above the store for his kinsmen, and provided aid, advice, comfort and shelter."[35]

In addition to income and visibility, the self-employed also have the flexibility required to pursue activism. In her study of Chaldeans in Detroit, Sengstock[36] notes that self-employment provides members of migrant communities interested in the goal of communal assistance with special advantages.

> If a man is employed in a large corporation, he cannot easily obtain employment for recently arrived relatives, especially if they do not know English. . . . With an ethnic occupation, the immigrant and his family are provided with a definite means of support. . . . The effect of an ethnic occupation extends not only to the family but to the entire community.

Given their unique orientations and concerns, ethnic women often created their own fraternal organizations. The black women's club movement was established in the 1890s as a means of promoting the well-being of black children in a segregated society and to "refute the negative images of black women then being advanced by many in the women's suffrage movement . . . who were afraid of losing white financial support if they allowed black women to partici-pate."[37] Jewish immigrant women participated in labor unions, political move-ments, and fraternal groups and created Hebrew Free Loan organizations, "the small pro-feminist investment banks that were set up around the country in the 1920s and 1930s as Jewish women's loan funds, lending money exclusively from women and to women for everything from dentists' bills to venture capital for entrepreneurs."[38] Immigrant women were also involved in the *landsmanshaftn* (hometown lodges) that were a basic component of the social and philanthropic life of immigrant Jews but generally in subordinate and segregated roles.[39] Not all accepted their secondary standing. Challenging the financial control of their hus-bands, the women's auxiliary of one Bronx-based group obtained a court order that required the organization to relinquish to women members the funds that they had contributed.[40]

As time passed, the entrepreneurs at the forefront of ethnic fraternal organiza-tions often became ambitious, sophisticated, and progressive rather than nostalgic in outlook. They not only provided resources but also shaped adaptation.

> While most local lodges had been formed by artisans and small merchants with the limited goal of mutual assistance, the drive toward national consolidations of fraternals was fueled by ambitious leaders who viewed these organizations as outlets for their en-trepreneurial energies and drives for personal gain and status. Emanating largely from those with more formal education, these career-oriented fraternalists adopted modern American business and investment procedures to increase the stability and efficiency of their growing ventures.[41]

However

> as the social distance between the classes in each group widened, those moving into
> higher social categories did not simply abandon those left behind. . . . Frequently,
> they made vigorous attempts to preach the advantages of hard work and efficiency they
> now believed explained their own success and the value of ethnic identity, an element
> which generated the cohesiveness necessary for many to succeed and attain positions of
> group leadership.[42]

Such discussion not only muted class and regional conflict within ethnic communities but also provided meaningful ties with the past and with coethnics.
These ties were much needed during times of rapid social change. Such organizations were popular among Swedes, Irish Catholics, Italians, Japanese, Jews, Yu-
goslavs, Chicanos, and Germans. While providing jobs and assistance for recent
arrivals, they also encouraged coethnics to adopt middle-class values and political
conservatism intended to further the goals of the ethnic middle class and avoid
offending American elites.

For example, in 1916, Italian business owners in San Francisco established
an Italian Welfare Agency to help newcomers from all regions. It stood in contrast
to the locally based mutual aid societies, which were parochial. Bank of America
founder A. P. Giannini worked to wean immigrants away from mutual
aid societies so that they would save in his "progressive" bank. Yugoslav and
Mexican middle classes discouraged labor activism among coethnic workers,
while the Japanese American bourgeoisie advocated the acceptance of
discrimination and residential segregation in order to avoid creating resentment
among whites.[43] In general, the fewer social and economic options available to
the rank and file, the greater the power of coethnic elites over them. For example,
pre–World War II American Chinatowns featured both robust ethnic economies
and despotic rulers. These interrelated conditions could be traced to the
discrimination, linguistic isolation, and ethnic loyalty characteristic of such
enclaves.[44]

However, communal dominance by the middle class was not universal. The
historian John Bukowczyk[45] notes that during a series of strikes in 1915 and 1916
against Standard Oil in Bayonne, New Jersey, the Polish American middle class
learned to support coethnic workers or bear the angry consequences. Accordingly, Polish merchants extended strikers credit, tavern keepers provided meeting
space, and a Polish attorney assisted with translation, leadership, and legal help.
These merchants received not only loyal patronage, but further, following a riot,
discovered that while several businesses owned by Jews and Irishmen had been
sacked, those run by fellow Poles were untouched.

Finally, as discussed in Chapter 3, it is important to note that in many ethnic
communities, distinctions between small entrepreneurs (e.g., barbers, proprietors
of newsstands, owners of fruit stands, repair shop owners, self-employed taxi dri-
vers, and garment assemblers) on the one hand, and wage laborers, on the other,
are often minimal. They live in the same apartment buildings, consume similar

quantities of the same products, socialize together, and often have comparable earnings.[46] During a lifetime, individuals frequently alternate between wage work and self-employment in response to changing economic conditions.[47] These exceptions noted, the ethnic middle class often sought to impose its agenda on co-ethnics. Nevertheless, agendas were pluralistic as competing leaders offered constituents a range of alternatives. "Inevitably, competition for members among local lodges intensified over time as various leaders sought to expand and sustain the base of influence and power."[48] Ethnic organizations moved beyond basic economic purposes to the achievement of political and ideological goals. In fact, the limited economic resources at these organizations' disposal motivated their adoption of noneconomic agendas. Often, the agendas involved what we now call ethnic mobilization. In nineteenth-century Cincinnati, for example, competing German American organizations offered different routes to the preservation of "Germanness." One hundred years later, affiliation-minded Southeast Asian refugees in California could select among a number of mutual assistance associations, each with its own take on the Vietnam War, preservation of cultural traditions, and community building in the United States.[49] Most recently, Hepner[50] describes the development of "Modern Ethiopianism," an alternative form of Rastafarianism (led by Asento Foxe, an employee of the New York State Correctional System) that offers believers a more conservative, orderly, and gender-equal approach to this faith than previously available.

Among blacks, Poles, Koreans, and several other groups, churches were the base of communal activism. In their classic study of Polish American resettlement, Thomas and Znaniecki emphasized two central points. First, the church provided a whole variety of important functions, extending far beyond the realm of religion to the provision of social services and a sense of community identification. Second, the specifically Polish character of the Church was essential to its role in the community. Although the Irish American Catholic Church was better established, had more extensive links to American society, and had a more educated staff, "its framework cannot be successfully utilized by the Poles . . . since they do not feel 'at home' in a parish whose prevalent language and mores are different and with whose members they have no social connections."[51] Churches themselves are often created by entrepreneurial immigrants, seeking to advance themselves by appealing to their compatriots' social and spiritual needs.[52]

Fraternal groups were established to achieve economic goals, and then added political purposes. In contrast, other ethnic organizations followed the opposite trajectory. The largest Polish American association, the Polish Roman Catholic Union, and the secular Polish National Alliance were both created to achieve ideological or religious goals, and added insurance programs at a later date.[53] Similarly, Cuban exiles initially created "organizations along political, religious, occupational and regional lines" and then, having established a tight-knit community, went on to build an ethnic economic enclave.[54]

ETHNIC ECONOMIES
AND ETHNIC PHILANTHROPY

Small-scale ethnic fraternal, mutual benefit, and self-help endeavors often expand into formalized philanthropic activities, involving the donation of both money and volunteer effort to communal, often charitable causes. Technically, philanthropy involves unrequited giving.[55] Yet, given our understanding of ethnic economies as symbiotic, it appears clear that donors do receive reciprocal benefits, in the form of prestige, useful social relationships (with both clients and fellow donors), and political power in return for their contributions.[56]

A variety of ethnic groups have created formalized philanthropic activities by which leading members of the community aggregate funds for collective causes. Notable among these is the American Jewish community. In 1990, American Jews raised more than $750 million for local and overseas needs. Although Jews usually make up no more than 10% of the population of a particular community, the local Jewish Federation campaign typically raises almost as much as the entire community's United Way campaign. Through philanthropy, Jews in America have built an impressive structure of communal institutions to educate their children, offer social services to their families, assist the elderly, resettle immigrants, support Israel, fight anti-Semitism, and provide a wide variety of recreational activities.

Goldscheider and Zuckerman[57] and several other scholars have pointed out that Jewish continuity and solidarity in the United States have relied on an interactive and synergetic relationship between communal attachment and institution building that was maintained through philanthropy: Jews who have valued their communities have given money to build community institutions. These institutions, in turn, have allowed for the reproduction of the community, thus creating a new generation of givers to maintain the process.[58]

Ritterband[59] asserts that "[f]or [fund-raising] solicitation to take place, one must associate with other Jews (at home or at work) through formal (affiliation with Jewish organizations) or informal ties, through a network of friends and business or professional contacts," while Tobin, Tobin, and Troderman[60] suggest that "[g]iving to Jewish philanthropies comes primarily from a sense of collective obligation."

> The data unequivocally suggest that strengthening Jewish communal ties will have long-term positive effects on Jewish philanthropy. Helping Jews meet other Jews, encouraging marriages between Jews, fostering Jewish neighborhoods: all of these efforts will promote giving to Jewish causes. The disintegration of Jewish neighborhoods and friendship circles, abetted by intermarriage, erodes giving to Jewish philanthropies.

Both Jewish religious teachings and Jewish experience emphasize a communal orientation. "Jewish tradition contains a vast literature that assumes the transcendent obligation to give."[61] Similarly, drawing on a long history of Jewish self-government in Europe and patterns of residential segregation and ethnic self-help (often reinforced by discrimination and intolerance from Gentiles), Jews have maintained a strong collective outlook in the United States. This collectivism has been reflected both in patterns of informal coethnic interaction and in the creation of a variety of religious and secular institutions that have reinforced Jews' feeling of mutual involvement and shared fate. In addition to collecting funds for these many causes, the social system of Jewish philanthropy, centered around the local Jewish Federation, provides an important vehicle by which Jews, who until recently were largely excluded from mainstream American institutions, could create their own status structure.[62]

Jewish and indeed most ethnic philanthropy works in ways that contrast with Anglo-American attitudes about money on two levels. First, the ethnic approach violates a norm about financial autonomy. Americans ordinarily keep personal financial information confidential.[63] However, within Jewish philanthropy, we find groups of men and women who do share intimate details of their lives, so much so that certain Jewish Federation activities are specifically designed for participants to share personal concerns—financial and otherwise—and conclude with an annual pledge.[64]

A second way that ethnic philanthropy contrasts with the larger society's assumptions about economic life is in its understanding of individual versus collective notions of ownership and responsibility. Within Jewish philanthropy, an individual's financial assets are not considered to be his or hers alone but, rather, are really property of the group. Federation colleagues assess an individual's holdings, suggest an appropriate level of giving (in light of the individual's own needs), and then collectively celebrate the gift. While the gift is seen as altruistic, at the same time it is also defined as collective property: the successful Jew is expected, even obliged, to share his or her wealth, connections, and talent with needy and less fortunate coethnics.[65] If a donor refuses to give at the appropriate level, he or she may be condemned or even excluded.[66]

In addition to Jews, numerous other ethnic groups are also active in philanthropy. We have already cited the vital role played by the Polish Catholic Church for Polish immigrants.[67] Black self-help and philanthropy, based largely in the church and the entrepreneurial middle class, established and supported a broad range of communal institutions including colleges, fraternal organizations, and loan funds.[68] Among them were the Freedman's Bank, with branches in more than 30 cities, and places of learning such as Spelman, Howard, Fisk, and Tuskegee. Self-help provided the basis for a range of black businesses, notably banks and insurance companies. These businesses were both essential and relatively free from competition, since white-owned firms often refused to serve blacks. In 1940, blacks held more life insurance in black insurance companies than was owned by the entire populations of several nations, including Poland, Brazil, Yugoslavia, and Mexico, all of which had populations exceeding that of black America.[69]

Between 1800 and 1900, the African Methodist Episcopal (A.M.E.) church built 20 colleges and universities. In 1908, the American Baptist Home

Missionary society established 23 black institutions of higher education, 14 of which were black owned. Further, the black community provided almost 20% of the funding for 5000 schools constructed by Sears Roebuck owner and philanthropist Julius Rosenwald for blacks.[70] Eight black fraternities and sororities formed between 1906 and 1924 "continue today to be active in philanthropy, sponsoring programs to mentor disadvantaged youths, for example, and raising money for scores of charitable endeavors." Various fraternal and mutual aid societies persist in providing similar benefits. One, the century-old Improved Benevolent Protective Order of Elks of the World, claims 450,000 members and supports a variety of causes for which it raises $1 million annually.[71] Since the 1970s, black charitable federations, such as the United Black Fund of America and the National Black United Fund, have become important venues. The former seeks to work with the United Way to ensure that black charities receive "a fair share" of a community's donations, while the latter, which raised more than $7 million in 1990, defines itself as a black alternative to the United Way.[72]

While most ethnic communal endeavors are devoted to assisting coethnics or coreligionists, ethnic philanthropy often benefits out-group members (admittedly, for reasons that are at least partly self-serving). For example, both Jewish and WASP philanthropic activities have sought to provide assistance to African Americans.[73] Similarly, hospitals, refugee resettlement agencies, schools and colleges, camps, homeless shelters, foster homes, food banks, youth programs, welfare services, and the like are created and supported by specific religious congregations to serve an ethnically diverse clientele.[74]

ETHNIC ECONOMIES AND POLITICAL LEADERSHIP

Ethnic economies provide important support for political leadership. Such support takes many forms, ranging from office holding to informal efforts to influence the political process on a group's behalf. As Light and Bonacich,[75] Min,[76] and others have pointed out, financial contributions from ethnic economies permit members of immigrant groups who are not eligible to vote to exert influence over American political decision making.[77]

Bounded ethnic communities can produce significant political autonomy. Stanford Lyman notes that

> Chinese communities in the United States have enjoyed a measure of self-government far exceeding that of other ethnic communities. . . . [A] merchant class soon became the ruling elite. . . . Because commercial success was so closely tied to social acceptance and moral probity in America, this elite enjoyed good relations with public officials. Chinatown merchants controlled immigrant associations, dispensed jobs and opportunities, settled disputes, and acted as an advocate for Chinese sojourners before white society.[78]

Resettlement, Socialization, and Mobilization

Leading figures in ethnic economies have directed the adaptive patterns of coethnics. Early this century, coreligionists' resettlement programs sought to diminish Old World traits and replace them with Americanisms. For example, Protestant, Jewish, and Catholic immigrants of the early twentieth century received strong pressure to adopt American outlooks and behavior patterns from established coreligionists who "[a]ll were advocates of . . . cooperation with the American political, economic and social establishment."[79]

This pattern is illustrated in the following discussion of Catholic and Jewish resettlement activities. Despite the manifold social, cultural, religious, and economic differences between Catholics and Jews (who constituted two of the major denominations of migrants during this time), we find some very close parallels between the two groups. At the turn of the century, established Catholics were mainly Irish, while the largest part of American Jewry was of German descent. Both groups were more Westernized and educated and had more exposure to Anglo-Saxon culture than their recently arrived southern and eastern European coreligionists. Accordingly, American Catholics and Jews encouraged the rapid Americanization of their immigrant brethren, partly in a sincere effort to aid "greenhorns," partly in an attempt to consolidate their power over the entire religious community, and partly out of fear that the presence of a large mass of unassimilated and often radical coreligionists would provoke hostility among native Protestants.[80]

> Catholics themselves embarked on Americanization campaigns in the 1920s. . . . [T]hey hoped that their . . . efforts would strengthen immigrant loyalty to the Church, . . . (act) as a means of defusing anti-Catholic sentiment. . . . And finally . . . many Catholic leaders were themselves infected with the nationalistic spirit that demanded the inculcation of patriotism and conformity to American values.[81]

German–American Jews followed a similar agenda, one heavily influenced by the settlement house movement and its emphasis on training immigrants to become self-reliant Americans. By creating institutions such as the United Hebrew Charities, the Educational Alliance (a community center), the Hebrew Immigrant Aid Society (HIAS), the Hawthorne School (a Jewish reformatory), and other Jewish communal organizations that have provided aid—ranging from job placement, interest-free loans, and health care to summer camps for recent immigrants—American Jews sought to transform eastern Europeans into Americans.

Early programs were sometimes harsh and condescending. An American Jewish publication asserted that new immigrants "must be Americanized in spite of themselves, in the mode prescribed by their friends and benefactors."[82] A major goal of the Americanizers was to "pull down the ghetto" in the Lower East Side and distribute the recently arrived around the nation, thus restricting their ability to reestablish Old World enclaves. While many of the mobility-seeking offspring of eastern European Jews complied with Americanizing activities, some were humiliated in the process. Others reacted by asserting their own identity and creating their own self-help institutions. With time, however, relations between the German and eastern European Jews smoothed, and a "wiser policy of gradual adjustment" was agreed upon—one in which immigrants themselves came to play a leading role.[83] Ultimately, conflicts were smaller than those within the Catholic community because the Jewish religion was not subject to the organizational centralization that put different nationalities of Catholics in confrontation with each other. More recently, Southeast Asian refugees who have been resettled by Evangelical Christian groups report being pressured to join the church of their sponsors.[84] Likewise, Soviet Jews, who in the eyes of their coethnic hosts lack religious knowledge and interest, sometimes complain of unwanted proselytization in the course of resettlement interactions.[85]

While conflicts between migrants and hosts have endured until the present, the sociologist Paul Ritterband[86] describes how current programs for Jewish immigrants follow an agenda that completely contradicts the approach directed toward turn-of-the-century arrivals.

> The 1880–1914 Russian Jewish immigrants were offered a network of settlement houses and other institutions designed by the earlier wave of German Jewish immigrants as a means of Americanizing their all too traditional and exotic co-religionists. By contrast, the contemporary American Jewish community, itself composed largely of descendants of earlier waves of East European immigrants, has attempted to Judaize the immigrants.

In both periods, conflicts developed as hosts directed new arrivals toward patterns of adaptation that were not of their own choosing.[87]

The elites of ethnic communities encouraged Americanization of coethnics for several self-interested reasons. As mentioned earlier, one was to avoid inflaming prejudice. German American Jews, for example, accurately predicted that a sizable influx of exotic, socialist, and Orthodox eastern European Jews would increase anti-Semitism, making life more difficult for them too. Accordingly, they created numerous resettlement programs, including the Galveston movement, which encouraged Jewish migrants to settle in Texas, far from New York, where an enormous community had already taken hold. For similar reasons, from 1908 until the early 1920s, Jewish communal leaders in New York undertook a broad-based effort called the Kehillah movement to foster Jewish adaptation and advancement during the peak years of immigration.[88]

Ethnic elites also encouraged the Americanization of coethnics, paradoxically, in order to preserve a coethnic constituency of workers, customers, and political supporters. Ethnic leaders astutely observed that coethnic migrants were rapidly adopting American customs, and if a way of combining traditional and American social forms was not developed, the ethnic mode would cease to exist altogether. As Glazer and Moynihan[89] and Greeley[90] note, Italian and Polish ethnic identities are largely a product of these groups' experiences in the United States—not the country of origin.[91] U.S.-based ethnic communities played an important role in the creation or transformation of these identities. Moreover, many newly arrived immigrants affiliate on the basis of localized feelings of connection to a family, a village, a region, or a particular religious leader or movement. American ethnic communities and organizations play a major role in transforming these specific and localized identities into more inclusive ones that are of greater political and economic utility in the new context. Once national ethnic associations took shape, goals had to be established that would transcend local interests and sustain an inclusive identity among newcomers from diverse regional and social backgrounds. "It was precisely this need that moved national fraternals to become one of the chief forces for generating a strong attachment" to groups' common origins, an attachment that was loose and poorly developed upon arrival.[92]

National fraternal organizations also encouraged Americanization because high rates of return by immigrants would deprive ethnic enterprises of their labor force and financial base and take from ethnic organizations their constituencies. Americanization, English language and sports programs were directed toward children. "National fraternals reached forward under the banner of Americanization and backward under the guise of ethnic identity in order to sustain the loyalty of large portions of immigrant communities."[93]

In all these activities, it is important to note that coethnic-run Americanizing programs were distinct from assimilation activities maintained by out-group members. American Jews and Catholics wanted their newly arrived coreligionists to speak English, dress like Americans, and express their political dispositions in American terms, but they most certainly did not want them to become Protestants. Rather, in direct opposition to assimilationists, exclusionists, and eugenicists, the goal of coethnic Americanization programs was to establish a viable ethnic community in the United States.[94]

Political Incorporation

Throughout U.S. history, ethnic groups have used communally based political power to fill their needs. The urban political machines of the nineteenth and twentieth centuries are an archetype. They provided benefits while socializing newcomers to the American political system. Based in specific communities, they maintained coalitions among a variety of ethnic groups. The basic building block of the political machine was the precinct captain. In direct communication with superiors in city hall, he maintained community contacts and provided jobs, benefits, gifts, and emergency aid in exchange for votes. This practice connected the ethnic working class to the municipal political structure. Thus, the political machine had a human face and the benefits it rendered yielded a practical basis for party building.

Of the many immigrant communities, Irish immigrants, who knew the English language and—due to their contact with the British—had a history of creating alternative political organizations, are most commonly associated with the great political machines. While the Irish nature of the political machine is overstated (Tammany Hall's "Boss Tweed" was Scottish), the Hibernians were well suited for building political machines. Established in the States prior to the vast turn-of-the-century migration, Irish Americans were able to organize and mediate between the many competing southern and eastern European nationalities that settled after 1880. As time passed, big-city machines reached out to non-European groups as well. For example, Mayor Richard Daley of Chicago, one of the last great bosses, derived much of his support from African Americans. Puerto Ricans, Mexicans, and other Latino groups, as well as Arabs and Asian Americans, have now become vital actors on the urban political landscape.[95]

Besides political machines, craft unions too have played an important role in the development of ethnic-controlled economies. During the late nineteenth century, unions were exclusionist.[96] However, the organized labor movement has also offered a key venue in which immigrant and ethnic group members have become organized and politically active, while helping them mobilize their communities and linking them to larger social institutions. For example, various industrial unions, the International Ladies Garment Workers Union (ILGWU), the United Farmworkers Union (UFW), and several public sector unions have played vital roles in bringing their ethnic constituencies into local politics while also advancing their economic interests.[97] However, with the general downturn in the entire labor movement since the late 1970s, unions have had diminishing influence in the lives of ethnic Americans in the last decades.

The political ascendancy of white ethnics was indicated by the election of Irish Catholic John F. Kennedy as president in 1960 and the passage of the Immigration Act of 1965 (against the opposition of "old American" interests such as the Daughters of the American Revolution and the National Association of Evangelicals). This law changed the national origins associated with U.S. immigration policy, thus permitting millions of previously excluded immigrants to enter the United States.[98]

From the 1950s through the 1970s, the Civil Rights movement, largely organized and led by blacks, resulted in a major expansion of opportunities for blacks and other ethnic Americans in a variety of public and private institutions. Chief accomplishments were the banning of most forms of de jure racial segregation, the abandonment of the separate-but-equal doctrine, the passage of the Voting Rights Act of 1965, and the societal rejection of racial bigotry. The Civil Rights movement and the Voting Rights Act also fostered the growth of black political power. From 1970 to 1992, the number of black elected officials grew fivefold nationwide, from fewer than 1500 to more than 7500. Major American institutions, including government agencies, the courts, public and private education, and some foundations, address the needs and concerns of an increasingly ethnically diverse society through a variety of programs such as multicultural education, affirmative action, bilingual education, and court-mandated redistricting. More recently, Latinos have made important strides in the political realm. Ironically, much of their recent mobilization was motivated by the anti-immigrant policies of the 1990s, such as California's Proposition 187 and welfare reform programs, which sought to deny benefits to noncitizens.[99]

Political action created opportunities. Affirmative action, equal opportunity, set-asides, civil service reforms, and public works contracts fostered the growth of ethnic economies in public and private sectors and offered numerous services to ethnic communities. Nowhere is the relationship between ethnic economies and politics more evident than in conflicts between urban minority groups lacking sizable ethnic ownership economies (especially African Americans, but also Afro-Caribbeans and Latin American groups) and noncoethnic entrepreneurs who serve them (Koreans, Chaldeans, Indians, Palestinians, and Jews). Activists have deployed protests, boycotts, political influence, and other strategies to obtain what they feel are respectful treatment, reasonable prices, reduced marketing of socially destructive products (liquor, cigarettes, and lottery tickets), a chance at owning their own shops, and, ultimately, community control. In response, entrepreneurs have organized themselves; installed security systems; provided jobs, free food, and entertainment for customers; and contributed donations to politicians and police. While leaders of clashing communities attempt to diffuse conflicts through discussions and religious services, tensions remain high, yielding violent outcomes. For example, in the Los Angeles riot of 1992, some 2000 Korean businesses were damaged or destroyed.[100] Involved parties are often remote from the political process, subject to demagoguery and distortion, and, in some situations, lack even citizenship and English competence.[101] Given the significant costs borne by the embroiled groups and the society at large, the need for addressing political conflicts surrounding ethnic economies is a high priority.[102]

ETHNIC ECONOMIES AND CULTURAL AND GEOGRAPHICAL SPACE

Upon entry to the United States, ethnic minority groups generally lack a familiar environment over which they have control. Accordingly, the creation of such a setting is often important for a group's development of a culture, base of power, and sense of turf in the new milieu. A combination of factors associated with ethnic economies—racial segregation, ethnic economic concentration, and patterns of residential clustering—have been vital to the formation of such environments in the United States.

Ethnic Economies and Ethnic Media

Usually established as a profit-making enterprise that advertises the goods and services of ethnic entrepreneurs, ethnic media are ethnic businesses. They play a major role in the creation of communal solidarity, offer valuable information, and shape group members' opinions. The role of print media in organizing ethnic life is well established. Book publishing, the recording industry, and the film industry also exert considerable influence. Ethnic food stores almost always distribute audio- and videotapes, CDs, books, newspapers, and magazines along with traditional foodstuffs in a location where they can be readily acquired by community members. Broadcast media, including radio and most recently cable television, offer a mixture of entertainment, advertisements, and political dialogue. Scholars interested in transnationalism frequently cite the importance of pervasive, rapid, and low-cost media as linking expatriate communities with their countries of origin on a daily basis. Technologies that bring distant countries socially, economically, and culturally closer include phone, fax, cable and satellite television, e-mail, international banking arrangements, video- and audiotape, motor vehicles, and inexpensive jet travel.

Because ethnic media are heavily dependent upon coethnic customers, these outlets play important roles in giving visibility and voice to ethnic issues, accomplishments, and personalities. For example, since the 1960s and 1970s, African Americans have worked to acquire ownership of media companies, ranging from recording and film production firms to radio stations and movie theater chains. Some have expanded economic and cultural autonomy. Others simply permitted performers to create and distribute works that had little likelihood of being produced by existing media companies. Reflecting on his reasons for purchasing a radio station in 1968, James Brown asserted:

> First, I thought black communities needed radio stations that really served them and represented them. . . . Second, I wanted my station to be a media training ground so black people could . . . learn advertising, programming and management at all levels. Third, as owner, I wanted to be a symbol of the black entrepreneur. . . . At that time there were around five hundred black-oriented radio stations in the country, but only five of them were owned by black people—and three of those were mine.[103]

As of 1997, minorities owned 2.8% of American commercial broadcast stations, a figure that has lately been declining. The only area of growth is in ownership of AM radio stations by Hispanics.[104]

Ilsoo Kim[105] notes that Koreans, like many recent migrant populations, lack the extent and degree of geographical concentration typical of earlier arrivals, who lived in bounded urban villages, Little Italies, and Chinatowns.[106] Lacking face-to-face contact, the ethnic media plays a vital role in unifying ethnic communities. "By informing geographically dispersed immigrants of community meetings and events, the media are the most powerful means of integrating and sustaining the community. . . . [W]ithout the ethnic media, the nonterritorial community could not exist."[107]

Hamid Naficy[108] elaborates on the unique ability of ethnic media to help exile groups simultaneously cope with adjustment to the host society and preservation of traditions and forms of association lost in flight. He describes how Iranians in Los Angeles have been active in the creation of an extensive ethnic media industry. Driven by advertisers and representing various points of view in terms of politics, gender, subethnicity, and taste, Iranian American media include radio, TV, films, music, theater, conferences, and even phone-accessed newscasts. As such, they constitute an important ethnic economy in their own right. Communal events such as conferences and performances allow the community to understand itself in the American setting and help "exiles find new friends, companions, lovers and especially future spouses."[109]

Ethnic Economies and Ethnic Neighborhoods

Ethnic neighborhoods, grounded in business districts and home ownership and sometimes reinforced by residential segregation, have played key roles in permitting ethnic groups to develop a sense of community and sovereignty. According to Olivier Zunz[110] in his study of Detroit,

> ethnic neighborhoods were the spatial anchor of the communities. . . . I have stressed ethnicity as the major force behind clustering and presented immigrants as actors building their own communities with their own labor and sweat on their own soil. I have also argued that home ownership provided the basis for community organization.

The presence of ethnic businesses within these locations has been important in establishing and defining such environments. In their research on Pittsburgh, the historians Bodnar, Simon, and Weber[111] demonstrate how the establishment of neighborhoods, undergirded by home ownership and business concentration, gave Italian and Polish ethnic groups important resources in shaping their adjustment. Coming from peasant backgrounds, these groups emphasized owning property. Accordingly, they created a variety of funding sources to offer coethnics mortgages. Home ownership protected families from restrictions, evictions, and profit gouging by landlords. If money was short, boarders could be taken in to cover mortgage payments. In turn, they could be evicted to make room for kinfolk.[112]

> The largest area of Polish-American fraternal investment was real estate. Fraternals promoted the goal of home ownership by lending money directly to members or by purchasing mortgages from banks and building associations. By 1927, the Polish Women's Alliance had over 86 percent of its assets invested in mortgages and the Polish National Alliance had over 85 percent.[113]

Similarly, Jews' dispersion from Manhattan into Brooklyn, the Bronx, and other suburban locations early in the twentieth century was linked to non-Jewish control over Manhattan's real estate and construction businesses. Jewish developers found more opportunities beyond Manhattan, where they created major settlements.[114] In fact, ethnic real estate developers, sometimes working with co-ethnic business and communal interests, have created many ethnic communities. Following San Francisco's destruction in the 1906 earthquake and fire, city fathers planned to relocate Chinatown to a less central location. However, quick action by the developer Look Tin Eli thwarted the plan. Obtaining a $3 million loan from Hong Kong contacts, he hired Americans to design and build a new enclave that would be

> more emphatically "Oriental" to draw tourists. The old Italianate buildings were replaced by Edwardian architecture embellished with theatrical chinoiserie. China-town, like the phoenix, rose from the ashes with a new facade, dreamed up by an American-born Chinese man, built by white architects, looking like a stage-set China that does not exist.[115]

Seventy years later and about 400 miles to the south, another famous Chinese American community took shape. Monterey Park, California, sometimes called the first suburban Chinatown, was to a large extent the product of Frederic Hsieh's imagination. Starting in 1977, Hsieh, who worked as an engineer by day and studied for his real estate license by night, began buying properties in the Los Angeles suburb and promoting the community as "the Chinese Beverly Hills" in Chinese language newspapers throughout Hong Kong and Taiwan. By 1990, the city had become 56% Asian.[116] Similarly, a coalition of Korean real estate developers and traders, the Korea Town Development Association, "engineered the creation and recognition of Koreatown" in Los Angeles by advertising the settlement to potential migrants in Seoul, currying favor with American politicians, and encouraging coethnic cooperation among Korean business owners.[117] Osofsky[118] describes how during the first decade of this century, the Afro-American Realty Company, headed by Philip A. Payton Jr., acquired property in Harlem and implemented the settlement of blacks. Finally, along with the role played by real estate developers, the post–World War II movement of established communal and commercial institutions—synagogues, Jewish community centers, favored shops, and professional offices—was vital to the establishment of Oak Park, a Detroit suburb that was more than 40% Jewish in 1955.[119]

Coethnic concentration and land ownership underlie communal solidarity in the rural Midwest much the same way as they do in urban settings. Studies by Salamon[120] and Gross[121] show that German Catholic communities followed unique traditions of association and inheritance. As a consequence, their landholding was more lasting and their villages more stable than in adjacent communities settled by Anglo-Saxons. Faced with declining farm incomes, the Amish have turned to wage labor and entrepreneurship as sources of income to maintain and even expand their ownership of farms in the face of urban encroachment.[122] Finally, several studies demonstrate that ethnic gangs maintain a strong sense of loyalty to local neighborhoods, providing philanthropy, jobs, security, and other benefits.[123] "There is the understanding, then, among the community that the gang is a resource that can be counted on, particularly in situations where some form of force is necessary."[124]

Wilson[125] and Drake and Cayton[126] have emphasized the importance of ethnic neighborhoods that were racially segregated, but vertically integrated in terms of class, as providing a location whereby rank-and-file members lived in relative proximity to coethnics with more extensive resources and social connections. Propinquity to a coethnic middle class helps less skilled, educated, and connected members gain access to resources (human, cultural, and social capital) and role models who can offer routes to upward mobility, often in the ethnic economy. To cite Wilson's classic formulation, prior to the 1960s,

> [l]ower-class, working-class and middle class black families all lived more or less in the same communities (albeit in different neighborhoods), sent their children to the same schools, availed themselves of the same recreational facilities and shopped at the same stores . . . The black middle-class professionals of the 1940s and 1950s (doctors, teachers, lawyers, social workers, ministers) lived in higher income neighborhoods of the ghetto and serviced the black community.[127]

Such "institutional ghettos" were characterized by an extensive degree of social organization and featured strong, interdependent social networks, personal responsibility for neighborhood problems, and participation in voluntary and formal organizations.[128] Due to the out-migration of more affluent residents, "today's ghetto neighborhoods are populated almost exclusively by the most disadvantaged segments of the black urban community"[129] with dire consequences for those who remain, including crime, violence, joblessness, and social isolation.[130]

Like Wilson, Zunz articulates the positive impact of class integration within an ethnic ghetto in his analysis of Detroit's Polonia between 1880 and 1920.

> The Polish neighborhood was not inhabited solely by poor Poles. . . . [T]he small percentage (5% of the Polish population) who made up the elite, the clergy, the few professionals, the commercial class all stayed within the community and contributed to its development. They were the ones who gave the largest sums of money to build churches and schools. . . . The predominantly working-class Polish neighborhood was built, at least in part, by the upper social stratum of the ethnic group. All members of this upper occupational stratum had experienced a classic form of upward mobility . . . from day labor to economic independence as shopkeepers and small proprietors. But success was achieved within the community; consequently, they did not leave their area of initial settlement to join native white Americans, Instead, social mobility was reinvested in the community and used as a means to reinforce ethnic identity.[131]

Unlike Detroit's Polonia or Chicago's clearly delimited "Bronzeville," Pittsburgh's black community was fragmented. The population was well organized and maintained several social and fraternal associations, an Afro-American building and loan association, a variety of businesses, a cooperative supermarket, and two black newspapers (one of which, the *Pittsburgh Courier*, developed a national readership). However, this community was unable to develop a sense of territorial control. "They did not concentrate enough to form even a small identifiable business district," and some key institutions were not even located in the black residential areas.[132] This lack of geographical concentration had significant implications. "Blacks arriving in Pittsburgh at the turn of the century were frustrated in their job search and denied the comfort and security provided by the existence of community."[133]

Ethnic Shops

Although narrowly focused studies of ethnic economies address only the income generation of ethnic businesses, the benefits these operations provide to communities go well beyond jobs and earnings. Rather, they provide many vital community functions.

> The presence of a small business district serving the needs of those in the immediate area also played a significant role in the process of community development. Self-employed businessmen symbolized the success some immigrants sought. They had status and represented stability—symbolically, if not always in fact—in a rapidly changing world. Their enterprises, in addition, became meeting places for the entire community, a source of gossip and a center of ideas. Their willingness to extend credit often made them the only friendly fortress in difficult times. Buying "on tick" or "on the book" often became the means of survival for beleaguered workers.[134]

In her classic work on American cities, Jane Jacobs notes that local small businesses play a key role in providing urban communities with safety, vitality, and foot traffic in addition to the goods and services they sell. They act as "the eyes" of a community. Moreover, because their owners are committed to the communities in which they are located, they provide social capital in the form of personal concern and caring. Hence, their presence can make a poor but active area safer and more attractive than a more affluent but less trafficked neighborhood. "Storekeepers and other small businessmen are typically strong proponents of peace and order themselves; they hate broken windows and holdups; they hate having customers made nervous about safety. They are great street watchers and sidewalk guardians if present in sufficient numbers."[135]

In fact, a review of the ethnic community literature in American sociology—from the early Chicago School to the present—reveals the extensive interconnection that exists between ethnic communities and their businesses. William Foote Whyte's *Street Corner Society*,[136] for example, makes known the importance of ethnic shops, restaurants, and bowling alleys (supported by both legitimate trade and illegal gambling activities) as key settings where communal life takes place for Italian youth in Boston. Gerald Suttles's *The Social Order of the Slum*[137] offers a rich and detailed description of the many functions that ethnic businesses play in the ethnically diverse "Addams" region of Chicago. The author notes that of the 267 businesses in the area, 107 were the sole property of a single ethnic group and that "among the residents of the area, the ideal form of commercial relations is one in which each ethnic group conducts its business entirely among its own members." This is because

> commercial relations with these people are intimate and all economic transactions are buried in the guise of friendship and sentiment. . . . Some people spend a good portion of the day bantering in these business places and then leave without buying anything. . . . Personal connections were seized upon to furnish customers. . . . All of these businesses grant favor to their customers, and the license they extend goes as far as to include types of clothing, ribaldry, drinking, gambling and rough-housing that would not be tolerated in more impersonal establishments.[138]

In *Blue Collar Community*,[139] William Kornblum devotes an extensive discussion to a factory town's multiethnic tavern culture, pointing out that "[t]he more enterprising tavern owner with an ethnic clientele often attempts to make his establishment the informal organizational headquarters of the group." In order to do so, he or she will have to improve the setting in order to make it appeal to families, not just workers. "Success at such an endeavor is often due to the prestige of the tavern's owner, including his or her leadership in other ethnic organizations or in larger community institutions."

Finally, in her ethnography of Soviet Jews in Brighton Beach, Brooklyn, Fran Markowitz[140] makes much of the importance of ethnic night clubs, which have become the social centers of Soviet Jewish communities in several settlements throughout the United States since the late 1970s.[141] Such settings provide an environment in which flashily dressed émigrés spend long evenings in celebration of religious and secular events in a style that combines their Russian, Jewish, and American identities.

> Russian restaurants exemplify to an extreme the core value of hospitality as they provide their patrons with comfort and sensual pleasures to excess. These restaurants are decorated with plush wallpaper, mirrors, flashing lights inlaid in the dance floor, long dining tables draped in linen and covered with china and flowers. . . . Women arrive heavily made-up in shiny lipstick and thick, black mascara. . . . The restaurants are institutionalized showplaces that bring Soviet émigrés together . . . because they provide arenas in which individuals can demonstrate success and measure themselves in terms of their fellow émigrés.[142]

As these several examples demonstrate, ethnic businesses are not simply places where customers purchase goods and services and owners earn a living. Instead, they are embedded in a wide variety of communal and personal relationships that are central to collective life. Business is the means whereby communal life is oriented. It is highly unlikely that such communal benefits would be made available through nonethnic chain businesses, such as a McDonald's or 7-Eleven, even though they could provide roughly equivalent goods and a comparable handful of minimum wage jobs to local residents.

Status Systems

The ethnic connection often links affluent members with the broader coethnic community. The rich seek recognition unavailable in the larger society, while the rank and file may become recipients of philanthropy. Due to unfamiliarity with American society, poor English skills, distinct cultural and religious orientations, and discrimination from natives, members of ethnic communities find the social institutions of the host society unwelcoming. For example, until the 1960s, many upscale vacation hotels, voluntary associations, country clubs, philanthropies, and other organizations excluded non-WASP participants (see Chapter 5). Although other organizations—such as churches—are more welcoming to ethnics, they maintain a social and linguistic style that members of ethnic groups find uncongenial. Warner and Wittner[143] demonstrate that many of America's recent immigrants continue to form ethnic congregations.

Accordingly, immigrant and ethnic elites often devise social settings that allow them to enjoy social prestige. In so doing, not only do they create agreeable contexts, but in addition, they use these organizations as vehicles to celebrate their accomplishments and achieve their communal goals.

In some cases, the number of ambitious individuals who seek notoriety through involvement in organizations outstrips available positions. When this happens, institutions may proliferate. Bodnar[144] cites the case of St. Stanislaus Kostka Polish Church in Brooklyn during the 1890s. "Secular leaders championed the formation of separate churches from St. Stanislaus in order to challenge clerical authority and promote their own status and business relationships. Because they wanted churches in which they could exert more control, they helped found splinter congregations."

Kim[145] and Min[146] describe a similar propensity among Korean churches formed since the 1970s. Kim notes that Korean churches offer established community members an opportunity to enjoy high repute in a manner generally unavailable in the larger society.

> Money alone does not guarantee successful [Korean] businessmen and professionals a commensurate status recognition in the larger society. . . . This sense of status alienation causes many successful professionals and businessmen to commit themselves deeply to church affairs as well as to other community activities. In these activities they can enjoy the prestige, granted by their fellow countrymen, that is denied them by their occupational or professional peers.[147]

Partly to pursue the goal of self-help, and partly because they have been excluded from mainstream organizations, Jews have developed an extensive and successful set of ethnic philanthropic institutions. In addition to raising funds for communal causes, such organizations provide a setting in which group members can occupy positions of prestige. In recent decades, Jews have had more access to the philanthropic activities of the larger society.[148] While the reduction in exclusion is in many ways a positive development, the increasing acceptance of Jews in mainstream philanthropic institutions has weakened the collective basis of coethnic organizations. As a case in point, the former president of a major city's Jewish Federation contrasts the present to an earlier period:

> Until the 1970s, there was a certain reality that [the Jewish] Federation provided an outlet for philanthropic giving and for community service in the Jewish community when the leadership was largely excluded from philanthropies in the general community. As a result of that, many key leaders rose to preeminence at a time when it would have been difficult for them to have achieved the same success in the general community.
>
> But now with Federation, if you give a gift of under $25,000, it is not viewed as overly significant. Whereas in the general community, if you give a $5,000 gift, it is viewed as extraordinary. So, therefore, you can buy much more attention, much more access on a pure economic basis for a lower dollar investment. And add to that the fact that the track to the top and to influence is a much shorter track in the general community, than it is in the Jewish community.
>
> In the old days, Federation was in a captive market where they could pick the finest fruit off the tree of talent. Now, they've got to compete for that talent in a very competitive market. So, I think that that's a major change. And with that, you have the fraying of the connectedness of the Jewish community with its religious roots and you have those people who say "Why should I bother being involved in the Jewish community . . ." So we've got a watershed movement in my opinion.

These statements notwithstanding, many Jews continue to express interest in the world of Jewish philanthropy, to which they devote significant amounts of time and effort and sizable contributions. In fact, interest is so great that many volunteers feel incapable of attaining the most prestigious positions in such organizations because they cannot contribute at the highest level. In their study of Jewish philanthropy, Phillips and Gold[149] found that one of the most commonly discussed challenges to the Jewish Federation was its image as a closed and elitist organization that favored the rich. This complaint was expressed even by those with relatively high incomes and long-term engagement in Jewish philanthropy. Several such volunteers felt their level of advancement within the Federation structure was restricted because of their inability to give at the highest level.

For example, Harry, an attorney, described resigning from a national board and redirecting his energies to his local community when the national organization evolved from "a meritocracy" that valued input from all participants to "an aristocracy" that focused on the concerns of the biggest donors: those from known philanthropic families who possessed inherited wealth.

> The national board was a very unique experience. The level of camaraderie was extremely high. We did a lot of brainstorming and rethinking about the Jewish community.
>
> But then the organization got very hung up in the necessity of raising dollars and never sought our role beyond that. The board was a meritocracy but the larger organization was an aristocracy.

> The so-called leaders were there because of the size of their bank rolls and not because of their brain power. Now I understand that that has to happen to a certain extent but I think it was overdone.
>
> There was a time when a lot more people, who didn't have huge bank rolls but who had other things to contribute, were involved in this board and they slowly got kind of pushed aside. I was certainly one of those people and so, maybe I have a certain bias but, you know, I don't have those kind of dollars.
>
> So I and a number of other people, really got very discouraged and frustrated by it and decided that there was no longer any useful contribution that we could make, so I disinvolved myself and then as a result decided to focus my attentions in my own community.
>
> That's a fact of fund-raising life. What I'm saying is, is that the organization had started to go in a direction of meritocracy and it turned back to an aristocratic approach, which I think is, going to be possibly, the death penalty for the organization.

Similarly, while female volunteers emphasize that their approach to Federation involvement is more collective and less status-driven than that of men, female respondents did complain about being obliged to perform duties that they felt were below them.[150] This is exemplified in Molly's reaction to a Los Angeles "phone-a-thon" session:

> I hate it that someone of my stature has to go and make phone calls with a bunch of people who don't know what they're doing. I went to a regular phone training session, and I sat next to an older woman and I made a phone call, and the person I called hung up. I said, "I hate it when someone hangs up," and this lady, in her 50s or 60s says, "You'll find that this happens. I've been doing this five years and people do this." And I said, "I've been doing this 22 years and I hate it. It's not worth my time."

As these quotes suggest, ethnic communal structures provide a setting wherein group members direct their pursuit of status. The fact that well-educated, U.S.-born persons with ample social and economic resources at their disposal continue to compete for prestige within these organizations demonstrates their importance and value. Although ethnic organizations were initially created to assist immigrants and oppressed minorities in their adaptation to a new and often hostile environment, many continue to be a focus of communal interest and involvement long after their initial purposes have been accomplished or taken over by institutions of the larger society. While such organizations continue to assist disadvantaged and indigent group members, they also provide a basis of social affiliation for their economically secure members.

STRENGTH AND SPECIALIZATION

Ethnic groups and their corresponding economies reveal significant diversity both in their level of communal development and in their areas of specialization. While we lack the data that would permit a systematic comparison of an array of ethnic communities, available literature does allow us to identify certain tendencies. Of course, communal strength and specialization are products of group characteristics and circumstances as well as the actions of group members. Historically, groups with considerable ethnic and/or class resources, inclusive ethnic economies, strong cultural identities, and limited access to the larger society (often the result of discrimination) have been noted for their powerful communities. These groups include Jews, Amish, Japanese Americans before World War II, and Mormons.

More recently, groups such as Cubans and Koreans have developed ethnic communities of significance, based on sizable ethnic economies, shared religion and ideology, and geographical concentration. Conflicts with both native whites and other ethnic groups have reinforced these groups' communal solidarity.[151] While Cubans are noted for both their political and economic power in south Florida, ethnic contention in New York and Los Angeles has caused Koreans to realize the limitations of focusing only on economic cooperation.[152] As a consequence, they have recently devoted more resources to developing political influence. The long-term prospects for communal development among these groups remains to be seen, because rapidly assimilating youth appear far less oriented toward ethnic concerns than their immigrant parents.[153]

While contemporary observers ordinarily associate ethnic communities with urban locations, many of the most autonomous ethnic groups have lived in rural or small town settings. For the Amish, self-isolation reduces the propensity for assimilation-fostering interactions or cultural conflicts with out-group members. Other agriculturally oriented religious groups also find rural settings best for preserving traditional forms. Such is the case among the Old Believers, Russian Fundamentalist Christians who migrated to the western United States after stays in Brazil, Turkey, and China. While several thousand joined other Russian refugees to build communities in Oregon's Willamette Valley, settlements also developed in remote regions of Alaska and Canada. Their members "hoped for more isolation to protect their children from the influences of American culture."[154] Some 90% of men in the Alaskan settlements are involved in fishing and even build their own boats. Preferring "independent work with their own people" to other employment, ethnic economies permit Old Believers to earn a living while remaining faithful to an array of religious stipulations.[155] Another rural ethnic group that has long maintained a unique culture, diet, dialect, and way of life is the Sea Islanders, an African American community residing on several islands off the southeastern coast. Having purchased land following manumission, Sea Islanders remained largely isolated from mainstream society until bridges were constructed to the mainland in the 1940s. Their singular culture and way of life includes both West African and North American influences and, as a consequence, has been of great interest for historians and folklorists.[156]

As these examples suggest, certain forms of discrimination and isolation have had the effect of strengthening ethnic communities. However, under other cir-

cumstances, hostility from the larger society has precluded the open display of ethnic identification. In extreme cases, antagonism has led to the dismantling of ethnic communities. Because of two world wars with Germany, Americans of
German origins—the group to which the largest number of Americans trace
their ancestry—became much less open in the celebration of their language and
customs. Similarly, due to communism and the cold war, "Russians remained the
people Americans loved to hate."[157] Aware of the negative image of their homeland, many Russian Americans felt forced to abandon their heritage in favor of
total assimilation. The consequences were disastrous for ethnic communal organizations as public displays of Russian heritage became taboo. The most extreme
case of the suppression of an ethnic community involved the wholesale intern-
ment of the Japanese American population during World War II, resulting in the
liquidation of the significant ethnic economy the group had established.[158]

Just as ethnic groups vary in terms of the strength of their ethnic communities,
they also develop communal activities in different dimensions. As noted earlier,
Jews have been active in philanthropic activities directed toward social services
at home and the support of Israel abroad. Catholic groups have developed an
impressive network of parochial schools, colleges, and universities as well as the
nation's largest system of nonprofit hospitals. Irish and African Americans have
refined extensive political skills and constituencies, especially in urban settings,
providing coethnics with government jobs and contracts.[159]

Several groups including Arabs, Poles, Haitians, African Americans, Irish, Armenians, Jews, Chinese, and Cubans have worked to shape political affairs in their
countries and regions of origin, often by exerting influence on the U.S. government.[160] A wide range of groups from Cambodians to Native Americans have
mobilized their communities to preserve cultural traditions and practices. Most
recently, evangelical Christians have emerged as a powerful political force, but one
more concerned with social policy than urban economies.[161]

CONCLUSIONS

In this chapter we have argued that ethnic economies and ethnic communities
provide each other with a wide array of benefits (as well as occasional disadvantages) that extend beyond aid in finding jobs or becoming self-employed. We
understand ethnic economies and ethnic communities as bound together by notions of mutual obligation and shared fate. Hence, beliefs of common identity
based in ancestry, religion, refugee status, nationality, and language may yield the
solidarity required to create an ethnic economy. Moreover, enduring notions of
solidarity may be retained long after a particular pattern of ethnic economic concentration has been abandoned.

The history of ethnic communities in American society indicates that nearly
every group pooled resources to create or support mutual assistance activities,

social welfare, education, media, cultural activities, religious institutions, neighborhood control, political leadership, and other benefits. Such benefits are vital bases of ethnic life and can be seen as helping many more persons than the number who find paying employment within the ethnic economy. In fact, many of those most directly involved in both producing and consuming benefits of ethnic communities, such as children, homemakers, the elderly, the sick, recent arrivals, and the unemployed are not formally employed at all.

In a capitalistic society, such as that of the United States, ethnic business owners and professionals have traditionally maintained the greatest influence in ethnic communities. However, workers employed in ethnic niches may also have important links to ethnic economies. Through involvement in unions, formal associations, and informal networks, such workers contribute significantly to ethnic communal life through their support of self-help activities and political movements.

In conclusion, we believe that while the benefits provided by ethnic economies to their communities cannot always be counted in dollars and cents, such benefits are nevertheless of great importance and must be considered when evaluating the impact of ethnic economies on social life.

Forms of Disadvantage

Disadvantage is the oldest explanation of superior entrepreneurship. This idea has played a serious role in the history of sociology. Weber maintained that the religious ethic of sectarian Protestants encouraged the universalistic business behavior characteristic of true bourgeois capitalism.[1] But even Weber[2] acknowledged that Protestant sectarians also selected entrepreneurship because tests of religious conformity excluded them from the civil service and the armed forces. This exclusion amounted to a labor force disadvantage arising from religious discrimination. Subjected to religious discrimination, Protestant sectarians turned to entrepreneurship. Therefore, Weber thought that labor force disadvantage supplemented the religious affinity of sectarian Protestantism for entrepreneurship.

Disputing Weber in a historic debate, Werner Sombart returned to the problem of capitalism's origin, attributing it to Jews, not Protestants.[3] Sombart[4] stressed the rationalism of the Jews as a cultural resource that had fitted them for entrepreneurship. However, Sombart[5] also mentioned the Jews' exclusion from medieval trade guilds, membership in which was open only to Christians. In consequence of this disadvantage, Sombart claimed, Jews were compelled to start their own firms and to operate hypercompetitively, thereby encouraging market capitalism's ultimate success. Thus, like Weber, Sombart split his explanation of entrepreneurship into a component of religious affinity and a component of labor force disadvantage born of religious discrimination. Both Weber and Sombart stressed the contribution of religious affinity to entrepreneurship, but both also mentioned the contribution of labor force disadvantage.

In the recent revival of interest in immigrant and ethnic entrepreneurship, the classic formula (disadvantage + affinities) at first persisted. Cultural influences initially received the most emphasis, but labor market disadvantage received secondary recognition. Light[6] stressed the "cultural repertoires" that influenced minority entrepreneurship in the United States before the World War II. But he also declared[7] prewar Chinese business firms "monuments to the discrimination that had created them." In a later publication that represented an important maturation of this literature, Light[8] formally distinguished disadvantage explanations from cultural ones, and pointed out the inadequacy of purely cultural explanations.

In the 1980s, cultural explanations went out of fashion in social science. Research stressed disadvantage to the point that this idea dominated the discourse, often to the exclusion of affinities. This position revised classical theory. Unlike Weber and Sombart, both of whom understood disadvantage explanations to complement affinities, the main explanation, researchers during the 1980s treated disadvantage as a way to avoid having to examine affinities at all. Indeed, Jones, McEvoy, and Barrett[9] declared it a "form of racist discrimination" even to discuss ethnocultural affinities in entrepreneurship when discrimination, a labor force disadvantage, also compels people to chance entrepreneurship. Other less extreme, writers simply ignore affinities, advancing disadvantage as the whole explanation for high rates of entrepreneurship.[10] Discussing entrepreneurial Pakistanis and East Indians in Britain, Aldrich et al.[11] declared that "because of natives whites' prejudice and hostility" Asians in Britain must "seek employment below their skill level or else create their own employment opportunity by forming a small business." Ladbury[12] found that Turkish Cypriots in London opened small businesses because "that was all they could get." Min[13] found that more than 90% of Korean entrepreneurs mentioned disadvantage as a major reason for their self-employment, and he assigned first importance to this cause. In Min's[14] opinion, "disadvantage in the American job market" was a principal cause of Korean entrepreneurship in Atlanta. Similarly, Lubin's[15] comparative study of Soviet immigrants in the United States and Israel also stressed disadvantage, not cultural repertoires. In her opinion,[16] the chief motivation for entrepreneurship among the immigrants arose from "lack of other employment options."

Phizacklea[17] declared entrepreneurship an "escape route" for minority men confined to "dead-end manual jobs by racism and racial discrimination." Except for racism, these men would have obtained better jobs for which they were objectively qualified. Therefore, Phizacklea[18] viewed their entrepreneurship "as a form of disguised unemployment." Blaschke and Ersoz[19] also turned to disadvantage in their account of Turkish entrepreneurship in West Berlin, concluding that "unemployment or the threat of unemployment" was the principal source of

Turkish entrepreneurship. "Other than hard-to-come-by dependent employment, Turkish nationals are only left with one option for economic survival—that is, starting self-employed businesses."

The business cycle also offers indirect support for disadvantage theory. The business cycle literature has commonly reported a countercyclical relationship between aggregate unemployment and self-employment such that self-employment rises in periods of increased unemployment and declines with the return of full employment.[20] One can also count upon the media to make this wise point whenever unemployment increases.[21] True, Becker[22] found the evidence mixed in his review of existing literature. However, his own time series statistical data, 1948– 1982, did support the countercyclical hypothesis in the nonagricultural sector. Also utilizing time series data, Steinmetz and Wright[23] found no relationship between unemployment and self-employment until the unemployment rate was interacted with a time variable. When interacted, both the unemployment rate and the interaction term became significant predictors of self-employment rates.

THEORIES OF DISADVANTAGE

Summarizing this one-dimensional, contemporary view, we dub it the simple disadvantage hypothesis. The *simple disadvantage hypothesis* expects disadvantage in the labor market to encourage self-employment independent of the resources of those disadvantaged. Jettisoning the classic formula for entrepreneurship (disadvantage + affinities), simple disadvantage became the baseline from which modern research proceeded. However, as simple disadvantage arguments proliferated, those offering them began to offer variations on the simple disadvantage hypothesis (a sign of theoretical maturation) that actually returned research to the classical formula.

Confronting the evidence, simple disadvantage theory encountered problems of uneven fit. Several researchers reported that simple disadvantage did not fit their data at all. Comparing Chinese and African Americans, Fairlie and Meyer[24] rejected disadvantage theory on the grounds that "self-employment rates are higher among more advantaged ethno-racial groups, contradicting the disadvantage theory."

Other researchers found that disadvantage did not have identical effects upon workers at all socioeconomic levels. Reviewing disadvantage research, Johnson found data sparse and support only partial. According to Johnson,[25] "non-manual workers" were more likely to undertake self-employment in response to unemployment than were manual workers. Among manual workers, Johnson found that the unskilled were "less likely to set up than skilled workers." Thus, unemployment's effects upon self-employment depended upon the skills of the unemployed, a resource constraint. Similarly, Razin and Langlois[26] found that disadvantaged access to salaried jobs only increased self-employment among Canadian minorities when disadvantage was connected to strong resources.

Haber[27] examined the relationship between unemployment and self-employment in the period 1979–1983, a recession. In this period, self-employment grew by 6.9%, whereas wage and salary employment increased only 1.3%. Haber also found that the greatest growth of self-employment occurred among employed workers who opened a side business. Haber[28] supposed that, when their hours were reduced during the recession, some wage and salary workers opened a side business to supplement their earnings from paid employment. Therefore, the effects of unemployment on self-employment were much less than those of underemployment. Haber supposed that the underemployed had more resources than did the unemployed; hence, they could more easily set up on their own account.

Studying the resurgence of self-employment in Europe, Keeble and Weaver[29] found results similar to those of Haber. Originally, they endorsed the "recession push" explanation they found in the existing literature. According to this explanation, unemployment, fear of unemployment, and blocked promotion opportunities compelled European workers to open their own business firms. Therefore, self-employment rates increased in Europe as economic conditions deteriorated. However, Keeble and Weaver[30] found that the occupational structure of localities influenced the extent to which local unemployment promoted self-employment. Managerial workers and others possessing higher educational qualifications were much more likely than others to undertake self-employment in response to unemployment or underemployment. Therefore, in localities with many managerial workers, unemployment and underemployment occasioned greater increase in self-employment than in other localities.

In his study of Vietnamese and Soviet Jewish immigrants in San Francisco, Gold[31] found "little evidence to indicate that small business is a direct alternative to unemployment." In Gold's opinion, the unemployed had a motive for self-employment all right, but they typically lacked the resources to succeed in it. Unemployed immigrants who tried self-employment usually failed. More commonly, the foreign born undertook self-employment because of "the low quality" of the jobs they could obtain, a situation of underemployment, not unemployment. When starting up their own businesses, the underemployed had access to the slender resources afforded by the disagreeable jobs they still held. The unemployed had no resources. Hence, the underemployed more commonly succeeded in developing viable business firms than did the unemployed.

Implicit in this literature we find a sophisticated version of disadvantage theory that transcends the classical view while incorporating all of its explanatory power. We call this implicit theory the resource-constraint variant of the disadvantage theory. The *resource-constraint variant* supposes that even the disadvantaged require resources to undertake and/or survive in self-employment. The resource-constraint formula for entrepreneurship is disadvantage + resources. On this view, disadvantage alone is insufficient to create entrepreneurs in the formal sector. The resource-constraint variant resembles the classical formula of disadvantage + affinities. The difference is the substitution of resources for affinities in the formula. Affinities must be ethnocultural in the hard sense.[32] That is, they must belong to historic systems of cultural meaning. The Protestant work ethic is an affinity in that sense. Resources include ethnocultural affinities, but they also include class resources as well as ethnocultural resources (such as social capital), which are not reducible to historic systems of cultural meaning. *Resources* is broader than *affinities* and represents, for this reason, a theoretical improvement that broadens the scope of classical theory.[33]

Although they offer alternative versions of how disadvantage causes entrepreneurship, the resource-constraint and simple disadvantage theories need not exclude one another. Conceivably, each fits different situations. Confronting labor force disadvantage, those with no resources turn to self-employment in the informal economy. A typical firm in the informal economy requires next to no resources. For example, fruit vendors at Los Angeles freeway entrances are self-employed, but their informal enterprise did not require extensive resources of money, skill, and knowledge. Anyone could do it. On the other hand, when people with resources confront disadvantage, they mobilize those resources to produce a bona fide business firm with premises, telephone, regular hours, and taxes to pay. A grocery store owner or dry cleaner requires resources that those merely disadvantaged simply lack. Lacking resources, they could not have responded to disadvantage by starting this firm.

TYPES OF DISADVANTAGE

Taking account of the difference between the resource-constraint variant and simple disadvantage theory, we also distinguish two types of disadvantage that the existing literature conflates. These types we call resource disadvantage and labor market disadvantage. Groups experience *resource disadvantage* when, as a result of some historical experience, such as centuries of slavery or peonage, their members enter the labor market with fewer resources than other groups. African Americans are in this position, as are Mexican immigrants. Resources include all attributes that improve the productivity of employees, including human capital, a positive work ethic, good diets, reliable health, contact networks, self-confidence, education, and so forth. Thus, if their group was or is prevented from obtaining education, group members enter the labor market with less education on the average than non-group members, a disadvantage that reduces their productivity. Even if these disadvantaged persons then earn the expected market return on their human capital, their incomes will be low because their human capital and productivity are low. Since their human capital is low because of prior exclusion, a condition that existed when they entered the labor market, we appropriately term these workers resource disadvantaged.

To illustrate the point, Table 8.1 compares the educational attainment of whites, Hispanics, and blacks in the United States in 1995. A higher percentage of

TABLE 8.1   Educational Attainment of Ethnoracial Categories for the United States, 1995

	High school graduates		College graduates	
	Men	Women	Men	Women
White	83.0%	83.0%	27.2%	21.0%
Black	73.4%	74.1%	13.6%	12.9%
Hispanic	52.9%	53.8%	10.1%	8.4%
Resource disadvantage ratios				
Black/white	88.4%	89.2%	50.0%	61.4%
Hispanic/white	63.7%	64.8%	37.1%	40.0%

Source: U.S. Bureau of the Census, *Statistical Abstract of the United States, 1996* (Washington, D.C.: GPO, 1996), Table 242.

white men and women had completed high school than had either black or Hispanic men and women. Similarly, a higher percentage of white men and women had completed 4 years of college than had either black or Hispanic men or women. Blacks and Hispanics had lower average educational attainments than did whites. The causes of this disadvantage lie largely in the historic past, but the consequences are contemporary. In this sense, relative to whites, blacks and Hispanics entered the labor market with lesser resources. They were resource disadvantaged.

We distinguish resource disadvantage from labor market disadvantage. *Labor market disadvantage* arises when groups receive below-expected returns on their human capital for reasons unrelated to productivity.[34] Their human capital may be extensive or minimal. That does not matter. Labor market disadvantage means that qualified workers get no job at all or they do not get a job commensurate with their experience and education. Bates refers to this situation as blocked mobility.[35] Discrimination is a classic cause of labor market disadvantage. For example, labor market disadvantage obtains when equally productive female workers earn less than their male counterparts. It also obtains when female workers do not receive promotions for which they are qualified. Hiring discrimination and a ceiling on promotions are prominent forms of labor market disadvantage that affect women. However, when unqualified and unproductive female workers earn low wages, they do not suffer from labor market disadvantage except to the extent that their wages are lower than equally unqualified and unproductive male workers. Naturally, their unqualified and unproductive situation may be itself the product of resource disadvantage, such as historic gender roles in society, but it is essential to distinguish disadvantage that arises in the labor market from disadvantage that arises earlier in society. A significant fraction of immigrant workers are subject to labor market disadvantage because they have accents and because their educational credentials are not understood or recognized by American employers.

TABLE 8.2   Unemployment Rate by Educational Attainment and Ethnoracial Category
for the United States, 1995

	Less than high school	Completed high school	Completed college	All persons
White	9.2%	4.6%	2.3%	4.3%
Black	13.7%	8.4%	4.1%	7.7%
Hispanic	10.9%	8.1%	3.7%	8.0%
Labor force disadvantage ratios				
Black/white	1.49%	1.82%	1.78%	1.79%
Hispanic/white	1.18%	1.76%	1.60%	1.86%

Source: U.S. Bureau of the Census, *Statistical Abstract of the United States, 1996* (Washington, D.C.:
GPO, 1996), Table 649.

Table 8.2 illustrates disadvantage in the labor market. When compared to
whites with comparable educational attainment, blacks and Hispanics had higher
unemployment rates in 1995. The ratio of their groups' education-adjusted unemployment rates relative to the white unemployment rate is an appropriate measure
of their disadvantage, and blacks had slightly higher ratios than Hispanics.

Black college graduates experienced the most disadvantage, 1.78 times the
white rate, and Hispanic nongraduates of high school the *least* labor force disadvantage, only 1.18 times the white rate. True, the unemployment rate of all three
ethnoracial categories declined with educational attainment, so that blacks and
Hispanics were at a resource disadvantage relative to whites because they had
lower average educational attainment. But blacks and Hispanics *also* had higher
labor market disadvantage than whites. In point of fact, blacks and Hispanics
experienced both labor market and resource disadvantage in 1995.

Labor market disadvantage and resource disadvantage are two different disadvantages. Any group can suffer from neither, from either, or from both. When
both are present, resource disadvantage may precede or follow labor market disadvantage. When resource disadvantage is in place before a worker enters the labor
market, resource disadvantage precedes labor market disadvantage. When a woman
who was not offered algebra in high school seeks a job, the consequences of her
inferior education will narrow her career horizon, increasing the likelihood of labor market disadvantage as well. On the other hand, today's resource disadvantage
can reflect yesterday's labor market disadvantage. For example, unfair treatment of
female workers in the 1950s produced a generation of contemporary women
who did not have the career role models they would otherwise have had. This
lack was a resource disadvantage that continues to hold back female workers in
the labor force, the daughters of those earlier women. In such cases, prior labor
force disadvantage caused current resource disadvantage.

That said, resource disadvantage is worse than labor market disadvantage in that those resource-deprived lack the resources to undertake formal sector self-employment in response to labor market disadvantage.[36] Because they provide at least some workers with the option of formal sector self-employment, entrepreneurial resources reduce the vulnerability of groups to abuse, discrimination, or exploitation in the labor market. For this reason, whatever else it also is, entrepreneurship is one self-defense of those treated unfairly in the labor market. Labor unions are another such defense. Arguably, labor unions provide a more comprehensive defense because they benefit and include a larger fraction of the labor force. Entrepreneurship's direct benefit affects a minority. Nonetheless, groups that have entrepreneurs and labor unions are better defended than groups that have only labor unions.

Naturally, those never subject to unfair treatment in the labor market need no defense. One might suppose that this advantaged class includes native whites, the majority group in American society. On a simple reckoning, native whites are not disadvantaged in the labor market at all. However, some native whites are women, who experience gender discrimination in the labor market. Moreover, all native whites, if they live past 40, face employer discrimination against older workers. Without entrepreneurial resources, older native whites have no defense when this nasty contingency arises. Finally, in many universities, white men are "invisible victims" of affirmative action quotas that offer them the choice of self-employment or resignation to reverse discrimination.[37] Granted, disadvantage of non-whites is worse than that of native whites, other things being equal, but the notion that native white men never face discrimination is absurd.[38]

Stressing resource endowments, the resources theory of entrepreneurship explains superior entrepreneurship by superior resources. But by implication resources theory also explains inferior entrepreneurship by inferior resources. Here, inferior resources means resource disadvantage, not labor market disadvantage. Resource-disadvantaged groups are unable to mount an entrepreneurial response *in the formal sector* to labor market disadvantage. Among these disadvantaged groups are blacks, Mexicans, Central Americans, Hmong, and some others, the least educated ethnoracial categories. Conversely, non-resource-disadvantaged groups (most Asians and foreign whites) more easily defeat labor market disadvantage by starting businesses of their own in the formal sector.[39] This capacity renders them sensitive to labor force disadvantage that the resource-disadvantaged must tolerate.

DISADVANTAGE MUST BE MEASURED

We now wish to rectify several conceptual and methodological flaws in the existing disadvantage literature. First, several researchers failed to define or to measure labor market disadvantage, simply assuming its presence from conditions thought to cause it. Evans claimed that the main disadvantage facing immigrant workers was nonfluency in the language of the host country.[40] In a series of papers, Evans[41] examined the occupational effects of weak English skills. She found that belonging to a non–English-language community increased the likelihood of an immigrant's self-employment. The reason, Evans[42] supposed, is that "people with weak skills" in English have an incentive to seek "employment from their compatriots because they can get better jobs inside the enclave than they could in the broader labour market." In turn, regardless of linguistic disadvantage, an entrepreneur benefits from the linguistic disability of coethnics because their linguistic disability creates a captive labor force of workers paid "below the market value of their skills." In this situation, coethnic entrepreneurs "spring up to hire them," thus causing high rates of entrepreneurship in linguistically disadvantaged groups.

Evans's commonsense view mistakes cause and effect. Conditions that cause labor market disadvantage are not the same as labor market disadvantage, their effect. Thus, inferior language skills, health disability, racial or gender discrimination, and the like cause labor market disadvantage. However, these situations are not labor market disadvantage, so they cannot measure it. Labor market disadvantage is the consequence of these conditions: higher than expected underemployment or unemployment among those who do not speak the language, who have health problems, who experience discrimination, or whatever. If we declare lack of English fluency a labor force disadvantage, we should have to declare individuals disadvantaged who earn more than their expected return on their human capital *despite* lack of fluency in English. *Groups* are not disadvantaged unless they actually suffer adverse consequences of mistreatment in the labor market.[43] Hispanics and blacks complain of mistreatment, and their education-adjusted unemployment rates do show a resulting disadvantage (Table 8.2). The best measure of labor market disadvantage of groups is the penalty disadvantage inflicts, unemployment, not the condition that draws a penalty. No penalty means no disadvantage. Big penalty means big disadvantage.

Infinite Causes

Second, the possible causes of labor market disadvantage are both transitory and infinite, so it is useless to enumerate them. In China, it became a disadvantage during the cultural revolution to have had educated parents, but, after the cultural revolution, it became an advantage again.[44] French employers discriminate against those whose knowledge of art and music does not meet a high class standard,[45] and American employers discriminate against men who know about these subjects. According to Henry Higgins in George Bernard Shaw's *Pygmalion,* British employers discriminate against cockney speakers. Japanese employers discriminate against *burakumin,* who are not, as far as non-Japanese can tell, any different from the employers. Hollywood studios discriminate against actresses with small busts, but modeling agencies discriminate against models with big busts.

The literature of entrepreneurship reflects the bewildering etiologies of disadvantage. Explaining Korean entrepreneurship, Min[46] turned to status incongruence, a form of underemployment. That is, he measured underemployment among Korean immigrant men by discrepancy between their work status in Korea and their work status in Atlanta on the one hand, and, on the other, by discrepancy between their educational background and their current work status. More than 90% of Min's[47] respondents had held white-collar or professional employment in Korea, but only 17% found white-collar or professional positions as their first U.S. job. In that sense, most Koreans were underemployed. Similarly, 68% of Korean entrepreneurs in Atlanta had completed 4 years of college or more, but 83% of Korean entrepreneurs were in manual occupations on their first American job. More than half of the Korean entrepreneurs were "status inconsistents with a high pre-immigrant occupation and a low occupation in this country."[48] Unsurprisingly, the Korean entrepreneurs also regarded their first American job as inferior in income and prestige to their entitlement. About half reported that this dissatisfaction drove them to undertake self-employment.

Light and Bonacich[49] offered an opportunity cost definition of labor force disadvantage. They reported that Korean wage and salary earners in Los Angeles earned only 70% of the return on their human capital that non-Korean workers earned. On the other hand, self-employed Koreans earned 92% of the return that non-Koreans obtained on their human capital. Either way, Koreans were disadvantaged. However, the Koreans' disadvantage was 22% greater in wage and salary employment than in self-employment. Arising from relative disadvantage, the obvious financial incentive explained the Koreans' overrepresentation in self-employment. This treatment of underemployment turned exclusively on below-expected wages rather than, as did Min's, upon subjective dissatisfaction with low-prestige jobs.

Kim, Hurh, and Fernandez[50] and Fernandez and Kim[51] defined disadvantage in terms of inferior returns upon college diplomas awarded by foreign universities. They distinguished college-educated Asians by those who had graduated from U.S. institutions and those who had graduated from foreign institutions, a distinction never drawn before. They found that, among three national origin groups, graduates of foreign universities were more frequently self-employed than graduates of American universities. This result suggests that foreign college graduates were underemployed in the American labor force and so turned in despair to self-employment.

Because the causes of disadvantage are infinitely expandable, we cannot measure disadvantage by enumerating its causes. However long, any list of possible labor force disadvantages can always be expanded by one. Therefore, as a research strategy, we must measure labor force disadvantage in terms of underemployment and unemployment, the penalties of disadvantage. Here, at least, closure is possible. Unemployment means long- and short-term joblessness among job-seeking workers. Unemployment provides workers no return upon their human capital, which, indeed, they might as well not possess. Unemployment is worse than underemployment. Underemployment means lower earnings than one's human capital normally commands, a disadvantage, but one that affords at least some return upon human capital. One cause of underemployment is short hours. People who work 10 hours weekly are likely to earn lower than expected returns upon their human capital even if their hourly wages are satisfactory. That kind of underemployment amounts to partial unemployment. Another kind of underemployment is low pay relative to qualifications. When immigrant doctors pump gasoline, they earn a fair wage for gasoline service station attendants, but their wage is a much lower than their expected return upon their human capital.

Another meaning of underemployment is purely subjective. People may reject jobs because the task is not one they deem appropriate for someone like them, because they dislike the boss, because they are not morning people, or any fanciful reason. Unsuitability occurs when workers earn an expected return on their human capital but reject their task. This is the usual situation of immigrant professionals who run garment factories or gasoline service stations: the money is satisfactory, but the work is *infra dignitatem*. We suppose that it is worse to be both underpaid and dissatisfied with the job than to be merely underpaid or merely dissatisfied. In any case, underemployment must become a state of conscious dissatisfaction before it has consequences. When objectively underemployed people are happy in their wretched jobs, ignorance is bliss, and underemployment produces no consequences in the labor market.

Disadvantage Is Continuous

Third, simple disadvantage literature has often failed to acknowledge degrees of disadvantage. Therefore, Oliver and Shapiro[52] correctly complain that some disadvantaged people are more disadvantaged than other disadvantaged people. However, conflating resource and labor market disadvantage as they do, Oliver and Shapiro cannot explain why, if blacks were more disadvantaged than others, they were not also more self-employed than others. Moreover, they fail to observe that Hispanics are more resource disadvantaged than blacks, who are only more labor market disadvantaged than Hispanics. In general, the merely resource disadvantaged are more disadvantaged than the merely labor market disadvantaged, the long-term unemployed are more disadvantaged than the short-term unemployed, and the unemployed are more disadvantaged than the underemployed. The unemployed are more disadvantaged because the underemployed earn a return on their education, skill, and work experience whereas the unemployed earn none. Among the unemployed, the long-term unemployed are more disadvantaged than the short-term unemployed if only because the long-term unemployed have depleted their resources in the course of protracted unemployment.[53]

Both the underemployed and the unemployed have objective grounds for dissatisfaction with their labor force status and, hence, for considering self-employment. But the underemployed have more choice about timing their entry into business than do the unemployed. They can wait until conditions are ripe rather than having to rush in desperation into overcrowded or unsuitable markets. Similarly, the underemployed can accrue financial resources and training for subsequent self-employment while working at their unsatisfactory jobs. Indeed, training underemployed coethnics for self-employment is a principal resource of small ethnic businesses.[54] In sum, the underemployed have more financial and skill resources for legitimate self-employment than do the permanently unemployed. Especially when the underemployed have higher educational credentials and job skills unused in their occupation, they possess important resources for self-employment. Because the permanently unemployed typically lack much human capital, they have a reduced capacity for self-employment even if their need is higher. Worse, the longer they are unemployed, the more their human capital falls behind what their age cohort's employed members command.

True, those more disadvantaged have more incentive to undertake self-employment than do those less disadvantaged. Increasing the subjective intensity of unemployment (temporary, protracted, and permanent) increases the economic attractiveness of self-employment. For the permanently unemployed underclass of great cities, emigration, begging, public welfare, crime, and self-employment offer the only alternatives to starvation.[55] Public welfare and self-employment are incompatible in law because welfare recipients are not permitted to receive benefits while obtaining income from a business. Fortunately, some agencies are trying to change this situation. Even though welfare and self-employment are not incompatible in practice, some welfare recipients unlawfully operate business enterprises on the side. Instead of expressing indignation about this freeloading minority, the ignorant political response, one might ask why *all* welfare recipients do not also operate a clandestine small business on the side. Fear of detection is probably not the only reason. Some welfare recipients operate no business because, thanks to public welfare, they need not. Welfare supplies their modest needs. In addition, however, many welfare recipients do not operate a side business because, despite the incentive, they lack the resources. Those who lack resources cannot undertake self-employment no matter how desperately they need income.

Even the Disadvantaged Require Resources

Simple disadvantage is enough to explain self-employment in the informal economy. The informal economy requires next to no resources. But even those sorely disadvantaged in the labor market need resources to undertake self-employment in the mainstream. Therefore, disadvantaged workers with more resources are the most likely to try or to succeed in self-employment. No matter how skilled or how educated, an unemployed person earns nothing. However, if highly skilled, the worker's economic loss is greater than if unskilled because an unskilled person earns a lower return on his or her human capital when fully employed. In this sense, unemployment represents a greater absolute economic loss for the trained and experienced than for the unskilled beginner. This idea explains Johnson's[56] findings that high-skilled workers were more likely to become self-employed than were low-skilled workers. Additionally, disadvantaged workers with skills and education have more resources at their disposal with which they can undertake their own business firm in response to labor market disadvantage. It therefore follows that labor force disadvantage promotes more entrepreneurship among those with resources than among those lacking them.

REVIEW

Based on this review and critique of the disadvantage literature, Table 8.3 summarizes our theoretical discussion.[57] Among groups suffering resource disadvantage, additional labor market disadvantage has no effect in stimulating compensatory entrepreneurship.[58] In this case, labor market disadvantage increases the need for self-employment without, however, providing the necessary resources. As W. S. Gilbert[59] put it, "they would if they could, but they are not able." Only among groups not resource disadvantaged does labor market disadvantage encourage entrepreneurship. Those not disadvantaged at all have the resources, but they lack the motive to undertake defensive entrepreneurship. Therefore, their self-employment rate is average.

Groups with high levels of entrepreneurship suffer labor force disadvantage without resource disadvantage. Their labor force disadvantage provides a motive for defensive self-employment, and their extensive resources provide the means. Abused in the labor market, they have the resources to start businesses of their own. Middleman minorities fit this model. Outsiders, and subject to discrimination,

TABLE 8.3   Disadvantage and Entrepreneurship

Group resource disadvantage	Group labor market disadvantage	
	Yes	No
Yes	Low entrepreneurship	Lowest entrepreneurship
Example	African Americans	
No	Highest entrepreneurship	Average entrepreneurship
Example	Middleman minorities	Native-born white men

middleman minorities have elaborated a cultural preparation for entrepreneurship that facilitates their defensive self-employment.[60] Indeed, in some cases, middleman minorities make a virtue of necessity, turning defensive entrepreneurship into a source of gigantic capitalist profit. But labor force disadvantage does not have the same energizing effect upon nonmiddleman groups that lack resources. Lacking resources of entrepreneurial self-defense, with few exceptions, black and Hispanic underdogs must endure whatever abuse employers dish out, escaping only into crime or the informal economy. Their labor market disadvantage generates high self-employment in those sectors, but their resource disadvantage excludes them from mainstream self-employment.

DISADVANTAGE AND THE INFORMAL ECONOMY

Comparing the four major ethnoracial categories, Light and Rosenstein[61] found consistent support for the resource-constraint version of disadvantage in their survey of 272 metropolitan areas of the United States. However, as they noted, the census data they employed could not look into the informal sector. Yet resource-constraint theory predicts much higher self-employment for blacks and Hispanics in the informal sector than in the mainstream economy. The informal economy simply demands fewer resources to enter than does the mainstream economy. Therefore, those suffering labor market disadvantage and resource disadvantage have motive and capability to start informal sector businesses. If so, blacks and Hispanics should demonstrate much higher self-employment rates in the informal sector than they do in the mainstream. Studies that focus on average self-employment in the formal sector, as did Light and Rosenstein's, simply cannot evaluate participation of ethnoracial groups and categories in the informal sector.

Partially to remedy this shortcoming, we introduce Table 8.4, which is also derived from census data. The firms enumerated in Table 8.4 are all in the formal sector; none is in the informal sector. Nonetheless, by arranging the formal sector firms in descending order of magnitude, we capture the result of declining resource requirements upon the ethnoracial composition of the self-employed. In the top panel, among firms with 100 or more employees, still considered small businesses, black and Hispanic entrepreneurs are very rare indeed. Together, they constitute only 1.8% of owners in this size class. In the next size class, firms with any employees, black and Hispanic entrepreneurs are more than twice as numerous. Together they represent 5.4% of all owners in the size class. In the next size class lower, firms with no employees, the representation of blacks and Hispanics doubles again. Black and Hispanic firms together represent 10.2% of nonemployer firms. Finally, when we look only at nonemployer firms whose owners worked fewer than 20 hours weekly, we are getting quite close to the informal sector. In this bottom tier of firms, blacks and Hispanics together represented 11.7% of firms. In short, as we proceed down the size classes, approaching the informal

TABLE 8.4   Business Firms as Percentage of Size Class for the United States by Race and Ethnoracial Category, 1987

Number of employees	Hispanic	Black	White men	Total
>100 employees	0.7	1.1	98.2	100
Any employees	2.9	2.5	94.6	100
No employees	5.0	5.2	89.7	100
No employees and works <20 hours/week	4.9	6.8	88.4	100
Gross receipts				
>$1,000,000	1.25	0.96	97.8	100
$100,000 to $999,999	2.5	1.62	95.8	100
$5000 to $99,999	4.6	4.44	90.9	100
<$5000	5.0	6.23	88.7	100
N	422,373	424,165	8,755,252	9,601,790

Source: U.S. Bureau of the Census, 1987 Economic Censuses, CBO87-1 Character of Business Owners (Washington, D.C.: GPO, 1992), Tables 11C and 12B.

sector, a promised land that, like Moses, we cannot enter, the representation of blacks and Hispanics in self-employment consistently increases just as the resource-constraint theory predicts.

The bottom panel of Table 8.4 offers a related but different test of the resource-constraint theory. In the top tier, among firms that grossed more than $1,000,000, blacks and Hispanics together constituted just 2.2% of all business owners. In the next tier down, among business firms with revenues between $100,000 and $999,999, the black and Hispanic owners represented 4.1% of all owners. Firms with gross revenues from $5000 to $99,000 are the next to the bottom size class. In this class, black and Hispanic owners were 9.0% of all owners. Finally, in the smallest size class of firms, those that grossed less than $5000, blacks and Hispanics constituted 11.2% of owners. Obviously formal sector firms grossing less than $5000 yearly are much closer to the informal sector than formal sector firms grossing $1,000,000 or more. As the size class decreased, the bottom panel also finds increasing representation of black and Hispanic entrepreneurs in the business population. This result is exactly what one would expect from the resource-constraint theory.

DISCUSSION

A long, large, and even historical body of literature has developed around the disadvantage theory. Weber and Sombart thought that entrepreneurship was a product of religiously inspired affinities plus disadvantage, but they stressed the affinities. In the 1980s, the classic formula was pared down to disadvantage alone. This stripped–down disadvantage literature has yielded widespread agreement that those disadvantaged in wage labor turn to entrepreneurship in self-protection. However, operating out of that consensus, contemporary researchers encountered many problems that suggest the desirability of retrieving and expanding the affinities argument. The concept of entrepreneurial resources includes the classical affinities variable, expanding it to include other material and cultural sources of entrepreneurship such as social capital and cultural capital. This usage distinguishes our disadvantage theory from Timothy Bates's economistic version, in which, he declares, ethnic resources play no role.[62]

We distinguish simple disadvantage theory, the model so popular in the 1980s, from a resource-constraint variant. Simple disadvantage theory predicts augmented self-employment in proportion to a group's disadvantage: the more disadvantaged, the more self-employment. Simple disadvantage theory does not invoke resource disparities. The resource-constraint version maintains, in contrast, that those most disadvantaged in the labor market often lack the resources to undertake self-employment in the mainstream. Therefore, it predicts the most formal sector self-employment among persons slightly disadvantaged who are not resource-disadvantaged. Here the resources provide the means, and the labor force disadvantage the motive. Entrepreneurship requires means as well as motive. In the simple disadvantage theory, the disadvantaged have ample motive for self-employment, but they often lack the means, material and cultural.

Census data assume firms of a sufficient size and permanence that census enumerators could find and measure them. The informal economy lies outside this range. The resources required to operate in the informal economy are appreciably fewer than those required in the mainstream economy. Selling pencils on the street requires only pencils and a tin cup. Manufacturing pencils requires millions in start-up capital, so it is no wonder that millionaires manufacture pencils and paupers sell them. One has to take resources into account when explaining participation in mainstream entrepreneurship. The simple disadvantage theory offers a satisfactory explanation for entrepreneurship in the informal economy. Indeed, those with resources would normally avoid the informal economy since their resources give them entry into the mainstream. We showed that as one descends the hierarchy of formal sector firms, from bigger to smaller, the participation of resource-deprived blacks and Hispanics increases. This finding is exactly what resource-constraint theory predicts; it implies, furthermore, that could we see participation rates in the informal sector, still the black hole of entrepreneurship research, we would find the resource-deprived more heavily participating than in the formal sector.

Although impressed by the superiority of the resource-constraint version for the formal sector, we do not jettison simple disadvantage theory. Rather, we propose that simple disadvantage theory explains participation in the informal economy, in which resource requirements are minimal anyway. That is why resource-deprived groups, such as blacks and Hispanics, are more active as en-trepreneurs in the informal economy than in the formal economy. Its resource-constraint variant better explains entrepreneurial participation in the economic mainstream that the census depicts. Although our results pertain to American immigrant and ethnic minorities, we find a direct line of intellectual continuity with classical theories that confirms and supports this individual analysis.

DISADVANTAGE AND THE ETHNIC-CONTROLLED ECONOMY

Disadvantage explanations have been most commonly applied to the analysis of ethnic ownership economies, wherein groups impeded in the larger labor market enter self-employment as an alternative to the absence or poor quality of work available in existing firms or the public sector. However, a significant body of research concerning ethnic niches also discusses the role of disadvantage as ulti-mately yielding an advantageous position—what Jiobu[63] calls *ethnic hegemony*—for group members in the ethnic-controlled economy.[64] Just as in the case of the ethnic ownership economy, simple disadvantage alone is generally not sufficient for the development of ethnic niches. Rather, it is groups characterized by a com-bination of disadvantage plus resources that develop advantageous ethnic niches.

Disadvantage yields benefit in the following manner: Certain ethnic and im-migrant groups suffer resource deficits in the labor market. They may be undocu-mented, lack English language skills, have little formal education, lack American diplomas and credentials, or lack familiarity with American work practices. These liabilities mean that desirable and well-paid jobs are unavailable (at least with wages commensurate with those for native-born white men). However, employers realize that despite these shortcomings, workers do have other strengths, such as a strong work ethic, and are willing to employ them, but often at substandard pay.[65] In fact, a sizable body of literature surveying employer attitudes demonstrates that employers in a wide range of industries prefer certain groups of immigrant and ethnic workers (most commonly Asians, West Indians, and Latinos) over native-born whites and blacks.[66]

In the opinion of employers, immigrant workers may lack "hard skills" such as literacy, numeracy, and technical, job-related skills. However, their ample en-dowment with "soft skills . . . such things as communication and people skills, teamwork skills, demeanor, motivation, flexibility, initiative, work attitudes, and effort" make up for their lack of the former.[67] As a result, ethnic minority groups have saturated certain occupations. They have been able to develop niches in unskilled labor, factory work, landscaping, domestic service, hotel and restaurant positions, garment assembly, and other endeavors.[68]

In other cases, immigrant and ethnic workers may possess hard skills, but due to the labor market disadvantage produced by discrimination and outsider status, may accept jobs refused by natives. For example, because they speak English, are well-educated, and satisfy affirmative action mandates, West Indians fill the ranks of government, nonprofit, and health care jobs in New York City. The West Indian hold over this niche is assured because such positions do not appeal to Americans, yet other immigrants lack the skills they require.[69] Similarly, immigrant and minority professionals often concentrate in niches rejected by native whites, such as government and public health.[70] When ethnic niches develop, incumbents may then use their concentration and solidarity to acquire perquisites including promotions, flexibility, increased wages and benefits, and the provision of coethnics with jobs.[71] "The majority must now deal with the minority group or do without."[72]

It is important to note that groups most successful in developing such niches are characterized by a combination of resource disadvantage and other assets, including soft or hard skills and strong ethnic networks. Groups that encounter labor market disadvantage to the extent that they are infrequently hired, such as inner-city black men, have no opportunity to develop a niche.[73] Others, including immigrant women working in domestic service or the garment industry, have been unable to develop significant control over their niches.[74] For these groups, disadvantage remains just that and does not yield ethnic-controlled niches.

CHAPTER 9

Credit Issues in the Ethnic Ownership Economy

Ethnic ownership economies operate in environments that sometimes contain legal and institutional obstacles. When such obstacles exist, ethnic economies survive despite the resistance of their environment, and they could prosper better were that resistance eliminated. The American financial system poses this kind of obstacle. Enmeshed in obsolete laws, and wedded to banks as the flagship institution, the American financial system constrains ethnic ownership economies, inhibiting their growth and preventing them from generating all the jobs and economic mobility that would otherwise be possible.[1] Under the circumstances, a policy-oriented review of ethnic economies profitably addresses the manner in which the American financial system undermines ethnic economies, the reasons for it, and appropriate reforms.

Although the American financial system delivers credit effectively to the mainstream,[2] it has consistently failed to deliver basic savings and credit *outside* the mainstream.[3] For at least a century, banks have neglected low-income customers, small business, inner cities and slums, immigrants, nonwhites, and even women.[4] Neglect means infrequent service outlets, inconvenient service, high costs, and institutional unwillingness to make small consumer or business loans at all.[5] This neglect constrains and inhibits the entrepreneurship of the disadvantaged, causing their ethnic economies to grow more slowly than would otherwise have occurred

213

or not at all. Neglect prevents informal sector firms from expanding into the formal sector. It prevents some formal sector firms from growing and stifles others altogether. In this way, the financial system opposes the economic development of the neediest and most vulnerable sectors of American society.

This complaint is not new. The founders of the credit union movement leveled it against banks in the first two decades of this century. As a result of institutional reforms then effectuated, the credit union movement has remedied the banking industry's neglect, bringing saving and credit facilities to affinity groups.[6] Credit unions are growing rapidly. The credit union movement experienced fivefold growth in assets between 1980 and 1995, whereas, in the same period, commercial banks only doubled their assets.[7] However, in 1995, the assets of credit unions still represented only 6% of the assets of commercial banks and saving associations in the United States.[8] Commercial banks and thrifts still carry principal responsibility for credit and saving in the American economy, and they continue to obstruct and inhibit the ability of ethnic communities to help themselves.

Indeed, despite the Community Reinvestment Act of 1977,[9] the financial situation has worsened in the past two decades. When, following Reagan-era deregulation, banks reduced their service presence in American inner cities, their already inadequate level of financial service deteriorated *even further*, and is now worse than it was before deregulation.[10] In the wake of the departing bank branches, check cashing outlets and pawn shops have proliferated in inner cities.[11] Excluding racketeer- and state-sponsored lotteries, whose real if destructive financial role is concealed from view,[12] check cashing outlets and pawn shops are now the financial agencies most available to inner-city residents.[13] Check cashing outlets charge customers 3% of face value just to cash a paycheck or a welfare check. Neither pawn shops nor check cashing outlets offer savings accounts. Therefore, in inner cities, financial management is more expensive and less convenient than elsewhere.

Evaluating this dreary situation, counterparts to which exist in other countries,[14] Muhammed Yunus, founder of the Grameen Bank, identifies the banking industry as a contributory *cause* of poverty, welfare dependency, and economic stagnation and their related social problems.[15] Unfortunately, his argument has force. After all, whatever they also involve, both poverty and economic development, its converse, are centrally about money, saving, and credit. Mismanaging one's money, not saving one's money, and not enjoying access to business or mortgage credit create poverty where poverty did not already exist and exacerbate poverty where it already exists. The opposite conditions promote personal affluence and local economic development through the growth of ethnic economies. Therefore, when financial institutions enable low-income people to manage their money wisely and to obtain credit to buy a home or to start a small business, then the financial institutions help to minimize poverty and to prosper ethnic ownership economies.

However, when a financial system not only does not support poor people's ability to manage their money, to save money, to buy a home, or to start a business, but actually inhibits them all, then, Muhammed Yunus concludes, the financial system *cocauses* the poverty of the poor, making it worse and more extensive than it otherwise had to be.[16] The most damaging practice is unwarranted withholding of credit from very small businesses. Very small businesses created nearly one-half of net new employment in the United States between 1990 and 1995. Small businesses created three-quarters of new net employment.[17] When banks ignore small and very small business, they sabotage the job-creation process, dooming millions unnecessarily to unemployment and poverty. This indictment is very serious because, if true, the banking and financial systems coproduce and exacerbate poverty; they do not just coexist with it.

THE BANKERS' COUNTERARGUMENT

But is Muhammed Yunus's dramatic conclusion entirely fair? In self-defense, bankers argue that banks cannot service the poor because of inescapably negative cost considerations: providing financial services to low-income communities is unprofitable.[18] Much evidence supports the industry's contention. In a comprehensive review article, Solomon asserts that "The costs [for banks] to originate and service a $1,000 loan approximate those associated with a $100,000 loan," but the returns are $1/1000$ as large. Banks are not charities; they require revenues that pay for their services. Moreover, banks have obligations to stockholders and depositors such that "they cannot and should not be required to extend credit if sound judgment suggests undue risk."[19] On this view, costly and inconvenient financial services are a regrettable but unavoidable consequence of the high cost of providing those services to low-income communities.[20]

In a sense, the bankers' rebuttal even understates the institutional problem because the financial problems of the poor are cultural as well as situational, and bankers mention only situational problems. Anyone must acknowledge in fairness that poor people do not understand money management and credit so well as the nonpoor.[21] A century ago, bankers condemned the improvidence and thriftlessness of the poor. Today, one obtains the same coverage, less pejoratively, by acknowledging the nonmembership of the poor in the middle-class culture of money management. By the middle-class culture of money management we mean the basic knowledge, skills, and attitudes that permit people effectively to manage their finances. These resources are an important component of the cultural capital of the middle class. If they acquire it at all, people acquire the culture of money management as human capital, cultural capital, or both.[22] That is, people acquire the money culture in school, families of orientation, or both. Since neither schools nor families communicate the money culture to poor people, poor people do not routinely acquire it. Lacking basic financial knowledge, the poor consume incompetently, gamble more, and save less than they otherwise could. Their own financial mismanagement renders poor people even more difficult for the mainstream financial system to service than their low incomes would strictly require.[23]

Many of the same, distressing circumstances apply also to women.[24] Women earn less than men, and, as a class, they understand money management less well than men. Therefore, many would require adult education in order to attain financial literacy.[25] The stock market guru Elaine Garzarelli is enough proof that women do not lack financial capability. However, at least in Western societies, the cultural capital handed women less frequently includes money management than does the cultural capital handed men of the same class.[26] The causes of this state of affairs may invite feminist outrage, but there they indisputably are.[27] Women's low wages and their ignorance of the money system render women less profitable bank customers than men. When women are also poor, and two-thirds of poor adults are women, the financial incompetence and vulnerability of women accentuates the financial incompetence and vulnerability of the poor. Moreover, even as business owners, women own smaller firms than men, can advance less collateral than men, and so make even less profitable bank customers than men.[28]

The problems of small business borrowers are somewhat different from those of either the poor or of women. Unlike poor women, small business borrowers do not lack financial skills. Small business owners' incomes are also not lower than those of wage and salary workers. Small business owners have bank accounts and credit cards. However, their business credit needs are too small for profitability. Banks earn little or nothing on small business loans. The cost of administration of small loans' approaches or reaches the bank's revenue from the loan. Therefore, banks avoid small business loans because the costs of the loans are as high or higher than the income they generate. When banks cannot profitably lend, small business firms cannot hire, unemployment results, and poverty increases. This outcome is unfortunate, but it is arguably not the fault of the banks.

PARADOXES OF BANKING

To the extent that high costs and low revenues prevent banks from serving the poor, women, and small business without subsidies, banks escape blame for the rejection these groups receive and for the additional poverty that flows from it.[29] This failure is society's problem, not the banks' problem. Facing this plausible argument, the temptation is to conclude that saving and credit cannot be delivered to the poor, to immigrants, to women, or to small business unless Congress subsidizes the delivery from taxes. Bankers also argue now that informal agencies are available to pick up the rejectees.[30]

However, bankers may exaggerate the unprofitability of underserved markets in order to whitewash their own misconduct. This is the tack that American critics of the banking industry have taken with respect to the unmet credit needs of racial minorities.[31] Without denying the high costs of servicing these problem constituencies, critics complain that bankers discriminate against minorities for social reasons and not just because they are not creditworthy.[32] Anne Shlay's pioneering study of lending in Chicago found that "credit markets were segregated by race" such that, net of creditworthiness, black and Hispanic neighborhoods received "far less conventional finance than comparable white neighborhoods."[33] Squires and Kim found that the likelihood of black applicants' credit obtaining approval varied directly with the proportion of black employees in the banks.[34] The critics' case was strengthened when the Boston Federal Reserve Bank, a pillar of the banking establishment, published its own study of 131 Boston-area banks. Results showed that blacks and Hispanics were 56% more likely than nonminorities to be denied a mortgage loan *net* of creditworthiness.[35]

This result confirms the independent contribution of social discrimination to loan denials, indicating a situation that requires immediate rectification. However, it only weakens and does not demolish the banking industry's self-justification.[36] Taken together, strictly economic and cost-relevant factors, such as previous bankruptcies and late payments, were vastly more important predictors of loan denials than was race. The Boston results suggest that bank decisions depended principally upon creditworthiness and only secondarily upon race. If creditworthiness is already the main determinant of loan denial, and the negative contribution of race is minor, then even the elimination of racially motivated denials will have, at best, a minor influence upon the rate of loan denials minorities receive.[37] Moreover, what about loan denials to small business and to women? We have still no comparable evidence that social discrimination plays a big role in these denials.[38]

Related to this issue is measurement of just how unreasonably bad is the service that banks now provide to low-income neighborhoods. By *unreasonably bad service* we mean service that is worse than it has to be in view of the costs of banking. Reasonably bad service is bad service that reflects the realistic cost constraints of servicing problem markets but that does not exaggerate the cost constraints. If existing banking service is much worse than it has to be, and bank profits too high, then reform offers some possibility for improving the service banks offer, thus strengthening ethnic ownership economies. We agree that reform would have this beneficial effect. However, existing evidence does *not* suggest that the service banks now offer low-income neighborhoods falls wildly short of reasonably bad service. To assess the extent of banker abuse of low-income neighborhoods, the Woodstock Institute undertook a study of business loans in the six-county Chicago area between 1993 and 1996. After calculating the ratio of new business loans to existing businesses in poor, medium, and rich neighborhoods, Immergluck and Mullen found that poor neighborhoods received only 76% as many business loans as they should have obtained. At the opposite extreme, rich neighborhoods received 7% more business loans than would have been indicated by their share of existing business firms.[39] These results indicate unreasonable underservice of poor neighborhoods, but the underservice is modest, not egregious. Moreover, when one considers size and profitability of loans, and not just their number, one concludes that the banks' service record is better than the Woodstock results imply. In that case, the Woodstock results actually suggest that

Chicago-area banks were not providing unreasonably bad service to low-income neighborhoods.

We agree that government must prohibit banker discrimination, a serious white-collar crime. Prison sentences are appropriate penalties for bankers who discriminate on the basis of race, class, or gender. That said, rather than demonizing bankers, as critics of the banking industry do, we conclude that banks are *unable* to deliver unsubsidized services to some markets because of cost considerations.[40] Therefore, the banks' potential for service improvement would be modest even were they run by angels rather than bankers. However, this conclusion does not imply that no financial institution can deliver services to problem markets. Possibly *banks* cannot deliver these services, but other nonbank financial institutions can. In this case, the inability of the American financial system to service the low-income communities would stem from excessive reliance upon banks rather than from the misconduct of bankers. After all, banks are only a part of any financial system. Just because banks cannot deliver services to the troubled markets, one cannot conclude that no self-sustaining, unsubsidized institutions can deliver services there. Possibly our problem is a one-size-fits-all financial system whose flagship institution, banks, cannot service certain markets. In that case, reform of the financial system would strengthen ethnic economies by expanding the scope of nonbank institutions.

MICROCREDIT AND INFORMAL CREDIT

In point of fact, the American financial system already contains two nonbank financial institutions that target and serve exactly the problem markets that banks avoid and serve badly when they serve them at all. These are microcredit and informal credit. Informal credit refers to rotating savings and credit associations (ROSCAs), the current nomenclature for what were once called rotating credit associations. The new terminology has one big advantage. The words reflect the institution's dual role in saving and credit, whereas the old term, *rotating credit association*, gave the erroneous impression, encouraged by Bates, that ROSCAs only provide credit.[41] In actuality, saving is the ROSCAs' main activity.[42] Found widely in Latin America, Central America, Africa, and Asia, ROSCAs have different names in different regions, and the practice also varies somewhat. For example, the Korean ROSCA is called *kye*, the Jamaican ROSCA *partners*, and the Haitian ROSCA *san*.[43] But all ROSCAs have in common their defining feature: a club whose members contribute to a fund that is rotated among the membership at successive meetings until all the members have received the fund and all but the last have enjoyed an advance upon saving. When all have received the joint fund, the club is terminated, and a new one formed, usually with substantial continuity of membership.

ROSCAs are old but not ancient; the oldest ROSCAs are about 400 years old, and their membership is predominantly female in most countries.[44] Modernization theorists of the 1960s predicted their imminent demise in collision with the supposedly superior financial institutions of advanced market capitalism, especially banks.[45] Haveman and Roa claim that modernization did wipe out indigenous ROSCAs in the United States, the parents of today's thrifts.[46] However, Third World ROSCAs have not only survived into the present, they are more pervasive than ever. "In a typical year, at least one-fifth of all households in Taiwan participate in ROSCAs."[47] Moreover, Third World ROSCA users are not principally remote peasants, insulated from modern financial institutions. Rather, the most likely ROSCA subscribers in the Third World are white-collar workers in big cities.[48] The survival and proliferation of ROSCAs in Third World cities signals a traditional financial institution that competes successfully with banks.

Unlike ROSCAs, microcredit is new in the world. Solomon defines *microcredit* as "a loan fund, usually organized as a nonprofit organization, [that] makes very small short-term working capital loans to people who wish to start or expand a small business."[49] The borrowers then repay the loan from the proceeds of the business. At the end of the loan cycles, the borrowers have repaid their loans with interest, but they still own the small businesses they started with their loans. The case of Mrs. K is typical. Mrs. K is a member of the Na Poe Village Bank in Northeast Thailand. This bank was created by the Catholic Relief Services. Like most women in her area, Mrs. K works in rice fields and raises pigs and chickens to sell on the market. Upon joining the village bank, Mrs. K got a $50 loan. Using this money, she bought more pigs; on the proceeds from the sale of these pigs, she repaid her loan. This repayment made her eligible for a $75 loan. With her $75 loan, she bought chickens and ducks and increased her silk weaving. By the end of the fourth loan cycle, Mrs. K had personal savings of $160, she owned a viable business of her own, she had improved her family's living standard, and she had even helped her oldest son to start his own silversmith business.[50]

The oldest of the microcredit agencies and the parent of the concept is the Grameen Bank of Bangladesh.[51] The Grameen Bank began in 1976, when its founder, Dr. Muhammed Yunus, loaned each of 42 impoverished Bangladeshis 62 cents, stipulating that recipients invest the loan in a business. Recipients purchased raw materials for weaving and potting businesses and earned from their microbusinesses the wherewithal to repay their loans. As of 1998, the Grameen Bank, of which Muhammed Yunus is still president, had 12,000 employees who staffed 1112 branches that served 2,300,000 borrowers in 36,000 villages of Bangladesh. Every month the Grameen Bank lent $35,000,000 in "tiny loans." Grameen Bank loans average $100, and the bank enjoys a repayment rate of 98%, higher than what the Bank of America obtains from its loans in California.[52]

The Grameen Bank is not really a bank; that is why it can target markets that real banks cannot service. True, Grameen Bank meets its operating expenses by collecting interest from loan recipients just as do banks. Moreover, this interest is pegged at market rates. However, Grameen Bank is a nonprofit organization, not a profit-making business. Second, Grameen Bank now loans *only* to impoverished *women*. Third, and most important, Grameen Bank expanded its relationship with customers far beyond the arm's-length convention of American business. Indeed, this extension is its unique innovation. Without utilizing encumbering legal contracts or even requiring collateral, Grameen Bank assigns borrowers to "solidarity groups" of five members. Each group member is responsible for the debts of the other four, and in case any group member defaults on her loan, the other four must repay her defaulted loan or lose eligibility for further loans from Grameen Bank. This compulsory interdependence powerfully encourages the formation of a moral community within the solidarity group.[53] Finally, Grameen Bank requires borrowers to modernize their social existence, pledging, for example, to send their children to school, to build a latrine, and to practice birth control. No one can become a Grameen borrower who does not join a solidarity group and pledge to modernize her family's lifestyle.

ROSCAs AND MICROCREDIT IN THE UNITED STATES

The extent of ROSCA use in the United States today is harder to ascertain than the extent of microcredit use. ROSCAs are informal; they do not report operating statistics. As a result, the *only* evidence about ROSCAs is social scientists' ethnographic research. This evidence certainly proves that ROSCAs are widespread in virtually all contemporary immigrant communities that originated in the Third World.[54] Among current immigrant groups for whom solid evidence of extensive ROSCA involvement in the United States now exists are Koreans, Vietnamese, Mexicans, Salvadorans, Guatemalans, Trinidadians, Jamaicans, Barbadans, and Ethiopians. Historical research also shows that ROSCAs were common among Asian and Caribbean immigrants in the United States in the first half of this century, but some of the groups that used ROSCAs then, such as the Japanese Americans, no longer do so. At least in the case of third-generation Chinese Americans, who have also stopped using ROSCAs, Wong attributes the dissociation to the availability of homes for collateral on any loans.[55]

ROSCAs serve immigrants, minorities, women, and small business, constituencies banks avoid. ROSCAs do *not* service the destitute, the unemployed, nor those without social capital. Of course, immigrant ROSCAs operate at economic levels appropriate to their participants. Wealthier immigrant groups, such as Koreans, have higher-stakes ROSCAs than do poor immigrants, such as Salvadorans. However, even within immigrant communities, ROSCAs adjust the stakes to suit the economic level of participants. For example, Korean ROSCAs that cater to business owners sometimes require monthly investments of $5000, whereas Salvadoran ROSCAs that cater to workers require monthly investments of $50. ROSCAs tap informal sources of creditworthiness, expanding the circle of the creditworthy beyond what banks can imitate. For example, ROSCAs can lend to a young person on the social collateral provided by parents, who, though not obliged by law to do so, are known to stand surety for that young person's debt. Banks cannot do that. However, even ROSCAs cannot lend money to impecunious and unemployed youths who lack creditworthy parents willing to stand surety for them. In general, ROSCAs serve those who have both dependable incomes *and* social capital; they cannot serve people who lack either one.

Unlike microcredit borrowers, who must invest in business firms, ROSCA members may use their loans for any purpose. Latinos in American cities mainly use ROSCA loans for consumption, especially weddings, *quincineras*, and consumer durables. Few Latinos apply ROSCAs to business purposes. Among Caribbean and Asian ROSCA users, the largest group also utilize ROSCA cash for consumption, but significant minorities involve ROSCA funds in their business operations. One way is up-front as equity capital; more commonly, ROSCA loans provide short-term credit to relieve cash-flow problems. ROSCA credit occasionally enters directly in home purchase, whether as downpayment or mortgage payment.[56] Of course, a big motive for forced and energetic saving in a ROSCA is downpayment on a home, so equity funds saved in ROSCAs commonly provide the downpayment for immigrant hómes. ROSCAs may explain the much more rapid growth of home ownership among poor immigrants than among impoverished native blacks and native whites.

MICROCREDIT IN THE UNITED STATES

The profile of microcredit in the United States is easier to document than is the profile of ROSCAs. Severens and Kays identified 328 microenterprise programs in 47 states in 1995.[57] These programs are new. Of these 328 agencies, 85% were less than 10 years old.[58] In their short lives, the 328 agencies had collectively loaned $126 million to 171,555 needy people. Microentrepreneurs received $35 million in 1995 alone. Of the 36,211 businesses that received assistance in that year, 38% were start-ups and the remainder existing businesses. Women and nonwhites were the majority of borrowers. Three-quarters of microcredit agencies had a borrower clientele that was predominantly women; 62% of borrowers were also nonwhite.

American microcredit shares with its international parent this basic contract: You must repay your loan, attend your training program, and manage your business in order to receive further assistance (Edgcomb, Klein, & Clark, 1996). However, American microcredit agencies have considerably diversified program activities beyond Grameen's group lending method. In fact, only a fifth of American microcredit programs continue the Grameen-inspired policy of group lending. American microcredit agencies offer forms of microcredit that do not derive from the Grameen parent. The first are credit-led individual loan programs that sometimes also offer technical assistance and training. Of all the microcredit programs, the credit-led individual loans most closely approximate banking. Their goal is to provide credit to those who, lacking access to bank credit, are nonetheless capable of developing and managing their businesses with minimal support. The agency provides that minimal support and seeks to recoup the cost from user fees.

The second American innovation is training-led strategies, in which successful clients gain access to credit after they complete their training.[59] Training-led strategies have two principal forms: business development strategies and welfare client strategies. The business development strategies require clients to develop a viable business plan before they access credit. Training of welfare clients has a similar structure, but its training period is more intensive, typically 80 hours as opposed to 28 hours. Moreover, the training program includes more personal assistance in recognition of the welfare clients' low educational levels. Finally, the training program requests welfare authorities to exempt trainees from legal prohibition against income generation or asset accumulation on the part of welfare recipients.

Of those that offer them at all, American microcredit agencies target Grameen-style group lending programs to the most marginal users. However, for reasons that are not understood, but probably include the prevalence of drug and alcohol addiction in the United States, group lending has been less effective in the United States than had been expected from the Grameen example. Balkin concludes that, compared with the poor of Bangladesh, the poor of the United States are also "relatively impoverished in social capital," and so are actually worse situated than the poor of Bangladesh.[60] We agree. As a result, repayment rates are lower in the American microcredit groups than in the Grameen Bank's groups. The American solidarity groups also have been harder to form and to keep together than the Bangladeshi groups. American groups have not exerted the kind of loan discipline over members that had been expected from the Grameen Bank experience, and cost-effectiveness has been less than expected as well.[61]

American microcredit staff members tend to select and promote the most creditworthy of the impoverished, not the least creditworthy as does the Grameen Bank. In view of the difficulty American microcredit agencies experience in forming solidarity groups, a problem we attribute to the troubled environment of social capital, they incline toward strategies that stress the individual client who obtains counseling and education. The most creditworthy of the disadvantaged clients offer the most successful and cost-effective prospects for individual training. Therefore, American microcredit agencies select those individuals to coach who have the highest likelihood of success in the program. American recipients of microcredit loans typically have more formal education and more job experience than the average welfare recipient and sometimes even more than the average American. Although living in poverty and on welfare, these microcredit trainees had class resources that the poorest Americans lack.[62] For these reasons, Bates and Servon declare that "microenterprise programs do more to help those who exist at the margins of the mainstream economy" than to help "those who are completely cut off."[63] Although a fair encapsulation of microcredit programs' performance to date, Bates and Servon's generalization does not distinguish between the three principal forms of American microcredit. Borrowers enrolled in Grameen-style solidarity groups are the poorest and least creditworthy of the microcredit clients. Therefore, the statistics to which Bates and Servon call attention probably apply to the 80% of microcredit programs that do not utilize the Grameen-style technique of solidarity groups. Less effective here than in Bangladesh, Grameen-style microcredit is not completely ineffective in the United States.

MICROCREDIT AND INFORMAL CREDIT

How do microcredit and ROSCAs make unsubsidized saving and credit available to people whom banks cannot service? This is a feat. Let us acknowledge that their success in this task is only partial. ROSCAs do not and cannot service those who lack social capital, jobs, or the tradition of participating in ROSCAs. These limitations restrict their scope. Conversely, unlike the Grameen Bank of Bangladesh, American microcredit agencies still require subsidies, albeit small and cost-effective ones. Microcredit agencies can, however, service people who lack jobs, social capital, and the cultural tradition of ROSCA participation. These advantages extend their potential clientele into groups that ROSCAs cannot reach any more than can banks. On the whole, ROSCAs and microcredit are not competing for the same clientele. The clients of microcredit agencies are poorer.

This said, microcredit and informal credit share more than just nondiscrimination against minorities.[64] Ultimately, Grameen-style microcredit and informal credit succeed in the underserved markets *because* they are not banks. The key difference between Grameen-style microcredit and informal credit on the one hand and banks on the other is the various institutions' different orientation to the borrowers' social capital. True, banks utilize formal credit agencies to assess creditworthiness. Credit agencies sell a commodified social capital, so one cannot say that banks make *no* use of social capital at all. However, banks neither build nor require social capital among borrowers, nor do banks accept social capital as loan collateral.[65] Bank customers enter the bank as individuals and no matter how many years they remain bank customers, they never build social capital with other customers.

In contrast, ROSCAs require applicants to present already existing social capital as a condition of borrowing.[66] Only those whose existing social capital guarantees their creditworthiness[67] will be accepted as ROSCA members. Reliance upon preexisting social capital permits ROSCAs to make noncollateralized loans because the collateral is the borrowers' social capital. The reason ROSCAs can extend the boundary of creditworthiness beyond what banks can attain is ultimately this capability: ROSCAs accept enforceable social capital as collateral. If banks could enforce existing social capital, they might accept it as collateral. In that case, banks could also make loans to the poor, to immigrants, to women, and to small business. However, banks cannot accept social capital as collateral, and so long as they remain banks they will never have that capability. ROSCAs succeed in their niche because they do something banks cannot.

Unlike ROSCAs, Grameen-style group lending programs do not require borrowers to present social capital as a ticket of admission. Those without social capital are welcome to join a microcredit solidarity group, a flexibility that considerably expands access beyond the limits of those eligible for ROSCA membership. However, Grameen-style microcredit agencies consciously impose social capital development upon borrowers as a condition of loan access.[68] Five-woman solidarity groups represent social capital that the Grameen-style agency created rather than social capital that female borrowers already enjoyed and then presented as collateral. Upon entry to the microcredit agency, the individual women are normally unacquainted and lack the solidarity that, once in place, finally confers creditworthiness. Because of mutual responsibility for loans and joint training exercises, microcredit borrowers acquire the enforceable social capital that alone makes them creditworthy, but they need not command that social capital as a ticket of admission to the agency. In this sense, the Grameen-style microcredit agency opens its doors to people neither banks nor ROSCAs could serve.

The poor normally lack jobs, education, and collateral, but they need not also lack social capital.[69] Even if they do lack social capital, the poor need not also lack the capacity to form social capital. When the poor have no collateral, banks cannot make them creditworthy, no matter what their social capital. When the poor lack collateral but have social capital, then ROSCAs can make them creditworthy anyway. When the poor lack collateral and social capital, but retain the capacity to form social capital, then Grameen-style microcredit can make them creditworthy. That is why microcredit agencies can reach people whom ROSCAs cannot. Problems arise when the poor, lacking collateral, also lack social capital and even lack the capacity to form social capital. Unfortunately, because of American social conditions, including the prevalence of addictions, and the extreme individualism of the American culture,[70] inability to form social capital occurs more frequently here than in Bangladesh. As a result, Grameen-style solidarity groups are harder to form and to maintain in North America than in Bangladesh. Therefore, American microcredit agencies cannot make all the poor creditworthy by creating social capital, the usual strategy in Bangladesh. Under the circumstances, American microcredit agencies have been compelled to change strategy. Training individuals displaces creation of social capital as the first priority. Agencies naturally prefer to train clients who already have the most human and cultural capital because they are easiest to train. In this manner, the American microcredit agencies select for training and loans the least impoverished of the poor rather than the most impoverished.

CONCLUSION

Banks have never provided financial services to immigrants, to the poor, to women, and to small business. In self-defense, bankers claim that the costs of servicing these markets surpass the revenue they yield. Unpersuaded, critics of the banking industry claim that social discrimination contributes to the banks' neglect of these markets. Reviewing the evidence, we find that social discrimination is a real but minor contributor to the poor service banks offer. The main contributor is the high cost banks face when servicing these problem markets. However, this conclusion does not prove that only subsidies can improve the access of immigrants, nonwhites, the poor, women, and small business to financial services.[71] Banks cannot service these markets but microcredit and informal credit can and, indeed, already do.

Grameen-style microcredit and informal credit are nonbank financial institutions that not only reach but actually target the banks' problem markets. As Table 9.1 specifies, enforceable social capital is the key to their ability to accomplish this feat. Banks do not accept social capital as loan collateral, but both informal credit and microcredit do. For this reason, both microcredit and informal credit can make loans to underserved groups to whom banks cannot lend. However, informal credit and microcredit vary greatly in which lenders they can accept. Informal credit requires prior and existing social capital among users as a condition of admission. Those who cannot be enforceably trusted cannot be admitted. In this practice, informal credit gives much more scope and range to social capital than do banks, whose operating vision is ultimately framed in liberal individualism. Unlike informal credit, however, Grameen-style microcredit does not require that clients present existing social capital at the time of entry. But Grameen-style microcredit does require clients to develop social capital as a condition of borrowing. The creation of enforceable trust permits Grameen-style microcredit agencies to expand the circle of creditworthiness to destitute people who, lacking all other resources, can at least build social capital.[72] This expansion enlarges the circle of the creditworthy beyond what even informal credit could reach because the very poorest individuals typically lack social capital.

In the American social context, one finds more poor people who, lacking collateral and social capital, even lack the capacity to form social capital. Caroline Moser supposes that impoverished people who lack social capital are the poorest

TABLE 9.1   ROSCAs and Microcredit: Access Requirements

	Banks	ROSCA	Grameen-style microcredit
Enforce social capital	No	Yes	Yes
Social capital provides loan collateral	No	Yes	Yes
Participation requires prior social capital	No	Yes	No
Participation builds social capital	No	Yes	Yes
Participation requires ability to form social capital	No	Yes	Yes

of the poor. We disagree; a worse poverty exists. When the poor lack social capital and even lack the capacity to form social capital, their situation is worse than when they only lack social capital. Such people are truly the poorest of the poor.[73] A cultural import from Bangladesh, Grameen-style microcredit cannot assist these poor people, so most American microcredit agencies have shifted their priority from creation of social capital to training trainable individuals. When training individuals becomes the goal, then agencies acquire an incentive to select from the pool of impoverished loan applicants those who require the least training. Training them is easier and cheaper than attempting to build social capital among those who cannot build it. However, this new strategy encounters the objection that the agency is selecting the least impoverished of the poor. Moreover, the training of individuals costs money, so the microcredit agencies require subsidies to offer it.

Contrasting banks on the one hand and, on the other, informal credit and microcredit, we find that each institution's orientation to social capital explains success or failure in the problem markets.[74] Except for institutional credit checks, a commodified social capital, banks ignore borrowers' uncommodified social capital. However, ROSCAs and Grameen-style microcredit lenders orient their entire strategy around social capital. Compared with this reorientation, the social discrimination of the bankers is of modest importance. This institutional difference in orientation explains why banks cannot service the problem markets whereas microcredit and informal credit can. Therefore, the chronic failure of the American financial system to deliver services to the problem markets arises from an excessive reliance upon banks. It is as though American society asked beavers to fly as well as to build dams, then criticized eager beavers for incompetence. To reach the problem markets, the American financial system needs to diversify institutional forms, expanding the role and scope of informal credit and microcredit without eliminating the vital role banks play in the mainstream. The trouble is, microcredit and informal credit are, relative to banks, still few in number, short of assets, and subject to obsolete laws that curtail their growth.[75] Therefore, the development of a balanced financial system, which better serves the needs of the poor, of women, and of small business, requires structural reform of banking.

Endnotes

Chapter 1

1. John Sibley Butler, *Self-Help and Entrepreneurship among Black Americans* (Albany: State University of New York, 1991), 209–17.
2. Ivan Light, Hadas Har-Chvi, and Kenneth Kan, "Black/Korean Conflict in Los Angeles," ch. 6 in Seamus Dunn, ed., *Managing Divided Cities* (Newbury Park, CA: Sage, 1994), 73.
3. Light, Har-Chvi, and Kan, *Managing Divided Cities,* 75.
4. "Indonesians Riot over Prices, Unemployment," *Los Angeles Times,* February 14, 1998, sec. A, p. 4.
5. "Once Again, Indonesia Starts Living Dangerously," *The Economist,* February 21, 1998, p. 37; "Taking the Blame," *The Economist,* February 28, 1998, p. 46. See also Keith B. Richburg, "Chinese Bear Brunt of Indonesia's Ills," *Manchester Guardian Weekly,* January 17, 1999, p. 20.
6. Ivan Light and Carolyn Rosenstein, *Race, Ethnicity, and Entrepreneurship in Urban America* (Hawthorne, N.Y.: Aldine de Gruyter, 1995), 205.
7. Werner Sombart, *The Jews and Modern Capitalism* (Glencoe, IL: Free Press, 1953), 33.
8. Max Weber, *Basic Concepts in Sociology* (New York, Greenwood Press, 1969), 109, 251–52; and H. H. Gerth and C. Wright Mills, *From Max Weber: Essays in Sociology* (New York: Oxford University Press, 1958), 189, 215.
9. For contemporary discussion of the economic role of Jews in Europe, see Hillel J. Kieval, "Middleman Minorities and Blood: Is There a Natural Economy of the Ritual Murder Accusation in Europe?", Ch. 8, and Victor Karady, "Jewish Entrepreneurship and Identity under Capitalism and Socialism in Central Europe," in Daniel Chirot and Anthony Reid, eds., *Essential Outsiders* (Seattle: University of Washington, 1997), 125–52.
10. One might suppose that Jews would welcome the honor of having invented capitalism. However, in Wilhelmian Germany, capitalism was hated on the feudal–landed right wing as well as on the socialist left wing. Therefore, capitalism's inventors would have been obnoxious to many Germans. To blame the Jews for inventing capitalism was, in that political climate, to lay opprobrium at their door, thus bolstering old-fashioned religious anti-Semitism with economic arguments. In point of fact, a generation later, Hitler's left-wing supporters did lay this historical opprobrium at the doorstep of the Jews. In recognition of *The Jews and Modern Capitalism,* Weber's contemporary and intellectual rival, Werner Sombart, received an honorary membership in Hitler's party. See Anthony D. Reid, "Entrepreneurial Minorities, Nationalism, and the State," in Daniel Chirot and Anthony Reid, eds., *Essential Outsiders,* ch. 2. On the whole controversy, see Karl-

Siegbert Reherg, "Das Bild des Judentums in der Fruehen Deutschen Soziologie," in Erhard Wrehn, eds., *Juden in der Soziologie* (Konstanz: Hartung-Gorre, 1989), 127–73.

11. Edna Bonacich and John Modell, *The Economic Basis of Ethnic Solidarity* (Los Angeles: University of California, 1981), 13.

12. Indeed, as Jane Winn observes, this intellectual climate still persists in development studies. See "Law, Culture, and Development: Relational Contract and the Informal Sector of Taiwan," in *Workshop on Enterprises, Social Relations, and Cultural Practices: Studies of the Chinese Societies* (Taipei: Academica Sinica, 1992).

13. Gerth and Mills, *From Max Weber: Essays in Sociology,* 189. See also Max Weber, *General Economic History* (New Brunswick, NJ: Transaction, 1981), ch. 6.

14. Robert Blauner, *Racial Oppression in America* (New York: Harper & Row, 1972), ch. 2.

15. Edna Bonacich, "A Theory of Middleman Minorities," *American Sociological Review* 38 (1973), 583–94.

16. Robin Cohen, *Global Diasporas* (Seattle: University of Washington, 1997), 101–4.

17. Rehberg, "Das Bild des Judentums in der Fruehen Deutschen Soziologie," 127–73; and Suzanne Model, "The Economic Progress of European and East Asian Americans," in Norman R. Yetman, ed., *Majority and Minority,* 5th ed. (Boston: Allyn & Bacon, 1991), 292–93.

18. Howard Paul Becker, *Man in Reciprocity* (New York: Praeger, 1956), 225–37.

19. Reid, "Entrepreneurial Minorities, Nationalism, and the State," 39, 58; and Walter Zenner, *Minorities in the Middle* (Albany: State University of New York, 1991), 7.

20. Abner Cohen, *Custom and Politics in Urban Africa* (Berkeley and Los Angeles: University of California Press, 1969), 8–9, 14–25.

21. F. Bechofer and B. Elliott, "The Petite Bourgeoisie in Late Capitalism," *Annual Review of Sociology* (1985): 185–86.

22. Clifford Geertz, "The Rotating Credit Association: A 'Middle Rung' in Development," *Economic Development and Cultural Change* 10 (1962), 241–63.

23. Jar-Der Luo, "The Significance of Networks in the Initiation of Small Businesses in Taiwan," *Sociological Forum* 12 (1997), 313; Dale W. Adams and M. L. Canavesi de Sahonero, "Rotating Savings and Credit Associations in Bolivia," *Savings and Development* 13 (1989), 219–36.

24. Leon Mayhew, "Ascription in Modern Societies," *Sociological Inquiry* 38 (1968), 105–20; Burton Benedict, "Family Firms and Economic Development," *Southwestern Journal of Anthropology* 24 (1968), 1–29; Wayne E. Nafziger, "The Effect of the Nigerian Extended Family on Entrepreneurial Activity," *Economic Development and Cultural Change* 18 (1969), 25–33; Brigitte Berger, "The Culture of Modern Entrepreneurship," in Brigitte Berger, *The Culture of Entrepreneurship* (San Francisco: ICS, 1991), 24.

25. Bonacich, "A Theory of Middleman Minorities," 583–94.

26. Jose Cobas, "Puerto Rican Reactions to Cuban Immigrants: Insights from Trading Minority Interpretations," *Ethnic and Racial Studies* 9 (1986), 535; Ivan Light and Edna Bonacich, *Immigrant Entrepreneurs* (Berkeley and Los Angeles: University of California Press, 1988), 17–20; Howard Aldrich and Roger Waldinger, "Ethnicity and Entrepreneurship," *Annual Review of Sociology* 16 (1990), 125.

27. Suzanne Berger defined the "traditional sector" of France and Italy as those groups whose "activities involve the production of goods with technologies, costs, capital-labor ratios, and patterns of ownership and management that are significantly different from those used in the production of the same goods by other, modern firms. . . . We are above all describing the class of small, independent property owners: farmers, shopkeepers, artisans, and certain small and medium businessmen." See "The Traditional Sector in France and Italy," ch. 4 in Suzanne Berger and Michael Piore, eds., *Dualism and Discontinuity in Industrial Societies* (Cambridge: Cambridge University Press, 1980), 91.

28. Ivan Light and Stavros Karageorgis, "The Ethnic Economy," in Neil Smelser and Richard Swedberg, eds., *Handbook of Economic Sociology* (New York: Russell Sage Foundation, 1994), 648.

29. Cobas, "Puerto Rican Reactions to Cuban Immigrants: Insights from Trading Minority Interpretations"; David J. O'Brien and Stephen S. Fugita, *Japanese American Ethnicity: The Persistence of Community* (Seattle: University of Washington Press, 1991), 200; and Zenner, *Minorities in the Middle.*

30. Martin Marger, "East Indians in Small Business: Middleman Minority or Ethnic Enclave?" *New Community* 16 (1990): 551–59.

31. Cobas, "Puerto Rican Reactions to Cuban Immigrants: Insights from Trading Minority Interpretations."

32. Light and Bonacich, *Immigrant Entrepreneurs*, 17–200.

33. Lever-Tracy, David Ip, and Noel Tracy, *The Chinese Diaspora and Mainland China* (New York: St. Martin's, 1996), ch. 14.

34. An intriguing parallel exists between this situation and the emergence of alternative medical therapies that challenge the medical mainstream. No one suggests that the alternative therapies, many derived from traditional remedies, can replace allopathic medicine, the "scientific" mainstream. On the other hand, acupuncture, transcendental meditation, yoga, tai chi chuan, homeopathy, herbalism, and other alternative medical systems cure selected ailments invulnerable to allopathic intervention while cost-effectively preventing the appearance of disease in other cases. These achievements have brought alternative medicine back into the armamentarium of pragmatic therapists.

35. Booker T. Washington, *The Negro in Business* (New York: Johnson Reprint Co., 1907).

36. W. E. Burghardt DuBois, *The Philadelphia Negro* (Philadelphia: University of Pennsylvania Press, 1899).

37. Shelley Green and Paul Pryde, *Black Entrepreneurship in America* (New Brunswick, NJ: Transaction, 1997), 20; and Kelleye Jones, "Johnson Publishing, Inc., A Case of Strategic Development," *Journal of Developmental Entrepreneurship* 2 (1997), 113–14.

38. Robert E. Weems, "Out of the Shadows: Business Enterprise and African American Historiography," *Business and Economic History* 26 (1997): 204.

39. Harold Cruse, *The Crisis of the Negro Intellectual* (New York: William Morrow, 1967), 19.

40. See, for example, Robert L. Woodson, "A Legacy of Entrepreneurship," in Robert L. Woodson, ed., *On the Road to Economic Freedom* (Washington, D.C.: Regnery Gateway, 1987), ch. 1.

41. Ivan Light, *Ethnic Enterprise in America* (Berkeley and Los Angeles: University of California Press, 1972), ch. 6; and John Sibley, *Entrepreneurship and Self-Help among Black Americans* (Albany, NY: State University of New York, 1991), chs. 1, 2.

42. Light, *Ethnic Enterprise in America*, ch. 5.

43. "All groups support at least some entrepreneurship; hence, the presence of self-employment does not meaningfully distinguish among them." Suzanne Model, "Ethnic Economy and Industry in Mid-Twentieth Century Gotham," *Social Problems* 44 (1997), 459.

44. Roger Waldinger, *Still the Promised City?* (Cambridge: Harvard University Press, 1996), 255; and Peter S. Li, "Self-Employment and Its Economic Return for Visible Minorities in Canada," in David M. Saunders, ed., *New Approaches to Employee Management, vol. 2, Discrimination in Employment* (Greenwich, CT: JAI Press Inc, 1994), 182.

45. Steven J. Gold, *Refugee Communities* (Newbury Park, CA: Sage, 1992), 180–81, 194.

46. Bonacich and Modell, *The Economic Basis of Ethnic Solidarity*, 45.

47. Jock Collins, "Cosmopolitan Capitalism: Ethnicity, Gender, and Australian Entrepreneurs," (Ph.D. diss., University of Wollongong, 1998), I: 4, 72.

48. Sie-Lun Wong, *Emigrant Entrepreneurs: Shanghai Industrialists in Hong Kong* (New York: Oxford University Press, 1988).

49. Ivan Light, Georges Sabagh, Mehdi Bozorgmehr, and Claudia Der-Martirosian, "Les quarte economies ethniques das iraniens a Los Angeles," *Revue europeenne des migrations internationales* 8 (1992).

50. Luis Guarnizo, *The Mexican Ethnic Economy in Los Angeles: Capitalist Accumulation, Class Restructuring, and the Transnationalization of Migration* (Davis, CA: California Communities Program of the University of California, 1998), 10.

51. Light and Karageorgis, "The Ethnic Economy," 647–71.

52. Bonacich and Modell, *The Economic Basis of Ethnic Solidarity*, chs. 12–14.

53. O'Brien and Fugita, *Japanese American Ethnicity: The Persistence of Community*, chap. 7.

54. Charles Hirschman, "America's Melting Pot Reconsidered," *Annual Review of Sociology* 9 (1983), 397–423.

55. Barbara Lal distinguishes ethnic entrepreneurs, who own businesses, from "ethnic identity entrepreneurs," who promote essentialized versions of ethnic identity out of occupational self-interest. "Ethnic Identity Entrepreneurs: Their Role in Transracial and Intercountry Adoptions," *Asian and Pacific Migration Journal* 6 (1997), 385–413.

56. Jeffrey G. Reitz, "Ethnic Concentrations in Labour Markets and Their Implications for Ethnic Inequality," in Raymond Aron *et al.*, eds., *Ethnic Groups and Social Inclusion: A Comparative Study of Resources and Constraints in an Urban Setting* (Toronto: University of Toronto Press, 1990), 138–39.

57. Neoliberals claim that an immigrant economy constrains immigrants' potential for upward mobility by restricting workers to an ethnic business sector. Guarnizo, *The Mexican Ethnic Economy in Los Angeles: Capitalist Accumulation, Class Restructuring, and the Transnationalization of Migration*, 3.

58. Jeffrey G. Reitz and Sherrilyn Sklar, "Culture, Race, and the Economic Assimilation of Immigrants," *Sociological Forum* 12 (1997), 269.

59. In fairness to the assimilation model, its predictions are a matter of speed as well as of direction. Conceivably, the assimilation model's predictions will ultimately prove as successful among nonwhites as they already have among whites. However, it will have taken longer to reach this point. See Ivan Light, "Ethnic Succession," in Charles F. Keyes, ed., *Ethnic Change* (Seattle: University of Washington Press, 1981), 68–69.

60. "Data from the 1991 Australian census shows that many [non-English-speaking background] immigrant groups continue to have a higher relative presence as employers and self-employed than do the Australian-born in the 1990s." High entrepreneurship groups in Australia include those from Korea, Greece, Italy, Germany, Holland, the Czech Republic, Slovakia, Taiwan, and Hungary. Low entrepreneurship groups in Australia include those from Japan, India, Sri Lanka, Vietnam, Indonesia, and Turkey. Average entrepreneurship groups include those from China, Singapore, Malaysia, Egypt, Lebanon, Poland, Ukraine, Yugoslavia, Canada, and the United States. Collins, "Cosmopolitan Capitalism: Ethnicity, Gender, and Australian Entrepreneurs," I:239.

61. Stephen Castles *et al.* identify similar but not identical patterns in Australia, another pluralistic market society. *The Global Milkbar and the Local Sweatshop: Ethnic Small Business and the Economic Restructuring of Sydney* (Wollongong, Australia: Office of Multicultural Affairs, Dept. of the Prime Minister and Cabinet, by the Centre for Multicultural Studies, University of Wollongong, 1991).

62. Frank Fratoe and R. L. Meeks, "Business Participation Rates of the 50 Largest U.S. Ancestry Groups: Preliminary Report," Research Division, Minority Business Development Agency of the U.S. Department of Commerce, 1995; Frank Fratoe, "A Sociological Analysis of Minority Business," *Review of Black Poltical Economy* 15 (1986), 6–29; Teresa A. Sullivan and Stephen D. McCracken, "Black Entrepreneurs: Patterns and Rates of Return to Self-Employment," *National Journal of Sociology* 2 (1988), 167–85; and Constance A. Hoffman and Martin N. Marger, "Patterns of Immigrant Enterprise in Six Metropolitan Areas," *Sociology and Social Research* 75 (1991), 144–57.

63. Morteza H. Ardebili, "The Economic Adaptation of Iranian Immigrants in the Kansas City Metropolitan Area," (Ph.D. diss., University of Kansas, 1986), 116; M. D. R. Evans, "Language Skill, Language Usage, and Opportunity: Immigrants in the Australian Labour Market," *Sociology* 21 (1987), 258; and Monica Boyd, "Family and Personal Networks in International Migration: Recent Developments and New Agendas," *International Migration Review* 23 (1989), 654.

64. Robert T. Averitt, *The Dual Economy: The Dynamics of American Industry Structure* (New York: W. W. Norton, 1968); and Robert M. Jiobu, "Ethnic Hegemony and the Japanese of California," *American Sociological Review* 53 (1988), 184–85.

65. Charles Tolbert, Patrick Horan, and E. M. Beck, "The Structure of Economic Segregation: A Dual Approach," *American Journal of Sociology* 85 (1980), 1095–1116.

66. Impossible because, where noncommunicating labor markets exist, employers will hire cheap noncoethnic labor in preference to expensive coethnic labor. As this practice spreads, the formerly noncommunicating labor markets merge into a single labor market.

67. Pierre Bourdieu condemns the practice of simplifying economic reality to make it agree with economic theory. ("L'essence du neoliberalisme," *Le Monde Diplomatique* March 1998: 3. Available: http://www.mondediplomatique.fr/md/1998/03/BOURDIEU/19167.html)

68. Teresa A. Sullivan, "Sociological Views of Labor Markets: Some Missed Opportunities and Neglected Dimensions," ch. 12 in Ivar Berg, ed., *Sociological Perspectives on Labor Markets* (New York: Academic Press, 1981), 342.

69. Alejandro Portes and Robert D. Manning, "The Immigrant Enclave: Theory and Empirical Examples," in Joane Nagel and Susan Olzak, eds., *Competitive Ethnic Relations* (Orlando: Academic Press, 1986), 61.

70. Arthur Sakamoto and Meichu D. Chen, "Further Evidence on Returns to Schooling by Establishment Size," *American Sociological Review* 56 (1991), 765–71; and Don Mar, "Another Look at the Enclave Economy Thesis," *Amerasia* 17 (1991), 13.

71. Light and Bonacich, *Immigrant Entrepreneurs*, ch. 1.

72. Ivan Light, "Immigrant and Ethnic Enterprise in North America," *Ethnic and Racial Studies* 7 (1984), 195–216.

73. Kenneth L. Wilson and Alejandro Portes, "Immigrant Enclaves: An Analysis of the Labor Market Experiences of Cubans in Miami," *American Journal of Sociology* 86 (1980), 297.

74. Wilson and Portes, "Immigrant Enclaves: An Analysis of the Labor Market Experiences of Cubans in Miami," 297–302.

75. Wilson and Portes, "Immigrant Enclaves: An Analysis of the Labor Market Experiences of Cubans in Miami," 306–7.

76. This was also the *point d'appui* of Thomas Bailey and Roger Waldinger, "Primary, Secondary, and Enclave Labor Markets: A Training Systems Approach," *American Sociological Review* 56 (1991), 432–45.

77. St. Clair Drake and Horace R. Cayton, *Black Metropolis* (New York: Harper & Row, 1962), 430–33.

78. Alejandro Portes, "Modes of Incorporation and Theories of Labor Immigration," in Mary Kritz, Charles Keely, and Silvano Tomasi, eds., *Global Trends in Migration* (New York: Center for Migration Studies, 1981).

79. "Enclaves consist of immigrant groups which concentrate in a distinct spatial location and organize a variety of enterprises serving their own ethnic market and/or the general population. Their basic characteristic is that a significant proportion of the immigrant labor force works in enterprises owned by other immigrants." Portes, "Modes of Incorporation and Theories of Labor Immigration," 290–91.

80. Wilson and Martin redefined Portes's concept of enclave economy. In order to permit intergroup comparisons, they developed an input–output model that permitted estimation of the extent to which vertical integration of firms permitted an enclave economy to capture respending. Although no one has subsequently followed up this line of research, their emphasis upon compact interdependence did become a permanent feature of the enclave literature. See Kenneth Wilson and W. Allen Martin, "Ethnic Enclaves: A Comparison of the Cuban and Black Economies in Miami," *American Journal of Sociology* 88 (1982), 135–60.

81. Alejandro Portes and Robert L. Bach, *Latin Journey* (Berkeley and Los Angeles: University of California Press, 1985), 203.

82. Portes, "Modes of Incorporation and Theories of Labor Immigration."

83. Portes and Bach, *Latin Journey,* 217.

84. Portes and Bach, *Latin Journey,* ch. 7.

85. Portes and Bach, *Latin Journey,* 187, 193.

86. Portes and Bach, *Latin Journey,* 268.

87. Portes and Bach, *Latin Journey,* 370.

88. Niles H. Hansen and Gilberto C. Cardenas, "Immigrant and Native Ethnic Enterprises in Mexi-

can American Neighborhoods: Differing Perceptions of Mexican Immigrant Workers," *International Migration Review* 22 (1988), 226–42.

89. Wilson and Portes, "Immigrant Enclaves: An Analysis of the Labor Market Experiences of Cubans in Miami," 301–2.

90. Wilson and Martin, "Ethnic Enclaves: A Comparison of the Cuban and Black Economies in Miami," 138.

91. Wilson and Martin, "Ethnic Enclaves: A Comparison of the Cuban and Black Economies in Miami," 154; Portes and Bach, *Latin Journey,* 267–68.

92. Ivan Light *et al.,* "Beyond the ethnic enclave economy," *Social Problems* 41 (1994), 601–16; Suzanne Model, "The Ethnic Economy: Cubans and Chinese Reconsidered," *Sociological Quarterly* 33 (1992), 63–82; Mar, "Another Look at the Enclave Economy Thesis"; Robert M. Alvarez, "Mexican Entrepreneurs and Market in the City of Los Angeles: A Case of an Immigrant Enclave," *Urban Anthropology* 19 (1990), 99–123; Ewa Morawska, "The Sociology and Historiography of Immigration," in Virginia Yans McLaughlin, ed., *Immigration Reconsidered: History, Sociology, and Politics* (New York: Oxford University Press, 1990), 202; Cobas, *Puerto Rican Reactions to Cuban Immigrants: Insights from Trading Minority Interpretations;* John R. Logan, Richard D. Alba, and Thomas L. McNulty, "Ethnic Economies in Metropolitan Regions: Miami and Beyond," *Social Forces* 72 (1994), 693.

93. Gerard Celas, "L'entrepreneurship et les haitiens de Montreal" (master's thesis, Université de Montréal, 1991), 122.

94. Logan, Alba, and McNulty, "Ethnic Economies in Metropolitan Regions: Miami and Beyond," 71.

95. This is also true of Iranians in Kansas City. Morteza H. Ardebili, "The Economic Adaptation of Iranian Immigrants in the Kansas City Metropolitan Area," 190.

96. Neil J. Smelser writes that "like all markets, the market for entrepreneurial services has a demand and a supply side." *The Sociology of Economic Life,* 2d ed. (Englewood Cliffs, NJ: Prentice-Hall, 1976), 126.

97. These issues are discussed in greater detail in Ivan Light and Carolyn Rosenstein, *Race, Ethnicity, and Entrepreneurship in Urban America* (New York: Aldine de Gruyter, 1995), 73–80, 115–21.

98. Roger Waldinger, Robin Ward, and Howard Aldrich, "Trend Report: Ethnic Business and Occupational Mobility in Advanced Societies," *Sociology* 19 (1985), 589.

99. Roger Waldinger, Robin Ward and Howard Aldrich. "Trend Report: Ethnic Business and Occupational Mobility in Advanced Societies," 32

100. "We emphasize the fit between immigrant firms and the environments in which they function, including not only economic and social conditions but also the unique historical conditions encountered at the time of immigration." Waldinger, Ward, and Aldrich, "Trend Report: Ethnic Business and Occupational Mobility in Advanced Societies," 32.

101. Gaye Tuchman and Harry Gene Levine, "New York Jews and Chinese Food: The Social Construction of an Ethnic Pattern," *Journal of Contemporary Ethnography* 22 (1993), 397.

102. See Eran Razin "Immigrant Entrepreneurs in Israel, Canada, and California," ch. 5 in Ivan Light and Parminder Bhacher, eds., Immigration and Entrepreneurship. (New Brunswick: Transaction, 1993), 101; Eran Razin, "Entrepreneurship among Foreign Immigrants in the Los Angeles and San Francisco Metropolitan Regions," *Urban Geography* 9 (1988), 283–301; Paul Ong, "An Ethnic Trade: Chinese Laundries in Early California," *Journal of Ethnic Studies* 8 (1981), 95–113.

103. Howard Aldrich, Trevor P. Jones, and David McEvoy, "Ethnic Advantage and Minority Businesses Development," in Robin Ward and Richard Jenkins, eds., *Ethnic Communities in Business* (New York: Cambridge University Press, 1984), ch. 11.

104. Aldrich, Jones, and McEvoy, "Ethnic Advantage and Minority Businesses Development," 205.

105. Of course, one might dispute the sweeping conclusion on other grounds. First, it is incompatible with the textbook claim that supply and demand resources always interact to produce entrepreneurship. Second, the researchers did not examine demographic or class resources on the supply side, nor did they look into intermetropolitan continuities of rank. These supply issues

might have required a modification of their lopsided conclusion, a contradiction to the text-book model, that only demand-side influences affected entrepreneurship in the British cities.

106. Roger D. Waldinger, *Through the Eye of the Needle* (New York: New York University, 1986), chs. 1, 4.
107. Thomas R. Bailey's study of New York City's restaurant industry encountered the same problem. *Immigrant and Native Workers* (Boulder: Westview Press, 1987), 22.
108. Given his design, Waldinger could not explain why, on the supply side, immigrant groups other than Dominicans and Chinese were not drawn into the garment industry, nor, on the demand side, whether other New York City industries did not offer more or equally favorable demand opportunities to Dominicans and Chinese.
109. Light and Rosenstein, *Race, Ethnicity, and Entrepreneurship in Urban America.*
110. Light and Rosenstein, *Race, Ethnicity, and Entrepreneurship in Urban America,* 93.
111. Eran Razin and Ivan Light, "Ethnic Entrepreneurs in America's Largest Metropolitan Areas," *Urban Affairs Review* 33 (1998): 332–60.
112. Jeffrey G. Reitz, *The Survival of Ethnic Groups* (Toronto: McGraw-Hill, 1980).
113. Robin Ward, "Ethnic Entrepreneurs in Britain and Europe," in Robert Goffee and Richard Scase, eds., *Entrepreneurship in Europe* (London: Croom Helm, 1987), ch 6.
114. Robert M. Jiobu, *Ethnicity and Assimilation* (Albany: State University of New York, 1988), 223.
115. Light and Bonacich, *Immigrant Entrepreneurs,* 193.
116. Min Zhou and John R. Logan, "Return on Human Capital in Ethnic Enclaves: New York City's Chinatown," *American Sociological Review* 54 (1989), 809–20.
117. Suzanne Model, "The Ethnic Economy: Cubans and Chinese Reconsidered," *Sociological Quarterly* 33 (1992), 63–82.
118. Logan, Alba, and McNulty, "Ethnic Economies in Metropolitan Regions: Miami and Beyond," 693.
119. "An ethnic economy could be defined as any situation where common ethnicity provides an economic advantage: in relations among owners in the same or complementary business sectors, between owners and workers, or even among workers in the same firm or industry regardless of the owner's ethnicity." Logan, Alba, and McNulty, "Ethnic Economies in Metropolitan Regions: Miami and Beyond," 693.
120. Timothy Bates, "Why Are Firms Owned by Asian Immigrants Lagging Behind Black-Owned Businesses?," *National Journal of Sociology* 10 (1996), 28; and Timothy Bates, *Race, Self-Employment, and Upward Mobility* (Baltimore: Johns Hopkins University Press, 1997), 104–5.
121. "I have argued that ethnicity has an external effect on the human-capital accumulation process." George J. Borjas, "Ethnicity, Neighborhoods, and Human-Capital Externalities," *American Economic Review* 85 (1995), 365. See also Thomas Sowell, *Race and Culture* (New York: Basic, 1994), ch. 4; and Gary S. Becker, *Accounting for Tastes* (Cambridge: Harvard University Press, 1996), 16.
122. The data Bates presents do not, however, support his theoretical generalization. "Blacks and Hispanics are significantly less likely than whites to enter self-employment, controlling for other factors. The other factors . . . are educational background, household wealth, work experience, age, gender, and marital status." *Race, Self-Employment, and Upward Mobility,* 31.
123. Peter S. Li, "Self-Employment and Its Economic Return for Visible Minorities in Canada," in David M. Saunders, ed., *New Approaches to Employee Management, Volume 2: Discrimination in Employment* (Greenwich, CT: JAI Press Inc., 1994), 189.
124. Light and Bonacich, *Immigrant Entrepreneurs,* 197.
125. Jiobu, *Ethnicity and Assimilation,* 223.
126. Dennis P. Clark, "The Expansion of the Public Sector and Irish Economic Development," in Scott Cummings, ed., *Self-Help in Urban America* (Washington, NY: Kennikat Press, 1980).
127. On nepotism at work, see Margaret Grieco, "Family Networks and the Closure of Employment," in Gloria Lee and Ray Loveridge, eds., *The Manufacture of Disadvantage* (Milton Keynes: Open University Press, 1987).

128. Thomas Kessner, *The Golden Poor: Italian and Jewish Mobility in New York City, 1880– 1915* (New York: Oxford University Press, 1977); and Suzanne Model, "Ethnic Bonds in the Workplace: Blacks, Italians, and Jews in New York City" (Ph.D. diss., University of Michigan, 1985).

129. Waldinger, *Still the Promised City?*, 302.

130. John Logan finds the same process at work in the private economy of New York City, 1920–1960, where white ethnics consciously built upon social networks to "find jobs, to attempt to control access to those jobs, to set up privileged relationships with suppliers and clients of business firms, to pool capital, and to do all the other things that affect success of failure in the economy." "White Ethnics in the New York Economy, 1920–1960," *Working Paper* 112 (New York: Russell Sage Foundation, 1997), 42.

131. Alejandro Portes, "Social Capital: Its Origins and Applications in Modern Sociology," *Annual Review of Sociology* 24 (1998): 13.

132. Waldinger, *Still the Promised City?*, 4.

133. Judy Scully, "A Stage Irish Identity—an Example of Symbolic Power," *New Community* 23 (1997), 385–98.

134. "The results show that, for both white and black youths, the most frequently used methods of search are checking with friends and relatives, and direct application without referrals. These are also the two most productive methods." Harry J. Holzer, "Informal Job Search and Black Youth Unemployment," *American Economic Review* 77 (1987), 446.

135. Logan, "White Ethnics in the New York Economy, 1920–1960," 43.

136. Stanley Lieberson and Mary C. Waters, *From Many Strands: Ethnic and Racial Groups in Contemporary America* (New York: Russell Sage, 1988), 127; see also Nathan Glazer and Daniel P. Moynihan, *Beyond the Melting Pot,* 2d ed. (Cambridge: MIT Press, 1970).

137. Robert L. Boyd, "Differences in the Earnings of Black Workers in the Private and Public Sectors," *The Social Science Journal* 30 (1993–1994), 409–429.

138. Robert L. Boyd, "A Contextual Analysis of Black Self-Employment in Large Metropolitan Areas, 1970–1980," *Social Forces* 70 (1991), 413.

139. In many cases, owners prefer to abdicate responsibility for hiring to employees, who perform for free a service the employers would otherwise have to administer at their own cost. The Bank of America's check cashing facility on Figueroa Street in Los Angeles once hired only Cubans on its second floor. The reason: the Cubans were good workers, and they assumed the responsibility for finding a replacement when any coethnic retired or quit.

140. Noah Lewin-Epstein and Moshe Semyonov, "Sheltered Labor Markets, Public Sector Employment, and Socioeconomic Returns to Education of Arabs in Israel," *American Journal of Sociology* 1994 (100), 622–51.

141. Edna Bonacich, "Making It in America," *Sociological Perspectives* 30 (1987), 459.

142. Roger Waldinger, "Ethnicity and Opportunity in the Plural City," in Roger Waldinger and Mehdi Bozorgmehr, eds., *Ethnic Los Angeles* (New York: Russell Sage, 1996), 449–51.

143. Our distinction recreates the same ownership vs. control terminology that Berle and Means (1967) utilized to discuss the modern corporation. However, the overlap is just fortuitous. We are not discussing ownership vs. control of corporations, but the manner in which ethnic groups extend their influence over whole economies. See Maurice Zeitlin, *The Large Corporation and Contemporary Classes* (New Brunswick, NJ: Rutgers University, 1989), chs. 1, 2.

144. Patricia G. Greene, "A Call for Conceptual Clarity," *National Journal of Sociology* 10 (1996), 50.

145. Light, "Ethnic Succession."

146. Waldinger uses the term *usurpationary closure* to designate coethnics' ability to exclude outsiders from hiring. The term *ethnic-controlled economy* includes this function, but also includes the ability of coethnic employees to feather their own nest in other ways. See Roger Waldinger, "Social Capital or Social Closure?: Immigrant Networks in the Labor Market," Working Paper Number 26 of the Lewis Center for Regional and Policy Studies, School of Public Policy and Social Research, University of California, Los Angeles, 1997.

147. "The modal labor market experience of immigrants is not in the ethnic economy nor the ethnic enclave economy, but in the open mainstream economy." Richard Alba and Victor Nee, "The Assimilation of Immigrant Groups: Concept Theory, and Evidence," Paper presented at the Conference on Becoming American/America Becoming: International Migration to the United States, sponsored by the Social Science Research Council, January 18–21, 1996, 71.

148. Li, "Self-Employment and Its Economic Return for Visible Minorities in Canada," 194–95.

149. Light, "Ethnic Succession," 79.

Chapter 2

1. If 2 Tibetans live in Wausau, and one works in the other's business, then the Tibetan ethnic ownership economy would occupy one hundred percent of the Tibetans. This uniformity could not arise if 100,000 Tibetans lived in Wausau.

2. Edna Bonacich and John Modell, *The Economic Basis of Ethnic Solidarity* (Los Angeles: University of California Press, 1980), Table 3:1.

3. "Sixty percent of the male Nisei in the mid-1960s were employees. Of these 10 percent were working in firms that they identified as Japanese American." Bonacich and Modell, *The Economic Basis of Ethnic Solidarity*, 111.

4. Steven J. Gold, "Patterns of Economic Cooperation Among Israeli Immigrants in Los Angeles," *International Migration Review* 105 (1994): 114–135.

5. Pyong Gap Min, "Some Positive Functions of Ethnic Business for an Immigrant Community: Koreans in Los Angeles." Final Report Submitted to the National Science Foundation, Sociology Division, 1996, 66.

6. Alejandro Portes, Juan M. Clark, and Manuel M. Lopez, "Six Years Later: The Process of Incorporation of Cuban Exiles in the United States, 1973–1979," *Cuban Studies* 11–12 (1982), 18.

7. On Koreans, see: Pyong Gap Min, *Caught in the Middle: Korean Communities in New York and Los Angeles* (Los Angeles: University of California Press, 1996).

8. Ivan Light, *Ethnic Enterprise in America* (Berkeley: University of California Press, 1972); Pyong Gap Min, "Filipino and Korean Immigrants in Small Business: A Comparative Analysis," *Amerasia* 13 (1986–1987): 53–71; and James T. Fawcett and Robert W. Gardner, "Asian Immigrant Entrepreneurs and Non-Entrepreneurs: A Comparative Study of Recent Korean and Filipino Immigrants," *Population and Environment: A Journal of Interdisciplinary Studies* 15 (1994), 211–238.

9. Yen-Fen Tseng, "Chinese Ethnic Economy: San Gabriel Valley, Los Angeles Country," *Journal of Urban Affairs* 16 (1994), 169–189.

10. Frank A. Fratoe and Ronald L. Meeks, "Business Participation Rates of the 50 Largest U.S. Ancestry Groups: Preliminary Report," (Washington, D.C.: Minority Business Development Agency of the U.S. Department of Commerce, 1985).

11. Comparing Tables 2.3 and 2.4, we see that Korean self-employment rates rose drastically between 1980 and 1990. In point of fact, the Koreans were establishing themselves in business in the 1980s so the big increase is probably attributable to a rapidly rising rate rather than to enumeration error.

12. In-Jin Yoon, *Own My Own* (Chicago: University of Chicago, 1997), 20–21.

13. Jock Collins, "Cosmopolitan Capitalism: Ethnicity, Gender and Australian Entrepreneurs," Vol 1, (PhD diss., University of Wollongong, 1998); Robert Kloosterman, Joanne van der Leun, and Jan Rath, "Across the Border: Immigrants' Economic Opportunities, Social Capital and Informal Business Activities," *Journal of Ethnic and Migration Studies* 24 (1998), 258.

14. Ivan Light and Carolyn Rosenstein, *Race, Ethnicity, and Entrepreneurship in Urban America* (Hawthorne New York: Aldine de Gruyter, 1995), ch. 2.

15. Maria De Lourdes Villar, "Hindrances to the Development of an Ethnic Economy Among Mexican Migrants," *Human Organization* 53 (1994), 263–268.

16. Yoon, *Own My Own*, 20–21.
17. Roger Waldinger, *Still the Promised City?* (Cambridge, MA: Harvard University, 1996), 303.
18. John R. Logan, Richard D. Alba, and Thomas McNulty, "Ethnic Economies in Metropolitan Regions: Miami and Beyond," *Social Forces* 72 (1994): 697; and Jeffrey G. Reitz, *The Survival of Ethnic Groups* (Toronto: McGraw Hill, 1990), Table 4.12; M.D. R. Evans, "Immigrant Entrepreneurship: Effects of Ethnic Market Size and Isolated Labor Pool," *American Sociological Review* 54 (1989), 957.
19. Logan, Alba, and McNulty, "Ethnic Economies in Metropolitan Regions: Miami and Beyond," 701.
20. Ivan Light, Georges Sabagh, Mehdi Bozorgmehr, and Claudia Der-Martirosian, "Beyond the Ethnic Enclave Economy," *Social Problems* 1 (1994), 65–80.
21. Gold, "Patterns of Economic Cooperation Among Israeli Immigrants in Los Angeles," 114–135.
22. Prodromos I. Panayiotopoulos, "Challenging Orthodoxies: Cypriot Entrepreneurs in the London Garment Industry," *New Community* 22 (1996), 437–460.
23. Colonialism creates this type. For instance, the British rubber industry in Malaya once resembled this description. While Malaya (now Malaysia) remained in the British empire, all the plantation owners were British; all their manual employees were non-British.
24. Bonacich and Modell, *The Economic Basis of Ethnic Solidarity*, 111.
25. Martine Guerguil, "Some Thoughts on the Definition of the Informal Sector," *CEPAL Review* 35 (1988): 57–65.
26. Saskia Sassen, *The Global City: New York, London, Tokyo* (Princeton, NJ: Princeton University, 1991), 79.
27. Ann Dryden Witte, "Beating the System?" in Susan Pozo, ed., *Exploring the Underground Economy* (Kalamazoo, Michigan: W.E. Upjohn Institute, 1996), 133–34.
28. "Another part of the informal economy is working illegally for others, rather than being self-employed. This usually means being paid in cash with no deductions for social security or any other benefits." Alex Stepick, *Pride Against Prejudice: Haitians in the United States* (Boston: Allyn & Bacon, 1998), 48.
29. Ivan Light, Richard Bernard, and Rebecca Kim, "The Garment Industry of Los Angeles," *International Migration Review* 33 (1999): 5–25.
30. Alejandro Portes and Alex Stepick, "Unwelcome Immigrants: The Labor Market Experiences of 1980 (Mariel) Cuban and Haitian Refugees in South Florida," *American Sociological Review* 50 (1985), 14–15.
31. Alejandro Portes, "The Informal Economy and Its Paradoxes," in Neil J. Smelser and Richard Swedberg, eds., *The Handbook of Economic Sociology* (Princeton, N.J.: Russell Sage, 1994), 438–443.
32. Portes, "The Informal Economy and Its Paradoxes," 440.
33. James D. Smith, "Measuring the Informal Economy," *The Annals of the American Academy of Political and Social Science* 493 (1987), 83–99; and Kevin McCrohan, James D. Smith, and Terry K. Adams, "Consumer Purchases in Informal Markets," *Journal of Retailing* 67 (1991). Cited from Portes 1994, "The Informal Economy and Its Paradoxes," 441.
34. $.83 \times .15 = .1245$.
35. Edgar Feige, "Defining and Estimating Underground and Informal Economies: The New Institutional Economics Approach," *World Development* 18 (1990), 989–1002.
36. Quoted from Portes, "The Informal Economy and Its Paradoxes," 441.
37. Portes, "The Informal Economy and Its Paradoxes," 438.
38. Bettylou Valentine, *Hustling and Other Hard Work* (New York: Free Press, 1978), 26, 118.
39. Marta Tienda and Rebecca Raijman, "Forging Mobility: Competition, Cooperation and Immigrants' Socioeconomic Progress," Paper Presented at the "Becoming American/America Becoming" Conference, Sanibel Island FL Jan. 21.
40. John Bodnar, *The Transplanted* (Bloomington: Indiana University, 1985), 82–83.

41. Min Zhou, "Employment Patterns of Immigrants in the U.S. Economy: Labor Force Participation and Underemployment," Working Paper 98–01 (Institute of Industrial Relations, University of California, Los Angeles, 1998), 19.
42. Kurt Bauman, "Characteristics of the Low-Income Self Employed," Proceedings of the Fourteenth Annual Meeting of the Industrial relations Association Chicago, Dec. 28–30, 1987, 340.
43. Tienda and Raijman, 52.
44. Michael S. Laguerre, "The Informal Economy in the San Francisco Bay Area," Working Paper 594: 1 (Berkeley: Institute of Urban and Regional Development of the University of California, 1993).
45. U.S. Bureau of the Census, *1987 Economic Censuses: Characteristics of Business Owners* CBO87-1 (Washington DC: USGPO, 1991), Table 11B.
46. Alex Stepick, "Miami's Two Informal Sectors," in Alejandro Portes, Manuel Castells, and Lauren A. Benton, eds., *The Informal Economy* (Baltimore: Johns Hopkins University, 1989), 116–125.
47. "Haitians become full-time informal sector entrepreneurs usually when they have no choice, when they lose or cannot obtain wage-labor employment." Alex Stepick, *Pride Against Prejudice: Haitians in the United States* (Boston: Allyn & Bacon, 1998), 45.
48. Stepick, "Pride Against Prejudice: Haitians in the United States," 122.
49. Stepick, "Miami's Two Informal Sectors," 122.
50. Loic Wacquant, "Inside the Zone: The Social Art of the Hustler in the Black American Ghetto," *Theory, Culture, and Society* 15 (1998), 1–36.
51. Of course, predatory crimes have an economic basis too, but they do not take the form of a business. Therefore, they are not illegal enterprises. Loic Wacquant blurs this distinction, lumping the sale of stolen merchandise, pillage, break-ins, and stealing cars with gambling, drug sales, pimping, and even murder for hire. "Inside the Zone: The Social Art of the Hustler in the Black American Ghetto," *Theory, Culture, and Society* 15 (1998), 1–36.
52. U. S. Bureau of the Census. *Statistical Abstract of the United States: 1996* (Washington DC: USGPO, 1996), Table 325.
53. Richard Freeman, "The Supply of Youths to Crime," in Susan Pozo, ed., *Exploring the Underground Economy* (Kalamazoo, MI: W.E. Upjohn Institute, 1996), 83.
54. Freeman, "The Supply of Youths to Crime," 83.
55. The Mafia is "clearly only a part of the world of stable, hierarchical criminal organizations. There are others, more or less ethnically homogeneous. . . . " 74. Peter Reuter, and Jonathan B. Rubinstein, "Fact Fancy, and Organized Crime," in Nikos Passas, ed., *Organized Crime* (Aldershot UK: Dartmouth. 1995), ch. 4; John M Hagedorn, "Home Boys, Dope Fiends, Legits, and New Jacks," *Criminology* 32 (1994): 197–219; Freeman, "The Supply of Youths to Crime," 97.
56. "Organized Crime: Streamlined for Success." *The Economist*, vol 345 (1997), 29–30.
57. Eran Razin and Ivan Light, "Ethnic Entrepreneurs in America's Largest Metropolitan Areas," *Urban Affairs Review* 33 (1998), 332–360.
58. Ivan Light, *Cities in World Perspectives* (New York: Macmillan, 1983), ch. 12.
59. Logan, Alba, and McNulty, "Ethnic Economies in Metropolitan Regions: Miami and Beyond," Appendix 2.
60. Logan, Alba, and McNulty, "Ethnic Economies in Metropolitan Regions: Miami and Beyond," 699.
61. $[451 \times 1.5p] + [909 \times 1p] = 100$
62. Ivan Light and Edna Bonacich found that one-third of Los Angeles industries had no Korean employees. Just on this basis alone, the Koreans would have to be overrepresented in the other two-thirds of occupations and so, indeed, they were. This evidence suggests the possibility that *all* Koreans worked in niche industries. *Immigrant Entrepreneurs* (Los Angeles: University of California, 1988), 182.
63. Jeffrey G. Reitz, "Ethnic Concentrations in Labor Markets and Their Implications for Ethnic Inequality," in Raymond Breton et al., eds., *Ethnic Identity and Equality* (Toronto: University of Toronto, 1990), 135–195.

64. Victor Nee, Jimy M. Sanders, and Scott Sernau, "Job Transitions in an Immigrant Metropolis: Ethnic Boundaries and the Mixed Economy," *American Sociological Review* 59 (1994), 849–872.

65. Germans utilize "high levels of human capital and resemblance to Canada's mainstream society to advance in the general labor market. While they were quite entrepreneurial, entrepreneurship was not necessarily the most beneficial path for them. Germans have been among the least likely to retain close ethnic ties across the generations and have abandoned ethnic concentrations in labor markets." Eran Razin and Andre Langlois, "Metropolitan Characteristics and Entrepreneurship Among Immigrants and Ethnic Groups in Canada," *International Migration Review* 30 (1996), 714.

66. Ivan Light's mother, then five years old, was ejected from the St. Louis Public Library in 1917 for the crime of speaking German.

67. Major assimilation theorists, nonetheless indicated that 73.8 percent of Chinese immigrants in San Francisco, 77.4 percent of Korean immigrants, and 18.6 percent of Filipino immigrants were in ethnic ownership economies. Nee, Sanders, and Sernau, "Job Transitions in an Immigrant Metropolis: Ethnic Boundaries and the Mixed Economy," 855.

68. Stanley Lieberson, *A Piece of the Pie* (Los Angeles: University of California, 1980), 316–319.

69. Oscar Handlin, *Boston's Immigrants,* 2nd ed. (Cambridge: Harvard University, 1969), 253.

70. Handlin, *Boston's Immigrants,* 2nd ed, Table XIV.

71. To label an economic resource "political" might have hostile or even racist implications in the anti-state culture of American society. See: Louk Hagendoorn, "Ethnic Categorization and Outgroup Exclusion: Cultural Values and Social Stereotypes" *Ethnic and Racial Studies* 16 (1993), 26–51. We imply no such hostility. Plato (not Marx) said that justice is the true purpose of the state. If so, a state should intervene in labor markets when intervention is necessary to assure justice. Aisha C. Blackshire-Belay, defends affirmative action in the academy on just these classical grounds. "The Status of Minority Faculty Members in the Academy," *Academe* 84 (1998), 30–36.

72. Daniel Bell, *The End of Ideology* (Glencoe IL: Free, Press, 1960), ch. 7.

73. James Fawcett and Robert W. Gardner, Asian Immigrant Entrepreneurs and Non-Entrepreneurs: A Comparative Study of Recent Korean and Filipino Immigrants," *Population and Environment: A Journal of Interdisciplinary Studies* 15 (1994), 237.

74. Alberto Martinelli, "Entrepreneurship and Management," in Neil Smelser and Richard Swedberg, eds., *Handbook of Economic Sociology* (Princeton: Princeton University, 1994), 487.

75. Steven Gold and Nazli Kibria, "Vietnamese Refugees and Blocked Mobility," *Asian and Pacific Migration Journal* 2 (1993), 36.

76. M.D.R. Evans, "Language Skills, Language Usage, and Opportunity: Immigrants in the Australian Labor Market," *Sociology* 21 (1987), 268.

77. Light and Rosenstein, *Race, Ethnicity and Entrepreneurship,* ch. 5; Min, *Caught in the Middle,* ch. 6.

78. Edna Bonacich argues that immigrant entrepreneurs are immoral because they exploit the cheap labor of distressed coethnics and prop up the capitalist ideology. "Making It in America," *Sociological Perspectives* 30 (1987), 446–466.

Chapter 3

1. If Eo is the jobs created in the ethnic ownership economy and G is the jobs in the general labor market for which ethnics may compete, then $G + Eo =$ the job supply, and $G + Eo > G$. If additionally, Ec is jobs captured in the ethnic-controlled economy, then $Ec + Eo + G > G + Eo > G$.

2. Chris Tilly and Charles Tilly, "Capitalist Work and Labor Markets," in Neil Smelser and Richard Swedberg, eds., *Handbook of Economic Sociology* (Princeton: Princeton University, 1994), 302, 304.

3. The very worst case would be to work in the general labor market for rewards inferior to those paid in the ethnic economy.

4. But here is a sample of the heat: "Because Light knew nothing about the Afro-American experience in banking and enterprise, his analysis will forever stand as misleading." John Sibley Butler, *Entrepreneurship and Self-Help Among Black Americans* (Albany: State University of New York, 1991), 125.

5. Alan Wolfe, *Marginalized in the Middle* (Chicago: University of Chicago, 1996), 46.

6. Alejandro Portes and Min Zhou, "Divergent Destinies: Immigration, Poverty, and Entrepreneurship in the United States," Written for the Project on Poverty, Inequality, and the Crisis of Social Policy of the Joint Center for Political and Economic Studies, Washington, DC. 1992: 492.

7. For classic statements, see: W. Lloyd Warner and Leo Srole, *The Social Systems of American Ethnic Groups* (New Haven: Yale University, 1945); and Milton Gordon, *Assimilation in American Life* (New York: Oxford University, 1964).

8. Jeffrey G. Reitz and Sherrilyn M. Sklar, "Culture, Race, and the Economic Assimilation of Immigrants," *Sociological Forum* 12 (1997), 233–234; Roger Waldinger, *Still the Promised City?* (Cambridge MA: Harvard University, 1996), 95; Charles Hirschman, "America's Melting Pot Reconsidered," *Annual Review of Sociology* 9 (1983), 400.

9. Portes and Zhou, "Gaining the Upper Hand," 492.

10. "The importance of ethnic enterprise in Asian American economic achievement is clearly suggested in our analysis. Self-employment among Asian Americans is generally associated with high earnings." Victor Nee and Jimy Sanders, "The Road to Parity: Determinants of the Socioeconomic Achievements of Asian Americans," *Ethnic and Racial Studies* 8 (1985), 85; see also, Portes and Zhou, "Gaining the Upper Hand," 511.

11. Edna Bonacich, "Making It in America," *Sociological Perspectives* 30 (1987), 446–466.

12. Ewa Morawska, *For Bread With Butter* (Cambridge: Cambridge University, 1985), 240.

13. " . . . . [Income] refers to flows of money, goods, or services, while assets refer to stocks of wealth or accumulations." Michael Sherraden, *Assets and the Poor* (Armonk, NY: M. E. Sharpe, 1991), 96.

14. Sherraden distinguishes tangible assets and intangible assets. Tangible assets include money, securities, real property, jewelry, machine & equipment, durable household goods, natural resources such as farmland, oil, minerals, copyrights and patents. Intangible assets include: access to credit, human capital, and cultural capital in the form of knowledge culturally significant subjects, such as vocabulary, accent, dress, appearance, informal social capital such as friends and family, formal social capital, and even political capital in the form of participation, power, and influence in the state. *Assets and the Poor: A New American Welfare Policy* (Armonk, NY: M.E. Sharpe, 1991), 102.

15. For example, a lady with a high income who spends more than she earns will amass debts that are negative wealth.

16. Melvin L. Oliver and Thomas M. Shapiro, "Wealth of a Nation: A Reassessment of Asset Inequality in America Shows a Least One Third of Households Are Asset-Poor," *American Journal of Economics and Sociology* 49 (1990), 143–144.

17. Melvin L. Oliver and Thomas M. Shapiro, *Black Wealth/White Wealth* (New York: Rutledge, 1997), 119.

18. To be sure, half of the self-employed fail in business within two years of starting, and three-quarters within five years. These strictures apply to the ones who succeed, not to the failures.

19. Francine D. Blau and John W. Graham, "Black-White Differences in Wealth and Asset Composition," *The Quarterly Journal of Economics* 105 (1990), 33.

20. Jock Collins, "Cosmopolitan Capitalism: Ethnicity, Gender and Australian Entrepreneurs," Vols 1 and 2, (PhD diss., 1998 University of Wollongong II-363).

21. Alejandro Portes and Robert Bach, *Latin Journey* (Berkeley: University of California, 1985).

22. Kenneth L. Wilson and Alejandro Portes, "Immigrant Enclaves: An Analysis of the Labor Market Experiences of Cubans in Miami," *American Journal of Sociology* 86 (1980), 314.

23. Portes and Bach, *Latin Journey*, ch. 6.

24. Jimy M. Sanders and Victor Nee, "Limits of Ethnic Solidarity in the Enclave Economy," *American Sociological Review* 52 (1987), 745–73.

25. Nee and Sanders, "The Road to Parity: Determinants of the Socioeconomic Achievements of Asian Americans," 75–93.

26. Min Zhou, *Chinatown: The Socioeconomic Potential of an Urban Enclave* (Philadelphia: Temple University Press, 1992), 115–116, 150.

27. Thomas R. Bailey and Roger Waldinger, "Primary, Secondary, and Enclave Labor Markets: A Training Systems Approach," *American Sociological Review* 56 (1991), 432–445.

28. Charles Choy Wong, "Black and Chinese Grocery Stores in Los Angeles' Black Ghetto," *Urban Life* 5 (1977), 439–64.

29. Jeffrey G. Reitz, "Ethnic Concentrations in Labour Markets and Their Implications for Ethnic Inequality," in Raymond Breton et al., eds., *Ethnic Identity and Equality* (Toronto: University of Toronto, 1990), 135–195.

30. Reitz, "Ethnic Concentrations," 175.

31. We mean higher net returns, not higher hourly returns. Bates points out that Asian American business owners work very long hours and so they earn higher net returns than blacks. But, the black owners actually earned higher returns per hour than the Asians. Alejandro Portes argues that "their relative return per dollar or per hour" misses the point. The bottom line is the "wealth accumulated by the entrepreneur, his social and economic status, and his influence in the community." "A Dissenting View: Pitfalls of Focusing on Relative Returns to Ethnic Enterprise," *National Journal of Sociology* 10 (1996), 45–47; and Timothy Bates, "Why Are Firms Owned by Asian Immigrants Lagging Behind Black-Owned Businesses?" *National Journal of Sociology* 10 (1996), 34.

32. Paul Maxim, "Immigrants, Visible Minorities, and Self-Employment," *Demography* 29 (1992), 182–183.

33. Portes and Zhou, "Gaining the Upper Hand,"; see also Nee and Sanders, "The Road to Parity: Determinants of the Socioeconomic Achievements of Asian Americans," 85.

34. Ivan Light and Elizabeth Roach, "Self-employment: Mobility Ladder or Economic Lifeboat?" in Roger Waldinger and Mehdi Bozorgmehr, eds., *Ethnic Los Angeles* (New York: Russell Sage Foundation, 1996), 203.

35. Maxim, "Immigrants, Visible Minorities, and Self Employment."

36. Norbert Wiley, "The Ethnic Mobility Trap and Stratification Theory," *Social Problems* 155 (1967), 147–59.

37. These are reviewed in Ivan Light and Stavros Karageorgis, "The Ethnic Economy," *Handbook of Economic Sociology* (Princeton: Princeton University, 1994), ch. 26.

38. Otherwise, participants are taking a pay cut to work in the ethnic ownership economy.

39. Portes and Bach, *Latin Journey*.

40. Sanders and Nee, "Limits of Ethnic Solidarity in the Enclave Economy."

41. Howard Aldrich and Roger Waldinger call this "organizing capacity." "Ethnicity and Entrepreneurship," *Annual Review of Sociology* 16 (1990), 112.

42. Matthew McKeever, "Reproduced Inequality: Participation and Success in the South African Informal Economy," *Social Forces* 4 (1998), 1209.

43. Portes and Zhou: 1992.

44. "This finding contradicts earlier dismissals of self-employment as irrelevant to the economic mobility of minorities or as a spurious consequence of human capital differences." Portes and Zhou, "Gaining the Upper Hand," 27.

45. Luis Eduardo Guarnizo, "The Mexican Ethnic Economy in Los Angeles: Capitalist Accumulation, Class Restructuring, and the Transnationalization of Migration," (Davis, CA: California Communities Program of the University of California, 1998), 7.

46. See also: Ivan Light and Elizabeth Roach, "Self-Employment: Mobility Ladder or Economic Lifeboat," ch. 7.

47. Because employer firms are less numerous than non-employer firms, an ethnic economy of 1,000 firms could not house 1,000 employer firms. The employer firms have to be some multiple (less than one) of all firms. This is an empirical, not a theoretical generalization. In principle,

an ethnic labor force of 1,000 workers could represent 1,000 employer firms each of whom hired no coethnic laborers. In this case, the size of the ethnic economy would be 100 percent, but its remuneration level would depend wholly upon business owners' returns and not at all upon wages. The wages would, after all, be paid to non-coethnics, and so would not affect the ethnic economy's remuneration level.

48. From Table 3.3.

49. If a significant proportion of coethnics are illegal, and uncounted, we overestimate the rate at which ethnic communities convert labor force into business firms. "Mexican workers, and particularly the undocumented, are a vital economic asset to the Chicano community, one that has contributed significantly to the development, maintenance, and recent expansion of the Chicano business sector and middle class." Gilberto Cardenas, Rodolfo O. de la Garza, and Niles Hansen. "Mexican Immigrants and the Chicano Ethnic Enterprise: Reconceptualizing an Old Problem," *Mexican Immigrants and Mexican Americans: An Evolving Relation* (Austin: Center for Mexican American Studies of the University of Texas, 1986), 158.

50. ". . . If we tripled black businesses that would not substantially reduce the black unemployment rate nor would it significantly increase black wealth in America." Kunjufu Jawanza, *Black Economics* (Chicago: African American Images, 1991), 159. Kunjufu's claim is clearly wrong here.

51. Steven Gold, *Refugee Communities* (Newbury Park, CA: Sage, 1992).

52. What counts here is the ratio between employees and gross payroll, not the observed payroll as a percentage of the expected payroll. As a percentage of expected payroll, observed payroll measures how much money was actually paid out in wages relative to how much would have been paid out had an ethnic economy generated employers, employees, and payroll at the same rate as the general economy. In this case, however, our interest is the relative performance of an ethnic economy in production of employees and of payroll. A poorer performance in production of payroll suggests wages that are lower than the general labor market paid.

53. Sanders and Nee, "Limits of Ethnic Solidarity in the Enclave Economy," 745–767.

54. McKeever, "Reproduced Inequality: Participation and Success in the South African Informal Economy."

55. Light and Karageorgis, "The Ethnic Economy," 652–655.

56. Ang Lee's feature-length film, "Pushing Hands" deals with underpaid workers in New York's Chinatown and their unscrupulous but coethnic employers.

57. Conditions in ethnic restaurants are truly deplorable. A federal investigatory team swept thru 43 randomly picked restaurants in Los Angeles Koreatown. Investigators found employees had been underpaid by $250,000. 41 of 43 restaurants had violated labor laws. Korean restaurant owners complain that they practice Korean labor customs, not American. K. Connie Kang, "41 Restaurants Violated Labor Laws." *Los Angeles Times,* Aug 22, 1998.

58. Of course, if they do not pay their workers the wages they owe them or if they pay wages below the legal minimum, they are operating in violation of the law. See: K. Connie Kang, "41 Restaurants Violated Labor Laws," Section B1; *idem,* "Ex-worker's Suit Seeks Back Wages," *Los Angeles Times,* Aug. 5, 1998.

59. Karl Marx defined exploitation as the owner's rate of profit where profit is money remaining after all the costs of the business have been paid, including the owner's labor charge. On Marx's definition, highly paid workers can be exploited worse than low-paid workers; and even low-paid workers are not exploited when the owner's profit is zero. Moreover, a profit exists only when a surplus remains after a business owner's labor charge and the opportunity cost of her capital have been deducted. On this accounting, hardly any ethnic minority or immigrant-owned businesses turn a profit. Without profit, they cannot exploit anyone. Karl Marx, "Wages, Price, and Profit." pp. 398–440 in Karl Marx and Frederick Engels: *Selected Works,* vol. 2 (Moscow: Foreign Languages Publishing House, 1962).

60. Francis A. J. Ianni, *A Family Business: Kinship and Social Control in Organized Crime* (New York: Russell Sage Foundation, 1972), 153.

61. Ronald Kessler, *The Sins of the Father* (New York: Warner Books, 1996), 35–38.

62. Daniel Bell, *The End of Ideology* (Glencoe, IL: Free Press, 1960), ch. 7; Rufus Schatzberg and Robert J. Kelly, *African-American Organized Crime* (New York: Garland, 1996), 231.
63. Jack Katz, *Seductions of Crime: Moral and Sensual Attractions in Doing Evil* (New York: Basic Books, 1988).
64. James M. O'Kane, *The Crooked Ladder* (New Brunswick, NJ: Transactions, 1992), 125; John M. Hagedorn, "Home Boys, Dope Fiends, Legits, and New Jacks," *Criminology* 32 (1994), 210.
65. Terrie E. Moffitt, "Adolescence-Limited and Life-Course-Persistent Anti-Social Behavior: A Developmental Taxonomy," *Psychological Review* 110 (1994), 675.
66. Suzanne Model, "The Ethnic Niches and the Structure of Opportunity: Immigrants and Minorities in New York City," in Michael B. Katz, ed., *The Underclass Debate* (Princeton: Princeton University, 1993), 165.
67. See: Daniel Bell, "The Capitalism of the Proletariat," ch 11 and "The Racket-Ridden Longshoremen," ch 9 in *The End of Ideology*.
68. Theodore Caplow, *The Sociology of Work* (Westport, CT: Greenwood Press, 1978).
69. Sometimes self-employed workers obtain the same restrictive control over a trade. Ronald Tsukashima discusses the advantages that Japanese Americans enjoyed in gardening as a result of ethnic cohesion. "Notes On Emerging Collective Action: Ethnic-Trade Guilds Among Japanese Americans in the Gardening Industry," *International Migration Review* 32 (1998), 374–400.
70. Waldinger, *Still the Promised City?,* 200.
71. Waldinger, *Still the Promised City?,* 209.
72. Model, "Ethnic Niches and the Structure of Opportunity: Immigrants and Minorities in New York City."
73. John R. Logan, "White Ethnics in the New York Economy, 1920–1960," Working Paper 112. (New York: Russell Sage Foundation, 1997).
74. Model also discussed benefits of clusters in the ethnic ownership economy. "The Ethnic Niches and the Structure of Opportunity: Immigrants and Minorities in New York City," 166–167.
75. Model, "The Ethnic Niches and the Structure of Opportunity: Immigrants and Minorities in New York City," 187.
76. Model, "The Ethnic Niches and the Structure of Opportunity: Immigrants and Minorities in New York City,"; and Robert L. Boyd, "Black and Asian Self-Employment in Large Metropolitan areas: a Comparative Analysis," *Social Problems* 37 (1990), 262–263; *idem*, "Differences in the Earnings of Black Workers in the Private and Public Sectors," *The Social Science Journal* 30 (1993), 133.
77. Model, "The Ethnic Niches and the Structure of Opportunity: Immigrants and Minorities in New York City," 183.
78. Logan, "White Ethnics in the New York Economy, 1920–1960," 35.
79. "The term niche refers to the over representation of ethnic and racial minorities in particular jobs." Model, "The Ethnic Niches and the Structure of Opportunity: Immigrants and Minorities in New York City," 164.
80. Logan, "White Ethnics in the New York Economy, 1920–1960," 42.
81. Reitz, "Ethnic Concentrations in Labour Markets and Their Implications for Ethnic Inequality," 176–177.
82. O'Kane, *The Crooked Ladder*, 83–84.
83. Mark Haller, "Illegal Enterprise: A Theoretical and Historical Interpretation," Organized Crime, edited by Nikos Pasas (Dartmouth: Aldershot, 1993), 221, 228–229: Ivan Light, "Numbers Gambling among Blacks: A Financial Institution," in Nikos Pasas, ed., *Organized Crime,* ch. 10.

Chapter 4

1. Howard Aldrich and Roger Waldinger call this capability "organizing capacity." "Ethnicity and Entrepreneurship," *Annual Review of* Sociology 16 (1989), 112.
2. Ethnic resources are also called ethno-cultural resources, and class resources are also called bourgeois resources. Ivan Light, "Immigrant and Ethnic Enterprise in North America," *Ethnic and*

Racial Studies 7(1984): 195–216; also Janet Chan, and Yuet-Wah Cheung, "Ethnic Resources and Business Enterprise: A Study of Chinese Businesses in Toronto," *Human Organization* 44, 142–54; Aldrich and Waldinger, "Ethnicity and Entrepreneurship," 127; Jeremy Boissevain, et al., "Ethnic Entrepreneurs and Ethnic Strategies," Ch. 5 in Roger Waldinger, Howard Aldrich, and Robin Ward, eds., *Ethnic Entrepreneurs* (Newbury Park: Sage, 1990); Martin Marger and Constance Hoffman, "Ethnic Enterprise in Ontario: Immigrant Participation in the Small Business Sector," *International Migration Review* 26 (1992), 968–81.

3. Erik Olin Wright, *Classes* (London: Verso, 1985), 150; Jock Collins, "Cosmopolitan Capitalism: Ethnicity, Gender and Australian Entrepreneurs." PhD diss., University of Wollongong, vol. 1, 26.

4. Wright, *Classes,* 44.

5. Bourdieu collapses gender, ethnicity, and generation into class, a strategy that conflates class resources and ethnic resources. See: Rogers Brubaker, "Rethinking Classical Theory: The Sociological Vision of Pierre Bourdieu," *Theory and Society* 14, 762.

6. Frank Parkin, *Marxism and Class Theory* (New York: Cornell University, 1979), 59

7. Michael Woolcock, "Social Capital and Economic Development: Toward a Theoretical Synthesis and Policy Framework," *Theory and Society* 27 (1998), 154.

8. Howard S. Becker developed the concept of occupational cultures; enterpreneurs have an occupational culture too. See: Howard S. Becker and James Carper, "The Elements of Identification with an Occupation," *American Sociological Review* 21 (1956):341–348; Howard S. Becker and Blanche Geer, "The Fate of Idealism in Medical School," *American Sociological Review* 23 (1958), 50–56.

9. Overlaps occur too. In-Jin Yoon points out that class culture often coincides "with the cultural values and attitudes of an ethnic group." He gives the example of Korean Americans all of whom, he claims, equally value education, hard work, and thrift, thus rendering these archetypically class values into cultural values. "The Changing Significance of Ethnic and Class resources in Immigrant Business." *International Migration Review* 25, 303–331.

11. Korean immigrants have an unusually hard time learning English claims Pyong Gap Min, implying the difficulty is linguistic in origin. Koreans speak English less well, says Min, than one would expect from their educational background. "Korean Immigrants in Los Angeles," in Ivan Light and Parminder Bhachu, eds., *Immigration and Entrepreneurship* (New Brunswick, NJ: transaction, 1993), 194.

11. Pierre Bourdieu, "Le Champ Economique," *Actes de la Recherche en Sciences Sociales* (September 1997), 56.

12. Theodore L. Cross, *Black Capitalism* (New York: Atheneum, 1969): 45ff; Ivan Light, *Ethnic Enterprise in America* (Los Angeles: University of California, 1972), ch. 2.

13. Melvin L. Oliver and Thomas M. Shapiro, *Black Wealth/White Wealth* (New York: Routledge, 1997), 45-50; John Sibley Butler, *Entrepreneurship and Self-Help among Black Americans* (Albany: State University of New York, 1991); Michael D. Woodard, *Black Entrepreneurs in America* (New Brunswick, NJ: Rutgers University, 1998), 34–56.

14. Ivan Light, *Ethnic Enterprise in America* (Los Angeles: University of California, 1972), esp. Chs. 2 and 3.

15. Alejandro Portes and Min Zhou, "Gaining the Upper Hand: Economic Mobility among Immigrant and Domestic Minorities," *Ethnic and Racial Studies* 15 (1992),491–522.

16. Ivan Light and Carolyn Rosenstein, *Race, Ethnicity, and Entrepreneurship in Urban America* (Hawthorne, NY: Aldine de Gruyter, 1995), 183.

17. Light, *Ethnic Enterprise in America,* 19–20.

18. "Actually, the practice among the majority of Negro businessmen is to start their businesses out of personal savings." Joseph Pierce, *Negro Business and Business Education* (New York: Harper and Brothers, 1947), 187.

19. Also true in Britain. See: Hilary Metcalf, Tariq Modood, and Satnam Virdee, *Asian Self-Employment in Britain* (London: Policy Studies Institute, 1997), 56–57.

20. Light, *Ethnic Enterprise,* ch. 2; Frank Fratoe, "Social Capital of Black Business Owners," *The Review of Black Political Economy* 16 (1988), 40

21. "The most famous of the organizations that have attempted to fill the breach in credit opportunities for women are the so-called rotating associations, almost always female dominated. . . . Small numbers of women will periodically contribute a portion of their earnings to a common fund; once in a regular cycle each woman will be able to draw a substantial amount of money from the fund to restock or otherwise improve her business." William C. Jordan, *Women and Credit in Pre-Industrial and Developing Societies* (Philadelphia: University of Pennsylvania, 1993), 100; also see: Jean-Pierre Hassoun. "Des Patrons Chinois à Paris," *Revue Française de Sociologie* 34(1993), 97–123; Dale Adams and M.L Canavesi de Sahonero. "Rotating Savings and Credit Association in Bolivia" *Savings and Development* 13 (1989), 219–36; John Campbell," The New New Englanders," *The Federal Reserve Bank of Boston Regional Review* 2 (1992), 17; Philip Kasinitz, *Caribbean New York* (Ithaca: Cornell University), 87.

22. "Ethnic Resources as Forms of Social Capital: A Study on Chinese Immigrant Entrepreneurs," Paper presented at the International Conference on Economic Governance in East Asia, organized by American Social Science Research Council and Institute of Anthropology and Sociology, Tsin-Hwa University, Taiwan, 1996), 10.

23. "Traditionally within the Amish community, private and family loans have financed new operations. Parents, relatives, or fellow church members extend credit to newly married couples or young families." Donald B. Kraybill and Steven M. Nolt, *Amish Enterprise: From Plows to Profits* (Baltimore: The Johns Hopkins University Press, 1995), 56. They also say (p. 156): "The church encourages members to make mutual aid their first priority. Successful business owners are expected to extend low-interest loans to fellow members."

24. "In 1996 Americans saved only 4.3% of disposable income, about half as much as was saved in 1967." "The Sorry State of Saving," *The Economist* 344 (1997), 15–16; see also: Jennifer Lee, "Entrepreneurship and Business development among African Americans, Koreans and Jews: Exploring Some Structural Differences," in Hector R. Cordero-Guzman, Ramon Grosfoguel, and Robert Smith, eds., *Transnational Communities and the Political Economy of New York in the 1990s* (Manuscript Book in Preparation).

25. Alejandro Portes, "The Social Origins of the Cuban Enclave Economy in Miami." *Sociological Perspectives* 30 (1987), 346; Gordon Redding, *The Spirit of Chinese Capitalism* (New York: Walter de Gruyter, 1990), ch. 7.

26. Kraybill and Nolt, *Amish Enterprise,* 110.

27. Catherine Zimmer and Howard Aldrich, "Resource Mobilization through Ethnic Networks: Kinship and Friendship Ties of Shopkeepers in England," *Sociological Perspectives* 30 (1987), 431–32.

28. Zimmer and Aldrich, "Resource Mobilization," 431.

29. "Greater borrowing from friends (some of which may represent RCAs) is consistent with the hypothesis that social resources available from group support networks disproportionately benefit Asian-immigrant firms." Timothy Bates, *Race, Self-Employment and Upward Mobility* (Baltimore: Johns Hopkins University Press, 1997), 126–127.

30. Philip Young and Ann Sontz, "Is Hard Work the Key to Success? A Socioeconomic Analysis of Immigrant Enterprise," *Review of Black Political Economy* 16 (1988), 17.

31. Shelly Tenenbaum, *A Credit to Their Community* (Detroit: Wayne State University, 1993). The Jewish Free Loan Association is still making free loans. Visit their website: http://www.freeloan.org.

32. Light, *Ethnic Enterprise,* 2; Jin-kyung Yoo, Korean Immigrant Entrepreneurs, ch. 6; Kyeyoung Park, *The Korean American Dream: Immigrants and Small Business in New York City* (Ithaca: Cornell University, 1997), 59; Violet Johnson, "Culture, Economic Stability, and Entrepreneurship: The Case of British West Indians in Boston." *New Migrants in the Marketplace,* edited by Marilyn Halter (Amherst: University of Massachusetts, 1995), 66.

33. Light, *Ethnic Enterprise in America,* ch. 2; Ivan Light, Jung-Kwuon Im, and Zhong Deng, "Korean Rotating Credit Associations in Los Angeles," *Amerasia* 16 (1991), 35–54.

34. Woolcock, "Social Capital and Economic Development," 154.

35. Steven Balkin, *Self-Employment for Low-Income People* (New York: Praeger, 1989), 15.
36. Gary S. Becker, *Human Capital,* 3d ed. (Chicago: University of Chicago, 1993), ch. 2.
37. Richard Rubinson and Irene Brown, "Education and the Economy," in Neil Smelser and Richard Swedberg, eds., *Handbook of Economic Sociology* (Princeton: Princeton University, 1994), 583–584.
38. Bates, *Race, Self-Employment, and Upward Mobility,* 30; Light and Rosenstein, *Race, Ethnicity and Entrepreneurship,* 130–131.
39. U. S. Bureau of the Census, *Statistical Abstract of the United States, 1996* (Washington, DC: U.S. Government Printing Office, 1996), Table 49.
40. Light and Rosenstein, *Race, Ethnicity, and Entrepreneurship,* 130.
41. James Coleman, "Social Capital in the Creation of Human Capital," *American Journal of Sociology* 94 (1988), 109
42. Collins, "Cosmopolitan Capitalism: Ethnicity, Gender and Australian Entrepreneurs," vol 2, 450.
43. Gary S. Becker, *Accounting for Tastes* (Cambridge: Harvard University, 1998), 5. Becker is dissatisfied with this narrow definition and seeks in this book to extend it.
44. In state socialist economies of the now-defunct Soviet type, the state paid students a stipend so students paid no opportunity cost or tuition.
45. This opportunity cost can mounts up even if a student's wage is small. At the minimum wage, a student would earn $9,000 in nine months, the usual academic year. In four years, the student would have failed to earn $36,000, an opportunity cost.
46. Pierre Bourdieu, and Jean-Claude Passeron, *Reproduction in Education, Society, and Culture* (London: Sage Publications, 1977), 73, 102.
47. Susan E. Mayer, *What Money Can't Buy: Family Income and Children's Life Chances* (Cambridge: Harvard University, 1997), 144.
48. Mayer, *What Money Can't Buy,* 42.
49. George Farkas, *Human Capital or Cultural Capital?* (New York: Aldine de Gruyter, 1996), 41–56.
50. ". . . the dispositions of agents, their habitus, that is, the mental structures through which they apprehend the social world, are essentially the product of the internalization of the structures of that world." Pierre Bourdieu, "Social Space and Symbolic Power." *Sociological Theory* 6 (1988), 18; also, Pierre Bourdieu, *Outline of a Theory of Practice* (Cambridge University Press, Cambridge, 1977), 77, 83.
51. Pierre Bourdieu, "Avenir de Classe et Causalité du Probable," *Revue Française de Sociologie* 15 (1974), 8.
52. Jozsef Borocz and Caleb Southworth, "Decomposing the Intellectuals' Class Power: Conversion of Cultural Capital to Income Hungary, 1986." *Social Forces* 74 (1996), 799. "And this cultural capital of origin is doubled again by the advantages it provides, such as cultural apprenticeship, table manners, the art of conversation, musical culture or the sense of suitability, tennis skill, accent, the precocity of one's acquisition of legitimate culture. The cultural capital of one's progenitors provides a sort of advance . . . which, right from the start, permits the newcomer to acquire culture from familiar examples." Bourdieu, *La Distinction,* 77. Translation by Ivan Light.
53. Bourdieu, "Les Trois Etats," 3; John B. Thompson, "Editor's Introduction," in Pierre Bourdieu, *Language and Symbolic Power* (Cambridge: Harvard University, 1991), 14.
54. "The choice of address, clothing, or cuisine are especially revelatory of one's social background because, situated outside the intervention of schools, they express, if you like, the naked taste beyond any express prescription or proscription." Bourdieu, *La Distinction,* 84–5. Translation by Ivan Light. Kay and Hagan find that women attorneys require stronger cultural capital than men attorneys to earn partnerships in prestigeous law firms. "Raising the Bar: The Gender Stratification of Law-Firm Capital," *American Sociological Review* 63 (1998), 728–743.
55. This definition is exclusive. High status knowledge that cannot be readily turned into financial gain is not cultural capital. Hence, the poor lack cultural capital even though they do not lack cultural knowledge.

56. Bourdieu, *La Distinction*, 88, 93.

57. See also Paul DiMaggio, "Social Structure, Institutions, and Cultural Good," in Pierre Bourdieu and James S. Coleman, eds., *Social Theory for a Changing Society* (Boulder: Westview Press, 1991), ch 4.

58. George Farkas, *Human Capital or Cultural Capital?* (New York: Aldine de Gruyter, 1996), 10–11.

59. Farkas, *Human Capital or Cultural Capital?*, 11.

60. "Cultural-capital theorists sometimes imply that the formative experiences of family upbringing and education launch into the world two classes of individuals whose destinies are from that time fixed. One class is endowed with a capacity to clothe themselves in the success-bringing symbolic apparatus of the dominant culture; the other class is doomed to the stigmatizing symbols of a dominated culture." David Halle, *Inside Culture* (Chicago: University of Chicago Press, 1993), 197.

61. Lamont and Lareau complain that the concept of cultural capital has lost its original meaning. Such reinterpretation, arising from public discussion, may signal the improvement of a flawed concept. Michele Lamont and Annette Lareau, "Cultural Capital: Allusions, Gaps, and Glissandos in Recent Theoretical Developments," *Sociological Theory* 6 (1988), 153–168.

62. Brigitte Berger, "The Culture of Modern Entrepreneurship," *The Culture of Entrepreneurship*, edited by Brigitte Berger. San Francisco: ICS Press, 1991), ch. 1.

63. This knowledge even survived 40 years of Hungarian socialism. Ivan Szelenyi, *Socialist Entrepreneurs: Embourgeoisement in Rulal Hungary* (Madison: University of Wisconsin, 1988), 210.

64. "We must not conceptualize a material inheritance that is not at the same time a cultural inheritance. Family property does not simply bear witness to the antiquity and continuity of the family's genealogy, thus consecrating its social identity, inseparable from its permanence. In addition, family wealth contributes to the family's moral reproduction. That is, it contributes to the transmission of values, of virtues, of competencies that legitimately belong to bourgeois dynasties." Bourdieu, *La Distinction*, 83. Translation by Ivan Light.

65. "Almost in all of the studies it was found that entrepreneur's father or some other close relative had been an entrepreneur. In any case, entrepreneurs have entrepreneurial parents more often than their proportion in the general population would suggest." Visa Huuskonen, "The Process of Becoming an Entrepreneur: A Theoretical Framework of Factors Influencing Entrepreneurs' Start-up Decisions (Preliminary Results)," in Heinz Klandt, ed., *Entrepreneurship and Business Development* (Aldershot: Avebury, 1993), 45–46.

66. Howard E. Aldrich, Linda A. Renzulli, and Nancy Langton, "Passing on Privilege: Resources Provided by Self-Employed Parents to their Self-Employed Children," *Research in Social Stratification and Mobility* 16 (1998), 293.

67. On Chinese children's role in family firms, see: Miri Song, "You're Becoming More and More English: Investigating Chinese Siblings' Cultural Identities," *New Community* 23 (1997), 343–362; *idem*, "Children's Labour in Ethnic Family Businesses: the Case of Chinese Take-Away Businesses in Britain," *Ethnic and Racial Studies* 20 (1997), 690–716.

68. "Most African American merchants I interviewed stated that they are the pioneers among their families and friends to own a business." Jennifer Lee, "Entrepreneurship and Business Development among African Americans, Koreans, and Jews," in Hector R. Cordero-Guzman, Ramon Grosfuguel, and Robert Smith, eds., *Transnational Communities and the Political Economy of New York in the 1990s* (Book Manuscript in Preparation).

69. See: Alejandro Portes, "Social Capital: Its Origins and Applications in Modern Sociology," *Annual Review of Sociology* 24 (1998), 1–24.

70. Elinor Ostrom, "Constituting Social Capital and Collective Action," *Journal of Theoretical Politics*, 6 (1994), 527–528.

71. Social capital derived from membership in an ethno-cultural group is discussed in the next chapter.

72. Jar-Der Luo, "The Significance of Networks in the Initiation of Small Businesses in Taiwan," *Sociological Forum* 12 (1997), 308.

73. Howard E. Aldrich, Amanda Brickman Elam, and Pat Ray Reese, "Strong Ties, Weak Ties and Strangers: Do Women Owners Differ from Men in their Use of Networking to Obtain Assistance?" in Sue Birley and Ian C. MacMillan, eds., *Entrepreneurship in a Global Context* (London and New York: Routledge, 1997), 1–25; Howard Aldrich, "Networking Among Women Entrepreneurs," in Oliver Hagan, Carol Rivchun, and Donald Sexton, eds., *Women-Owned Businesses* (New York: Praeger, 1989), 103–132; Dae Young Kim, "Beyond Coethnic Solidarity: Mexican and Ecuadorean Employment in Korean-owned Businesses in New York City," *Racial and Ethnic Studies*, forthcoming in 1999; Josef Bruederl and Peter Preisendoerfer, "Network Support and the Success of Newly Founded Businesses," *Small Business Economics* 10 (1998), 213–225; Mette Thuno, "The Chinese in Denmark," in Gregor Benton and Frank W. Pieke, eds., *The Chinese in Europe* (New York: St. Martin's Press, 1999) ch. 7; Jin-Kyung Yoo, *Korean Immigrant Entrepreneurs* (New York: Garland, 1999), ch. 5; Claudia Der-Martirosian, "Immigrant Self-employment and Social Capital," *International Migration Review* forthcoming in 1999; Light and Karageorgis, "The Ethnic Economy," 661.

74. Walter W. Powell and Laurel Smith-Doerr, "Networks and Economic Life," in Neil Smelser and Richard Swedberg, eds., *Handbook of Economic Sociology* (Princeton: Princeton University, 1994), 385; M. Patricia Fernandez-Kelly, "Social and Cultural Capital in the Urban Ghetto: Implications for the Economic Sociology of Immigration," in Alejandro Portes, ed., *The Economic Sociology of Immigration* (New York: Russell Sage Foundation, 1995), 216.

75. Sam Walton and John Huey, *Made in America* (New York: Doubleday, 1992), 21.

76. Donald Trump, *The Art of the Deal* (New York: Random House, 1987), 75.

77. The next chapter deals with social capital to which one has access thanks to ethno-cultural background.

78. Roberto M. Fernandez and Nancy Weinberg, "Sifting and Sorting: Personal Contacts and Hiring in a Retail Bank," *American Sociological Review* 62 (1997), 883–902.

79. Aldrich, Renzulli, and Langton, "Passing on Privilege," 298.

80. Yanjie Bian, "Bringing Strong Ties Back In: Indirect Connection, Bridges, and Job Search in China," *American Sociological Review* 61 (1996), 739–758.

81. Mayfair Mei-Hui Yang, "The Gift Economy and State Power in China," *Comparative Studies in Society and History* 31 (1989), 35.

82. Kwang-Kuo Hwang, "Face and Favor: The Chinese Power Game," *American Journal of* Sociology 92 (1987), 949.

83. "We can read daily in the newspapers about politicians and entrepreneurs giving gifts with the silent purpose of gaining votes or orders." Aafke Elisabeth Komter, "Reciprocity as a Principle of Exclusion: Gift Giving in the Netherlands," *Sociology* 30 (1996), 304.

84. ". . . Commodity exchange establishes objective quantitative relationships between the objects transacted, and not personal qualitative relationships between the objects transacted, and not personal qualitative relationships between the subjects in gift exchange . . . . Therefore, it is in this very space of personal relationship established by the gift that the art of guanxi unleashes its countertechniques of power." Mayfair Mei-Hui Yang, "The Gift Economy and State Power in China," *Comparative Studies in Society and History* 31 (1989), 38–39.

85. "Guanxi is based on reciprocity, the traditional concept of *bao*, where one does favours for others as 'social investments,' clearly expecting something in return. It is not a cold exchange, but is intertwined with *renqing* (human feeling, empathy) which raises it to a higher plane, and may also be based on a degree of *ganqing* (affect)." Thomas Gold, "After Comradeship: Personal Relations in China Since the Cultural Revolution," *The China Quarterly* 104 (1985), 660.

86. Coleman, "Social Capital," 109.

87. Conversely, those with more years of educational attainment have and deploy more social capital. Therefore, income benefits that economists attribute to the enhanced productivity of human capital owners might stem in whole or part from their social capital. ". . . The key insight of network studies is that the resources available through contacts vary, and the advantages and numbers of contacts clearly increase with education." Walter W. Powell and Laurel Smith-Doerr,

"Networks and Economic Life," in Neil Smelser and Richard Swedberg, eds., *Handbook of Economic Sociology* (Princeton: Princeton University Press), 373

88. Aldrich, Renzulli, and Langton distinguish only two forms of capital, physical and financial, and entrepreneurial. By entrepreneurial capital they mean human capital plus "attitudes, values, skills, and emotions that are relevant to business ownership." They exclude social capital from this definition, but acknowledge its influence. "Passing on Privilege," 295, 298

89. Alejandro Portes, "The Social Origins of the Cuban Enclave Economy in Miami," *Sociological Perspectives* 30 (1987), 340–372.

90. Their achievement was analogous to that of the post-war Hungarian bourgeoisie which, stripped of its wealth by the communist government, emerged a generation later with independent property, strictly on the basis of their class culture, Szelenyi, *Socialist Entrepreneurs*, 210

91. This same mistake induces the Germans to refer to the rebuilding of their postwar economy as an "economic miracle." In actuality, impoverished, bombed-out Germans of 1946 still had their human capital, social capital, and culture capital, and these resources permitted them to rebuild their devastated economy.

92. Stepick, *Pride*, 19

93. "Superstar Toni Braxton Tells Why She Filed for Bankruptcy." *Jet* magazine March 23, 1998. Available: http://web.lexis-nexis. Says Braxton, "I allowed my finances to become everyone else's finances; that's pretty much how I got here." See also: "Playboy Interview: Mike Tyson," *Playboy* magazine Nov. 1, 1998. Available: http://web.lexis-nexis. Says Tyson, "I don't trip about no fucking money." Loic Wacquant explains also that managers and promoters cheat the boxers, who do not understand the financial side of their profession. "A Fleshpeddler at Work: Power, Pain, and Profit in the Prizefighting Economy," *Theory and Society* 27 (1998), 1–42.

94. "It was like, once upon a time, I could have owned a Wendy's; now, I can't even eat at one." Loic Wacquant, "Inside the Zone: The Social Art of the Hustler in the Black American Ghetto," 28. Theory, Culture, and society 15:28.

95. Bates, *Race*, 14, 15.

96. Karl Marx, *Capital* (Moscow: Foreign Languages Publishing House, 1965), Vol. 1, 146 (chapter 4).

97. Other economists acknowledge the importance of social capital; indeed, they have provided some of the best evidence. Stephen Knack and Philip Keefer, "Does Social Capital Have an Economic Payoff? A Cross Country Investigation," *The Quarterly Journal of Economics* 112 (1997), 1283.

98. Bates acknowledges also "social resources" that "flow from ethnic solidarity," and which "may help" entrepreneurs. But Bates identifies human and social capital as the only class resources, Bates, *Race, Self-Employment and Upward Mobility*, 14, 15.

99. Bates wrongly identifies social capital with "a captive or protected market." Bates, *Race, Self-Employment and Upward Mobility*, 56.

100. For a critique of Bates' view, see: Salome Raheim, "Rejoinder: toward a broader understanding of the needs of African American entrepreneurs," *Journal of Developmental Entrepreneurship* 1 (1996), 17–26.

101. Timothy Bates and Lisa Servon, "Why Loans Won't Save the Poor," Inc Magazine Archives [Online]. Available: http://www.inc.com/incmagazine/archives/0460271.html. Richard Taub disagrees. See: "Making the Adaptation Across Cultures and Societies: A Report on an Attempt to Clone the Grameen Bank in Southern Arkansas," *Journal of Developmental Entrepreneurship* 3 (1998), 66.

102. Prodromos Panayiotopoulos, and Chris Gerry, "Youth enterprise promotion in the Commonwealth developing countries," *Third World Planning Review* 19 (1997), 225.

103. This is classical liberalism whose case for inequality rests upon the view that by identifying *and* rewarding "a wealth-creating few," we enhance the material welfare of all. Parkin, *Marxism and Class Theory*, 186.

104. Indeed, the language of social science elegantly explains what neo-classical economists must simply posit.

105. Shelley Green and Paul Pryde, *Black Entrepreneurship in America* (New Brunswick, NJ: Transaction, 1997), 170–171.
106. Alex Stepick, *Pride Against Prejudice* (Boston: Allyn and Bacon, 1998), 37–39, 42.
107. Sondra Beverly, "How Can the Poor Save? Theory and Evidence on Saving in Low-Income Households," (St. Louis: Working Paper 97–3 of the Center for Social Development of Washington University, 1997), 21–22.
108. Visit their website: http://www.emkf.org/entrepreneurship/index.html
109. "Ethnicity has an external effect on the human-capital accumulation process. Persons raised in advantageous ethnic environments will be exposed to social and economic factors that increase their productivity, and the larger or more frequent the amount of this exposure, the higher the resulting "quality" of the worker." George J. Borjas, "Ethnicity, Neighborhoods, and Human-Capital Externalities," *The American Economic Review* 85 (1995), 365; Gary S. Becker, *Accounting for Tastes* (Cambridge: Harvard University, 1996), 4.
110. "A person's personal and social capital form part of his total stock of human capital." Becker, *Accounting*, 4.
111. Li-Chen Cheng and Deborah Page-Adams, "Educational, Assets, and Intergenerational Well-being: The case of Female Headed Families." (St. Louis: Working Paper 96–3 of the Center for Social Development, Washington University, 1996), 11.
112. "Scholarly studies have failed to produce hard evidence that entrepreneurship in the present-day United States is an effective strategy for bootstrapping one's way out of poverty." Timothy Bates, "Why are firms owned by Asian immigrants lagging behind Black-Owned Businesses?" *National Journal of Sociology* 10:35. Bates to the contrary, the work of Alejandro Portes and his associates proves that Cubans in Miami bootstrapped themselves out of poverty. If it be objected that the Cubans lacked money, but had non-financial resources, then the objection supports our theoretical claim.
113. Peter Maas, *Underboss: Sammy the Bull Gravano's Story of Life in the Mafia* (New York: Harper Collins, 1997), esp. chs. 1–3; "Organised Crime: Streamlined for Success," *The Economist* 345 (Oct 11, 1997), 29–30. In the formal sector, the West Indians have used entrepreneurship to escape from poverty. Nancy Foner, "Race and Color: Jamaican Migrants in London and New York City." *International Migration Review* 19 (1985), 708–727.
114. Viviana A. Zelizer, *The Social Meaning of Money* (Princeton: Princeton University, 1997), 120.
115. Michael Sherraden distinguishes "tangible and intangible assets," including among the latter social capital and cultural capital. See: *Assets and the Poor* (Armonk N.Y.: M. E. Sharpe, 1991), 102–104. We endorse Sherraden's determination to add intangibles to the list of assets that poor people have. However, Sherradeen's distinction does not capture the origin (ethno-cultural or class) of the non- financial assets some poor families have. Also see: Janet Chan and Yuet-wah Cheung. "Ethnic Resources and Business Enterprise: A Study of Chinese Businesses in Toronto," *Human Organization* (1985), 44, 142–154; Ivan Light and Edna Bonacich, *Immigrant Entrepreneurs* (Berkeley and Los Angeles: University of California, 1988), ch 7.
116. Kim, Hurh, and Fernandez properly observe that to explain inter-group differences in self-employment in terms of resources, one must specify the resources. Yoon operationalized ethnic resources as follows: an entrepreneur received loans from family and/or friends; participated in a rotating credit association; was in partnership with a coethnic; participated in a business network of family and kin; has coethnic suppliers; worked long hours of unpaid labor. Yoon defined class resources with the following variables: an entrepreneur used personal savings to finance his or her own business, brought money with her or him from homeland, obtained bank or government loans for his or her business. Kwang Chung Kim, Won Moo Hurh, and Marilyn Fernandez, "Intra-group Differences in Business Participation: Three Asian Immigrant group," *International Migration Review* 23 (1098), pp. 73–95; Yoon, "Changing Significance." See also: Yen-Fen Tseng, "Ethnic Resources as Forms of Social Capital: A Study on Chinese Immigrant Entrepreneurs." Paper presented at the International Conference on Economic Governance in East Asia, organized by American Social Science Research Council and Institute of Anthropology and Sociology, Tsin-Hwa University, Taiwan, 1996.

117. Ewa Morawska, "Small Town, Slow Pace: Transformations of the Religious Life in the Jewish Community of Johnstown, Pennsylvania (1920–1940)," *Comparative Social Research* 13 (1991), 127–178.

118. Caesar Mavratsas, "Greek-American Economic Culture: The Intensification of Economic Life and a Parallel Process of Puritanization." in Marilyn Halter, ed., *New Migrants in the Marketplace* (Amherst: University of Massachusetts, 1995), 99.

119. Taiwanese wage earners view their jobs as "a temporary part in a career and a means to eventual entrepreneurship." Richard Stites," Industrial Work as an Entrepreneurial Strategy," *Modern China* 11 (1985), 242.

120. Frank W. Young, "A Macrosociological Interpretation of Entrepreneurship," in Peter Kilby, ed., *Entrepreneurship and Economic Development* (New York: Free Press), 142; Pnina Werbner, "Business on Trust: Pakistani Entrepreneurship in the Manchester Garment Trade," in Robin Ward and Richard Jenkins, eds., *Ethnic Communities in Business* (Cambridge: Cambridge University Press, 1984), 167; Nancy Foner. "Race and Color: Jamaican Migrants in London and New York City," *International Migration Review* 19 (1985), 717.

121. The same type of claim is made for numerous groups other than the Chinese. See also: Darrel Hess, "Korean Garment Manufacturing in Los Angeles," MA Thesis, Dept of Geography University of California at Los Angeles, June, (1990), 11; Jose Cobas, "Six Problems in the Sociology of the Ethnic Economy," *Sociological Perspectives* 32, 409; Philip Young and Ann Sontz, "Is Hard Work the Key to Success? A Socioeconomic Analysis of Immigrant Enterprise," *Review of Black Political Economy* 16 (1988), 11–31; Alejandro Portes. "The Social Origins of the Cuban Enclave Economy in Miami," *Sociological Prespectives* (1987) 30, 340–372; Foner, "Race and Color" 717. Mirriam Wells, "Ethnic Groups and Knowledge Systems in Agriculture" *Economic Development and Cultural Change* 39 (1991), 739–771; Hassoun, "Des Patrons Chinois," 97–123; Ellen Oxfeld Basu. "Profit, Loss, and Fate" *Modern China* 17 (1991), 227–259; Bernard Wong, "The Role of Ethnicity in Enclave Enterprises: A Study of the Chinese Garment Factories in New York City," *Human Organization* 46 (1987), 120–130; Stevan Harrell, "Why Do the Chinese Work so Hard? Reflections on an Entrepreneurial Ethic," *Modern China* (1985), 203–226; Stites, "Industrial Work," *Modern China* (1985), 227–246; Siu-lun Wong. "Chinese Entrepreneurs and Business Trust," *University of Hong Kong Supplement to the Gazette* 37 (1990), 25–34.

122. Peggy Levitt, "I Call Everyone Cousin: The Social Basis for Latino Small Business," in Marilyn Halter, ed., *New Immigrants in the Marketplace* (Amherst: University of Massachusetts, 1995), 133; Scott Cummings. "Collectivism: The Unique Legacy of Immigrant Economic Development," in Scott Cummings, ed., *Self-Help in Urban America* (Pt Washington, NY: Kennikat Press, 1980), 5–32; Fratoe, "Social Capital of Black Business Owners," 40.

123. Martin Marger, "Social and Human capital in Immigrant Adaptation: The Case of Canadian Business Immigrants," Paper presented at the "Social Capital Conference" held at Michigan State University, April 21 1998; see also: Martin N. Marger, "East Indians in Small Business: Middleman Minority or Ethnic Enclave?" *New Community* 16 (1990), 551–559.

124. Bruederl and Preisendorfer, "Network Support," 213–225.

125. "Clearly it is to family and kin rather than ethnic community-based sources that these business owners have turned, lacking sufficient self-generated capital." Marger, "Social and Human Capital," 549; Compare Marger with the anthropologists' version of kinship. See: Karen Leonard and Chandra S. Tibrewal, "Asian Indians in Southern California: Occupations and Ethnicity," in Ivan Light and Parminder Bhachu, eds., *Immigration and Entrepreneurship* (New Brunswick, NJ: Transaction Publishers, 1993), 150–151.

126. Such a case would utilize a class-only explanation, type 1 in Table 4.5.

127. Some of the initial Cuban business owners in Miami were Jews. Haitians make use of rotating credit systems. Both of these features refer back to ethno-cultural influences upon the ownership economies. Alejandro Portes, "The Social Origins of the Cuban Enclave Economy of Mi-

ami," *Sociological Perspectives* 30 (1987), 358. On Haitians, see: Michel Laguerre, "Rotating Credit Associations and the Diasporic Economy," *Journal of Developmental Entrepreneurship* 3 (1998), 23–34.

128. David W Engstrom and William McCready. "Asian Immigrant Entrepreneurs in Chicago" Center for Urban Research and Policy Studies of the University of Chicago, 1990, 26.

129. In-Jin Yoon, "Changing Significance," 303–331.

Chapter 5

1. Ivan Light, "Immigrant and Ethnic Enterprise in North America." *Ethnic and Racial Studies* 17 (2) (1984), 201.

2. Andrés T. Tapia, nd "Latino Church Grapples with Growing Pains." Christianity Todayhttp://www.loritapia.com/andrestapia/HTML/latinos/amen_conf_ct.htm

3. Luis León, "Born Again in East LA: The Congregation as Border Space," pp. 163-196 in R. Stephen Warner and Judith G. Wittner, eds., *Gatherings in the Diaspora: Religious Communities and the New Immigration* (Philadelphia. Temple University Press, 1998), p. 189. However, in abandoning Catholicism, these converts are also giving up certain ethnic resources, such as access to Catholic schools, colleges and social service agencies that have played an important role in the upward mobility of Catholic migrants.

4. J. Alan Winter, "Keeping the Cost of Living Jewishly Affordable," in David M. Gordis and Yoav Ben-Horin eds., *Jewish Identity in America* (Los Angeles: Wilstein Institute, 1990), 253–266.

5. Reflecting the importance of class resources in defining ethnicity, Carey McWilliams describes how established and relatively affluent persons of Mexican ancestry in the Southwestern U.S. were known as "Spanish-Americans" in contrast to poorer coethnics who were known simply as "Mexicans" despite their similar backgrounds. Steven Gold observed white Californians making similar distinctions in the 1970 and 1980s. Carey McWilliams, *North From Mexico* (New York: Greenwood Press, 1968), 121–6.

6. Chester Barnard, *The Functions of the Executive* (Cambridge, MA: Harvard University Press, 1938).

7. bell hooks, "Keeping Close to Home: Class and Education," in Virginia Cyrus, ed., *Experiencing Race, Class and Gender in the United States,* 2nd edition (Mountain View, CA: Mayfield, 1997), 126–133.

8. Rosabeth Moss Kanter, *Men and Women of the Corporation* (New York: Basic Books, 1977), 54.

9. Digby E. Baltzell, *Philadelphia Gentlemen: The Making of a National Upper Class.* (New York: The Free Press, 1957); Steven Gold and Bruce A. Phillips, "Mobility and Continuity among Eastern European Jews" in Silvia Pedraza and Rubén G. Rumbaut, eds., *Origins and Destinies: Immigration, Race and Ethnicity in America* (Belmont, CA: Wadsworth, 1996), 182–194; Howard G. Schneiderman, "The Protestant Establishment: Its History, Its Legacy—Its Future," in Silvia Pedraza and Rubén G. Rumbaut, eds., *Origins and Destinies: Immigration, Race and Ethnicity in America* (Belmont, CA: Wadsworth, 1996), 141–151; Harold L. Wilensky and Anne T. Lawrence, "Job Assignment in Modern Societies: A Re-examination of the Ascription-Achievement Hypothesis," in Amos Hawley, ed., *Societal Growth: Processes and Implications* (New York: The Free Press-Macmillan, 1979), 202–248.

10. Ann Swidler, "Culture in Action," *American Sociological Review* 51 (2) (1986), 273; William Julius Wilson, *When Work Disappears: The World of the New Urban Poor* (New York: Knopf, 1996).

11. Ivan Light, "Immigrant and Ethnic Enterprise in North America." *Ethnic and Racial Studies* 17 (2) (1984), 195–216.

12. Steven Gold and Bruce A. Phillips, "Mobility and Continuity among Eastern European Jews" in Silvia Pedraza and Rubén G. Rumbaut, eds., *Origins and Destinies: Immigration, Race and Ethnicity in America* (Belmont, CA: Wadsworth, 1996), 182–194; Pierrette Hondagneu-Sotelo, *Gendered Transitions: Mexican Experiences of Immigration* (Berkeley: University of California Press, 1994;

Robin H. Ward, "Orientation and Opportunity: An Interpretation of Asian Enterprise in Western Society." Paper presented at Annual Meeting of the American Sociological Association. (New York, August 30 — September 3, (1983).

13. Aubrey J. Bonnet, "An Examination of Rotating Credit Associations Among Black West Indian Immigrants in Brooklyn." in Roy S. Bryce-Laporte, ed., *Source Book on New Immigration* (New Brunswick, NJ: Transaction Books, 1980), 271–283; Ivan Light, *Ethnic Enterprise in America: Business and Welfare among Chinese, Japanese and Blacks* (Berkeley: University of California Press, 1972); Shelly Tenenbaum, *A Credit to their Community: Jewish Loan Societies in the United States 1880–1945* (Detroit: Wayne State University Press, 1993); Carlos Vélez-Ibañez, *Bonds of Mutual Trust: The Cultural System of Rotating Credit Associations among Urban Mexicans and Chicanos* (New Brunswick: Rutgers University Press, 1983).

14. For example, ethnic groups willing to lend money, work on religious holidays, accept financial risk, work in undesirable locations or engage in ritually "polluted" occupations have access to economic opportunities over those refusing to participate in such. John Sibley Butler, *Entrepreneurship and Self-Help Among Black Americans* (Albany: SUNY Press, 1991); Robert K. Merton, *Social Theory and Social Structure* (Glencoe IL.: The Free Press of Glencoe, 1949); Ellen Oxfeld, *Blood, Sweat and Mahjong: Family and Enterprise in an Overseas Chinese Community* (Ithaca: Cornell University Press, 1993); Abram L. Harris, *The Negro as Capitalist* (College Park, MD: McGrath, 1936); Max Weber, *The Protestant Ethic and the Spirit of Capitalism* (New York: Scribners, 1958).

15. Abner Cohen, *Custom and Politics in Urban Africa* (Berkeley: University of California Press, 1969); Francois Nielsen, "Towards a Theory of Ethnic Solidarity in Modern Societies," *American Sociological Review* 50 (2) (1985), 133–149; Orlando Patterson, *Ethnic Chauvinism: The Reactionary Impulse* (New York: Stein and Day, 1977); Alejandro Portes, "The Rise of Ethnicity: Determinants of Ethnic Perceptions Among Cuban Exiles in Miami." *American Sociological Review* 49 (1984), 383–397.

16. Fredrik Barth, *Ethnic Groups and Boundaries* (Boston: Little Brown and Company, 1969); Stephen Cornell, "The Variable Ties That Bind: Content and Circumstance in Ethnic Processes." *Ethnic and Racial Studies* 19 (2) (1996), 265–289; Michèle Lamont, *Money, Morals and Manners: The Culture of the French and the American Upper-Middle Class* (Chicago: University of Chicago Press, 1992).

17. Ivan Light and Carolyn Rosenstein, *Race, Ethnicity and Entrepreneurship in Urban America* (New York: Aldine De Gruyter, 1995), 19.

18. Steven Gold, "Soviet Jews in the United States." *American Jewish Yearbook* 94 (1994), 3–57; Caesar Mavratsas, "Greek- American Economic Culture: The Intensification of Economic Life and a Parallel Process of Puritanization," in Marilyn Halter (ed.), *New Migrants in the Marketplace: Boston's Ethnic Entrepreneurs* (Amherst: The University of Massachusetts Press, 1995), 97–119; Pyong-Gap Min, 1988 Ethnic Business Enterprise: Korean Small Business in Atlanta. Staten Island, NY: Center for Migration Studies.

19. Ann Swidler, "Culture in Action" *American Sociological Review* 51 (2) (1986), 273; Stephen Cornell, "The Variable Ties That Bind: Content and Circumstance in Ethnic Processes." *Ethnic and Racial Studies* 19 (2) (1996), 265–289; Michèle Lamont, *Money, Morals and Manners: The Culture of the French and the American Upper-Middle Class* (Chicago: University of Chicago Press, 1992).

20. It is conceivable that someone could acquire ethnic skills by hiring a tutor. However, if the student was a non-coethnic and paid to learn them, the resulting skills would be a product of class resources, not ethnic resources, since anyone with adequate funds could hire an instructor. Ethnicity would play no special role in their acquisition.

21. Eugene Roosens, *Creating Ethnicity: The Process of Ethnogenesis* (Newbury Park, CA: Sage, 1989); David Wellman, *Portraits of White Racism* (New York: Cambridge University Press, 1977); Donald Kraybill and Steven M. Nolt, *Amish Enterprise* (Baltimore: Johns Hopkins University Press, 1995).

22. Raymond Breton, "Institutional Completeness of Ethnic Communities and the Personal Relations of Immigrants," *American Journal of Sociology* 84 (1964), 293–318; Janet Chan, B.L. and

Yuet-Wah Cheung, "Ethnic Resources and Business Enterprise: A Study of Chinese Businesses in Toronto," *Human Organization* 44 (1985), 142–154.

23. Michael Hechter, *Principles of Group Solidarity* (Berkeley: University of California Press, 1987).

24. Howard G. Schneiderman, "The Protestant Establishment: Its History, Its Legacy—Its Future," in Silvia Pedraza and Rubén G. Rumbaut (eds.), *Origins and Destinies: Immigration, Race and Ethnicity in America* (Belmont, CA: Wadsworth, 1996), 145.

25. Alejandro Portes, "The Social Origins of the Cuban Enclave Economy of Miami," *Sociological Perspectives* 30 (4), 340–372; James S. Coleman, "Social Capital in the Creation of Human Capital," *American Journal of Sociology* 94 Supplement S95–S120; Steven Gold, *Refugee Communities: A Comparative Field Study* (Newbury Park, CA: Sage, 1992); Ivan Light, and Edna Bonacich, *Immigrant Entrepreneurs.* (Berkeley: University of California Press, 1988).

26. Shelly Tenenbaum, *A Credit to their Community: Jewish Loan Societies in the United States 1880–1945* (Detroit: Wayne State University Press, 1993); Muhammed Yunus, "Grameen Bank: Microlending for Economic Development" in Mark Breslow, Jim Campen, Ellen Frank, John Miller, and Abby Scher, eds., *Real World Banking,* 3d ed. (Somerville, MA: Dollars and Sense, 1997), 50–52.

27. Alejandro Portes and Julia Sensenbrenner, "Embeddedness and Immigration: Notes on the Social Determinants of Economic Action," *American Journal of Sociology* 98 (6) (1993), 1322; James S. Coleman, "Social Capital in the Creation of Human Capital," *American Journal of Sociology* 94 (1988), Supplement S95–S120; Mark Granovetter, "The Economic Sociology of Firms and Entrepreneurship," in Alejandro Portes (ed.), *The Economic Sociology of Immigration: Essays on Networks, Ethnicity and Entrepreneurship* (New York: Russell Sage Foundation, 1995), 128–165; Pierre Bourdieu and Loïc J. D. Wacquant, *An Invitation to Reflexive Sociology* (Chicago: University of Chicago Press, 1992), 119; Robert Putnam, "Bowling Alone: America's Declining Social Capital," *Journal of Democracy* 6 (1), 65–78; Alejandro Portes, "Social Capital: Its Origins and Applications in Modern Society," *Annual Review of Sociology* 24 (1998), 1–24.

28. Ivan Light, and Edna Bonacich, *Immigrant Entrepreneurs* (Berkeley: University of California Press, 1988); Thomas Bailey and Roger Waldinger, "Primary, Secondary and Enclave Labor Markets: A Training Systems Approach," *American Sociological Review* 56 (4) (1991), 432–445.

29. Abner Cohen and James Coleman show how the trust and reliability associated with ethnic transactions give ethnic entrepreneurs a significant advantage over economic actors relying on impersonal market relations when trading highly perishable food products and theft-prone precious stones. Abner Cohen, *Custom and Politics in Urban Africa* (Berkeley: University of California Press, 1969); James S. Coleman, "Social Capital in the Creation of Human Capital," *American Journal of Sociology* 94 (1988), Supplement S95–S120.

30. John K. Leba, *The Vietnamese Entrepreneurs in the U.S.A.* (1985). Houston: Zielecks; Alejandro Portes, and Julia Sensenbrenner, "Embeddedness and Immigration: Notes on the Social Determinants of Economic Action," *American Journal of Sociology* 98 (6) (1993), 1320–1350; Michael Hechter, *Principles of Group Solidarity* (Berkeley: University of California Press, 1987).

31. Bernard Wong, *Ethnicity and Entrepreneurship: The New Chinese Immigrants in the San Francisco Bay Area* (Boston: Allyn and Bacon, 1998), 75.

32. Steven Gold, "Patterns of Economic Cooperation among Israeli Immigrants in Los Angeles," *International Migration Review* 28 (105) (1994), 128.

33. While blue collar employment is generally considered a low-paying occupation, many Israeli men in Los Angeles work in real estate construction and remodeling. This occupation is well paid and accessed through an extensive ethnic network. Steven Gold, "Patterns of Economic Cooperation among Israeli Immigrants in Los Angeles," 114–15.

34. Mehdi, Bozorgmehr, Claudia Der-Martirosian, and Georges Sabagh, "Middle Easterners: A New Kind of Immigrant," in Roger Waldinger and Mehdi Bozorgmehr (eds.), *Ethnic Los Angeles* (New York: Russell Sage Foundation, 1996), 345–378.

35. Steven Gold, "Gender and Social Capital Among Israeli Immigrants in Los Angeles," *Diaspora* 4 (3) (1995), 267–301.

36. Mehdi, Bozorgmehr, Claudia Der-Martirosian and Georges Sabagh, "Middle Easterners: A New Kind of Immigrant," 345–378.

37. Steven Gold, 1994 "Patterns of Economic Cooperation among Israeli Immigrants in Los Angeles," 114–35; Steven Gold, *Refugee Communities: A Comparative Field Study* 1 (Newbury Park: Sage, 1992); Ivan Light, Georges Sabagh, Mehdi Bozorgmehr, and Claudia Der-Martirosian, "Beyond the Ethnic Enclave Economy," *Social Problems* 41 (1994), 65–80.

38. After all, if everyone in a given context has access to a given resource, its possession confers no competitive advantage. Mark Granovetter, "The Economic Sociology of Firms and Entrepreneurship." in Alejandro Portes (ed.), *The Economic Sociology of Immigration: Essays on Networks, Ethnicity and Entrepreneurship* (New York: Russell Sage Foundation, 1995), 142.

39. Ellen Oxfeld, *Blood, Sweat and Mahjong: Family and Enterprise in an Overseas Chinese Community* (Ithaca: Cornell University Press, 1993).

40. Patterns of group life associated with coupling and de-coupling are especially notable among middleman minority groups (See chapter 2).

41. Stanley Lieberson, *A Piece of the Pie* (Berkeley: University of California Press, 1980), 379.

42. Herbert Gans, "Second Generation Decline: Scenarios for the Economic and Ethnic Futures of the Post-1965 American Immigrants," *Ethnic and Racial Studies* 15 (2) (1992), 173–192.

43. Roger Waldinger, *Through the Eye of the Needle* (New York: NYU Press, 1986).

44. St. Clair Drake and Horace R. Cayton, *Black Metropolis* (New York: Harcourt Brace and Company, 1945); Robert L. Boyd, "The Allocation of Black Workers into the Public Sector," *Sociological Focus* 27 (1) (1994), 35–51; David M. Grant, Melvin L. Oliver, and Angela D. James, "African Americans: Social and Economic Bifurcation," in Roger Waldinger and Mehdi Bozorgmehr (eds.), *Ethnic Los Angeles* (New York: Russell Sage Foundation, 1996), 379–411; Cheryl Lynn Goldberg, *Or Does it Explode? Black Harlem in the Great Depression* (New York: Oxford, 1991); Roger Waldinger, *Still the Promised City? African-Americans and New Immigrants in Postindustrial New York* (Cambridge, MA: Harvard University Press, 1996).

45. Calvin Goldscheider and Frances E. Kobrin, "Ethnic Continuity and the Process of Self-Employment," *Ethnicity* 7 (1980), 256–278.

46. William J. Wilson, *The Truly Disadvantaged* (Chicago: University of Chicago Press, 1987); William J. Wilson, *When Work Disappears: The World of the New Urban Poor* (New York: Knopf, 1996).

47. In-Jin Yoon, *On My Own: Korean Businesses and Race Relations in America* (Chicago: University of Chicago Press, 1997), 142.

48. Luu Trankiem, "Economic Development Opportunities for Indochinese Refugees in Orange County," *California Community Foundation,* 60.

49. Sonya Salamon, *Prairie Patrimony: Family, Farming and Community in the Midwest* (Chapel Hill: University of North Carolina Press, 1992).

50. Shirley Ardner, "Women Making Money Go Round: ROSCAs Revisited," in Shirley Ardner and Sandra Burman (eds.), *Money Go Rounds: The Importance of Savings and Credit Associations for Women* (Oxford, 1995); Carlos Vélez-Ibañez, *Bonds of Mutual Trust: The Cultural System of Rotating Credit Associations among Urban Mexicans and Chicanos* (New Brunswick: Rutgers University Press, 1983); Ivan Light, *Ethnic Enterprise in America: Business and Welfare among Chinese, Japanese and Blacks* (Berkeley: University of California Press, 1972).

51. Shirley Ardner, "Women Making Money Go Round: ROSCAs Revisited," in Shirley Ardner and Sandra Burman (eds.), *Money Go Rounds: The Importance of Savings and Credit Associations for Women* (Oxford: Berg, 1995), 1.

52. Carlos Vélez-Ibañez, *Bonds of Mutual Trust: The Cultural System of Rotating Credit Associations among urban Mexicans and Chicanos* (New Brunswick: Rutgers University Press, 1983), 2.

53. Carlos Vélez-Ibañez, *Bonds of Mutual Trust: The Cultural System of Rotating Credit Associations among Urban Mexicans and Chicanos,* 90–91.

54. Ivan Light, *Ethnic Enterprise in America: Business and Welfare among Chinese, Japanese and Blacks* (Berkeley: University of California Press, 1972), 23.

55. Min found that only 4 of 159 Korean business owners in Atlanta and 3 out of 86 entrepreneurs in New York City used any *kye* (Korean rotating credit association) money for business capitalization. "Though many Korean immigrants participate in a *kye*, they intend mainly to accumulate savings and socialize with friends rather than to accumulate business capital." Pyong-Gap Min, *Caught in The Middle: Korean Communities in New York and Los Angeles.* (Berkeley: University of California Press, 1996).

56. Kyeyoung Park, *The Korean American Dream: Immigrants and Small Business in New York City* (Ithaca: Cornell University Press, 1997); Ivan Light and Zhong Deng, "Gender Differences in ROSCA Participation within Korean Business Households in Los Angeles," in Shirley Ardner and Sandra Burman (eds.), *Money Go Rounds: The Importance of Savings and Credit Associations for Women* (Oxford: Berg, 1995), 222.

57. Johanna Lessinger, "Investing or Going Home?: A Transnational Strategy among Indian Immigrants in the United States," in Nina Glick Schiller, Linda Basch, and Cristina Blac-Szanton (eds.), *Towards a Transnational Perspective on Migration: Race, Class, Ethnicity and Nationalism Reconsidered* (New York: New York Academy of Sciences, 1992), 53–80.

58. Shelly Tenenbaum, *A Credit to their Community: Jewish Loan Societies in the United States 1880–1945* (Detroit: Wayne State University Press, 1993).

59. Lubomyr Y. Luciuk, "A Continuing Presence: North America's Ukranians," in Robin Cohen (ed.), *The Cambridge Survey of World Migration* (Cambridge: Cambridge University Press, 1995), 109–113; Frank Renkiewicz, "The Profits of Nonprofit Capitalism: Polish Fraternalism and Beneficial Insurance in America," in Scott Cummings (ed.), *Self-Help in Urban America: Patterns of Minority Business Enterprise* (Port Washington, N.Y.: Kennikat Press, 1980), 113–129; Joseph Stipanovich, "Collective Economic Activity Among Serb, Croat, and Slovene Immigrants in the United States," in Scott Cummings (ed.), *Self-Help in Urban America: Patterns of Minority Business Enterprise* (Port Washington, N.Y.: Kennikat Press, 1980), 160–176; M. Mark Stolarik, "A Place for Everyone: Slovak Fraternal-Benefit Societies," in Scott Cummings (ed.), *Self-Help in Urban America: Patterns of Minority Business Enterprise* (Port Washington, N.Y.: Kennikat Press, 1980), 130–141; John Sibley Butler, *Entrepreneurship and Self-Help Among Black Americans* (Albany: SUNY Press, 1991).

60. Marcia Millman, *Warm Hearts, Cold Cash* (New York: The Free Press, 1991).

61. Nazli Kibria, *Family Tightrope: The Changing Lives of Vietnamese Americans* (Princeton, N.J.: Princeton University Press, 1993), 77.

62. Ewa Morawska, "East Europeans on the Move," in Robin Cohen (ed.), *The Cambridge Survey of World Migration.* (Cambridge: Cambridge University Press, 1995), 97–102; Jon Gjerde, "The Scandinavian Migrants," in Robin Cohen (ed.), *The Cambridge Survey of World Migration.* (Cambridge: Cambridge University Press, 1995), 85–90.

63. Pierrette Hondagneu-Sotelo, *Gendered Transitions: Mexican Experiences of Immigration* (Berkeley: University of California Press, 1994).

64. Michael J. Piore, *Birds of Passage* (New York: Cambridge University Press, 1979).

65. Sarah J. Mahler, *Salvadorans in Suburbia: Symbiosis and Conflict* (Boston: Allyn and Bacon, 1995), 74; Saskia Sassen, "The Informal Economy," in John Hull Mollenkopf and Manuel Castells (eds.), *Dual City: Restructuring New York* (New York: Russell Sage Foundation, 1991), 79–101.

66. Peggy Levitt, *"A Todos Les Llamo Primo* (I Call Everyone Cousin): The Social Basis for Latin Small Businesses," in Marilyn Halter (ed.), *New Migrants in the Marketplace: Boston's Ethnic Entrepreneurs.* (Amherst: The University of Massachusetts Press, 1995), 120–140.

67. William Kornblum, *Blue Collar Community* (Chicago: University of Chicago Press, 1974); Hector Delgado, *New Immigrants, Old Unions: Organizing Undocumented Workers in Los Angeles.* (Philadelphia: Temple University Press, 1993); Dennis P. Clark, "The Expansion of the Public Sector and Irish Economic Development," in Scott Cummings (ed.), *Self-Help in Urban America: Patterns of Minority Business Enterprise.* (Port Washington, N.Y.: Kennikat Press, 1980), 177–187; Ronald Takaki, *A Different Mirror: A History of Multicultural America* (Boston: Little Brown, 1993).

68. Thomas Bailey and Roger Waldinger, "Primary, Secondary and Enclave Labor Markets: A Training Systems Approach," *American Sociological Review* 56 (4) (1991), 432–445; Alejandro Portes and Robert Bach, *Latin Journey: Cuban and Mexican Immigrants in the United States* (Berkeley: University of California Press, 1985); Illsoo Kim, *New Urban Immigrants: The Korean Community in New York*. (Princeton, N.J.: Princeton University Press, 1981).

69. Thomas Bailey and Roger Waldinger, "Primary, Secondary and Enclave Labor Markets: A Training Systems Approach," *American Sociological Review* 56 (4) (1991), 435.

70. Jenna Weissman Joselit, *Our Gang: Jewish Crime and the New York Jewish Community, 1900–1940* (Bloomington: Indiana University Press, 1983); Stanford Lyman, *Chinese Americans.* (New York: Random House, 1974).

71. Dae Young Kim, "Beyond Co-ethnic Solidarity: Mexican and Ecuadorian Employment in Korean-Owned Businesses in New York City," *Ethnic and Racial Studies* 22 (3) (1999), 581–605; Steven Gold, "Patterns of Economic Cooperation among Israeli Immigrants in Los Angeles," *International Migration Review* 28 (105) (1994), 114–135; Steven Gold, "Chinese-Vietnamese Entrepreneurs in California," in Paul Ong, Edna Bonacich and Lucy Cheng (eds.), *The New Asian Immigration in Los Angeles and Global Restructuring* (Philadelphia: Temple University Press, 1994), 196–226.

72. Harold L. Wilensky and Anne T. Lawrence, "Job Assignment in Modern Societies: A Re-examination of the Ascription-Achievement Hypothesis," in Amos Hawley (ed.), *Societal Growth: Processes and Implications* (New York: The Free Press-Macmillan, 1979), 215.

73. William J. Wilson, *When Work Disappears: The World of the New Urban Poor* (New York: Knopf, 1996); Mary C. Waters, "West Indian Immigrants, African Americans and Whites in the Workplace: Different Perspectives on American Race Relations." Paper presented at the American Sociological Association Annual Meeting, Los Angeles, August, 1995; Harry J. Holzer, "Informal Job Search and Black Youth Unemployment," *American Economic Review* 27 (3) (1987), 446–452; Roger Waldinger, "The 'Other Side' of Embeddedness: A Case-Study of The Interplay of Economy and Ethnicity," *Ethnic and Racial Studies* 18 (3), 555–580.

74. Ed Wheeler, "Black Gold." Paper Presented at International Visual Sociology Association Annual Meeting, Rochester (July), 1988.

75. Roger Waldinger, "The Making of an Immigrant Niche." *International Migration Review* 28 (105) (1994), 15.

76. Ivan Light, *Ethnic Enterprise in America: Business and Welfare among Chinese, Japanese and Blacks,* 12.

77. John R. Logan, Richard D. Alba and Thomas L. McNulty, "Ethnic Economies in Metropolitan Regions: Miami and Beyond," *Social Forces* 72 (3) (1994), 691–724; Alejandro Portes and Robert D. Manning, "The Immigrant Enclave: Theory and Empirical Examples," in Susan Olzak and Joane Nagel (eds.), *Competitive Ethnic Relations* (Orlando: Academic Press, Inc, 1986), 47–68.

78. Timothy Bates, *Race, Self-Employment and Upward Mobility: An Illusive American Dream* (Baltimore: John Hopkins University Press, 1997).

79. Ivan Light, *Ethnic Enterprise in America: Business and Welfare among Chinese, Japanese and Blacks* (Berkeley: University of California Press, 1972); Stanford Lyman, *Chinese Americans* (New York: Random House, 1972); Louis Wirth, *The Ghetto* (Chicago: University of Chicago Press, 1928); Thomas P. Sowell, *Ethnic America* (New York: Basic Books, 1981); Donald Kraybill and Steven M. Nolt, *Amish Enterprise* (Baltimore: Johns Hopkins University Press, 1995); Edna Bonacich and John Modell, *The Economic Basis of Ethnic Solidarity: Small Business in the Japanese-American Community* (Berkeley: University of California Press, 1980).

80. U.S. Census 1990.

81. Fred Shuster, "No Static From Latino Radio Market." *Los Angeles Daily News* (http://www.latino.com/life/0605arad.html) (1996), 3. The relative size of entrepreneurial ethnic groups also determines the nature of ethnic economies. If the population is quite small, then almost the entire community can find jobs in the ethnic niche, and problems of co-ethnic competition are likely to be minor. As group size increases, there will be a greater availability of

co-ethnic labor, and if it is very large, only a fraction will be employable in an ethnic niche. Hence, a group's demographic features can be an ethnic resource. Stanley Lieberson, *A Piece of the Pie* (Berkeley: University of California Press, 1980), 380.

82. Fred Shuster, "No Static From Latino Radio Market," *Los Angeles Daily News* (http://www.latino.com/life/0605arad.html) (1996), 1.

83. In-Jin Yoon, *On My Own: Korean Businesses and Race Relations in America* (Chicago: University of Chicago Press, 1997); Pyong-Gap Min, *Caught in The Middle: Korean Communities in New York and Los Angeles* (Berkeley: University of California Press, 1996); James H. Johnson, Jr., Cloyzelle K. Jones, Walter C. Farrell, Jr. and Melvin L. Oliver, "The Los Angeles Rebellion: A Retrospective View," *Economic Development Quarterly* 6 (4) (November, 1992), 356–372.

84. Saskia Sassen, "The Informal Economy" in John Hull Mollenkopf and Manuel Castells (eds.), *Dual City: Restructuring New York.* (New York Russell Sage Foundation, 1991), 79–101.

85. Yen-Fen Tseng, "Beyond Little Taipei': The Development of Taiwanese Immigrant Businesses in Los Angeles," *International Migration Review* 29 (109) (1995), 33–58.

86. Illsoo Kim, *New Urban Immigrants: The Korean Community in New York* (Princeton, N.J.: Princeton University Press, 1981).

87. Pyong-Gap Min, *Caught in The Middle: Korean Communities in New York and Los Angeles,* 55–56.

88. Matt Richtel, "New Israelis Get Computers to Aid Assimilation," *New York Times* (January 21, 1998).

89. Steven Gold, "Chinese-Vietnamese Entrepreneurs in California," in Paul Ong, Edna Bonacich and Lucy Cheng (eds.), *The New Asian Immigration in Los Angeles and Global Restructuring.* (Temple University Press, 1994), 196–226.

90. Kenneth L. Wilson and W. Allen Martin, "Ethnic Enclaves: A Comparison of the Cuban and Black Economies in Miami," *American Journal of Sociology* 88 (1) (1982), 135–160.

91. John Sibley Butler, *Entrepreneurship and Self-Help Among Black Americans* (Albany: SUNY Press, 1991), 17.

92. Marcus D. Pohlmann, *Black Politics in Conservative America.* (New York: Longman, 1990), 45.

93. Grant, Melvin L. Oliver and Angela D. James, "African Americans: Social and Economic Bifurcation," in Roger Waldinger and Mehdi Bozorgmehr (eds.), *Ethnic Los Angeles* (New York: Russell Sage Foundation, 1996), 379–411.

94. Ronald Takaki, *A Different Mirror: A History of Multicultural America* (Boston: Little Brown, 1993), 162; Dennis P. Clark, "The Expansion of the Public Sector and Irish Economic Development," in Scott Cummings (ed.), *Self-Help in Urban America: Patterns of Minority Business Enterprise* (Port Washington, N.Y.: Kennikat, 1980), 177–187.

95. Since the late 1980s, legislation and court decisions have resulted in a drastic reduction in set aside programs. Michael D. Woodard, *Black Entrepreneurs in America: Stories of Struggle and Success* (New Brunswick, N.J.: Rutgers University Press, 1997), 29, 225–226; MBDA, ND MBDA Business Communities http/www.mbda.gov. stats.html/Hassidic. Further, the definition of just who qualifies as a minority is the result of political decision-making.

96. Timothy Bates, *Race, Self-Employment and Upward Mobility: An Illusive American Dream,* 174–184.

97. Philip Kasinitz, *Caribbean New York* (Ithaca: Cornell University Press, 1992), 98; Philip Kasinitz and Milton Vickerman, "Ethnic Niches and Racial Traps, Jamaicans in the New York Regional Economy" paper presented at Social Science History Association, Chicago, November 16, 1995, 13–14.

98. Felix Padilla, "Latino Ethnicity in the City of Chicago," in Susan Olzak and Joane Nagel (eds.), *Competitive Ethnic Relations* (Orlando: Academic Press, Inc., 1986), 153–172.

99. William Wei, *The Asian American Movement* (Philadelphia: Temple University Press, 1993); John Horton, with the assistance of Jose Calderon, Mary Pardo, Leland Saito, Linda Shaw and Yen-Fen Tseng, *The Politics of Diversity: Immigration, Resistance and Change in Monterey Park, California* (Philadelphia: Temple University Press, 1995); Yen Le Espiritu, *Asian American Panethnicity:* (Philadelphia: Temple University Press, 1992); Timothy P. Fong, *The First Suburban Chinatown: The Remaking of Monterey Park, California* (Philadelphia: Temple University Press, 1994).

100. Martin Marger, *Race and Ethnic Relations: American and Global Perspectives* (4th edition). (Belmont, CA: Wadsworth, 1997), 162.

101. Pyong-Gap Min, *Caught in The Middle: Korean Communities in New York and Los Angeles,* 164–165.

102. Steven Gold, *Refugee Communities: A Comparative Field Study* (Newbury Park: Sage, 1992); Alejandro Portes and Rubén G. Rumbaut, *Immigrant America: A Portrait* (2nd Edition) (Berkeley: University of California Press, 1996); David M. Riemers, *Still the Golden Door: The Third World Comes to America* (New York: Columbia University Press, 1985).

103. ORR: Office of Refugee Resettlement, 1995 Report to Congress: Refugee Resettlement Program.

104. Steven Gold, "Religious Agencies, Immigrant Resettlement and Social Justice," in *Research in Social Policy,* Vol. 5 Social Justice Philanthropy (1997), 47–65; Mohammed E. Ahrari (ed.), *Ethnic Groups and U.S. Foreign Policy* (New York: Greenwood Press, 1987).

105. Jeremy Hein, "State Incorporation of Migrants and the Reproduction of a Middleman Minority among Indochinese Refugees," *The Sociological Quarterly* 29 (3) (1988), 463–478.

106. Steven Gold, *Refugee Communities: A Comparative Field Study* (Newbury Park: Sage, 1992).

107. Ron Kelley and Jonathan Friedlander (eds.), *Irangeles: Iranians in Los Angeles* (Berkeley: University of California Press, 1993); Christine R. Finnan and Rhonda Cooperstein, "Southeast Asian Refugee Resettlement at the Local Level," Menlo Park, California: SRI International. According to the 1990 census, the self-employment rate for Iranians is 18.7 percent (#6 overall in the U.S.); 17.6 for Armenians (#7 overall, although this number includes non-refugees who have been in the U.S. for generations); 11.4 percent of Cubans (#45 overall); 10.8 percent for Chinese (#50 overall) and 15 and 25 percent for Soviet Jews living in New York and Los Angeles, respectively. All of these groups exceed the national average for self-employment which is 10.2 percent. While the Vietnamese self-employment rate of 8 percent in 1990 was below the national average, it more than doubled from 3.1 percent since 1980, suggesting that this group's ethnic-owned economy is growing at a rapid rate, and as of this writing, has likely exceeded the national average. In Jin Yoon, *On My Own: Korean Businesses and Race Relations in America* (Chicago: University of Chicago Press, 1997), 18–20; Steven Gold, "Soviet Jews in the United States." *American Jewish Yearbook* 94 (1994), 3–57.

108. Donald Kraybill and Steven M. Nolt, *Amish Enterprise* (Baltimore: Johns Hopkins University Press, 1995), 17.

109. Jack Katz, *Seductions of Crime* (New York: Basic Books, 1988); Ivan Light, "The Ethnic Vice Industry 1880–1944," *American Sociological Review* 42 (1977), 464–479.

110. Alejandro Portes and Rubén G. Rumbaut, *Immigrant America: A Portrait* (Berkeley: University of California Press, 1990), 3–4.

111. Stanford Lyman, *Chinese Americans* (New York: Random House, 1974), 135; Clifford Geertz, *Peddlers and Princes* (Chicago: University of Chicago Press, 1963); Mark Granovetter, "The Economic Sociology of Firms and Entrepreneurship," in Alejandro Portes (ed.), *The Economic Sociology of Immigration: Essays on Networks, Ethnicity and Entrepreneurship* (New York: Russell Sage Foundation, 1995), 128–165; Peggy Levitt, "*A Todos Les Llamo Primo* (I Call Everyone Cousin): The Social Basis for Latin Small Businesses," in Marilyn Halter (ed.), *New Migrants in the Marketplace: Boston's Ethnic Entrepreneurs* (Amherst: The University of Massachusetts Press, 1995), 120–140.

112. Steven Gold, "Economic Cooperation among Israeli Immigrants in Los Angeles," *International Migration Review* 28 105 (1994), 124.

113. Alejandro Portes and Robert Bach, *Latin Journey: Cuban and Mexican Immigrants in the United States* (Berkeley: University of California Press, 1985); Phyllis J. Johnson, "The Impact of Ethnic Communities on the Employment of Southeast Asian Refugees," *Amerasia* 14 (1) (1988), 1–22; Jacqueline Desbarats, "Ethnic Differences in Adaptation: Sino-Vietnamese Refugees in the United States," *International Migration Review* 20 (2) (1986), 405–427.

114. Dinker Raval, "East Indian Small Businesses in the U.S.: Perception, Problems and Adjustments," *American Journal of Small Business* 7 (3) (1983), 39–44.

115. Mary C. Sengstock, *Chaldean-Americans: Changing Conceptions of Ethnic Identity* (Staten Island, NY: Center for Migration Studies, 1982); Thomas Bailey and Roger Waldinger, "Primary, Secondary and Enclave Labor Markets: A Training Systems Approach," *American Sociological Review* 56 (4) (1991), 432–445; Alejandro Portes and Robert Bach, *Latin Journey: Cuban and Mexican Immigrants in the United States* (Berkeley: University of California Press, 1985).

116. Edna Bonacich, "Making it in America: A Social Evaluation of the Ethics of Immigrant Entrepreneurship," *Sociological Perspectives* 30 (4) (1987), 446–466.

Chapter 6

1. Max Weber, *Economy and Society* (Berkeley: University of California Press, 1978) cited in Jimmy M. Sanders and Victor Nee, "Limits of Ethnic Solidarity in the Ethnic Enclave Economy," *American Sociological Review* 52 (1987), 745–767.

2. Orlando Patterson, *Ethnic Chauvinism: The Reactionary Impulse* (New York: Stein and Day, 1977). William J. Wilson, *When Work Disappears: The World of the New Urban Poor* (New York: Knopf, 1996).

3. Ruth Milkman and Eleanor Townsley, Ch. 24, "Gender and Economy," in Neil Smelser and Richard Swedberg (eds.), *Handbook of Economic Sociology* (Princeton, NJ: Princeton University Press/Russell Sage Foundation, 1994); Annie Phizacklea, "Entrepreneurship, Ethnicity, and Gender," in Sallie Westwood and Parminder Bhachu (eds.), *Enterprising Women: Ethnicity, Economy, and Gender Relations* (London and New York: Routledge, 1988), pp. 20–33; Rae Lesser Blumberg, "Introduction: The Triple Overlap of Gender Stratification, Economy, and the Family," in Rae Lesser Blumberg (ed.), *Gender, Family, and Economy: The Triple Overlap* (Newbury Park: Sage, 1991), 7–32.

4. James S. Coleman, "Social Capital in the Creation of Human Capital," *American Journal of Sociology* 94, Supplement S95-S120, 1988; Ruth Milkman and Eleanor Townsley, "Gender and the Economy," Ch. 24, in Neil Smelser and Richard Swedberg (eds.), *Handbook of Economic Sociology* (Princeton, NJ: Princeton University Press/Russell Sage Foundation, 1994).

5. The Census defines a family as a domestic group of two or more people united by bonds of blood, adoption, or marriage. U.S. Bureau of the Census, 1990. Janet L. Bokemeier, "Rediscovering Families and Households: Restructuring Rural Society and Rural Sociology," *Rural Sociology* 60 (1), (1997), pp. 1–20.

6. While a large number of textbooks about ethnic families have been published in recent years, these offer very little information about the specific economic status and patterns associated with various ethnic families.

7. Pyong-Gap Min, "The Korean-American Family" in Charles H. Mindel, Robert Habenstein, and Roosevelt Wright, Jr. (eds.), *Ethnic Families in America,* 3rd ed. (New York: Elsevier, 1988), 199–229.

8. Ann Swidler, "Culture in Action," *American Sociological Review* 51 (2) (1986), 273–286.

9. Rubén G. Rumbaut, "Introduction: Immigration and Incorporation," *Sociological Perspectives* 40 (3) (1997), 334.

10. M. Patricia Fernández-Kelly and Anna M. García, "Power Surrendered, Power Restored: The Politics of Work and Family Among Hispanic Garment Workers in California and Florida" in Louise A. Tilly and Patricia Gurin (eds.), *Women, Politics, and Change* (New York: Russell Sage, 1990), 130–149.

11. For example, there are more Filipino women in the United States than men. In contrast, the number of Southeast Asian (Vietnamese, Laotian, and Cambodian) men significantly exceeds that

of co-national women. For all Filipinos in the United States as of 1980, there were 232,385 males and 269,055 females, a 16 percent difference. See Luciano Mangiafico, *Contemporary American Immigrants: Patterns of Filipino, Korean, and Chinese Settlement in the United States* (New York: Praeger, 1988). In 1984, there were approximately 204,000 male Southeast Asian refugees in the United States between the ages of 12 and 44, but only 156,000 females in the same age group, a 24 percent difference. See Bill Balvanz, "Determination of the Number of Southeast Asian Refugee Births and Pregnancies by California County," *Migration World* 16 (3) (1988), 7–16.

12. Steven Gold, *From the Workers' State to the Golden State: Jews From the Former Soviet Union in California* (Boston: Allyn and Bacon, 1995). Lisandro Pérez, "Immigrant Economic Adjustment and Family Organization," *International Migration Review* 20 (1) (1986), 4–20. Barry R. Chiswick, "Differences in Education and Earnings Across Racial and Ethnic Groups: Tastes, Discrimination, and Investments in Child Quality," *Quarterly Journal of Economics* CIII (3) (August 1988), 571–597.

13. James S. Coleman, "Social Capital in the Creation of Human Capital," *American Journal of Sociology* 94, Supplement S95–S120, 1988.

14. Elliott R. Barkan, *And Still They Come: Immigrants and American Society: 1920 to the 1990s* (Wheeling, IL: Harland Davidson, 1996), 207.

15. Donna Gabaccia, *From the Other Side: Women, Gender, and Immigrant Life in the US., 1820–1990* (Bloomington and Indianapolis: Indiana University Press, 1994). These are general tendencies. Each ethnic group reveals its own characteristics and patterns of economic life.

16. Donna Gabaccia, *From the Other Side: Women, Gender, and Immigrant Life in the U.S., 1820–1990* (Bloomington and Indianapolis: Indiana University Press, 1994), 31–33.

17. Ruth Milkman and Eleanor Townsley, "Gender and the Economy," Ch. 24, in Neil Smelser and Richard Swedberg (eds.), *Handbook of Economic Sociology* (Princeton, NJ: Princeton University Press/Russell Sage Foundation, 1994), 603.

18. 1992 Economic Census.

19. National Foundation for Women Business Owners (NFWBO), "Woman-Owned businesses to provide more jobs than Fortune 500," http://www.att.com/press/0392/920331.bsa.html, 1992. NFWBO, "Women Business Owners Make Progress in Access to Capital; Still Lag Men-Owned Businesses in Credit Levels," http://www.nfwbo.org/nfwbo/rr010.htm, 1996.

20. Lief Jensen, "Secondary Earner Strategies and Family Poverty: Immigrant-Native Differentials, 1960–1980," *International Migration Review* 25 (1) (1991), 113–140.

21. Heidi Hartmann, "The Unhappy Marriage of Marxism and Feminism" in Roger S. Gottlieb (ed.), *An Anthology of Western Marxism* (New York: Oxford University Press, 1989), 316–317; Randall Collins, "Women and The Production of Status Cultures," in Michèle Lamont and Marcel Fournier (eds.), *Cultivating Differences: Symbolic Boundaries and the Making of Inequality* (Chicago: University of Chicago Press, 1991), 213–231.

22. Donna Gabaccia, *From the Other Side: Women, Gender, and Immigrant Life in the U.S., 1820–1990* (Bloomington and Indianapolis: Indiana University Press, 1994), xv.

23. William J. Wilson, *When Work Disappears: The World of the New Urban Poor* (New York: Knopf, 1996).

24. National Committee on Pay Equity, The Wage Gap, Briefing Paper no. 1 (Washington DC: National Conference on Pay Equity, 1989), p. 4, cited in Ruth Milkman and Eleanor Townsley, "Gender and the Economy," Ch. 24, in Neil Smelser and Richard Swedberg (eds.), *Handbook of Economic Sociology* (Princeton, NJ: Princeton University Press/Russell Sage Foundation, 1994), 604.

25. Mary G. Powers and William Seltzer, "Occupational Status and Mobility Among Undocumented Immigrants by Gender," *International Migration Review* 32 (1) (1998), 21–55.

26. Donna Gabaccia, *From the Other Side: Women, Gender, and Immigrant Life in the U.S., 1820–1990* (Bloomington and Indianapolis: Indiana University Press, 1994), 441.

27. Douglas Massey, Joaquin Arango, Graeme Hugo, Ali Kouaouci, Adela Pellegrino and J. Edward Taylor, "Theories of International Migration: A Review and Appraisal," *Population and Development Review* 19(3) (1993), 443.

28. Shirley Ardner, "Women Making Money Go Round: ROSCAs Revisited" in Shirley Ardner and Sandra Burman (eds.), *Money Go Rounds: The Importance of Savings and Credit Associations for Women.* (Oxford, 1995); Carlos Vélez-Ibañez, *Bonds of Mutual Trust: The Cultural System of Rotating Credit Associations among Urban Mexicans and Chicanos.* (New Brunswick: Rutgers University Press, 1983); Ruth Milkman and Eleanor Townsley, "Gender and the Economy," Ch. 24, in Neil Smelser and Richard Swedberg (eds.), *Handbook of Economic Sociology* (Princeton, NJ: Princeton University Press/Russell Sage Foundation, 1994).

29. William J. Wilson, *When Work Disappears: The World of the New Urban Poor* (New York: Knopf, 1996).

30. Allen J. Scott, "The Manufacturing Economy: Ethnic and Gender Divisions of Labor," in Roger Waldinger and Mehdi Bozorgmehr (eds.), *Ethnic Los Angeles* (New York: Russell Sage Foundation, 1996), 222–224.

31. Nancy Foner, *The Caregiving Dilemma: Work in an American Nursing Home* (Berkeley: University of California, 1994). Paul Ong and Tania Azores, "The Migration and Incorporation of Filipino Nurses," in Paul Ong, Edna Bonacich, and Lucie Cheng, (eds.), *The New Asian Immigration in Los Angeles and Global Restructuring* (Philadelphia: Temple University Press, 1994), 154–195; Sheba George, "Caroling with the Keralites: The Negotiation of Gendered Space in an Indian Immigrant Community," in R. Stephen Warner and Judith G. Wittner (eds.), *Gatherings in the Diaspora: Religious Communities and the New Immigration* (Philadelphia: Temple University Press, 1998), 265–294.

32. Shirley Ardner and Sandra Burman (eds.), *Money Go Rounds: The Importance of Savings and Credit Associations for Women* (Oxford: Berg, 1995).

33. Miri Song, "Children's Labour in Ethnic Family Businesses: The Case of Chinese Take-Away Businesses in Britain," *Ethnic and Racial Studies* 20 (4) (1997), 690–716; David Parker, *Through Different Eyes: The Cultural Identities of Young Chinese People in Britain.* (Aldershot: Avebury, 1995); Jimy M. Sanders and Victor Nee, "Social Capital, Human Capital, and Immigrant Self-Employment," *American Sociological Review* 61 (2) (1996), 241.

34. Alejandro Portes and Rubén G. Rumbaut, *Immigrant America: A Portrait,* 2nd ed. (Berkeley: University of California Press, 1996).

35. Jimy M. Sanders and Victor Nee, "Social Capital, Human Capital, and Immigrant Self-Employment," *American Sociological Review* 61 (2) (1996), 240–241.

36. U.S. Small Business Administration Office of Advocacy, Small Business in the American Economy (Washington, DC: U.S. Government Printing Office, 1988), 101.

37. Blacks, especially those with education and skills, have access to government jobs (in the ethnic-controlled economy) while Asian immigrants generally do not. Robert L. Boyd, "Black and Asian Self-Employment in Large Metropolitan Areas: A Comparative Analysis," *Social Problems* 37 (2) (1990), 268.

38. Lief Jensen, "Secondary Earner Strategies and Family Poverty: Immigrant-Native Differentials, 1960–1980," *International Migration Review* 25 (1) (1991), 137.

39. Robert D. Mare and Christopher Winship, "Ethnic and Racial Patterns of Educational Attainment and School Enrollment," in Gary Sandefur and Marta Tienda (eds.), *Poverty and Social Policy: The Minority Experience* (New York: Plenum, 1988), cited in Barry R. Chiswick, "Differences in Education and Earnings Across Racial and Ethnic Groups: Tastes, Discrimination, and Investments in Child Quality," *Quarterly Journal of Economics* CIII 3 (August) (1988), 587.

40. Nathan Caplan, John K. Whitmore, and Marcella H. Choy, "Indochinese Refugee Families and Academic Achievement" *Scientific American* 266, N(2). (February, 1992), 36–42; Min Zhou, and Carl L. Bankston, III, *Growing Up American: How Vietnamese Children Adapt to Life in the United States.* (New York: Russell Sage Foundation, 1998).

41. Daniel Lichter, Gretchen Cornwell, and David Eggebeen, "Harvesting Human Capital: Family Structure and Education Among Rural Youth," *Rural Sociology* 58 (1993), 53–75, cited in Janet L. Bokemeier, "Rediscovering Families and Households: Restructuring Rural Society and Rural Sociology," *Rural Sociology* 62 (1) (1997), 10; U.S. Bureau of the Census. Alejandro Portes and Rubén G. Rumbaut, *Immigrant America: A Portrait,* 2nd ed. (Berkeley: University of California Press, 1996).

42. Donna Gabaccia, *From the Other Side: Women, Gender, and Immigrant Life in the U.S., 1820–1990* (Bloomington and Indianapolis: Indiana University Press, 1994), 54.

43. Greta A. Gilbertson, "Women's Labor and Enclave Employment: The Case of Dominican and Colombian Women in NYC," *International Migration Review* 29 (3) (1995), 668.

44. Min Zhou, Chinatown: The Socioeconomic Potential of an Urban Enclave (Philadelphia: Temple University Press, 1992). Arlene Dallalfar, "Iranian Women as Immigrant Entrepreneurs," *Gender and Society* 8 (4) (1994), 541–561.

45. Min Zhou and John R. Logan, "Returns on Human Capital in Ethnic Enclaves," *American Sociological Review* 54 (5) (1989), 818.

46. M. Patricia Fernández-Kelly and Anna M. García, "Power Surrendered, Power Restored: The Politics of Work and Family Among Hispanic Garment Workers in California and Florida" in Louise A. Tilly and Patricia Gurin (eds.), *Women, Politics, and Change* (New York: Russell Sage, 1990), p. 146.

47. Sheba George, "Caroling with the Keralites: The Negotiation of Gendered Space in an Indian Immigrant Community," in R. Stephen Warner and Judith G. Wittner (eds.), *Gatherings in the Diaspora: Religious Communities and the New Immigration* (Philadelphia: Temple University Press, 1998), pp. 265–294.

48. Donna Gabaccia, *From the Other Side: Women, Gender, and Immigrant Life in the U.S., 1820–1990* (Bloomington and Indianapolis: Indiana University Press, 1994), p. xv.

49. Donna Gabaccia, *From the Other Side: Women, Gender, and Immigrant Life in the U.S., 1820–1990,* xv; Ellen Oxfeld, *Blood, Sweat and Mahjong* (Ithaca: Cornell University Press, 1993).

50. Judith Stacey, *Brave New Families: Stories of Domestic Upheaval in Late Twentieth Century America* (New York: Basic, 1991).

51. U. S. Department of Labor, 1991.

52. Statistical Abstract of the U.S., 1992, p. 388.

53. Janet L. Bokemeier, "Rediscovering Families and Households: Restructuring Rural Society and Rural Sociology," *Rural Sociology* 60 (1) (1997), 16.

54. William J. Wilson, *The Truly Disadvantaged* (Chicago: University of Chicago Press, 1987). Charles Murray, Losing Ground: America Social Policy 1950–1980 (New York: Basic Books, 1984). Ruth Sidel, *Women and Children Last* (New York: Penguin, 1986).

55. Michael Fix and Jeffery S. Passel, *Immigration and Immigrants: Setting the Record Straight* (Washington DC: The Urban Institute, 1994).

56. Michael Fix and Jeffery S. Passel, *Immigration and Immigrants: Setting the Record Straight,* Table A-1, p. 76.

57. Donna Gabaccia, *From the Other Side: Women, Gender, and Immigrant Life in the U.S., 1820–1990* (Bloomington and Indianapolis: Indiana University Press, 1994), p. 37.

58. Kitty Calavita, *Inside the State: The Bracero Program, Immigration and the I.N.S.* (New York: Routledge, 1992), p. 59.

59. Stephen Castles and Godula Kosack, *Immigrant Workers and Class Structure in Western Europe* (Oxford: Oxford University Press, 1973).

60. Phyllis Moen and Elaine Wethington, "The Concept of Family Adaptive Strategies," *Annual Review of Sociology,* Vol. 18, 1992, p. 234.

61. Douglas, Massey Joaquin Arango, Graeme Hugo, Ali Kouaouci, Adela Pellegrino and J. Edward Taylor, "Theories of International Migration: A Review and Appraisal," *Population and Development Review* 19(3) (1993), 436.

62. Douglas Massey, Joaquin Arango, Graeme Hugo, Ali Kouaouci, Adela Pellegrino and J. Edward Taylor, "Theories of International Migration: A Review and Appraisal," 438.

63. Katherine M. Donato, "Current Trends and Patterns of Female Migration: Evidence From Mexico," *International Migration Review* 27 (4), 1993, 767.

64. Julia Wrigley, "Immigrant Women as Child Care Providers," in Ivan Light and Richard Isralowitz (eds.), *Immigrant Entrepreneurs and Immigrant Absorption in the United States and Israel* (Aldershot, UK: Ashgate, 1997), 117–139; Donna Gabaccia, *From the Other Side: Women, Gender, and Immigrant Life in the U.S., 1820–1990*, 34.

65. Terry Golway, *The Irish in America* (New York: Hyperion, 1997).

66. Mehdi Bozorgmehr, Claudia Der-Martirosian, and Georges Sabagh, "Middle Easterners: A New Kind of Immigrant," in Roger Waldinger and Mehdi Bozorgmehr (eds.), *Ethnic Los Angeles* (New York: Russell Sage Foundation, 1996), 356.

67. U.S. Congress, Senate Report on Conditions of Women and Child Wage Earners, vol. 2; Men's Ready Made Clothing, S. Doc. 645, 61st Cong., 2d Sess. (Washington, D.C., Government Printing Office, 1911) pp. 35, 221 cited in Miriam Cohen, *Workshop to Office: Two Generations of Italian Women in New York City, 1900–1950* (Ithaca, NY: Cornell University Press, 1993), 48–9.

68. Miriam Cohen, *Workshop to Office: Two Generations of Italian Women in New York City, 1900–1950*, 48–9, 76.

69. Donald Kraybill and Steven M. Nolt, *Amish Enterprise* (Baltimore: Johns Hopkins University Press, 1995); Nathan Glazer and Daniel Patrick Moynihan, *Beyond the Melting Pot* (Cambridge: The MIT Press, 1963); Steven Gold, *Refugee Communities: A Comparative Field Study* (Newbury Park, CA: Sage, 1992). Miri Song, "Children's Labour in Ethnic Family Businesses: The Case of Chinese Take-Away Businesses in Britain," *Ethnic and Racial Studies* (20) (4), 1997, 690–716.

70. Ruth Milkman and Eleanor Townsley, Ch. 24, "Gender and Economy," in Neil Smelser and Richard Swedberg (eds.), *Handbook of Economic Sociology* (Princeton, NJ: Princeton University Press/Russell Sage Foundation, 1994).

71. Margaret A. Gibson, "Punjabi Orchard Farmers: An Immigrant Enclave in Rural California," *International Migration Review* 22 (1), (1988), 39.

72. Ellen Oxfeld, *Blood, Sweat and Mahjong* (Ithaca: Cornell University Press, 1993), 204–205.

73. M. Patricia Fernández-Kelly and Anna M. García, "Power Surrendered, Power Restored: The Politics of Work and Family Among Hispanic Garment Workers in California and Florida, Louise A. Tilly and Patricia Gurin (eds.), *Women, Politics, and Change* (New York: Russell Sage, 1990) p. 131.

74. M. Patricia Fernández-Kelly and Anna M. García, "Power Surrendered, Power Restored: The Politics of Work and Family Among Hispanic Garment Workers in California and Florida," 131.

75. M. Patricia Fernández-Kelly and Anna M. García, "Power Surrendered, Power Restored: The Politics of Work and Family Among Hispanic Garment Workers in California and Florida," 131.

76. M. Patricia Fernández-Kelly and Anna M. García, "Power Surrendered, Power Restored: The Politics of Work and Family Among Hispanic Garment Workers in California and Florida," 131.

77. M. Patricia Fernández-Kelly and Anna M. García, "Power Surrendered, Power Restored: The Politics of Work and Family Among Hispanic Garment Workers in California and Florida," 147.

78. Philip Kasinitz and Milton Vickerman, "Ethnic Niches and Racial Traps, Jamaicans in the New York Regional Economy." Paper presented at Social Science History Association, Chicago, November 16, 1995. Pauline Agbayani-Siewart and Linda Revilla, "Filipino Americans," in Pyong Gap Min (ed.), *Asian Americans: Contemporary Trends and Issues* (Newbury Park, CA: Sage, 1995), 134–168.

79. Philip Kasinitz and Milton Vickerman, "Ethnic Niches and Racial Traps, Jamaicans in the New York Regional Economy." Paper presented at Social Science History Association, Chicago, No-

vember 16, 1995. Paul Ong and Tania Azores, "The Migration and Incorporation of Filipino Nurses," in Paul Ong, Edna Bonacich, and Lucie Cheng (eds.), *The New Asian Immigration in Los Angeles and Global Restructuring* (Philadelphia: Temple University Press, 1994), 154–195; The rate of self-employment per 1000 employed persons age 16+ is 180 for Koreans, 40 for Jamaicans, 33 and for Filipinos. The national average for all foreign born is 68. 1990 Census, cited in Alejandro Portes and Rubé G. Rumbaut, *Immigrant America: A Portrait,* 2nd ed. (Berkeley: University of California Press, 1996), 72. Among both Filipinos and Caribbeans, women have higher rates of professional employment than men. Elliott R. Barkan, *And Still They Come: Immigrants and American Society: 1920 to the 1990s* (Wheeling, IL: Harland Davidson, 1996), 207.

80. Steven J. Gold and Bruce A. Phillips, "Israelis in the United States," *American Jewish Yearbook,* 1996, 51–101; For example, foreign-born Koreans and foreign-born Israeli men in Los Angeles both have a self-employment rate of about 35 percent. However, only 14 percent of Israeli women are self-employed. However, 53 percent work as managers and professionals (1990 Census figures, cited in Mehdi Bozorgmehr, Claudia Der-Martirosian, and Georges Sabagh, "Middle Easterners: A New Kind of Immigrant," in Roger Waldinger and Mehdi Bozorgmehr (eds.), *Ethnic Los Angeles* (New York: Russell Sage Foundation, 1996), 356.

81. Elliott R. Barkan, *And Still They Come: Immigrants and American Society: 1920 to the 1990s* (Wheeling, IL: Harland Davidson, 1996), 205.

82. Bernard Wong, *Ethnicity and Entrepreneurship: The New Chinese Immigrants in the San Francisco Bay Area,* (Boston: Allyn and Bacon, 1998), 66.

83. Steven Gold, *Refugee Communities: A Comparative Field Study* (Newbury Park, CA: Sage, 1992), 180.

84. U.S. Small Business Administration Office of Advocacy, Small Business in the American Economy (Washington, DC: U.S. Government Printing Office, 1988), 173.

85. Bernard Wong, *Ethnicity and Entrepreneurship: The New Chinese Immigrants in the San Francisco Bay Area,* 67.

86. U.S. Small Business Administration Office of Advocacy, Small Business in the American Economy (Washington, DC: U.S. Government Printing Office, 1988), 174–76. U.S. Bureau of the Census, 1987.

87. Pyong-Gap Min, "The Korean-American Family," in Charles H. Mindel, Robert Habenstein, and Roosevelt Wright, Jr. (eds.), *Ethnic Families in America,* 3rd ed. (New York: Elsevier, 1988), 206–207.

88. Pyong-Gap Min, "The Korean-American Family," 211–213.

89. Rae Lesser Blumberg, "Introduction: The Triple Overlap of Gender Stratification, Economy, and the Family," in Rae Lesser Blumberg (ed.), *Gender, Family, and Economy: The Triple Overlap* (Newbury Park: Sage, 1991), 7–32.

90. Pyong-Gap Min, "The Korean-American Family," 213.

91. Walter P. Zenner, *Minorities in the Middle: A Cross-Cultural Analysis* (Albany: Suny Press, 1991), 139.

92. Miri Song, "Children's Labour in Ethnic Family Businesses: The Case of Chinese Take-Away Businesses in Britain," *Ethnic and Racial Studies.* (20) (4), 1997, 690–716.

93. John Sibley Butler, *Entrepreneurship and Self-Help Among Black Americans* (Albany: SUNY Press, 1991). Donna Gabaccia, *From the Other Side: Women, Gender, and Immigrant Life in the U.S., 1820–1990,* 51.

94. Greta A. Gilbertson, "Women's Labor and Enclave Employment: The Case of Dominican and Colombian Women in NYC," *International Migration Review.* 29 (3) (1995), 657–670. Annie Phizacklea, "Entreprenuership, Ethnicity, and Gender," in Sallie Westwood and Parminder Bhachu (eds.), *Enterprising Women: Ethnicity, Economy, and Gender Relations* (London and New York: Routledge, 1988), 20–33.

95. Pyong-Gap Min, *Changes and Conflicts: Korean Immigrant Families in New York* (Boston: Allyn and Bacon, 1998).

96. Rae Lesser Blumberg, "Introduction: The Triple Overlap of Gender Stratification, Economy, and the Family," 22.

97. National Foundation for Women Business Owners (NFWBO), "Minority Women-Owned Firms Increase in 50 Metro Areas" http://www.nfwbo.org/rr012.htm

98. National Foundation for Women Business Owners (NFWBO), "Minority Women-Owned Firms Thriving," http://www.nfwbo.org/nfwbo/rr014.htm, 1997.

99. National Foundation for Women Business Owners (NFWBO), "Women of All Races Share Entrepreneurial Spirit," http://www.nfwbo.org/nfwbo/rr020.htm, 1998.

100. National Foundation for Women Business Owners (NFWBO), "Minority Women-Owned Firms Thriving," http://www.nfwbo.org/nfwbo/rr014.htm, 1997.

101. National Foundation for Women Business Owners (NFWBO), "Women of All Races Share Entrepreneurial Spirit,"http://www.nfwbo.org/nfwbo/rr020.htm, 1998.

102. National Foundation for Women Business Owners (NFWBO), "Women Business Owners Make Progress in Access to Capital; Still Lag Men-Owned Businesses in Credit Levels" http://www.nfwbo.org/nfwbo/rr010.htm, 1996, p. 1.

103. U.S. Small Business Administration Office of Advocacy, Small Business in the American Economy (Washington, DC: U.S. Government Printing Office, 1988) p. 130.

104. U.S. Small Business Administration Office of Advocacy, Small Business in the American Economy, 132.

105. U.S. Small Business Administration Office of Advocacy, Small Business in the American Economy, 132.

106. U.S. Small Business Administration Office of Advocacy, Small Business in the American Economy, 142.

107. National Foundation for Women Business Owners (NFWBO), "Women of All Races Share Entrepreneurial Spirit," http://www.nfwbo.org/nfwbo/rr020.htm, 1998.

108. Edna Bonacich, "Making it in America: A Social Evaluation of the Ethnics of Immigrant Entrepreneurship," *Sociological Perspectives* 40 (4) (1987), 446–455.

109. Timothy Bates, *Race, Self-Employment and Upward Mobility: An Illusive American Dream* (Baltimore: John Hopkins University Press, 1997).

110. U.S. Small Business Administration (SBA), "Statistics on Women Business Ownership," http://www.sbaonline.sba.gov/womeninbusiness/stats96.html, 1996, p.1.

111. Nina Glick-Schiller, Linda Basch, and Cristina Blanc-Szanton, "Transnationalism: A New Analytic Framework for Understanding Migration," in Nina Glick Schiller, Linda Basch, and Cristina Blanc-Szanton (eds.), *Towards a Transnational Perspective on Migration: Race, Class, Ethnicity and Nationalism Reconsidered* (New York: New York Academy of Sciences, 1992), 1–24.

112. Linda Basch, Nina Glick Schiller, and Cristina Blanc-Szanton, *Nations Unbound: Transnational Projects, Postcolonial Predicaments, and Deterritorialized Nation States* (Basel, Switzerland: Gordon and Breach Publishers, 1994), 7.

113. Saskia Sassen, "The Informal Economy," in John Hull Mollenkopf and Manuel Castells (eds.), *Dual City: Restructuring New York* (New York: Russell Sage Foundation, 1991), 79–101; Ivan Light and Edna Bonacich, *Immigrant Entrepreneurs* (Berkeley: University of California Press, 1988).

114. Alejandro Portes, "Los Angeles in the Context of the New Immigration," Working Paper No. 18, Lewis Center for Regional Policy Studies, School of Public Policy and Social Research, University of California, January 1997.

115. Steven Gold, "Chinese-Vietnamese Entrepreneurs in California," in Paul Ong, Edna Bonacich and Lucy Cheng (eds.), *The New Asian Immigration in Los Angeles and Global Restructuring* (Philadelphia: Temple University Press, 1994), 196–226; Pyong-Gap Min, *Caught in the Middle: Korean Communities in New York and Los Angeles* (Berkeley: University of California Press, 1996).

116. Alejandro Portes, "Transnational Communities: Their Emergence and Significance in the Contemporary World System," Working Paper No. 16, Program in Comparative International Development, Department of Sociology, The Johns Hopkins University, 1995. Yasemin Nugoglu

Soysal, *Limits of Citizenship: Migrants and Postnational Membership in Europe* (Chicago: University of Chicago Press, 1994), 14.

117. Donald Nonini and Aihwa Ong, "Introduction: Chinese Transnationalism as an Alternative Modernity," in Aihwa Ong and Donald Nonini (eds.), *Ungrounded Empires: The Cultural Politics of Modern Chinese Transnationalism* (New York: Routledge, 1997), 19.

118. Nina Glick-Schiller, Linda Basch, and Cristina Blanc-Szanton, "Transnationalism: A New Analytic Framework for Understanding Migration," in Nina Glick Schiller, Linda Basch, and Cristina Blanc-Szanton (eds.), *Towards a Transnational Perspective on Migration: Race, Class, Ethnicity and Nationalism Reconsidered* (New York: New York Academy of Sciences, 1992), p. 3.; Michael Peter Smith and Luis Eduardo Guarnizo (eds.) *Transnationalism from Below* (New Brunswick, NJ: Transaction, 1998).

119. Steven Gold, "Transnationalism and Vocabularies of Motive in International Migration: The Case of Israelis in the U.S.," *Sociological Perspectives* 40 (3) (1997), 409–426; Johanna Lessinger, *From the Ganges to the Hudson* (Boston: Allyn and Bacon, 1995); Pyong-Gap Min, *Changes and Conflicts: Korean Immigrant Families in New York* (Boston. Allyn and Bacon, 1998).

120. Bernard Wong, *Ethnicity and Entrepreneurship: The New Chinese Immigrants in the San Francisco Bay Area* (Boston: Allyn and Bacon, 1998), 91.

121. Alex Stepick, *Pride Against Prejudice: Haitians in the United States* (Boston: Allyn and Bacon, 1998), 32.

122. Pyong-Gap Min, *Changes and Conflicts: Korean Immigrant Families in New York* (Boston: Allyn and Bacon, 1998).

123. Steven Gold, "Transnationalism and Vocabularies of Motive in International Migration: The Case of Israelis in the U.S.," 409–426; Diane L. Wolf, "Family Secrets: Transnational Struggles among Children of Filipino Immigrants," *Sociological Perspectives*. 40 (3) (1997), 455–480; Pierrette Hondagneu-Sotelo and Ernestine Avila, "I'm Here, But I'm There': The Meanings of Transnational Motherhood," *Gender and Society,* 11, (5), 1997, 548–571.

124. Calvin Goldscheider and Frances E. Kobrin, "Ethnic Continuity and the Process of Self-Employment," *Ethnicity* 7, 1980, 256–278; Miri Song, "Children's Labour in Ethnic Family Businesses: The Case of Chinese Take-Away Businesses in Britain," *Ethnic and Racial Studies* (20), (4), 1997, 690–716.

125. Donna Fenn, "Benchmark: Sources of Conflict in Family Business," http://www.inc.com/inc-magazine/archives/07950962.html, 1995.

126. Lillian Rubin, *Families on the Faultline* (New York: Harper Collins, 1994); Pyong-Gap Min, *Changes and Conflicts: Korean Immigrant Families in New York* (Boston: Allyn and Bacon, 1998); Steven Gold, *From the Workers' State to the Golden State: Jews From the Former Soviet Union in California* (Boston: Allyn and Bacon, 1995).

127. Stephen John Gross, "Handing Down the Form: Values, Strategies, and Outcomes in Inheritance Practices Among Rural German-Americans," *Journal of Family History* 21 (2), (1996), 192–217.

128. Sonya Salamon, *Prairie Patrimony: Family, Farming and Community in the Midwest* (Chapel Hill: University of North Carolina Press, 1992), 255.

129. Sonya Salamon, *Prairie Patrimony: Family, Farming and Community in the Midwest*, 253.

130. Barry R. Chiswick, "Differences in Education and Earnings Across Racial and Ethnic Groups: Tastes, Discrimination, and Investments in Child Quality," *Quarterly Journal of Economics*. CIII(3), (August 1988), 590–591.

131. Barry R. Chiswick, "Differences in Education and Earnings Across Racial and Ethnic Groups: Tastes, Discrimination, and Investments in Child Quality," 590; The noted family pattern, however, appears to rely on class resources (education, nonworking mother) as well as other contextual factors including urban residence and a two-parent family. Consequently, such investment in child quality may be unavailable to ethnic families lacking these resources.

132. James Diego Vigil, *Barrio Gangs: Street Life and Identity in Southern California* (Austin: University of Texas Press, 1988).

133. Bruce A. Phillips and Steven J. Gold, "The Communal Dimensions of Federation Involvement: A Qualitative Study of Jewish Philanthropy," draft report to the Aspen Foundation, grant number 94–1–nsrf–18, 1996.

134. Calvin Goldscheider and Frances E. Kobrin, "Ethnic Continuity and the Process of Self-Employment," *Ethnicity* (7), 1980, 256–278; Barry Kosmin and Paul Ritterband, *Contemporary Jewish Philanthropy in America* (Savage, MD: Rowman and Littlefield, 1991).

135. Sylvia Barack Fishman, "In Many Voices: Diversity and Commonality among American Jewish Women" in *The National Commission on American Jewish Women, Voices for Change: Future Directions for American Jewish Women* (Waltham: Brandeis University, Cohen Center for Modern Jewish Studies, 1995), 43–76; Alice Goldstein, "Dimensions of Giving: Volunteer Activity and Contributions of the Jewish Women of Rhode Island," in Barry A. Kosmin and Paul Ritterband (eds.), *Contemporary Jewish Philanthropy in America* (Savage, MD: Roman and Littlefield, 1991), 93–116; Bethamie Horowitz, "From Attaining Position to Providing Direction: Jewish Women and The Jewish Communal World," in *The National Commission on American Jewish Women, Voices for Change: Future Directions for American Jewish Women* (Waltham: Brandeis University, Cohen Center for Modern Jewish Studies, 1995), 81–86; Brenda Brown Lipitz, "Life in the Stalled Lane: Women in Jewish Communal Organizations," in *The National Commission on American Jewish Women, Voices for Change: Future Directions for American Jewish Women* (Waltham: Brandeis University, Cohen Center for Modern Jewish Studies, 1995), 87–97.

136. Rubén G. Rumbaut, "Paradoxes and Orthodoxies of Assimilation," *Sociological Perspectives* 40 (3) (1997), 483–511.

137. Alejandro Portes and Min Zhou, "The New Second Generation: Segmented Assimilation and Its Variants," *The Annals* 530 (1993) 74–96; Signithia Fordham, *Blacked Out: Dilemmas of Race, Identity and Success at Capital High* (Chicago: University of Chicago Press, 1996); Carola Suárez-Orozco and Marcelo Surez-Orozco, *Transformations: Immigration, Family and Achievement Motivation among Latino Adolescents* (Stanford: Stanford University Press, 1996).

138. Min Zhou and Carl L. Bankston, III, "Social Capital and the Adaptation of the Second Generation: The Case of Vietnamese Youth in New Orleans," *International Migration Review,* 28 (4) (1994), 840.

139. Min Zhou and Carl L. Bankston, III, "Social Capital and the Adaptation of the Second Generation: The Case of Vietnamese Youth in New Orleans," 843.

140. Min Zhou and Carl L. Bankston, III, "Social Capital and the Adaptation of the Second Generation: The Case of Vietnamese Youth in New Orleans," 842–843.

141. Janet L. Bokemeier, "Rediscovering Families and Households: Restructuring Rural Society and Rural Sociology," *Rural Sociology* 60 (1) (1997), 7; Pierrette Hondagneu-Sotelo, *Gendered Transitions: Mexican Experiences of Immigration* (Berkeley: University of California Press, 1994); Shelly Tenenbaum, *A Credit to Their Community: Jewish Loan Societies in the United States 1880–1945* (Detroit: Wayne State University Press, 1993); Ivan Light, *Ethnic Enterprise in America: Business and Welfare Among Chinese, Japanese, and Blacks* (Berkeley: University of California Press, 1972).

142. Silvia Pedraza, "Women and Migration: The Social Consequences of Gender," *Annual Review of Sociology* (17) (1991), 303–325. Caroline B. Brettell and Rita James Simon, "Immigrant Women: An Introduction," in Rita James Simon and Caroline B. Brettell (eds.), *International Migration: The Female Experience* (Totowa, NJ: Rowman and Allanheld, 1986), 3–20.

143. Pierrette Hondagneu-Sotelo, "Overcoming Patriarchal Constraints: The Reconstruction of Gender Relations Among Mexican Immigrant Women and Men," *Gender & Society* 6 (3) (1992), 393–415.

144. Annie Phizacklea, "Entreprenuership, Ethnicity, and Gender," in Sallie Westwood and Parminder Bhachu (eds.), *Enterprising Women: Ethnicity, Economy, and Gender Relations* (London and New York: Routledge, 1988), 22.

145. Hye-Kyung Lee and Stavros Karageorgis, "Korean and Filipino Immigrant Women in the Los Angeles Labor Market," in Ivan Light and Richard Isralowitz (eds.), *Immigrant Entrepreneurs and Immigrant Absorption in the United States and Israel* (Aldershot, UK: Ashgate, 1997), 151.

146. Pyong-Gap Min, *Changes and Conflicts Korean Immigrant Families in New York* (Boston: Allyn and Bacon, 1998); Greta A. Gilbertson, "Women's Labor and Enclave Employment: The Case of Dominican and Colombian Women in NYC," *International Migration Review* 29 (3) (1995), 657–670.

147. Steven Gold, "Gender and Social Capital Among Israeli Immigrants in Los Angeles," *Diaspora* 4 (3) (1995), 267–301; Steven J. Gold and Bruce A. Phillips, "Israelis in the United States," *American Jewish Yearbook,* 1996, 51–101.

148. Israeli women do, however, engage in important communal activities which contribute to co-ethnic men's economic endeavors.

149. Mehdi Bozorgmehr, Claudia Der-Martirosian, and Georges Sabagh, "Middle Easterners: A New Kind of Immigrant," in Roger Waldinger and Mehdi Bozorgmehr (eds.), *Ethnic Los Angeles* (New York: Russell Sage Foundation, 1996), 356.

150. Nazli Kibria, *Family Tightrope: The Changing Lives of Vietnamese Americans* (Princeton, NJ: Princeton University Press, 1993); Arlene Dallalfar, "Iranian Women as Immigrant Entrepreneurs," *Gender and Society.* 8 (4) (1994), 541–561; Micaela Di Leonardo, *The Varieties of Ethnic Experience* (Ithaca: Cornell University Press, 1984); Min Zhou and John R. Logan, "Returns on Human Capital in Ethnic Enclaves," *American Sociological Review* 54 (5) (1989), 809–820; Shelly Tenenbaum, *A Credit to Their Community: Jewish Loan Societies in the United States 1880–1945* (Detroit: Wayne State University Press, 1993); Sossie Andezian, "Women's Roles in Organizing Symbolic Life," in Rita James Simon and Caroline B. Brettell (eds.), *International Migration: The Female Experience* (Totowa, NJ: Rowman and Allanheld, 1986), 254–65; Sherri Grasmuck and Patricia Pessar, *Between Two Islands: Dominican International Migration* (Berkeley: University of California Press, 1991).

151. Pierrette Hondagneu-Sotelo, "Overcoming Patriarchal Constraints: The Reconstruction of Gender Relations Among Mexican Immigrant Women and Men," *Gender & Society* 6 (3) (1992), 396.

152. Lillian Rubin, *Families on the Faultline* (New York: Harper Collins, 1994).

153. Thanh V. Tran and Thang D. Nguyen, "Gender and Satisfaction with the Host Society Among Indochinese Refugees," *International Migration Review* (28), (2), 1994, 333–34.

154. Lillian Rubin, *Worlds of Pain* (New York: Basic, 1976) Rae Lesser Blumberg, "Introduction: The Triple Overlap of Gender Stratification, Economy, and the Family," in Rae Lesser Blumberg (ed.), *Gender, Family, and Economy: The Triple Overlap* (Newbury Park: Sage, 1991), 23.

155. Randall Collins, "Women and the Production of Status Cultures," in Michèle Lamont and Marcel Fournier (eds.), *Cultivating Differences: Symbolic Boundaries and the Making of Inequality* (Chicago: University of Chicago Press, 1991), 213–31. Randall Collins, "Women and Men in the Class Structure," in Rae Lesser Blumberg (ed.), *Gender, Family, and Economy: The Triple Overlap* (Newbury Park: Sage, 1991), 52–73. Nazli Kibria, *Family Tightrope: The Changing Lives of Vietnamese Americans* (Princeton, NJ: Princeton University Press, 1993).

156. Pnina Werbner, "Taking and Giving: Working Women and Female Bonds in a Pakistani Immigrant Neighborhood," in Sallie Westwood and Parminder Bhachu (eds.), *Enterprising Women: Ethnicity, Economy and Gender Relations* (London and New York: Routledge, 1988), 177–202.

157. Mary Waters, "Ethnic and Racial Identities of Second Generation Black Immigrants in New York City," *International Migration Review* 28 (4) (1994), 804.

158. Rae Lesser Blumberg, "Introduction: The Triple Overlap of Gender Stratification, Economy, and the Family," in Rae Lesser Blumberg (ed.), *Gender, Family, and Economy: The Triple Overlap* (Newbury Park: Sage, 1991), 23.

159. Silvia Pedraza, "Women and Migration: The Social Consequences of Gender," *Annual Review of Sociology* 17 (1991), 303–325.

160. Sherri Grasmuck and Patricia Pessar, *Between Two Islands: Dominican International Migration* (Berkeley: University of California Press, 1991). Pierrette Hondagneu-Sotelo, *Gendered Transitions: Mexican Experiences of Immigration* (Berkeley: University of California Press, 1994); Pnina

Werbner, "Taking and Giving: Working Women and Female Bonds in a Pakistani Immigrant Neighborhood," in Sallie Westwood and Parminder Bhachu (eds.), *Enterprising Women: Ethnicity, Economy and Gender Relations* (London and New York: Routledge, 1988), 180.

161. Nazli Kibria, *Family Tightrope: The Changing Lives of Vietnamese Americans* (Princeton, NJ: Princeton University Press, 1993); Pierrette Hondagneu-Sotelo, *Gendered Transitions: Mexican Experiences of Immigration* (Berkeley: University of California Press, 1994).

162. Donna Gabaccia, *From the Other Side: Women, Gender, and Immigrant Life in the U.S., 1820–1990*, xv.

163. Steven Gold, "Gender and Social Capital Among Israeli Immigrants in Los Angeles," *Diaspora* 4, (3), 1995, 267–301.

164. Pyong-Gap Min, *Changes and Conflicts: Korean Immigrant Families in New York* (Boston: Allyn and Bacon, 1998); Steven Gold, *Refugee Communities: A Comparative Field Study* (Newbury Park, CA: Sage, 1992); Sheba George, "Caroling with the Keralites: The Negotiation of Gendered Space in an Indian Immigrant Community," in R. Stephen Warner and Judith G. Wittner (eds.), *Gatherings in the Diaspora: Religious Communities and the New Immigration* (Philadelphia: Temple University Press, 1998), 265–294.

165. Michael Baker and Dwanyne Benjamin, "The Role of the Family in Immigrants; Labor-Market Activity: An Evaluation of Alternative Explanations," *The American Economic Review* (87) (4), September 1997, 725.

166. Pyong-Gap Min, *Changes and Conflicts: Korean Immigrant Families in New York* (Boston: Allyn and Bacon, 1998); Steven Gold, "Gender and Social Capital Among Israeli Immigrants in Los Angeles," *Diaspora* (4) (3), 1995, 267–301.

167. Arlene Dallalfar, "Iranian Women as Immigrant Entrepreneurs," *Gender and Society* (8) (4), (1994), 541–561.

168. James S. Coleman, "Social Capital in the Creation of Human Capital," *American Journal of Sociology*, 94, Supplement S95–S120, 1988.

169. Pyong-Gap Min, *Changes and Conflicts: Korean Immigrant Families in New York,* 73.

170. Diane L. Wolf, "Family Secrets: Transnational Struggles among Children of Filipino Immigrants," *Sociological Perspectives* (40) (3), 1997, 463.

171. Min Zhou, and Carl L. Bankston, III *Growing Up American: How Vietnamese Children Adapt to Life in the United States* (New York: Russell Sage Foundation, 1987). 171–174.

172. Roberta G. Simmons, *Moving into Adolescence* (New York: Aldine de Gruyter, 1987).

173. Black women have rates of college attendance exceeding those of co-ethnic males. Black women with 4 years of college earn more than comparably educated white women, due in large part to their concentration in government jobs (an ethnic-controlled niche). Andrew Hacker, *Two Nations: Black and White, Separate, Hostile and Unequal* (New York: Scribners, 1992) 95; 178.

174. Manju Sheth, "Asian Indian Americans," in Pyong Gap Min (ed.), *Asian Americans: Contemporary Trends and Issues* (Newbury Park, CA: Sage, 1995), 191; Pnina Werbner, "Taking and Giving: Working Women and Female Bonds in a Pakistani Immigrant Neighborhood," in Sallie Westwood and Parminder Bhachu (eds.), *Enterprising Women: Ethnicity, Economy and Gender Relations* (London and New York: Routledge, 1988), 180.

175. Donna Gabaccia, *From the Other Side: Women, Gender, and Immigrant Life in the U.S., 1820–1990*, 63.

176. Donna Gabaccia, *From the Other Side: Women, Gender, and Immigrant Life in the U.S., 1820–1990*, 69.

177. Donna Gabaccia, *From the Other Side: Women, Gender, and Immigrant Life in the U.S., 1820–1990*, 69.

178. Donna Gabaccia, *From the Other Side: Women, Gender, and Immigrant Life in the U.S., 1820–1990*, 71.

179. Lucy Cheng and Philip Q. Yang, "Asians: The `Model Minority' Deconstructed," in Roger Waldinger and Mehdi Bozorgmehr (eds.), *Ethnic Los Angeles* (New York: Russell Sage Foundation, 1996), 340.

180. Steven J. Gold and Bruce A. Phillips, "Mobility and Continuity Among Eastern European Jews," in Silvia Pedraza and Rubén G. Rumbaut (eds.), *Origins and Destinies: Immigration, Race and Ethnicity in America* (Belmont, CA: Wadsworth, 1996), 182–194.

181. Pyong-Gap Min, *Changes and Conflicts: Korean Immigrant Families in New York*, 199–229; Steven Gold, *Refugee Communities: A Comparative Field Study* (Newbury Park, CA: Sage, 1992); Steven Gold, "Gender and Social Capital Among Israeli Immigrants in Los Angeles," *Diaspora*. (4) (3), 1995, 267–301; Nazli Kibria, *Family Tightrope: The Changing Lives of Vietnamese Americans* (Princeton, NJ: Princeton University Press, 1993); William T. Liu, Maryanne Lamanna, and Alice Mirata, *Transition to Nowhere: Vietnamese Refugees in America* (Nashville: Charter House, 1979); J. Donald Cohon, Jr., "Psychological Adaptation and Dysfunction among Refugees," *International Migration Review* 15 (1) (1981), 255–275.

182. William J. Wilson, *The Truly Disadvantaged* (Chicago: University of Chicago Press, 1987); Andrew Hacker, *Two Nations* (New York: Scribners, 1992).

183. Diane L. Wolf, "Family Secrets: Transnational Struggles among Children of Filipino Immigrants," *Sociological Perspectives*. 40 (3) (1997), 455–480; Maxine Hong-Kingston, *China Men* (New York: Vintage International, 1979); John Okada, *No-No Boy* (Seattle: University of Washington Press, 1976).

184. Donna Gabaccia, *From the Other Side: Women, Gender, and Immigrant Life in the U.S., 1820–1990*, 134.

Chapter 7

1. St. Clair Drake and Horace Cayton, *Black Metropolis* (New York: Harcourt, Brace and Company, 1945); Louis Wirth, *The Ghetto* (Chicago: University of Chicago Press, 1928).

2. Peggy Levitt, "*A Todos Les Llamo Primo* (I Call Everyone Cousin): The Social Basis for Latin Small Businesses," in Marilyn Halter (ed.), *New Migrants in the Marketplace: Boston's Ethnic Entrepreneurs* (Amherst: The University of Massachusetts Press, 1995), 135.

3. Robert Bellah, Richard Madsen, William M. Sullivan, Ann Swidler, and Steven M. Tipton, *Habits of the Heart: Individualism and Commitment in American Life* (Berkeley: University of California Press, 1985), 72–73.

4. Alejandro Portes, "The Social Origins of the Cuban Enclave Economy of Miami," *Sociological Perspectives* 30 (4) (1987), 340–372.

5. James S. Coleman, "Social Capital in the Creation of Human Capital," *American Journal of Sociology* 94 (1988), Supplement S95–S120; Nazli Kibria, *Family Tightrope* (Princeton: Princeton University Press, 1993); William J. Wilson, *When Work Disappears: The World of the New Urban Poor* (New York: Knopf, 1996).

6. Ivan Light, *Ethnic Enterprise in America: Business and Welfare Among Chinese, Japanese and Blacks* (Berkeley: University of California Press, 1972), 110–111.

7. Steven J. Gold, "Patterns of Economic Cooperation among Israeli Immigrants in Los Angeless," *International Migration Review* 28 (105) (1994), 114–135; Carlos Vélez–Ibañez, *Bonds of Mutual Trust: The Cultural System of Rotating Credit Associations Among Urban Mexicans and Chicanos* (New Brunswick: Rutgers University Press, 1983).

8. Shelly Tenenbaum, *A Credit to Their Community: Jewish Loan Societies in the United States 1880–1945* (Detroit: Wayne State University Press, 1993).

9. Paul Ritterband, "The Determinants of Jewish Charitable Giving in the Last Part of the Twentieth Century," in Barry A. Kosmin and Paul Ritterband (eds.), *Contemporary Jewish Philanthropy in America* (Savage, MD: Roman and Littlefield, 1991), 57–74; Linda S. Walbridge, *Without Forgetting the Imam: Lebanese Shi'ism in an American Community* (Detroit: Wayne State University Press, 1997).

10. George J. Borjas, "Ethnicity, Neighborhoods and Human–Capital Externalities," *American Economic Review* 85 (3) (1995), 365–390; St. Clair Drake and Horace Cayton, *Black Metropolis* (New York: Harcourt, Brace and Company, 1945); Yen Le Espiritu, *Asian American Panethnicity* (Philadelphia: Temple University Press, 1993); Arthur A. Goren, *New York Jews and the Quest for Community: The Kehillah Experiment 1908–1922* (New York: Columbia University Press, 1970); Alejandro Portes and Julia Sensenbrenner, "Embeddedness and Immigration: Notes on the Social Determinants of Economic Action," *American Journal of Sociology* 98 (6) (1993), 1320–1350.

11. Martin Sanchez–Jankowski, *Islands in the Street* (Berkeley: University of California Press, 1991).

12. John Bodnar, Roger Simon, and Michael P. Weber, *Lives of Their Own: Blacks, Italians, and Poles in Pittsburgh, 1900–1960* (Urbana: University of Illinois Press, 1982); Olivier Zunz, *The Changing Face of Inequality: Urbanization, Industrial Development and Immigrants in Detroit 1880–1920* (Chicago: University of Chicago Press, 1982); Ivan Light, *Ethnic Enterprise in America: Business and Welfare Among Chinese, Japanese and Blacks* (Berkeley: University of California Press, 1972); John Sibley Butler, *Entrepreneurship and Self-Help Among Black Americans* (Albany: SUNY Press, 1991); Pyong-Gap Min, *Caught in the Middle: Korean Communities in New York and Los Angeles* (Berkeley: University of California Press, 1996).

13. William Kornblum, *Blue Collar Community* (Chicago: University of Chicago Press, 1974).

14. Edward Kantowicz, "Politics," in Stephen Thernstrom (ed.), *The Harvard Encyclopedia of American Ethnic Groups* (Cambridge: Harvard University Press, 1980), 803–813.

15. Hector Delgado, *New Immigrants, Old Unions: Organizing Undocumented Workers in Los Angeles* (Philadelphia: Temple University Press, 1993).

16. Sherry Gorelick, *City College and the Jewish Poor* (New York: Schocken Books, 1982).

17. Michael Karni, "Finnish-American Cooperativism: The Radical Years, 1917–30," in Scott Cummings (ed.), *Self-Help in Urban America: Patterns of Minority Business Enterprise* (Port Washington, NY: Kennikat Press, 1980), 145–59.

18. Michael Karni, "Finnish–American Cooperativism: The Radical Years, 1917–30," 147.

19. Michael Karni, "Finnish-American Cooperativism: The Radical Years, 1917–30," 151.

20. Steven J. Gold, *Refugee Communities: A Comparative Field Study* (Newbury Park, CA: Sage, 1992); Steven J. Gold, "Patterns of Economic Cooperation Among Israeli Immigrants in Los Angeles," *International Migration Review* 28 (105) (1994), 114–35; Ivan Light, Georges Sabagh, Mehdi Bozorgmehr, and Claudia Der–Martirosian, "Beyond the Ethnic Enclave Economy," *Social Problems* 41 (1994), 65–80; Illsoo Kim, *New Urban Immigrants: The Korean Community in New York* (Princeton, NJ: Princeton University Press, 1981); Irving Howe, *World of Our Fathers* (New York: Harcourt, Brace, Javonovich, 1976); Michael R. Weisser, *A Brotherhood of Memory: Jewish Landsmanshaftn* (Ithaca: Cornell University Press, 1989); Stanford Lyman, *Chinese Americans* (New York: Random House, 1974).

21. Raymond Breton, "Institutional Completeness of Ethnic Communities and the Personal Relations of Immigrants," *American Journal of Sociology* 84 (1964), 293–318; Ivan Light, *Ethnic Enterprise in America: Business and Welfare Among Chinese, Japanese and Blacks* (Berkeley: University of California Press, 1972); William Kornblum, *Blue Collar Community* (Chicago: University of Chicago Press, 1974); John Sibley Butler, *Entrepreneurship and Self-Help Among Black Americans* (Albany: SUNY Press, 1991); Luis León, "Born Again in East LA: The Congregation as Border Space," in R. Stephen Warner and Judith G. Wittner (eds.), *Gatherings in the Diaspora: Religious Communities and the New Immigration* (Philadelphia. Temple University Press, 1998), 163–196; Randal L. Hepner, "The House That Rasta Built: Church-Building and Fundamentalism Among New York Rastafarians" in R. Stephen Warner and Judith G. Wittner (eds.), *Gatherings in the Diaspora: Religious Communities and the New Immigration* (Philadelphia: Temple University Press, 1998), 197–234.

22. Roger Waldinger, *Still the Promised City? African-Americans and New Immigrants in Postindustrial New York* (Cambridge, MA: Harvard University Press, 1996), 99–101.

23. Deborah Dash Moore, *To the Golden Cities: Pursuing the American Jewish Dream in Miami and L.A.* (Cambridge, MA: Harvard University Press, 1994); Alejandro Portes, "The Social Origins of the Cuban Enclave Economy of Miami," *Sociological Perspectives* 30 (4) (1987), 340–372; Philip Kasinitz, *Caribbean New York* (Ithaca: Cornell University Press, 1992); Stanford Lyman, *Chinese Americans* (New York: Random House, 1974); Ivan Light, Georges Sabagh, Mehdi Bozorgmehr, and Claudia Der-Martirosian, "Beyond the Ethnic Enclave Economy," *Social Problems* 41 (1994), 65–80; Luis Edward Guarnizo, *The Mexican Ethnic Economy in Los Angeles: Capitalist Accumulations, Class Restructuring, and the Transnationalization of Migration* (Davis, CA: California Communities Program, University of California–Davis, 1998).

24. Suzanne Model, "The Ethnic Niche and the Structure of Opportunity: Immigrants and Minorities in New York City," in Michael B. Katz (ed.), *The Underclass Debate: Views from History* (Princeton: Princeton University Press, 1993), 161–193.

25. Timothy Bates, *Race, Self-Employment and Upward Mobility: An Illusive American Dream* (Baltimore: Johns Hopkins University Press, 1997), 255.

26. John Bodnar, *The Transplanted: A History of Immigrants in Urban America* (Bloomington: University of Indiana Press, 1985), 137.

27. Ivan Light, *Ethnic Enterprise in America: Business and Welfare Among Chinese, Japanese and Blacks* (Berkeley: University of California Press, 1972); Stephen Warner and Judith G. Wittner (eds.), *Gatherings in the Diaspora: Religious Communities and the New Immigration* (Philadelphia: Temple University Press, 1998).

28. Alejandro Portes, "The Social Origins of the Cuban Enclave Economy of Miami," *Sociological Perspectives* 30 (4) (1987), 340–372.

29. Arthur H. Fauset, *Black Gods of the Metropolis* (Philadelphia: University of Pennsylvania Press, 1944); Deborah Dash Moore, *To the Golden Cities: Pursuing the American Jewish Dream in Miami and L.A.* (Cambridge, MA: Harvard University Press, 1994); Joane Nagel, *American Indian Ethnic Renewal* (New York: Oxford University Press, 1996); Zaragosa Vargas, *Proletarians of the North: A History of Mexican Industrial Workers in Detroit and the Midwest, 1917–1933* (Berkeley: University of California Press, 1993).

30. Scott Cummings (ed.), *Self-Help in Urban America: Patterns of Minority Business Enterprise* (Port Washington, NY: Kennikat Press, 1980).

31. W. I. Thomas and Florian Znaniecki, *The Polish Peasant in Europe and America* (New York: Richard Badger, 1920), 1519–1520.

32. John Bodnar, *The Transplanted: A History of Immigrants in Urban America* (Bloomington: University of Indiana Press, 1985), 120.

33. John Bodnar, *The Transplanted: A History of Immigrants in Urban America,* 123.

34. John Bodnar, *The Transplanted: A History of Immigrants in Urban America,* 124.

35. Stanford Lyman, *Chinese Americans* (New York: Random House, 1974), 30.

36. Mary C. Sengstock, *Chaldean–Americans: Changing Conceptions of Ethnic Identity* (Staten Island, NY: Center for Migration Studies, 1982), 34–35.

37. Emmett D. Carson, *A Hand Up: Black Philanthropy and Self-Help in America* (Washington, DC: Joint Center for Political and Economic Studies, 1993), 20.

38. Susan Weidman Schneider, "Women, Money and Power," in *The National Commission on American Jewish Women, Voices for Change: Future Directions for American Jewish Women* (Waltham: Brandeis University, Cohen Center for Modern Jewish Studies, 1995), 99; Shelly Tenenbaum, *A Credit to their Community: Jewish Loan Societies in the United States 1880–1945* (Detroit: Wayne State University Press, 1993).

39. Michael R. Weisser, *A Brotherhood of Memory: Jewish Landsmanshaftn* (Ithaca: Cornell University Press, 1989), 259.

40. Michael R. Weisser, *A Brotherhood of Memory: Jewish Landsmanshaftn,* 268–69.

41. John Bodnar, *The Transplanted: A History of Immigrants in Urban America*, 128.

42. John Bodnar, *The Transplanted: A History of Immigrants in Urban America*, 139.

43. John Bodnar, *The Transplanted: A History of Immigrants in Urban America*, 140.

44. Ivan Light, *Ethnic Enterprise in America: Business and Welfare Among Chinese, Japanese and Blacks* (Berkeley: University of California Press, 1972); Stanford Lyman, *Chinese Americans* (New York: Random House, 1974); Ngan-Ling Chow, "Family, Economy and the State: A Legacy of Struggle for Chinese American Women," in Silvia Pedraza and Rubén G. Rumbaut (eds.), *Origins and Destinies: Immigration, Race and Ethnicity in America* (Belmont, CA: Wadsworth, 1996), 110–24.

45. John J. Bukowczyk, "The Transformation of Working-Class Ethnicity: Corporate Control, Americanization, and the Polish Immigrant Middle Class in Bayonne, New Jersey 1915–1925," *Labor History* 25 (1) (Winter 1984), 70–71.

46. For example, two of the most common occupations for Arab-Americans in the Detroit area — the ethnic grocery business and auto assembly — are accessed through ethnic contacts. Aspiring business owners acquire investment capital while working in the auto industry. Entrepreneurs exhausted by the long hours and risks involved in self-employment find an alternative income in the auto plants. So interconnected are self-employment and auto work that it would be a distortion to discuss the Arab-Americans' ethnic economy without including each element. Sameer Y. Abraham and Nabeel Abraham, *Arabs in the New World* (Detroit: Wayne State University Center for Urban Studies, 1983).

47. National Foundation for Women Business Owners (NFWBO), "Women of All Races Share Entrepreneurial Spirit," http://www.nfwbo.org/nfwbo/rr020.htm, 1998. Bernice Mennis, "Jewish and Working Class," in Virginia Cyrus (ed.), *Experiencing Race, Class, and Gender in the United States*, 2nd ed. (Mountain View, CA: Mayfield, 1997), 133–136.

48. John Bodnar, *The Transplanted: A History of Immigrants in Urban America* (Bloomington: University of Indiana Press, 1985), 125.

49. Steven J. Gold, *Refugee Communities: A Comparative Field Study* (Newbury Park, CA: Sage, 1992); Christine R. Finnan and Rhonda Cooperstein, *Southeast Asian Refugee Resettlement at the Local Level* (Menlo Park, California: SRI International, 1983).

50. Randal L. Hepner, "The House That Rasta Built: Church-Building and Fundamentalism Among New York Rastafarians," in R. Stephen Warner and Judith G. Wittner (eds.), *Gatherings in the Diaspora: Religious Communities and the New Immigration* (Philadelphia: Temple University Press, 1998), 197–234.

51. W. I. Thomas and Florian Znaniecki, *The Polish Peasant in Europe and America* (New York: Richard Badger, 1920), 1526.

52. St. Clair Drake and Horace Cayton, *Black Metropolis* (New York: Harcourt, Brace and Company, 1945); Luis León, "Born Again in East LA: The Congregation as Border Space," in R. Stephen Warner and Judith G. Wittner (eds.), *Gatherings in the Diaspora: Religious Communities and the New Immigration* (Philadelphia: Temple University Press, 1998), 163–196.

53. John Bodnar, *The Transplanted: A History of Immigrants in Urban America* (Bloomington: University of Indiana Press, 1985), 126.

54. Alejandro Portes, "The Social Origins of the Cuban Enclave Economy of Miami," *Sociological Perspectives* 30 (4) (1987), 358.

55. Francie Ostrower, *Why the Wealthy Give: The Culture of Elite Philanthropy* (Princeton: Princeton University Press, 1995), 4–5; Barry A. Kosmin and Paul Ritterband (eds.), *Contemporary Jewish Philanthropy in America* (Savage, MD: Roman and Littlefield, 1991).

56. Barry R. Chiswick, "An Economic Analysis of Philanthropy," in Barry A. Kosmin and Paul Ritterband (eds.), *Contemporary Jewish Philanthropy in America* (Savage, MD: Roman and Littlefield, 1991), 2–16.

57. Calvin Goldscheider and Alan S. Zuckerman, *The Transformation of the Jews* (Chicago: University of Chicago Press, 1984).

58. Steven Gold and Bruce A. Phillips, "Mobility and Continuity Among Eastern European Jews," in Silvia Pedraza and Rubén G. Rumbaut (eds.), *Origins and Destinies: Immigration, Race, and Ethnicity in America* (Belmont, CA: Wadsworth, 1996), 182–194; Seymour Martin Lipset, "A Unique People in an Exceptional Country," in Seymour Martin Lipset (ed.), *American Pluralism and the Jewish Community* (New Brunswick, NJ: Transaction, 1990), 3–29; Marc J. Swatez, "Machers': Fundraising and Leadership in the Chicago Jewish Community," doctoral dissertation, Northwestern University, 1993; Walter P. Zenner, *Minorities in the Middle: A Cross-Cultural Analysis* (Albany: Suny Press, 1991).

59. Paul Ritterband, "The Determinants of Jewish Charitable Giving in the Last Part of the Twentieth Century," in Barry A. Kosmin and Paul Ritterband (eds.), *Contemporary Jewish Philanthropy in America* (Savage, MD: Roman and Littlefield, 1991), 61.

60. Gary A. Tobin, Adam Z. Tobin, and Lorin Troderman, *American Jewish Philanthropy in the 1990s* (Waltham, MA: Cohen Center for Modern Jewish Studies, Brandeis University, 1995), 4.

61. Paul Ritterband, "The Determinants of Jewish Charitable Giving in the Last Part of the Twentieth Century," in Barry A. Kosmin and Paul Ritterband (eds.), *Contemporary Jewish Philanthropy in America* (Savage, MD: Roman and Littlefield, 1991), 59.

62. Jack Werthheimer, "Jewish Organizational Life in the United States Since 1945," *American Jewish Yearbook 95* (1995), 3–98.

63. Marcia Millman, *Warm Hearts, Cold Cash* (New York: The Free Press, 1991).

64. Carl Bakal, *Charity U.S.A.: An Investigation Into the Hidden World of the Multi-Billion Dollar Charity Industry* (New York: Times Books, 1979); Bruce A. Phillips and Steven J. Gold, "The Communal Dimensions of Federation Involvement: A Qualitative Study of Jewish Philanthropy," draft report to the Aspen Foundation, grant number 94–1–nsrf–18, 1996.

65. Bruce A. Phillips and Steven J. Gold, "The Communal Dimensions of Federation Involvement: A Qualitative Study of Jewish Philanthropy," draft report to the Aspen Foundation, grant number 94–1–nsrf–18, 1996.

66. In Phillips and Gold's study of Jewish philanthropy, several respondents described how they could no longer relate to former friends who were uninterested in the Jewish community or unwilling to contribute to Jewish causes. In the words of one man: "When we got heavily involved initially back in the mid-70s, it caused us to significantly change the people that we were good friends with. If they weren't interested in matters relating to the Jewish community, you just begin to find that your value system and their value system started to spread apart. But also, if you had a chance to sit and talk with friends and you were all excited about Israel and they didn't give a damn or you were interested in saving Soviet Jews or whatever the issue was, and they were interested in buying their new Cadillac, you will tend to drift apart." Bruce A. Phillips and Steven J. Gold, "The Communal Dimensions of Federation Involvement: A Qualitative Study of Jewish Philanthropy," draft report to the Aspen Foundation, grant number 94–1–nsrf–18, 1996, 23.

67. W. I. Thomas and Florian Znaniecki, *The Polish Peasant in Europe and America* (New York: Richard Badger, 1920); John Bodnar, Roger Simon, and Michael P. Weber, *Lives of Their Own: Blacks, Italians, and Poles in Pittsburgh, 1900–1960* (Urbana: University of Illinois Press, 1982).

68. John Sibley Butler, *Entrepreneurship and Self-Help Among Black Americans* (Albany: SUNY Press, 1991).

69. John Sibley Butler, *Entrepreneurship and Self-Help Among Black Americans*.

70. Emmett D. Carson, *A Hand Up: Black Philanthropy and Self-Help in America* (Washington, DC: Joint Center for Political and Economic Studies, 1993), 17.

71. Emmett D. Carson, *A Hand Up: Black Philanthropy and Self-Help in America,* 25, 41.

72. Emmett D. Carson, *A Hand Up: Black Philanthropy and Self-Help in America,* 46.

73. Susan A. Ostrander, "Charitable Foundations, Social Movements, and Social Justice Funding," *Research in Social Policy* 5 (1997), 169–190; Richard L. Zweigenhaft and G. William Domhoff, "Sophisticated Conservatives and the Integration of Prep Schools: The Creation, Funding, and Evolution of the 'A Better Chance' Program," *Research in Social Policy* 5, 223–240.

74. Southern California Writers' Program, *Los Angeles: A Guide to the City and Its Environs*, 2nd ed. (New York: Hastings House, 1951), 73.

75. Ivan Light, and Edna Bonacich, *Immigrant Entrepreneurs* (Berkeley: University of California Press, 1988).

76. Pyong-Gap Min, Pyong-Gap, *Caught in the Middle: Korean Communities in New York and Los Angeles* (Berkeley: University of California Press, 1996).

77. Political contributions by non-citizens have been the topic of significant controversy of late, suggesting that this type of political influence has come under increased scrutiny and may be of limited value.

78. Stanford Lyman, *Chinese Americans* (New York: Random House, 1974), 29–30.

79. Randall M. Miller, "Introduction," in Randall M. Miller and Thomas D. Marzik (eds.), *Immigrants and Religion in Urban America* (Philadelphia: Temple University Press, 1977), xvi; The secular settlement house movement had much the same agenda.

80. Lynn Dumenil, "The Tribal Twenties: 'Assimilated' Catholics' Response to Anti-Catholicism in the 1920s," *Journal of American Ethnic History* 11 (1) (1991), 21–49; Bernard Farber, Charles H. Mindel and Bernard Lazerwitz, "The Jewish American Family," in Charles H. Mindel, Robert Habenstein, and Roosevelt Wright, Jr. (eds.), *Ethnic Families in America*, 3rd ed. (New York: Elsevier, 1988) 400–437; Jenna Weissman Joselit, *Our Gang: Jewish Crime and the New York Jewish Community, 1900–1940* (Bloomington: Indiana University Press, 1983); Randall M. Miller, "Introduction," in Randall M. Miller and Thomas D. Marzik (eds.), *Immigrants and Religion in Urban America* (Philadelphia: Temple University Press, 1977), xi–xxii.

81. Lynn Dumenil, "The Tribal Twenties: 'Assimilated' Catholics' Response to Anti-Catholicism in the 1920s," *Journal of American Ethnic History* 11 (1) (1991), 30–31.

82. Irving Howe, *World of Our Fathers* (New York: Harcourt, Brace, Javonovich, 1976), 235.

83. Irving Howe, *World of Our Fathers,* 236.

84. J. Westermeyer, T. F. Vang, and J. Neider, "Refugees Who Do and Do Not Seek Psychiatric Care: An Analysis of Premigratory and Postmigratory Characteristics," *Journal of Nervous and Mental Disorders* 171 (2) (1983), 86–91.

85. Steven J. Gold, "Dealing With Frustration: A Study of Interactions Between Resettlement Staff and Refugees," in Scott Morgan and Elizabeth Colson (eds.), *People in Upheaval* (New York: Center For Migration Studies, 1987); Steven J. Gold, *Refugee Communities: A Comparative Field Study* (Newbury Park, CA: Sage, 1992); Fran Markowitz, *A Community in Spite of Itself: Soviet Jewish Émigrés in New York* (Washington, DC: Smithsonian, 1993).

86. Paul Ritterband, "Jewish Identity Among Russian Immigrants in the U.S.," in Noah Lewin–Epstein, Yaacov Ro'i, and Paul Ritterband (eds.), *Russian Jews on Three Continents: Migration and Resettlement* (London: Frank Cass, 1997), 333.

87. Irving Howe, *World of Our Fathers* (New York: Harcourt, Brace, Javonovich, 1976); Steven J. Gold, *From the Workers' State to the Golden State: Jews from the Former Soviet Union in California* (Boston: Allyn and Bacon, 1995).

88. Arthur A. Goren, *New York Jews and the Quest for Community: The Kehillah Experiment 1908–1922* (New York: Columbia University Press, 1970).

89. Nathan Glazer and Daniel Patrick Moynihan, *Beyond the Melting Pot* (Cambridge: The MIT Press, 1963).

90. Andrew Greeley, *Ethnicity in the U.S.* (New York: John Wiley, 1974).

91. Alejandro Portes, "Los Angeles in the Context of the New Immigration," Working Paper No. 18, the Lewis Center for Regional Policy Studies, School of Public Policy and Social Research, University of California, Los Angeles, January 1997.

92. John Bodnar, *The Transplanted: A History of Immigrants in Urban America,* 128.

93. John Bodnar, *The Transplanted: A History of Immigrants in Urban America,* 128.

94. Irving Howe, *World of Our Fathers* (New York: Harcourt, Brace, Javonovich, 1976); Rita J. Simon, *In the Golden Land: A Century of Russian and Soviet Jewish Immigration in America* (Westport, Connecticut: Praeger, 1997).

95. Edward I. Kantowicz, "Politics" in Stephen Thernstrom (ed.), *The Harvard Encyclopedia of American Ethnic Groups* (Cambridge: Harvard University Press, 1980), 803–813.

96. A. T. Lane, *Solidarity or Survival? American Labor and European Immigrants 1830–1924* (New York: Greenwood Press, 1987).

97. William Kornblum, *Blue Collar Community* (Chicago: University of Chicago Press, 1974).

98. David M. Reimers, *Still the Golden Door: The Third World Comes to America* (New York: Columbia University Press, 1985).

99. Rubén G. Rumbaut, "Transformations: The Post-Immigrant Generation in an Age of Diversity," paper presented at the East Sociological Society Meeting, Philadelphia, March 21, 1998.

100. Paul Ong, Kye Young Park, and Yasmin Tong, "Korean-Black Conflict and the State," in Paul Ong, Edna Bonacich, and Lucy Cheng (eds.), *The New Asian Immigration in Los Angeles and Global Restructuring* (Philadelphia: Temple University Press, 1994), 280.

101. In–Jin Yoon, *On My Own: Korean Businesses and Race Relations in America* (Chicago: University of Chicago Press, 1997); Pyong-Gap Min, *Caught in the Middle: Korean Communities in New York and Los Angeles* (Berkeley: University of California Press, 1996); Rukeia Draw, *Black/Chaldean Conflict in Detroit,* unpublished manuscript (Department of Sociology, Michigan State University, 1998); Mary C. Sengstock, *Chaldean-Americans: Changing Conceptions of Ethnic Identity* (Staten Island, NY: Center for Migration Studies, 1982); Ivan Light and Edna Bonacich, *Immigrant Entrepreneurs* (Berkeley: University of California Press, 1988); Philip Kasinitz and Bruce Haynes, "The Fire at Freddy's," *CommonQuest* 1 (2) (Fall 1996), 24–34.

102. James H. Johnson, Jr., Cloyzelle K. Jones, Walter C. Farrell, Jr., and Melvin L. Oliver, "The Los Angeles Rebellion: A Retrospective View," *Economic Development Quarterly* 6 (4), November 1992, 356–172.

103. James Brown with Bruce Tucker, *James Brown: The Godfather of Soul* (New York: Collier, 1986), 178–179.

104. Larry Irving (Assistant Secretary for Communications and Information, National Telecommunications and Information Administration, Department of Commerce), "The Big Chill: Has Minority Ownership Been Put on Ice?" Remarks at the National Association of Black–Owned Broadcasters' annual meeting. September 11, 1997, at Washington, DC. http://www.ntia.doc.gov/ntiahome/speeches/91197nabob.htm.

105. Illsoo Kim, *New Urban Immigrants: The Korean Community in New York* (Princeton, NJ: Princeton University Press, 1981).

106. While Chinatowns, Little Koreas, Little Odessas, Little Saigons, Little Indias and Little Havanas continue to grow in American cities, such enclaves are generally business districts wherein only a fraction of the coethnic population resides — generally, recent arrivals. Instead, community members often live in distant, less ethnically-defined suburbs, visiting the ethnic center only for shopping, dining, business or during communal celebrations. Mehdi Bororgmehr, "Internal Ethnicity: Iranians in Los Angeles" *Sociological Perspectives* 40(3) (1997), 387–408; Timothy P. Fong, *The First Suburban Chinatown: The Remaking of Monterey Park, California* (Philadelphia: Temple University Press, 1994); Steven Gold, *Refugee Communities: A Comparative Field Study* (Newbury Park, CA: Sage, 1992); Pyong-Gap Min, *Caught in The Middle: Korean Communities in New York and Los Angeles* (Berkeley: University of California Press, 1996).

107. Illsoo Kim, *New Urban Immigrants: The Korean Community in New York* (Princeton, NJ: Princeton University Press, 1981), 262.

108. Hamid Naficy, "Popular Culture of Iranian Exiles in Los Angeles," in Ron Kelley, Jonathan Friedlander, and Anita Colby (eds.), *Irangeles: Iranians in Los Angeles* (Berkeley: University of California Press, 1993), 325–364.

109. Hamid Naficy, "Popular Culture of Iranian Exiles in Los Angeles," 358.

110. Olivier Zunz, *The Changing Face of Inequality: Urbanization, Industrial Development and Immigrants in Detroit 1880–1920* (Chicago, University of Chicago Press, 1982), 178.

111. John Bodnar, Roger Simon, and Michael P. Weber, *Lives of Their Own: Blacks, Italians and Poles in Pittsburgh, 1900–1960* (Urbana: University of Illinois Press, 1982).

112. John Bodnar, Roger Simon, and Michael P. Weber, *Lives of Their Own: Blacks, Italians and Poles in Pittsburgh, 1900–1960,* 154.

113. John Bodnar, *The Transplanted: A History of Immigrants in Urban America* (Bloomington: University of Indiana Press, 1985), 127.

114. Michael R. Weisser, *A Brotherhood of Memory: Jewish Landsmanshaftn* (Ithaca: Cornell University Press, 1989), 78; Rita J. Simon, *In the Golden Land: A Century of Russian and Soviet Jewish Immigration in America* (Westport, CT: Praeger, 1997).

115. http://www.pbs.org/kqed/chinatown/story.html#earthquake

116. Timothy P. Fong, *The First Suburban Chinatown: The Remaking of Monterey Park* (Philadelphia, Temple University Press, 1994), 29–31.

117. Ivan Light and Edna Bonacich, *Immigrant Entrepreneurs* (Berkeley: University of California Press, 1988), 200–201.

118. Gilbert Osofsky, *Harlem: The Making of a Ghetto: Negro New York 1890–1930* (New York: Harper Torchbooks, 1968), 94–104.

119. Sidney Bolkosky, *Harmony & Dissonance: Voices of Jewish Identity in Detroit, 1914–1967* (Detroit: Wayne State University Press 1991), 298–299.

120. Sonya Salamon, *Prairie Patrimony: Family, Farming and Community in the Midwest* (Chapel Hill: University of North Carolina Press, 1992).

121. Stephen John Gross, "Handing Down the Form: Values, Strategies, and Outcomes in Inheritance Practices Among Rural German–Americans," *Journal of Family History* 21 (2) (1996), 192–217.

122. Donald Kraybill and Steven M. Nolt, *Amish Enterprise* (Baltimore: Johns Hopkins University Press, 1995).

123. Jack Katz, *Seductions of Crime* (New York: Basic Books, 1988).

124. Martin Sanchez–Jankowski, *Islands in the Street* (Berkeley: University of California Press, 1991), 124.

125. William J. Wilson, *The Truly Disadvantaged* (Chicago: University of Chicago Press, 1987).

126. St. Clair Drake and Horace Cayton, *Black Metropolis* (New York: Harcourt, Brace and Company, 1945).

127. William J. Wilson, *The Truly Disadvantaged* (Chicago: University of Chicago Press, 1987), 7.

128. William J. Wilson, *When Work Disappears: The World of the New Urban Poor* (New York: Knopf, 1996), 20.

129. William J. Wilson, *The Truly Disadvantaged* (Chicago: University of Chicago Press, 1987), 8.

130. William J. Wilson, *When Work Disappears: The World of the New Urban Poor,* 24.

131. Olivier Zunz, *The Changing Face of Inequality: Urbanization, Industrial Development, and Immigrants in Detroit 1880–1920* (Chicago: University of Chicago Press, 1982), 194.

132. John Bodnar, Roger Simon, and Michael P. Weber, *Lives of their Own: Blacks, Italians, and Poles in Pittsburgh, 1900–1960* (Urbana: University of Illinois Press, 1982), 78–79.

133. John Bodnar, Roger Simon, and Michael P. Weber, *Lives of their Own: Blacks, Italians, and Poles in Pittsburgh, 1900–1960,* 82.

134. John Bodnar, Roger Simon, and Michael P. Weber, *Lives of their Own: Blacks, Italians, and Poles in Pittsburgh, 1900–1960,* 81.

135. Jane Jacobs, *The Death and Life of Great American Cities* (New York: Anchor, 1992), 37.

136. William F. Whyte, *Street Corner Society* (Chicago: University of Chicago Press, 1955).

137. Gerald Suttles, *The Social Order of the Slum* (Chicago: University of Chicago Press, 1968), 47–49.

138. Gerald Suttles, *The Social Order of the Slum,* 84–85.

139. William Kornblum, *Blue Collar Community* (Chicago: University of Chicago Press, 1974), 89.

140. Fran Markowitz, *A Community in Spite of Itself: Soviet Jewish Emigres in New York* (Washington, DC: Smithsonian, 1993).

141. Steven J. Gold, *From the Workers' State to the Golden State: Jews from the Former Soviet Union in California* (Boston: Allyn and Bacon, 1995).

142. Fran Markowitz, *A Community in Spite of Itself: Soviet Jewish Emigrés in New York* (Washington, DC: Smithsonian, 1993), 237–38.

143. Stephen Warner and Judith G. Wittner (eds.) *Gatherings in The Diaspora: Religious Communities and the New Immigration* (Philadelphia. Temple University Press, 1998).

144. John Bodnar, *The Transplanted: A History of Immigrants in Urban America,* 156.

145. Illsoo Kim, *New Urban Immigrants: The Korean Community in New York* (Princeton, NJ: Princeton University Press, 1981).

146. Pyong-Gap Min, *Changes and Conflicts: Korean Immigrant Families in New York* (Boston: Allyn and Bacon, 1998).

147. Illsoo Kim, *New Urban Immigrants: The Korean Community in New York,* 204–205.

148. Francie Ostrower, *Why the Wealthy Give: The Culture of Elite Philanthropy* (Princeton: Princeton University Press, 1995).

149. Bruce A. Phillips and Steven J. Gold, "The Communal Dimensions of Federation Involvement: A Qualitative Study of Jewish Philanthropy," draft report to the Aspen Foundation, grant number 94–1–nsrf–18, 1996.

150. Steven J. Gold, "Women's Changing Place in Jewish Philanthropy," *Contemporary Jewry* 18 (1997), 60–75.

151. Pyong-Gap Min, *Caught in the Middle: Korean Communities in New York and Los Angeles* (Berkeley: University of California Press, 1996); Ivan Light and Edna Bonacich, *Immigrant Entrepreneurs* (Berkeley: University of California Press, 1988); Alejandro Portes, "The Social Origins of the Cuban Enclave Economy of Miami," *Sociological Perspectives* 30 (4) (1987) 340–372; Guillermo J. Grenier, Alex Stepick, Debbie Draznin, Aileen La Borwit, and Steve Morris, "On Machines and Bureaucracy: Controlling Ethnic Interaction in Miami's Apparel and Construction Industries," in Louise Lamphere (ed.), *Structuring Diversity: Ethnographic Perspectives on the New Immigration* (Chicago: University of Chicago Press, 1992), 65–93.

152. Pyong-Gap Min, *Caught in the Middle: Korean Communities in New York and Los Angeles.*

153. Rubén G. Rumbaut, "Transformations: The Post-Immigrant Generation in an Age of Diversity," paper presented at the East Sociological Society meeting, March 21, 1998, in Philadelphia. Karen J. Chai, "Competing for the Second Generation: English-Language Ministry at a Korean Protestant Church," in R. Stephen Warner and Judith G. Wittner (eds.), *Gatherings in the Diaspora: Religious Communities and the New Immigration* (Philadelphia. Temple University Press, 1998), 295–331; Maria Cristina Garcia, *Havana USA: Cuban Exiles and Cuban Americans in South Florida, 1959–1994* (Berkeley: University of California Press, 1996)

154. Susan Wiley Hardwick, *Russian Refuge: Religion, Migration, and Settlement on the North American Pacific Rim* (Chicago: University of Chicago Press, 1993), 123.

155. Susan Wiley Hardwick, *Russian Refuge: Religion, Migration, and Settlement on the North American Pacific Rim,* 118.

156. Patricia Guthrie, "Sea Islanders," in David Levinson and Melvin Ember (eds.), *American Immigrant Cultures: Builders of a Nation,* Vol. 2 (New York: MacMillan Reference, 1997), 779–784.

157. Susan Wiley Hardwick, *Russian Refuge: Religion, Migration, and Settlement on the North American Pacific Rim,* 4–5; Paul Robert Magocsi, "Russians," in Stephen Thernstrom (ed.), *Harvard Encylopedia of American Ethnic Groups* (Cambridge: Harvard–Belknap Press, 1980), 885–894.

158. Ivan Light, *Ethnic Enterprise in America: Business and Welfare Among Chinese, Japanese, and Blacks* (Berkeley: University of California Press, 1972); Ronald Takaki, *A Different Mirror: A History of Multicultural America* (Boston: Little Brown, 1993).

159. William J. Wilson, *The Declining Significance of Race* (Chicago: University of Chicago Press, 1978); William J. Wilson, *The Truly Disadvantaged* (Chicago: University of Chicago Press, 1987); Ronald Takaki, *A Different Mirror: A History of Multicultural America* (Boston: Little Brown, 1993); Dennis P. Clark, "The Expansion of the Public Sector and Irish Economic Development," in Scott Cummings (ed.), *Self–Help in Urban America: Patterns of Minority Business Enterprise* (Port Washington, N.Y.: Kennikat Press, 1980); Nathan Glazer and Daniel Patrick Moynihan, *Beyond the Melting Pot* (Cambridge: The MIT Press, 1963); Roger Waldinger, *Still the Promised City? African-*

Americans and New Immigrants in Postindustrial New York (Cambridge, MA: Harvard University Press, 1996); Timothy Bates, *Race, Self-Employment and Upward Mobility: An Illusive American Dream* (Baltimore: Johns Hopkins University Press, 1997).

160. Mohammed E. Ahrari (ed.), *Ethnic Groups and U.S. Foreign Policy* (New York: Greenwood Press, 1987); Stanford Lyman, *Chinese Americans* (New York: Random House, 1974); Linda Basch, Nina Glick Schiller, and Cristina Blanc-Szanton, *Nations Unbound: Transnational Projects, Postcolonial Predicaments, and Deterritorialized Nation States* (Basel, Switzerland: Gordon and Breach Publishers, 1994).

161. Nancy T. Ammerman, "North American Protestant Fundamentalism," in Martin E. Marty and R. Scott Appleby (eds.), *Fundamentalisms Observed* (Chicago: University of Chicago Press, 1991), 1–65.

Chapter 8

1. Even earlier, writing "On the Jewish Question," Karl Marx implies disadvantage theory when he asserts that European Jews were disliked because they were non-Christians *and* because of their propensity towards "huckstering." Jews developed economic power to compensate for their marginal political status, making them even more despised. (Robert Tucker, ed., *The Marx-Engels Reader*, 2nd ed. [New York: Norton 1978], 26–52.)

2. Max Weber, *The Protestant Ethic and the Spirit of Capitalism*. Translated by Talcott Parsons (New York: Scribners, 1958), 37–39.

3. Talcott Parsons, "Capitalism in Recent German Literature: Sombart and Weber," *The Journal of Political Economy* 6 (1928), 641–666.

4. Werner Sombart, *The Jews and Modern Capitalism* (Glencoe, IL: Free Press, 1951), 274.

5. Werner Sombart, *The Jews and Modern Capitalism* (Glencoe, IL: Free Press, 1951), 300–301.

6. Ivan Light, *Ethnic Enterprise in America* (Berkeley and Los Angeles: University of California, 1972), 43–44.

7. Ivan Light, *Ethnic Enterprise in America,* 8.

8. Ivan Light, "Disadvantaged Minorities in Self-Employment," *International Journal of Comparative Sociology* 20 (1979), 31–45.

9. Trevor Jones, David McEvoy, and Giles Barrett, "Labour Intensive Practices in the Ethnic Minority Firm," in J. Atkinson and D. Storey (eds.), *Employment, the Small Firm, and the Labour Market* (London: Routledge), 190.

10. Nathan Glazer referred to disadvantage plus affinity to account for American Jews' high rates of self-employment. "The Jew prefers a situation where his own merit receives objective confirmation, and he is not dependent on the good will or personal reaction of a person who may happen to not like Jews . . . the young immigrant going into business could, despite his accent, produce clothing as good as that produced by longer established Americans, and more cheaply . . . But . . . trying to rise to the vice presidency of a huge corporation, he certainly would have found the going harder." Nathan Glazer, "Social Characteristics of American Jews 1654–1954," *American Jewish Yearbook* 56 (1955), 28.

11. Howard Aldrich, John Cater, Trevor Jones, and David McEvoy, "From Periphery to Peripheral: The South Asian Petite Bourgeoisie in England," *Research in Sociology of Work* 2 (1983), 8.

12. Sarah Ladbury, "Choice, Chance or No Alternative? Turkish Cypriots in Business in London," in Robin Ward and Richard Jenkins (eds.), *Ethnic Communities in Business* (Cambridge: Cambridge University, 1984), 105.

13. Pyong-Gap Min, "From White Collar Occupations to Small Business: Korean Immigrants' Occupational Adjustment," *The Sociological Quarterly* 25 (1984), 343.

14. Pyong-Gap Min, "From White Collar Occupations to Small Business: Korean Immigrants' Occupational Adjustment," 335.

15. Nancy Lubin, "Small Business Owners," in Rita J. Simon (ed.), *New Lives: The Adjustment of Soviet and Jewish Immigrants in the U.S. and Israel* (Lexington, MA: Lexington Books, 1985).

16. Nancy Lubin, "Small Business Owners," 157.

17. Annie Phizacklea, "Entrepreneurship, Ethnicity, and Gender," in Sallie Westwood and Parminder Bhachu (eds.), *Enterprising Women* (London and New York: Routledge, 1988).

18. Annie Phizacklea, "Entrepreneurship, Ethnicity, and Gender," 21.

19. Jochen Blaschke and Ahmet Ersoz, "Life Histories: The Establishment of Turkish Small Businesses in West Berlin." Unpublished paper. City University of New York, April 1986.

20. John E. Bregger, "Self-Employed in the United States, 1948–1962," *Monthly Labor Review* 86 (1963), 37–43; Ivan Light, *Cities in World Perspective* (New York: Macmillan, 1983), 367.

21. Penelope McMillan, "New Entrepreneurs Try Marketplace," *Los Angeles Times* (13 December 1982), Sec. 2, p. 1; Jacqueline Mitchell, "Fear of Layoff Spurs Employees to Launch Part-Time Businesses," *Wall Street Journal* (25 May 1990), Sec. 1, p. 1.

22. Eugene H. Becker, "Self-Employed Workers: An Update to 1983," *Monthly Labor Review* 107 (1984), 14–18.

23. George Steinmetz and Erik Olin Wright, "The Fall and Rise of the Petty Bourgeoisie: Changing Patterns of Self-Employment in the Postwar United States," *American Journal of Sociology* 94 (1989), 973–1018.

24. Robert Fairlie and Bruce D. Meyer, "Ethnic and Racial Self-Employment Differences and Possible Explanations," *The Journal of Human Resources* 31 (1996), 785.

25. Peter Johnson, "Unemployment and Self-Employment: A Survey," *Industrial Relations Journal* 12 (1981), 5–15.

26. Eran Razin and Andre Langlois, "Metropolitan Characteristics and Entrepreneurship Among Immigrants and Ethnic Groups in Canada," *International Migration Review* 30 (1996), 703–727.

27. Sheldon Haber, "A New Perspective on Business Ownership." Report prepared for U.S. Small Business Administration, Office of Advocacy, by Simon and Company, 1985, under Contract #SBA 8559-AER-84.

28. Sheldon Haber, "A New Perspective on Business Ownership," 12.

29. David Keeble and Egbert Weaver, *New Firms and Regional Development in Europe* (London: Croom Helm, 1986), 10–19.

30. David Keeble and Egbert Weaver, *New Firms and Regional Development in Europe.*

31. Steven J. Gold, *Refugee Communities: A Comparative Field Study* (Newbury Park, CA: Sage, 1992), 174–175.

32. The distinction between hard and soft cultural theory is discussed in Ivan Light, "Asian Enterprise in America," in Scott Cummings (ed.), *Self-Help in America* (Port Washington, NY: Kennikat, 1980), 33–57.

33. In emphasizing ethnic resources and social capital, disadvantage theory in its various forms would be considered invalid by both Marxists and neo-classical economists, who dismiss the importance of collective resources in creating ethnic economies. Timothy Bates, *Race, Self-Employment and Upward Mobility* (Baltimore: Johns Hopkins University, 1997), and Sherry Gorelick, *City College and the Jewish Poor* (New York: Schocken Books, 1982). While rejecting the simple disadvantage version, we believe that groups characterized by both disadvantages and resources can develop ethnic economies. Ivan Light and Carolyn Rosenstein, *Race, Ethnicity, and Entrepreneurship in Urban America* (Hawthorne, NY: Aldine de Gruyter, 1995); Saskia Sassen, "The Informal Economy," in John Hull Mollenkopf and Manuel Castells, *Dual City: Restructuring New York* (New York: Russell Sage Foundation, 1991); and Alex Stepick, *Pride Against Prejudice: Haitians in the United States* (Boston: Allyn and Bacon, 1998).

34. Economists call this outcome market failure. See Thomas Sowell, *Race and Economics* (New York: David Mckay, 1975), Ch. 6.

35. Timothy Bates, *Race, Self-Employment and Upward Mobility* (Baltimore: Johns Hopkins University, 1997), 84.

36. A starving pauper lacks the knowledge to farm, but starvation affords him the motive.

37. Frederick W. Lynch, *Invisible Victims: White Males and the Crisis of Affirmative Action* (Westport, CT: Greenwood Press, 1989).

38. Who is more disadvantaged in the labor market: an 18 year old black man who has completed high school or a 62 year old white man who has the same educational credential? What if the older white man is also disabled, alcoholic, ex-convict, and a homosexual? If we keep piling on the disabilities, the white man's disadvantage finally exceeds the black man's.

39. Timothy Bates, *Race, Ethnicity and Self-Employment* (Baltimore: Johns Hopkins University, 1997), 91–95.

40. Sengstock explained the entrepreneurship of Roman Catholic Chaldeans in Detroit who were "forced into the grocery business" because they lacked marketable skills, and knew little English. (Mary Catherine Sengstock, "Maintenance of Social Interaction Patterns in an Ethnic Group." Ph.D. diss., Washington University, 1967, 187.)

41. M. D. R. Evans, "Language Skill, Language Usage, and Opportunity: Immigrants in the Australian Labour Market," *Sociology* 21 (1987), 253–74; M. D. R. Evans, "Immigrant Entrepreneurship: Effects of Ethnic Market Size and Isolated Labor Pool," *American Sociological Review* (1989).

42. M. D. R. Evans, "Immigrant Entrepreneurship: Effects of Ethnic Market Size and Isolated Labor Pool," *American Sociological Review* (1989), 270.

43. Individuals may be disadvantaged even when they receive better than expected treatment in the labor market. Such a person may have succeeded despite discrimination. But we cannot make the same claim of groups.

44. Zhong Deng, "Status Attainment in China." Ph. D. diss., University of California at Los Angeles, 1993.

45. Pierre Bourdieu, *La Distinction* (Paris: Editions de Minuit, 1979).

46. Pyong-Gap Min, *Ethnic Business Enterprise: Korean Small Business in Atlanta* (New York: Center for Migration Studies, 1988), 35–36, 56–61.

47. Pyong-Gap Min, *Ethnic Business Enterprise: Korean Small Business in Atlanta,* 57.

48. Pyong-Gap Min, *Ethnic Business Enterprise: Korean Small Business in Atlanta,* 59.

49. Ivan Light and Edna Bonacich, *Immigrant Entrepreneurs* (Berkeley and Los Angeles: University of California, 1988), Table 35.

50. Kwang Chung Kim, Won Moo Hurh, and Marilyn Fernandez, "Intra-Group Differences in Business Participation: Three Asian Immigrant Groups," *International Migration Review* 23 (1989), 73–95.

51. Marilyn Fernandez and Kwang Chung Kim, "Self-Employment Rates of Asian Immigrant Groups: An Analysis of Intragroup and Intergroup Differences," *International Migration Review* 32 (3) (1988), 654–681.

52. Melvin Oliver and Thomas Shapiro, *Black Wealth/White Wealth: A New Perspective on Racial Inequality*. (New York: Routledge 1995), 45.

53. Michael Podgursky and Paul Swaim, "Duration of Joblessness Following Displacement," *Industrial Relations* 26 (1987), 224–225.

54. Jose A. Cobas, Mikel Aickin, and Douglas S. Jardine, "Industrial Segmentation, the Ethnic Economy, and Job Mobility: The Case of Cuban Exiles in Florida," *Quality and Quantity* 27 (1993), 249–270; Thomas Bailey and Roger Waldinger, "Primary, Secondary, and Enclave Labor Markets: A Training Systems Approach," *American Sociological Review* 56 (1991), 432–445.

55. Crime offers an illegal alternative. The relationship of labor force disadvantage and self-employment parallels what Terrence P. Thornberry and R. L. Christenson ("Unemployment and Criminal Involvement: An Investigation of Reciprocal Causal Structures," *American Sociological Review* 49, p. 400), find between unemployment and crime.

56. Peter Johnson, "Unemployment and Self-Employment: A Survey," *Industrial Relations Journal* 12 (1981), 5–15.

57. Resemblances to Merton's anomie paradigm are inescapable. Entrepreneurship is a kind of innovation. Merton thought that innovation arose from the combination of blocked access to institutionalized means and introjection of cultural goals. Translated into the entrepreneurship lexicon, Merton's view becomes the simple disadvantage theory: subject to discrimination in the labor market, ambitious people turn to entrepreneurship. The trouble is, we hasten to point out,

people who have introjected the cultural goals may lack the requisite resources in which case innovation becomes retreatism. Robert King Merton, *Social Theory and Social Structure* (New York: Free Press, 1957), 140.

58. Entrepreneurship means legal activities accessible to measurement. Those engaged in the informal or illegal economy are likely to claim unemployment rather than to reveal their participation in the informal economy. Those without resources, therefore, lack access to the "legal" economic structure, and when they have the added burden of labor market disadvantage, they may have access only to the informal or illegal economic structure. In fact, resource disadvantage and labor market disadvantage may provide the motivation for their engagement in such activities.

59. W. S. Gilbert, *Plays and Poems of W. S. Gilbert* (New York: Random House, 1932).

60. Edna Bonacich, "A Theory of Middleman Minorities," *American Sociological Review* 38 (1973), 583–594; Jonathan H. Turner and Edna Bonacich, "Toward a Composite Theory of Middleman Minorities," *Ethnicity* 7 (1980), 144–158.

61. Ivan Light and Carolyn Rosenstein, *Race, Ethnicity, and Entrepreneurship in Urban America* (Hawthorne, NY: Aldine de Gruyter, 1995), 176.

62. Timothy Bates, *Race, Self-Employment, and Upward Mobility* (Baltimore: Johns Hopkins University, 1997), 95.

63. Robert M. Jiobu, "Ethnic Hegemony and the Japanese of California," *American Sociological Review* 53 (3) (1988), 353–367.

64. Herbert Gans, "Second Generation Decline: Scenarios for the Economic and the Ethnic Futures of the Post-1965 American Immigrants," *Ethnic and Racial Studies* 15 (2), 173–192; Roger Waldinger, *Still the Promised City? African-Americans and New Immigrants in Postindustrial New York* (Cambridge, MA: Harvard University Press, 1996); Roger Waldinger and Mehdi Bozorgmehr (eds.), *Ethnic Los Angeles* (New York: Russell Sage Foundation, 1996); Mary C. Waters, "West Indian Immigrants, African Americans and Whites in the Workplace: Different Perspectives on American Race Relations," Paper presented at the American Sociological Association Annual Meeting, Los Angeles, August 1994; Hector Delgado, *New Immigrants, Old Unions: Organizing Undocumented Workers in Los Angeles* (Philadelphia: Temple University Press, 1993).

65. Douglas Massey, Joaquin Arango, Graeme Hugo, Ali Kouaouci, Adela Pellegrino, and J. Edward Taylor, "Theories of International Migration: A Review and Appraisal," *Population and Development Review* 19 (3) (1993), 431–466.

66. Joleen Kirschenman and Kathryn M. Neckerman, "We'd Love to Hire Them, But . . . ': The Meaning of Race for Employers," in Christopher Jencks and Paul E. Peterson (eds.), *The Urban Underclass* (Washington, DC: Brookings Institution, 1991), 203–32; William J. Wilson, *When Work Disappears: The World of the New Urban Poor* (New York: Knopf, 1996); Steven J. Gold, "Israeli Immigrants in the U.S.: The Question of Community," *Qualitative Sociology* 17 (4) (1994), 325–363; Roger Waldinger, "The 'Other Side' of Embeddedness: A Case-Study of the Interplay of Economy and Ethnicity," *Ethnic and Racial Studies* 18 (3) (1995), 555–580; Allen J. Scott, "The Manufacturing Economy: Ethnic and Gender Divisions of Labor," in Roger Waldinger and Mehdi Bozorgmehr (eds.), *Ethnic Los Angeles* (New York: Russell Sage Foundation, 1996); Guillermo J. Grenier, Alex Stepick, Debbie Draznin, Aileen La Borwit, and Steve Morris, "On Machines and Bureaucracy: Controlling Ethnic Interaction in Miami's Apparel and Construction Industries," in Louise Lamphere (ed.), *Structuring Diversity: Ethnographic Perspectives on the New Immigration* (Chicago: University of Chicago Press, 1992), 65–93.

67. Philip Moss and Chris Tilly, " 'Soft' Skills and Race: An Investigation of Black Men's Employment Problems," (New York: Russell Sage Foundation, 1995) (http://epn.org/sage/rstill.html).

68. Roger Waldinger, *Still the Promised City? African-Americans and New Immigrants in Postindustrial New York* (Cambridge, MA: Harvard University Press, 1996), Ch. 15; Robert M. Jiobu, "Ethnic Hegemony and the Japanese of California," *American Sociological Review* 53 (3) 353–367; Philip Kasinitz, *Caribbean New York* (Ithaca: Cornell University Press, 1992).

69. Nancy Foner, *The Caregiving Dilemma: Work in an American Nursing Home* (Berkeley: University of California Press, 1994); Philip Kasinitz and Milton Vickerman, "Ethnic Niches and Racial Traps," Jamaicans in the New York Regional Economy." Paper presented at Social Science History Association, Chicago, 16 November 1995.

70. Ivan Light and Edna Bonacich, *Immigrant Entrepreneurs* (Berkeley and Los Angeles: University of California, 1988); Pyong-Gap Min, *Caught in the Middle: Korean Communities in New York and Los Angeles* (Berkeley: University of California Press, 1996); Roger Waldinger, "The Making of an Immigrant Niche," *International Migration Review* 28 (105) (1994), 3–30; Bradley Parlin, *Immigrant Professionals in the United States* (New York: Praeger, 1976); Paul Ong and Tania Azores, "The Migration and Incorporation of Filipino Nurses," in Paul Ong, Edna Bonacich, and Lucie Cheng, (eds.), *The New Asian Immigration in Los Angeles and Global Restructuring* (Philadelphia: Temple University Press, 1994), 154–195; David M. Grant, Melvin L. Oliver, and Angela D. James, "African Americans: Social and Economic Bifurcation," in Roger Waldinger and Mehdi Bozorgmehr (eds.), *Ethnic Los Angeles* (New York: Russell Sage Foundation, 1996), 379–411; Timothy Bates, *Race, Self-Employment and Upward Mobility* (Baltimore: Johns Hopkins University, 1997).

71. Roger Waldinger, "The Making of an Immigrant Niche," *International Migration Review* 28 (105) (1994), 3–30; Mary C. Waters, "West Indian Immigrants, African Americans and Whites in the Workplace: Different Perspectives on American Race Relations." Paper presented at the American Sociological Association Annual Meeting, Los Angeles, August 1994; Hector Delgado, *New Immigrants, Old Unions: Organizing Undocumented Workers in Los Angeles* (Philadelphia: Temple University Press, 1993); Herbert Gans, "Second Generation Decline: Scenarios for the Economic and Ethnic Futures of the Post-1965 American Immigrants," *Ethnic and Racial Studies* 15 (2) (1992), 173–192.

72. Robert M. Jiobu, "Ethnic Hegemony and the Japanese of California," *American Sociological Review* 53 (3) (1988), 356.

73. William J. Wilson, *When Work Disappears: The World of the New Urban Poor* (New York: Knopf, 1996); Harry J. Holzer, "Informal Job Search and Black Youth Unemployment," *American Economic Review* 27 (3) (1987), 446–452; Philip Moss and Chris Tilly, " 'Soft' Skills and Race: An Investigation of Black Men's Employment Problems" (New York: Russell Sage Foundation, 1995), [http://epn.org/sage/rstill.html].

74. M. Patricia Fernández-Kelly and Anna M. Garcia, "Power Surrendered, Power Restored: The Politics of Work and Family Among Hispanic Garment Workers in California and Florida," in Louise A. Tilly and Patricia Gurin (eds.), *Women, Politics and Change* (New York: Russell Sage, 1990), 130–149; Pierrette Hondagneu-Sotelo, *Gendered Transitions: Mexican Experiences of Immigration* (Berkeley: University of California Press, 1994).

Chapter 9

1. Daniel Immergluck and Erin Mullen, "Getting Down to Business." (Chicago: Woodstock Institute, 1998), 1.

2. The financial system delivers credit so effectively that a third of California households owe it $10,000 or more, excluding mortgages. See: Don Lee, and Debora Vrana, "Consumer Debt Rising Steeply in Southland," *Los Angeles Times* (Dec. 10, 1995: section 1), p. 1; Robert D. Manning, "Can't Leave Home Without It: Charting the Social and Economic Currents of the Credit Card Society," Paper presented at the Annual Meeting of the American Sociological Association meeting, Toronto, Canada, Aug. 4, 1997.

3. Savings and loan associations originated because banks were unwilling to "to make loans to individuals for home construction." Heather A. Haveman, and Hayagreeva Roa, "Structuring a Theory of Moral Sentiments: Institutional and Organizational Coevolution in the

Early Thrift Industry," *American Journal of Sociology* 102 (1997), 1608. Commercial banks were uninterested in individuals and home mortgages. See also: Daniel Immergluck, "Business as Usual," *Inc Magazine Archives*. Online. Internet. June 23, 1997. Available: http://www.inc.com/incmagazine/archives/04941143.html

4. ". . . gaps exist in the availability of capital for small-business development and for housing. The greatest evidence of gaps is for long-term and unsecured debt for small and moderately sized businesses, equity financing for new businesses and early stage businesses that are unlikely to go public and for small businesses that want to develop new products, loans for nontraditional organizations . . . loans of all types to businesses in low-income neighborhoods, and home-mortgage loans to minorities." Julia Ann Parzen, and Michael Hall Kieschnick, *Credit Where It's Due* (Philadelphia: Temple University, 1992), 37–38. Their complaint is much less true of mortgage credit now than it once was. Since the Community Reinvestment Act became law in 1977, mortgage loans to minority and low-income home buyers have soared. Just between 1991 and 1995, home purchase loans to whites increased 66%, but loans to blacks increased 300% and to Hispanics 200%. See: Gregory D. Squires, *Capital Communities in Black and White* (New York: State University of New York, 1994), 67–71; Jim Campen, "Lending Insights: Hard Proof that Banks Discriminate," Ch. 5 in *Real World Banking*, 3rd edition, edited by Marc Breslow, Jim Campen, Ellen Frank, John Miller, and Abby Scher (Somerville MA: Dollars and Sense, 1997), 42–43. See also: Elaine Edgcomb, Joyce Klein, and Peggy Clark, *The Practice of Microenterprise in the U.S.* (New York: Aspen Institute, 1996), 15; William D. Bradford, "Commercial Banks and Inner City Economic Development: Theory, Comments and Development of a Model," *Review of Black Political Economy* 4 (3) (1973), 21–40.

5. "There are three banks and four savings and loans with a combination of seven branches in South Central. Only two of the three banks with South Central branches made single family loans in the study area. One of these two banks, Bank of America, issued only one loan in the area. Of the four savings and loan institutions, only two contributed significantly to single family home lending." David Rzepinski, "South Central Home Loan Study," Master's Thesis, University of California, Los Angeles, 1989, p. 4.

6. J. Carroll Moody and Gilbert C. Fite, *The Credit Union Movement, 1850–1970* (Lincoln: University of Nebraska, 1971), 75.

7. U. S. Department of Commerce, Bureau of the Census, *Statistical Abstract of the United States 1996* (Washington, D.C.: U.S. Government Printing Office, 1996), Tables 778, 783.

8. *Statistical Abstract of the United States, 1996,* Table 775

9. Squires, *Capital Communities,* 67–71.

10. Gregory D. Squires, and Sally O'Conner, "Fringe Banking in Milwaukee: The Rise of Check-Cashing Businesses and the Emergence of a Two-Tiered Banking System," Paper presented at the 1997 Annual Meeting of the American Sociological Association, Aug. 11, Toronto.

11. John R. Wilke, "Back-Door Loans: Some Banks' Money Flows Into Poor Areas– and Causes Anguish," *The Wall Street Journal* (October 21, 1991: sect. A), 1; John Caskey, *Fringe Banking* (New York: Russell Sage, 1994), 93; Saskia Sassen, "The Informal Economy: Between New Developments and Old Regulations," *Yale Law Review* 103 (1997), 2296–2297; James F. Peltz, "Rights Group Finds Mortgage Lending Bias," *Los Angeles Times* (Dec. 24, 1997, section D), 1.

12. Ivan Light, "Numbers Gambling among Blacks: A Financial Institution," *American Sociological Review* 42 (1977), 892–904; Brett Pulley, "Living off the Daily Dream of Winning a Lottery Prize," *New York Times* (May 22, 1999, sect. 1), p. 1

13. Michael Hudson, "Fringe Banks that Exploit the Poor," in Mark Breslow, Jim Campen, Ellen Frank, John Miller, and Abby Scher (eds.), *Real World Banking*, 3rd ed. (Somerville, MA: Dollars and Sense, 1997), 46–52.

14. Ayse Pamuk, "Informal Institutional Arrangements in Credit, Land Markets, and Infrastructure in Trinidad," Paper presented at the Lincoln Institute of Landpolicy Workshop on Urban Land Market Reform, Cambridge MA July 7, 1988.

15. Muhammed Yunus, "Grameen Bank: Microlending for Economic Development," in Mark Bres-
     low, Jim Campen, Ellen Frank, John Miller, and Abby Scher (eds.), *Real World Banking,* 3d ed.
     (Somerville, MA: Dollars and Sense, 1997), 50–52; Muhammed Yunus, "Towards Creating a
     Poverty Free World," *Grameen Dialogue* 29 (January, 1997); 1–2; Muhammed Yunus, "Credit
     where Credit's Due," *The Guardian Weekly* (Nov. 8, 1998), 20.
16. ". . . Poverty is not created by the poor, nor is it sustained by them. The roots of poverty lie in
     our institutions, concepts, and theoretical frameworks." Muhammed Yunus, "Grameen Bank," 1
17. *The State of Small Business: 1998* (Washington D.C.: U.S. Small Business Administration, 1998), ch. 2
18. David Malmquist, Fred Phillips-Patrick, and Clifford Rossi, "The Economics of Low-Income
     Mortgage Lending," *Journal of Financial Services Research* 11 (1997), 179; Bruce Posner, "Be-
     hind the Boom in Microloans." *Inc Magazine Archives* April (1994), 114 +. Online. Internet.
     June 23, 1997. Available: http://www.inc.com/incmagazine/archives/04941143.html;
     Michael Woolcock, "Learning from Failures of Microfinance: What Unsuccessful Cases Tell
     Us about how Group-Based Programs Work." *American Journal of Economics and Sociology*,
     forthcoming in 1999.
19. Katherine L. Bradbury, Karl E. Case, and Constance R. Dunham, "Geographic Patterns of Mort-
     gage Lending in Boston, 1982-1987," *New England Economic Review* Sept/Oct (1989), 3.
20. "Locked Out or Priced Out?" *The Economist* 344 (1997), 56–57
21. "Lack of saving potential is not necessarily the biggest obstacle which prevents low-income
     groups from saving. Frequent causes are mistrust of financing institutions or simply, lack of access
     to banking. . . ." U.N. Center for Human Settlements, *Mobilization of Financial Resources for
     Low-Income Groups* (Nairobi: Habitat, 1989), 8.
22. Sondra Beverly, "How Can the Poor Save? Theory and Evidence on Saving in Low-Income
     Households," Working Paper 97–3, Center for Social Development, Washington University,
     1997, p. 28; S. Cohen, "Consumer Socialization: Children's Saving and Spending," *Childhood
     Education* 70 (1994), 244–246.
23. Brett Puley, "Living Off the Daily Dream of Winning a Lottery Prize," *New York Times* (May 22,
     1999, sect 1), 1. In William Hogarth's lithographic series entitled "The Rake's Progress," a rich
     young man dissipates his fortune on drink and whores. In the eighteenth century Hogarth al-
     ready knew that even the wealthy sometimes mismanage their finances. From a moralistic point
     of view, never far away in the United States, the poverty of those who ignored the money
     culture they had learned is more reprehensible than the poverty of those to whom the money
     culture was never offered.
24. William C. Jordan, *Women and Credit in Pre-Industrial and Developing Societies* (Philadelphia:
     University of Pennsylvania, 1993).
25. Lisa J. Servon, "Microenterprise Programs and Women: Entrepreneurship as Individual Empow-
     erment," *Journal of Developmental Entrepreneurship* 1 (1996), 31–55.
26. In East Asian societies, women have principal responsibility for managing family finances. This
     assignment strengthens women's financial competence. See: Ivan Light and Zhong Deng,
     "Gender Differences in RCA Participation within Korean Business Households in Los Angeles,"
     Money Go-Rounds: The Importance of Rotating Credit Associations for Women, edited by Shirley
     Ardener and Sandra Burman (Oxford and Washington: Berg, 1995), ch. 14.
27. Akiya Param, "In Our View," *Women and Money* 2 (April, 1998).
28. L. Fabowle, B. Orser, A. Riding, and C. Swift, "Gender, Structural Factors, and Credit Terms
     Between Canadian Small Businesses and Financial Institutions," Working Paper, Faculty of
     Business, Ryerson Polytechnic University, 1994.
29. In the case of small business owners, who are not poor themselves, we mean the poverty of those
     long-term unemployed who never obtained the jobs the small business owners would have
     created had banks lent them money.
30. A claim that is, as their own data reveal, only partially true because some ethno-racial groups are
     better provided with informal lending capacity than are others. See: Philip Bond and Robert

Townsend, "Formal and Informal Financing in a Chicago Ethnic Neighborhood," *Economic Perspectives* 20 (1996), 1, 24.

31. G. M. Chen, and J. A. Cole, "The Myths, Facts and Theories of the Ethnic Small Scale Enterprise Financing," *Review of Black Political Economy* 16 (1988), 111–123; Caren Grown, and Timothy Bates, "Commercial Bank Lending Practices and the Development of Black-Owned Construction Companies," *Journal of Urban Affairs* 14 (1992), 25–41.

32. "Few would argue that lenders shouldn't be able to charge higher rates to cover what are clearly the higher risks and costs of doing business with customers who have shaky credit histories or unstable incomes." Hudson, "Fringe Banks," p. 47. See also: Samuel L. Myers, and Tsze Chan, "Racial Discrimination in Housing Markets: Accounting for Credit Risk," *Social Science Quarterly* 76 (1995), 543–561; Lynn Elaine Browne and Geoffrey M.B. Tootell, "Mortgage Lending in Boston–A Response to the Critics," *New England Economic Review* Sept/Oct (1995), 55; Eric Rosenblatt, "A Reconsideration of Discrimination in Mortgage Underwriting with Data from a National Mortgage Bank," *Journal of Financial Services* 11 (1997), 128.

33. Anne B. Shlay, "Not in That Neighborhood: The Effects of Population and Housing on the Distribution of Mortgage Finance within the Chicago SMSA," *Social Science Research* 17 (1988), 159.

34. Gregory D. Squires, and Sunwoong Kim, "Does Anybody Who Works Here Look Like Me? Mortgage Lending, Race, and Lender Employment," *Social Science Quarterly* 76 (1995), 823–838.

35. Alicia J. Munnell, Lynn E. Browne, James McEneaney, and Geoffrey M. B. Tootell, "Mortgage Lending in Boston: Interpreting HMDA Data," Boston: Federal Reserve Bank of Boston, Working Paper No. 92–7, 1992; Katherine L. Bradbury, Karl E. Case, and Constance R. Dunham, "Geographic Patterns of Mortgage Lending in Boston, 1982–1987," *New England Economic Review* (Sept/Oct 1989), 3–31; Jim Campen, "Lending Insights: Hard Proof that Banks Discriminate." Ch 5 in Marc Breslow, Jim Campen, Ellen Frank, John Miller, and Abby Scher (eds.), *Real World Banking*, 3d edition. (Somerville MA: Dollars and Sense, 1997), 40.

36. Charles W. Calomiris, Charles M. Kahn, and Stanley D. Longhofer, "Housing-Finance Intervention and Private Incentives: Helping Minorities and the Poor," *Journal of Money, Credit, and Banking* 26 (1994), 652–653; Henry Buist, Isaac F. Megbolugbe, and Tina R. Trent, "Racial Homeownership Patterns, the Mortgage Market, and Public Policy," *Journal of Housing Research* 5 (1994), 114.

37. Similarly, the Woodstock Institute found that the rate of bank loans per 100 small businesses in low-income areas of Chicago was 81% of the rate in medium-income areas in 1996. This result implies that, were even were lending equalized, the low-income area could expect only 19 percent increase in its loan record. Immergluck and Mullen, "Getting Down to Business," p. 5. We are *not* arguing against the equalization of lending conditions.

38. In fact, some evidence finds men less likely to obtain mortgage loans than women. See: Cynthia K. Sanders, Edward Scanlon, and Shirley R. Emerson, "Mortgage Lending: Is Gender a Factor?" Working Paper 97–4 of the Center for Social Development, Washington University, 1997.

39. Daniel Immergluck and Erin Mullen, "New Small Business Data Show Loans Going to Higher-Income Neighborhoods in Chicago Area," *Reinvestment Alert* [Woodstock Institute] 11 (1997), 1–10.

40. Even banks set up to reach the inner-city cannot do it. The Los Angeles Community Development Bank "has fallen far short of its mandate to channel loans to the inner city's smallest businesses, with some programs failing to finalize a single deal . . . . " Lee Romney, "Bank Lags on Inner-City Loan Results," *Los Angeles Times* (Dec. 8, 1998, section A), 1. See also: David Puglielli, 1997. "The World Bank and Microfinance." Available: http://stu.beloit.edu/~ pugliell/microlending/paper.html

41. Timothy Bates, *Race, Self-Employment & Upward Mobility* (Baltimore: Johns Hopkins University, 1997), 122.

42. Kyeyoung Park, *The Korean American Dream: Immigrants and Small Business in New York City* (Ithaca: Cornell University, 1996), 59; Herbert Kempson and Elaine Kempson, *Credit Use and Ethnic Minorities* (London: Policy Studies Institute, 1996), 30–34; 58–61.

43. Jin-Kyung Yoo, *Korean Immigrant Entrepreneurs* (New York: Garland, 1999), chs. 6, 7; Louis Sterling, "Partners: the Social Organization of Rotating Savings and Credit Associations among Exilic Jamaicans," *Sociology* 29 (1995), 653–666; Michel S. Laguerre, "Rotating Credit Associations and the Diasporic Economy," *Journal of Developmental Entrepreneurship* 3: 24; *Idem. American Odyssey: Haitians in New York City* (Ithaca: Cornell University, 1984), 89.

44. Jean Besson, "Women's Use of ROSCAs in the Caribbean: Reassessing the Literature," in Shirley Ardener and Sandra Burman (eds.), *Money-Go-Rounds: The Importance of Rotating Savings and Credit Associations for Women* (Berg Publishers Limited: Oxford, 1995), 263–288.

45. Clifford Geertz, Clifford, "The Rotating Credit Association: a Middle Rung' in Development," *Economic Development and Cultural Change* 10 (1962), 241–263.

46. Heather A. Haveman and Hayagreeva Roa, "Structuring a Theory of Moral Sentiments: Institutional and Organizational Coevolution in the Early Thrift Industry," *American Journal of Sociology* 102 (1997), 1617.

47. Alec R. Levenson and Timothy Besley, "The Anatomy of an Informal Financial Market: ROSCA Participation in Taiwan," (Los Angeles: Milken Institute for Job and Capital Formation, Working Paper 95–8, 1995), 1.

48. Dale W. Adams and M. L. Canavesi de Sahonero, "Rotating Savings and Credit Associations in Bolivia," *Savings and Development* 13 (1989), 227, 231.

49. Lewis D. Solomon, "Microenterprise: Human Reconstruction in America's Inner Cities." Online. Internet. June 23, 1997. Available: http://www.dlcppi.org/texts/social/microent.txt

50. Source: http://devcap.org/February 3, 1997.

51. Alex Counts, *Give Us Credit* (New York: Random House, 1996).

52. Muhammed Yunus, "Credit Where Credit's Due," *The Guardian Weekly* (November 8, 1998), 20.

53. Chi-kan Richard Hung, "Southern Innovation, Northern Adaptation: The Experience of Group-Based Microcredit Programs in the US" (PhD diss., Indiana University, 1997), 15.

54. "Virtually all the immigrants in this study were familiar with revolving loan funds, and many Koreans participated in kye and Dominicans in san. Although there were numerous reports of the use of kye and san to start or expand businesses, to buy cars or furniture, and to finance a wedding or an education, their use for home purchases was relatively uncommon. Only a few Korean immigrants mentioned that they or their acquaintances had used funds accumulated through kye as a significant part of their downpayment. "Stephen J. Johnson, and Morsina Katimin, "Homeownership Aspirations and Experiences: Immigrant Koreans and Dominicans in Northern Queens, New York City," *Citiscape: a Journal of Housing and Urban Development* 3 (1997), 87.

55. Bernard Wong, "The Role of Ethnicity in Enclave Enterprises: A Study of the Chinese Garment Factories in New York City," *Human Organization* 46 (1987), 120–130.

56. Johnston and Katimin, "Homeownership Aspirations," 63–90.

57. Alexander C. Severens, and Amy J. Kays, *1996 Directory of U.S. Microenterprise Programs* (Washington D.C.: The Aspen Institute, 1997), xv.

58. Severens and Kayes, xvii

59. Margaret A. Johnson, "An Overview of Basic Issues Facing Microenterprise Practices in the United States," *Journal of Developmental Entrepreneurship* 3 (1998), 11–17.

60. Steven Balkin, "A Grameen Bank Replication: the Full Circle Fund of the Women's Self-Employment Project of Chicago," in N. M. Wahid (ed.), *The Grameen Bank: Poverty Relief in Bangladesh* (Boulder: Westview, 1993), 253–254.

61. Richard P. Taub, "Making the Adaptation across Cultures and Societies: A Report on an Attempt to Clone the Grameen Bank in Southern Arkansas," *Journal of Developmental Entrepreneurship* 3 (1998), 53–69. See also: Peggy Clark and Amy Keys, *Microenterprise and the Poor* (Washington D.C.: The Aspen Institute, 1999), 68.

62. Martha E. Mangelsdorf, "Against the Odds," *Inc Magazine Archives* August. Online. Internet. June 23, 1997. Available: http://www.inc.com/incmagazine/archives/08910221.html; Robert E. Friedman, Brian Grossman, and Puchka Sahay, *Building Assets: Self-Employment for Welfare Recipi-*

ents (Washington D.C.: Corporation for Enterprise Development, 1995), 2; Clark and Keys, *Microenterprise*, 14.

63. Timothy Bates, and Lisa Servon, "Why Loans Won't Save the Poor," *Inc Magazine Archives*. Online. Internet. June 23, 1997. Available: http://www.inc.com/incmagazine/archives/04960271 .html

64. "Informal [credit] markets are *prima facie* evidence of failure because the presumed most efficient market institution is a formal financial sector composed of banks, cooperatives, or other intermediaries that can bring together efficiently large numbers of lenders and borrowers." Nicole Woosley Biggart, Richard P. Castanias, II and Paul R. Davis, "Institutional Foundations of Rotating Savings and Credit Associations: A Socioeconomic Perspective," Unpublished manuscript, University of California at Davis, 1997), 3.

65. This is the classic definition of a bank. "The Dayton plan also suffered from the stigma of being merely a bank." Bank was a pejorative term because relationships among participants were those of debtor and lender rather than cooperating peers. Haveman and Roa, "Structuring a Theory of Moral Sentiments," 1641

66. Mexico's Autofin is a commercial firm that has learned how to associate mutually unknown borrowers in a ROSCA-like self-financing groups of 125 persons. Founded in 1978, Autofin offers car and home financing to poor borrowers, most from the informal sector, who make several monthly contributions to a pool before finally becoming eligible to receive the total fund. As of October, 1998, Autofin had delivered 1,280 cars and $15,700,000 of home finance to borrowers "who would never qualify for bank credit but whose [repayment] performance is fine." James F. Smith, "Purchasing Power to the People," *Los Angeles Times* (Nov. 29, 1998, section C), 1.

67. "ROSCAs operate on the principle of mutual trust. Consequently, they are formed by individuals who know each other well and most importantly trust each other." Fredrick O. Wanyama, "Informal Credit Institutions in the Local Political Arena: The Case of Rotating Savings and Credit Associations in Vihiga District, Western Kenya," Paper presented at the Nordic Africa Institute Conference, Rosendal, Norway, June 11, 1998.

68. "The Working Capital mission states that the [microenterprise] program uses groups to build communities of people who have little or no other access to resources." Lisa J. Servon, "Credit and Social Capital: The Community Development Potential of U.S. Microcredit Programs," *Housing Policy Debate* 9 (1998), 134; Sudarshan Synghal, "How in the World Can We Lend to the Poor? A Case Study of Group Lending among the Urban Poor in the U.S." (Ph.D. diss. Boston University, 1994), 113.

69. M. Patricia Fernandez Kelly, "Social and Cultural Capital in the Urban Ghetto: Implications for the Economic Sociology of Immigration," in Alejandro Portes (ed.), *The Economic Sociology of Immigration* (New York: Russell Sage Foundation, 1995), 216.

70. Robert D. Putnam, "The Prosperous Community: Social Capital and Public Life," *The American Prospect* 13 (1993), 35–37.

71. We do not object to cost-effective public subsidies. We are merely observing that microcredit and informal credit can fill the gap too.

72. Alejandro Portes, and Julia Sensenbrenner, "Embeddedness and Immigration: Notes on the Social Determinants of Economic Action," *American Journal of Sociology* 98 (1993), 1325.

73. Caroline Moser, *Confronting Crisis* (Washington D. C.: The World Bank, 1996), 204, fn 105.

74. Denise Lynne Anthony, "Investing in Trust: Building Cooperation and Social Capital in Microcredit Borrowing Groups," (PhD. diss, University of Connecticut, 1997), 61.

75. Steven Balkin, *Self-Employment For Low-Income People* (New York: Praeger Publishers, 1989), 160; Ivan Light, "Self Help for the Urban Poor," *The American Enterprise* 7 (1996), 50–52.

Selected Bibliography: 50 Key Sources on Ethnic Economies

In compiling this list of references, we combined two lists of 25 works, one published prior to 1986 and one after. We did this to include a good mix of both historical and contemporary writings. A full bibliography is available at the book's website: http://www.apcatalog.com

Aldrich, H., and Waldinger, R. (1990). Ethnicity and entrepreneurship. *Annual Review of Sociology, 16,* 111–135.

Ardner, S., and Burman, S. (Eds.). (1995). *Money go rounds: The importance of savings and credit associations for women.* Oxford: Berg.

Barnett, M. L. (Spring 1960). Kinship as a factor affecting Cantonese economic adaptation in the United States, *Human Organization, 19*(1), 40–48.

Bates, T. (1997). *Race, self-employment, and upward mobility: An illusive American dream.* Baltimore: Johns Hopkins University Press.

Bell, D. (1960). Crime as an American way of life. In *The end of ideology* (Ch. 7). Glencoe, IL: Free Press.

Bonacich, E. (1973). A theory of middleman minorities. *American Sociological Review, 38,* 583–594.

Bonacich, E., and Modell, J. (1981). *The economic basis of ethnic solidarity: A study of Japanese Americans.* Berkeley and Los Angeles: University of California Press.

Boyd, R. M. (1991). A contextual analysis of black self-employment in large metropolitan areas, 1970–1980. *Social Forces, 70,* 409–429.

Butler, J. S. (1991). *Entrepreneurship and self-help among black Americans.* Albany: State University of New York Press.

Chan, J., and Cheung, Y.-W. (1985). Ethnic resources and business enterprise: A study of Chinese businesses in Toronto. *Human Organization, 44,* 142–154.

Cohen, A. (1969). *Custom and politics in urban Africa.* Berkeley and Los Angeles: University of California Press.

Cummings, S. (Ed.). (1980). *Self-help in urban America: Patterns of minority business enterprise.* New York: Kenikart Press.

Drake, S. C., and Cayton, H. (1962). *Black metropolis,* Chs. 16 and 17. New York: Harper & Row.

Edgcomb, E., Klein, J., and Clark, P. (1996). *The practice of microenterprise in the U.S.* New York: Aspen Institute.

Friedman, M. (1959). The handling of money: A note on the background to the economic sophistication of overseas Chinese. *Man, 59,* 64–65.

Glazer, N., and Moynihan, D. P. (1970). *Beyond the melting pot: The Negroes, Puerto Ricans, Jews, Italians, and Irish of New York City.* Cambridge: MIT Press.

Gold, S. J. (1994). Patterns of economic cooperation among Israeli immigrants in Los Angeles. *International Migration Review, 28,* 105, 114–135.

Goldscheider, C., and Kobrin, F. (1980). Ethnic continuity and the process of self-employment. *Ethnicity, 7,* 256–278.

Harris, A. L. (1936). *The Negro as capitalist.* Philadelphia: American Academy of Political and Social Science.

Ianni, F. (1972). *A family business: Kinship and social control in organized crime.* New York: Russell Sage Foundation.

Jiobu, R. M. (1988). Ethnic hegemony and the Japanese of California. *American Sociological Review, 53*(3), 353–367.

Kinzer, R. H., and Sagarin, E. (1950). *The Negro in American business.* New York: Greenburg.

Kraybill, D. B., and Nolt, S. M. (1995). *Amish enterprise: From plows to profits.* Baltimore: Johns Hopkins University Press.

Light, I. H. (1972). *Ethnic enterprise in America.* Berkeley and Los Angeles: University of California Press.

Light, I. (1977). The ethnic vice district. *American Sociological Review, 43,* 892–904.

Light, I. (1977). Numbers gambling among blacks: A financial institution. *American Sociological Review, 42,* 892–904.

Light, I. (1979). Disadvantaged minorities in self-employment. *International Journal of Comparative Sociology, 20,* 31–45.

Light, I., and Bonacich, E. (1988). *Immigrant entrepreneurs.* Berkeley and Los Angeles: University of California Press.

Light, I., and Rosenstein, C. (1995). *Race, ethnicity, and entrepreneurship in urban America.* Hawthorne, NY: Aldine de Gruyter.

Logan, J. R., Alba, R. D., and McNulty, T. L. (1994). Ethnic economies in metropolitan regions: Miami and beyond. *Social Forces, 72*(3), 691–724.

Lovell-Troy, L. A. (1981). Ethnic occupational structure: Greeks in the pizza business. *Ethnicity, 8,* 82–95.

Min, P. G. (1996). *Caught in the middle: Korean communities in New York and Los Angeles.* Berkeley and Los Angeles: University of California Press.

Model, S. (1993). The ethnic niche and the structure of opportunity: Immigrants and minorities in New York City. In Michael B. Katz (Ed.), *The underclass debate: Views from history* (pp. 161–193). Princeton: Princeton University Press.

Oliver, M., and Shapiro, T. M. (1997). *Black wealth/white wealth.* New York: Routledge.

Portes, A., and Bach, R. (1985). *Latin journey: Cuban and Mexican immigrants in the United States.* Berkeley and Los Angeles: University of California Press.

Portes, A., and Sensenbrenner, J. (1993). Embeddedness and immigration: Notes on the social determinants of economic action. *American Journal of Sociology, 98*(6), 1320–1350.

Salamon, S. (1992). *Prairie patrimony: Family, farming, and community in the Midwest.* Chapel Hill: University of North Carolina Press.

Sanders, J. M., and Nee, V. (1987). Limits of ethnic solidarity in the ethnic enclave economy. *American Sociological Review, 52,* 745–767.

Solomon, L. D. (1993). Microenterprise: Human reconstruction in America's inner cities. *Harvard Journal of Law and Public Policy, 15,* 191–221.

Tenenbaum, S. (1993). *A credit to their community: Jewish loan societies in the United States 1880–1945.* Detroit, MI: Wayne State University Press.

Vélez-Ibañez, C. (1981). *Bonds of mutual trust.* New Brunswick, NJ: Rutgers University Press.

Waldinger, R. (1996). *Still the promised city? African-Americans and new immigrants in postindustrial New York.* Cambridge, MA: Harvard University Press.

Waldinger, R., Aldrich, H., Ward, R., and Associates. (1990). *Ethnic entrepreneurs: Immigrant business in industrial societies.* Newbury Park, CA: Sage.

Waldinger, R., and Bozorgmehr, M. (Eds.). (1996). *Ethnic Los Angeles.* New York: Russell Sage Foundation.

Ward, R., and Jenkins, R. (Eds.). (1984). *Ethnic communities in business: Strategies for economic survival.* Cambridge: Cambridge University Press.

Weber, M. (1958). *The Protestant ethic and spirit of capitalism.* New York: Charles Scribner's Sons. (Original work published 1906)

Westwood, S., and Bhachu, P. (Eds.). (1988). *Enterprising women: Ethnicity, economy, and gender relations.* London and New York: Routledge.

Wilson, K., and Martin, W. A. (1982). Ethnic enclaves: A comparison of the Cuban and black economies in Miami. *American Journal of Sociology, 88,* 135–160.

Wilson, K., and Portes, A. (1980). Immigrant enclaves: An analysis of the labor market experience of Cubans in Miami. *American Journal of Sociology, 86,* 295–319.

Yoon, I. J. (1997). *On my own: Korean businesses and race relations in America.* Chicago: University of Chicago Press.

Zenner, W. P. (1991). *Minorities in the middle: A cross-cultural analysis.* Albany: State University of New York Press.

Zhou, M. (1992). *Chinatown: The socioeconomic potential of an urban enclave.* Philadelphia: Temple University Press.

Index